W9-BVA-992

Saint Peter's University Library
Withdrawn

SOUNDINGS

Soundings

SOME EARLY AMERICAN WRITERS

by

LEWIS LEARY

Athens

THE UNIVERSITY OF GEORGIA PRESS

Library of Congress Catalog Card Number: 73–90847
International Standard Book Number: 0–8203–0350–x
The University of Georgia Press, Athens 30602
Copyright © 1975 by the University of Georgia Press
All rights reserved
Set in 12 on 13 pt. Linotype Caslon Old Face
Printed in the United States of America

FOR
KENNETH SILVERMAN
TO EXPAND AND AMEND

Contents

✻✺ ✺✻

Acknowledgments

✿ ✿

"Benjamin Franklin and the Requirements of Literature" contains some material which appears in my introduction to *The Autobiography of Benjamin Franklin* (New York: Collier Books, 1962), © The Crowell-Collier Publishing Company, 1962, and other material from "Benjamin Franklin" in *The Comic Imagination in American Literature,* edited by Louis D. Rubin, Jr. (New Brunswick, N.J.: Rutgers University Press, 1973).

"Nathaniel Tucker: Expatriate Patriot" is adapted from chapters in my *The Literary Life of Nathaniel Tucker, 1750–1807* (Durham, N.C.: Duke University Press, 1951), and appears in part as an introduction to *The Complete Published Poems of Nathaniel Tucker together with Columbinus: A Mask* (Delmar, N.Y.: Scholars' Facsimiles & Reprints, 1973, © 1973 Scholars' Facsimiles & Reprints, Inc. All rights reserved).

"Samuel Low: New York's First Poet" appeared in the *Bulletin of the New York Public Library* 74 (September 1970): 468–480.

"Royall Tyler: First Gentleman of the American Theater" is adapted from a lecture given on 17 April 1970 at the American Theater Festival at C. W. Post College.

"Charles Crawford: A Forgotten Poet of Early Philadelphia" appeared in the *Pennsylvania Magazine of History and Biography* 83 (July 1959): 293–306.

"Joseph Brown Ladd of Charleston" appeared in *Americana* 36 (October 1942): 571–588.

"Philip Freneau: A Reassessment" appeared in *Major Writers of Early American Literature,* edited by Everett Emerson (Madison: University of Wisconsin Press, © 1972 by the Regents of the University of Wisconsin), pp. 245–271.

"Hugh Henry Brackenridge's *Modern Chivalry*" is adapted from my introduction to *Modern Chivalry* (New Haven, Conn.: College and University Press, 1965).

ACKNOWLEDGMENTS

"John Blair Linn, 1777–1805" appeared in the *William and Mary Quarterly*, n.s. 5 (April 1947): 136–176.

"Thomas Branagan: Republican Rhetoric and Romanticism in America" appeared in the *Pennsylvania Magazine of History and Biography* 77 (July 1953): 232–252.

"James Fenimore Cooper's Lover's Quarrel with America" is adapted from my introduction to *Home as Found* (New York: Capricorn Books, 1961).

"Washington Irving: An End and a New Beginning" is revised from *Washington Irving* (Minneapolis: University of Minnesota Press, Pamphlets on American Writers, no. 25, 1963).

SOUNDINGS

DISTRIBUTION

Introduction

❧❦

THE essays here gathered represent a concern stretching over many years with the beginning of literature in the United States, an area of investigation which when I entered it had been little explored by modern students. Since then its landscape has been better charted, much of the undergrowth has been cleared, and the few writers of merit stand out now in truer proportion. Leon Howard in *The Connecticut Wits* has clarified the place and pretensions of active young men who rose to fame in New Haven. Carl and Jessica Bridenbaugh have uncovered much of the literary culture of Philadelphia in the age of Franklin. Richard Beale Davis has illuminated the cultural life of Thomas Jefferson's Virginia. Much more is now being supplied, mostly by younger persons, many of them our students, who will fill in the details in the generous overall view supplied by Howard Mumford Jones in *O Strange New World* and by Russel B. Nye in *American Literary History, 1607–1830*. The essays which are now here offered are meant to fill in gaps and crevices of opinion or information. My hope is that they may prove useful or provocative to others who may choose to explore further into what is to me the exciting period of our literary beginnnings.

For it was an exciting time. The 1780s saw, not only the emergence of a new nation, but also the beginnings of a new literature, which slowly, very slowly, and not until many years later, quickened to robust and vigorous life. On the same vessel which in 1783 brought to New York its first copy of the Treaty of Paris which defined the terms of peace between England and the new United States came the expatriate Hector St. John Crèvecoeur whose *Letters of an American Farmer* had asked in

I

London the year before that question which people have been attempting to answer ever since: "Who is the American, this new man?" Who am I? What is my destiny? What shall be, as Emerson was to put it, the substance of my shrift? What is my responsibility to myself, and what to my country? If I am not I, who will be?

And Crèvecoeur, who had been exiled from his homestead in upstate New York during the last years of the war, answered the question for his time, for the 1780s, and the answer seemed satisfying then. The American, said Crèvecoeur, was a man who had faith in the future of a country where decent simplicity, frugality, and opportunity went hand in hand, a land where there "are no aristocratical families, no courts, no kings, no bishops, no ecclesiastical domination"—so many of those things which in a later generation Henry James would find fault with his countrymen for doing without. It was a pioneer land stretching limitless toward unconquered resources for the filling of pockets and the improvement of minds. It was a land, in short, of great intentions which were spoken of with large rhetorical flourishes, and without shame. Its foundation, said Washington as he said farewell to his troops at Newburgh, "was not laid in a gloomy age of ignorance, but in an epocha when the rights of mankind were better understood, and more clearly defined than at any other period." As "proprietors of a vast continent, . . . abounding with all the necessaries of life," America seemed to him "designed by Providence for the display of human greatness."

The new country was a child of the eighteenth-century enlightenment, and its Declaration of Independence was one of the first documents of an emerging romanticism. Men were equal, and endowed with inalienable rights, which included the various kinds of happiness offered in the new world. Indeed, so fervent and persuasive were accounts of the bounty and felicity of this new world, and so heightened the rhetoric in which its promise was set forth, that Benjamin Franklin was moved in 1784 to warn, in a pamphlet of "Information for Those Who Wish to Remove to America," against the "wild imaginations" of get-rich-quick promises: "America," he said, "is a land of labour," and by no means a never-never land where streets are "paved with half peck loaves, the houses tiled with pancakes, and where the fowls fly about ready to be roasted, crying come eat me!" For times were hard in postwar America, and money was scarce, but patriot countrymen were confident that through frugality, hard work, and the avoidance of dissipating pleasures of tavern or playhouse, it would finally fulfill every promise.

Meanwhile, patriot voices were raised in patriotic song, for a great country deserved a great literature. "May we not please ourselves," said one ardent commentator, "with the expectation of seeing, even in our own day . . . a Parnassus, on some sunny hills of the west,—whence streams will issue that will gladden and refresh the fountains of poetry." There native bards "will equal the daring sublimity of Homer," as they "eternize in song their native pools and rivers." Young Samuel Low, a bank clerk in New York, greeted the end of warfare with assurance that literature, too long confined to "European climes," would now cross westward to the new, though not yet united, states.

Other young poets sent forth the same courageous call, that, not only would a western "Homer and a Milton rise / In all the pomp and majesty of song," but also a "second Pope" who would so inspire American genius that every stream would "murmur to the magic sound / Of song heroic." Among the first to sing, though neither wildly nor well, was Col. David Humphreys, who had been Washington's aide-de-camp, and who filled the postwar press with forthrightly gesticulating verses which called for patriotism, industry, and thrift. Somewhat better was Philip Freneau, now in his early thirties, who during the war had put aside a career in poetry to lay waste his talent by excoriating the enemy as "infernal miscreants," "foes to the rights of freedom and of man." When the peace came, Freneau sought privacy again as a poet, writing new songs, in a different tone, and gathering his early verses into volumes which neither the requirements of war nor the wartime shortage of paper had previously allowed.

In Connecticut doughty and talkative Timothy Dwight, who had been a chaplain during the war, completed and published the long epic on which he had been working for at least ten years.

He called it *The Conquest of Canaän,* and it told in laborious couplets of Joshua's leading the Israelites to the promised land, but it was dedicated to George Washington and it contained intrusive lines praising other patriot heroes so that people were glad to read it as allegory, for Joshua certainly was Washington, and the promised land America. And his countrymen responded also to the popular challenge of a song in which Dwight challenged, "Columbia, Columbia, to glory arise, / The Queen of the world, and the child of the skies."

Equally fervent in patriotism and literary ambition, young Joel Barlow, still in his twenties when the war ended, was dashing back and forth between Hartford and New York and Philadelphia, charming almost everyone he met, as he peddled subscriptions for his long poem, which had been started before the war when he was a student at Yale and which, when finally published in 1787 as *The Vision of Columbus*—the vision of what the new-discovered world might become—was dedicated to America's most faithful wartime ally, His Most Christian Majesty, Louis the Sixteenth, King of France and Navarre. Barlow's college classmate, the tall, redheaded, humorless, and compulsively hardworking Noah Webster, was also on the move, bouncing back and forth among Atlantic seacoast cities seeking purchasers, printers, and copyright for the spellers, grammars, and readers which would insure his countrymen, he said, against being "indebted to Great Britain for books to learn our children."

None of these postwar volumes, except Webster's long-lived *Blue-Back Speller,* did particularly well; probably none sold more than five hundred copies. And with reason: though they spoke of a nation, there was yet no nation, only scattered and isolated groups, not yet used to being called states. People of these former colonies were war-weary and impoverished. Each city was separated from almost every other city by miles on miles of undeveloped country, through which wound deep-rutted, muddy roads. And how few of these people there were. At the end of the 1780s there were four million of them, scattered over an area of nine hundred thousand square miles between the Great Lakes on the north and the southern limits of

Georgia, and westward to the Mississippi, most of them in villages and farm sites along the Atlantic coast. But of these four million, about one million were black, most of them slaves, and a large, probably undeterminable, number of the rest were illiterate or only partially educated, for during the eight years of war scores of schools and colleges had been closed, so that almost a whole school generation was undertrained in learning.

A generous estimate might suggest that in the whole of the new country there were probably fewer than two million people —less than the population of Philadelphia today—who were capable of reading or had possibilities for producing what we or they would call literature. Even the larger cities in which they clustered were small, and commerce between them—including the distribution of books—was slow and cumbersome. Two days of travel was good time between New York and Philadelphia or Boston. Philadelphia was the largest: it had forty thousand inhabitants—about the size of Poughkeepsie, New York, or Richmond, Indiana, today. New York boasted twenty-three thousand people in 1786—Marietta, Georgia, or Walla Walla, Washington, does better now. Boston had eighteen thousand inhabitants, about as many as Tarrytown, New York, or Emporia, Kansas. Charleston, loaded with blacks, had fewer people than Sequin, Texas, or East Massapequa, Long Island. How many copies, even of the best of modern books, do you suppose could be sold in Sequin or East Massapequa?

These late 1780s were a time for a pause, and a catching up, and for new beginnings. Thomas Paine had retired from pamphlet warfare to the New Jersey countryside, where he puttered over plans for an extension bridge that would span the Schuylkill River, and bombarded Congress with suggestions that he be appointed, and paid, as the official historian of the Revolution. Hugh Henry Brackenridge, who ten years later would question pretensions of democracy in *Modern Chivalry*, had left Philadelphia for a career at Pittsburgh on the western frontier. Francis Hopkinson, whose rollicking "The Battle of the Kegs" had briefly made a laughingstock of British military tactics, was in Bordentown working over designs for the Great Seal of the new United States. Alexander Hamilton and James Madison ex-

5

plained in *The Federalist* papers what a constitution which would unite the states should contain.

Much was to be done that was practical and necessary. There was, as James Madison said, little time for literature. "It is not the *vocation* of Americans to cultivate polite literature," said a contributor to the Philadelphia *Port Folio* in 1801. "They are too much absorbed in commerce, speculation." Literature was left to women, clergymen, and young men who were too ill for other occupation. Much that was published appeared pseudonymously, for as William Wirt is said to have warned St. George Tucker, one's reputation as a practical man in whom people could have confidence was not enhanced by being known as a writer. "In our country," explained a commentator in 1809, "men of powerful and brilliant talents . . . are generally hurried into the vortex of business; and neglect the flowers of poesy, for the fruits of wealth and independence."

William Linn in 1791 wrote rhapsodically of *The Blessings of America* whose western wilderness would become "like Eden, and her desert like the garden of the Lord," where joy and gladness should be found, thanksgiving, "and the joy of melody." That was good enough, and true perhaps, but conquering the new lands left little immediate room for melody, or poetry of any kind other than what one carried with him, in head or pocket. "The lovers of poetry, in America, still look for the gratification of their taste to the productions of the British bards," said Charles Brockden Brown's *Monthly Magazine and American Review* in 1799. Six years later the *Monthly Anthology* in Boston complained that "In literature we are yet in our infancy." Yet it was "not for want of learning or genius, that the American poets are so little regarded. . . . It is because, amidst the mutual clamours of contending parties, not one reader in a thousand cares three cents about the poetical or literary honour of his country."

People did of course care, some very greatly. Philip Freneau in 1786 had wondered angrily, "Can we ever be thought to have learning or grace, / Unless it be sent from that damnable place," which was England. A few years later, Noah Webster challenged: "Americans unshackle your minds, and act like independent beings. You have been children long enough, subject to the control, and subservient to the interest of a haughty parent. . . . Americans must believe, and act from the belief, that it is dishonorable to waste life in mimicking the follies of other nations and basking in the sunshine of foreign glory." It was just as Washington Irving appeared on the scene in 1809 with Diedrich Knickerbocker's *History of New York*, lavishly imitative but for this moment tentatively exploring native manners, that Joseph Buckminster calmly foresaw that the "men of letters who are to direct our taste, mold our genius, and inspire our emulation . . . have not yet shown themselves in the world. But . . . the generation which is to succeed us will be formed on better models."

He was right, of course. During the next few decades the new country grew in stature, confidence, and achievement. By the time Irving began seriously to write, it had almost doubled in size, and in self-appreciation also, and in readership. When James Fenimore Cooper published his first novel, it contained almost ten million people, most of whom seemed to care—as Cooper did also—more about how life should be lived than how it should be written about. During the lifetime of these two men, the United States remained a provincial, coastline-hugging country whose frontier was only partially explored, and was written of very little at all. The long struggle for literary independence was won finally by the generation which succeeded them.

Irving and Cooper may be thought to have helped usher in a literature which was new enough and attractive enough to tempt imitators, and tough enough to withstand most attacks against it. Those others who preceded them spoke less clearly, with less effective lasting charm, but in small ways or large helped push their new country, sometimes falteringly but always vauntingly, toward the nineteenth century. I have enjoyed making the acquaintance of all of them and am happy now to introduce them or explain them to my friends.

LEWIS LEARY

Benjamin Franklin

AND THE REQUIREMENTS OF LITERATURE

❧ ❧

In speaking about almost anything American, Benjamin Franklin is a good man to begin with. Years before the United States existed, he started things of which his countrymen continue to be proud—like libraries, civic clubs, volunteer fire departments, effective street lighting, and efficient heating devices. He was solidly American, ingenious, practical, ambitious, and successful. His *Autobiography* testifies that his feet were firm on the ground, but he did not stand still. No man of his time went so far, and few have gone farther. But, because he not only started things, but also let it be known that he did, Franklin may sometimes be credited with more than he deserves. That is one reason why he stands confidently at the head of any native literary procession. Talking about himself, he produced his country's first masterwork.

Like Walt Whitman and Mark Twain and Ernest Hemingway, Franklin created a public image so attractive and palpable that it obscures the man who made it. Whatever influences of time or place or circumstance combined to produce the successful and whimsical and plainspoken homespun favorite remembered as Ben Franklin, the projection of this character was a literary exploit of important magnitude. "He knew what he was about, this sharp little man," said D. H. Lawrence. "He set up the first dummy American."[1] Certainly Horatio Alger could not have done so well in celebrating the stereotyped rise from rags to riches if Franklin had not invented it. Neither Alger nor Franklin was bothered that, like almost all of Franklin's devices, the invention was mechanical. This was something never forgotten from his boyhood in Cotton Mather's backsliding Boston, that everything was susceptible of being set in a row and counted.

When Thomas Carlyle called him the father of all Yankees,[2] he meant something of that sort, and when Leigh Hunt explained that "Americans are Englishmen with the poetry and romance taken out of them," he meant much the same.[3] Carl Van Doren has spoken of Franklin's magnificent centrality and of the flexible equilibrium of his talents because, too busy or too wise to become any one thing, Franklin managed all things, including himself, with casual efficiency: "Mind and will, talent and art, strength and ease, wit and grace met in him as if nature had been lavish and happy when he was shaped. Nothing seems to have been left out except a passionate desire, as in most men of genius, to be all ruler, all soldier, all saint, all poet, all scholar, all some one gift or merit or success."[4]

Perhaps in colonial America more than in most places, versatility was a becoming goal—that and self-control, recognition of limits beyond which, as Hemingway later was to explain, no man could successfully venture. Franklin painstakingly defined himself as a man who kept within bounds, discovering such satisfaction in handling what was set before him that he seldom was tempted to stretch for more. Reality was what he could see or feel, even at the end of a kite string, and he was too sensible to suspect that gods of the sky might smite him down in reprisal. That was what Melville must have meant when he said that Franklin's mind was grave, but never serious.

Rightfully proud of the range of his experience, Franklin was pleased when other people mistook breadth for depth, but he never fooled himself, nor let himself down. When something was to be said, he prepared it carefully so that it could be said well, for Franklin recognized his deficiencies. He did not extemporize easily. Like Mark Twain, he was best in monologue, skilled at fitting tales to special situations and, if uninterrupted, could spin out a pretty compliment or an effective satire. In temperament a tranquil man, he is not known often to have been disturbed by unpleasant dreams, though he had wit enough to pretend amorous nighttime fantasies for recitation in flirtatious badinage with appreciative ladies. It did not seem strange to him that French women preferred to be kissed on the neck rather than on cheek or lips where make-up might be disordered.

Contented with surfaces because surfaces served him well, Franklin probably would have understood Melville's admiration for men who dived deeply, for a lady's kindness or to inevitable failure, but he would not have shared it. Better safe, he might have said, than sorry. He would have been pleased at Melville's description of him as "printer, postmaster, almanac maker, essayist, chemist, orator, tinker, statesman, humorist, philosopher, parlor man, political economist, professor of housewifery, ambassador, projector, maxim-monger, herb-doctor, wit:—Jack of all trades, master of each and mastered by none—the type and genius of his land." He might have nodded sagely, pretending to understand when Melville went on to say, "Franklin was everything but a poet,"[5] but he would certainly have known exactly what Carl Van Doren meant when a century later he described Franklin as the best writer in America.

Contemporaries like John Adams, who was not always sure that he was fond of Franklin or approved of him, recognized that clearly:

> He had wit at will. He had humor that, when he pleased, was delicate and delightful. He had satire that was good-natured or caustic, Horace, Swift, or Rabelais, at his pleasure. He had talents for irony, allegory, and fable, that he could adapt with great skill to the promotion of moral and political truth. He was master of that infantine simplicity which the French call *naïveté*, which never fails to charm, in Phaedrus and La Fontaine, from the cradle to the grave.

By the end of the American Revolution, Franklin's reputation, said Adams, was "more universal than that of Leibnitz, Newton, Frederick, or Voltaire."[6] Medallions were struck off in his honor, set in the lids of snuff boxes or worn as brooches or on rings. Portraits, busts, and popular prints "have made your father's face," Franklin wrote to his daughter, "as well known as that of the moon; so that he durst not do anything that will cause him to run away, as his phiz would discover him wherever he should venture to show it."[7] Scarcely a coachman or footman, a lady's chambermaid or a scullion in the kitchen, said Adams, "did not consider him as a friend of human kind. When they spoke of him, they seemed to think he was to restore the golden age."[8]

More than Washington or Jefferson or any man since, Franklin was the true American, a latter-day Columbus who revealed the new world to the old, a kind of god who "snatched the lightning from the sky and the scepter from tyrants."[9] None better represented the simple, noble men of whom Rousseau had spoken, who lived close to nature, faithful to her laws, uncontaminated by artificialities of court or town. Dressed plainly, his stockings wrinkled, his hair unpowdered, and his spectacles (bifocals of his own invention) askew on his nose, Franklin met kings and courtiers with simple dignity as a representative new man, one of those whom his friend Hector St. John Crèvecoeur described in *Letters from an American Farmer* as clad in homespun, unpretentious but wise, ingenious, and free. Having left ancient prejudices and old-world manners behind, these western pilgrims called Americans carried with them the hope of the world, in arts and sciences, in vigor and industry: "they finish the great circle," enforcing ageless certainties of natural nobility.[10] Franklin was portent of what man everywhere might be. He had no need, like Joaquin Miller a century later, to prove his western vitality by scampering about on all fours in Mayfair drawing rooms nipping at the ankles of admiring ladies. Walt Whitman's open shirt, Mark Twain's dazzling white suit, or Hemingway's obstreperous masculinity would not have fitted him well. His was a more subtly devised image, and more compelling.

Born in Boston on 6 January (17 January, new style), 1706, the fifteenth of his father's seventeen children and the youngest of ten sons, he remembered himself as a precocious boy, robust and inquisitive, so quick at reading that his father considered making a clergyman of him, "intending me as tythe of his sons to the service of the church."[11] At seven he made verses. At eight he entered Boston's best grammar school where he crammed two years' work into one. But his father had a change in mind about the ministry: that would mean college, and the elder Franklin had a workingman's suspicion that education at Harvard was not worth the expense. Better to learn to write legibly and do sums accurately. After another year of struggling to master these practical skills, and doing badly in arithmetic, Franklin at the age of ten left school to work in his father's soap-boiling and candlemaking shop.

Unsatisfied with cutting wicks and filling molds with tallow, Benjamin at twelve was apprenticed to his printer brother James, and within not many months became a professional writer—which is to say, he wrote for profit:

> I now took a fancy to poetry and made some little pieces. My brother thinking it might turn to account, encouraged me and induced me to compose two occasional ballads. One was called the "Lighthouse Tragedy," . . . the other was a "Sailor's Song on the Taking of the Famous *Teach*, or Blackbeard, the Pirate." They were wretched stuff, in street ballad style; and when they were printed, he sent me about town to sell them. The first sold prodigiously, the event being recent and having made a great noise.

"This success," the boy confessed, "flattered my vanity."

But his practical father again discouraged him, "ridiculing my performances and telling me verse-makers were generally beggars. Thus," said Franklin, "I escaped being a poet and probably a very bad one." But making verses was useful because it increased one's stock of works and provided exercise in their management—this Franklin may have learned from his neighbor Cotton Mather who suggested that young scholars sharpen their senses and polish their style by an occasional occupation with rhyme, at the same time warning them to be "not so set upon poetry as to be always pouring on the passionate and measured pages" and, particularly, to beware of "a boundless and sickly appetite" for "muses that are not better than harlots."

Words like these may have been heard directly from Dr. Mather's mouth, for tradition insists that young Franklin was in and out of the clergyman's study, a favorite protégé, more promising than either of the good man's sons or even his poetaster nephew, Mather Byles. "From my infancy," Franklin testified, "I was passionately fond of reading, and all the little money that came into my hands was laid out in the purchasing of books." He read *Pilgrim's Progress*, and then bought everything else of Bunyan's he could find. When these were read, he traded them for the shelfful of volumes in Burton's *Historical Collections*. To save money for more books, he became a vegetarian, living on biscuit and raisins, potatoes and rice, washed down with pump water, and felt much better for it.

What he could not buy he borrowed, from Matthew Adams, a merchant of literary tastes who frequented the Franklin printing shop, or from friendly apprentices to booksellers who slipped him occasional volumes from their masters' shelves, which Franklin would sit up all night to read so that he could return them early in the morning before they were missed. He read Plutarch's *Lives*, Locke's *Essay Concerning the Human Understanding*, Xenophon's *Memorabilia*, and the popular deistic writings of the Earl of Shaftesbury and the free-thinking theologian, Anthony Collins. Defoe's practical *Essay on Projects* and Cotton Mather's *Essays to Do Good* gave him "a turn of thinking," he said, "that had an influence on some of the principal future events of my life."

What Franklin read is probably less important to remember than why he read. He went to books for self-improvement, cramming up on the arithmetic he had not done well with in school, learning from history how other men had succeeded, from philosophy why. Literature was a storehouse containing the accumulated experience of man; it presented examples of excellence which a young man might emulate in the hope of developing a persuasive style of his own. When Franklin in his 'teens discovered the *Spectator*, he read it over and over, and was delighted with it:

> I thought the writing excellent and wished if possible to imitate it. With that in view, I took some of the papers, and making short hints of the sentiment of each sentence, laid them by a few days, and then without looking at the book, tried to complete the papers again by expressing each hinted sentiment at length as fully as it had been expressed before, in any suitable words that should occur to me. Then I compared my *Spectator* with the original, discovered some of my faults, and corrected them.

How practical and sensible he was, even then. Literature was something to be learned, and poetry something to be used. "Therefore," he continued,

I took some of the tales of the *Spectator* and turned them into verse, and after a time, when I had pretty well forgotten the prose, turned them back again. I also sometimes jumbled my collection of hints into confusion, and after some weeks endeavoured to reduce them into the best order before I began to form the full sentences and complete the paper. This was to teach me method in the arrangement of the thoughts. By comparing my work afterwards with the original, I discovered many faults and corrected them; but I sometimes had the pleasure of fancying that in certain particulars of small import I had been lucky enough to improve the method or the language, and this encouraged me to think that I might possibly in time come to be a tolerable English writer, of which I was extremely ambitious.

Opportunity to put such patient practice to use soon presented itself. In 1721 James Franklin established the *New England Courant,* the third newspaper to appear in Boston, indeed in all the American colonies. More lively than its local competitors, it was supported by a free-thinking group of local wits—"A Clan of Honest Wags," they called themselves, though Cotton Mather who was often the butt of their ridicule dismissed them as "another Hell-Fire Club." Dedicated to the eradication of dullness and opposition to leadership by the clergy, they wrote, London-style, as Ichabod Henroost, Tabitha Talkative, or Homespun Jack, about the charms of women, the evils of gossip, or the pompous pedantry of pulpit manners.

"Hearing their conversation," said sixteen-year-old Benjamin, "I was excited to try my hand among them. But being still a boy and suspecting that my brother would object to printing anything of mine in his paper if he knew it to be mine, I contrived to disguise my hand; and writing an anonymous paper, I put it at night under the door of the printing house." Discovered the next morning, read aloud and approved, the first of the Dogood Papers was printed in the *Courant* on Monday, 26 March 1722. The date marks the beginning of Franklin's long public career as a man of letters.

With these essays a literature of America was born, and Franklin was its single large generative force. His neighbor Cotton Mather wrote more than he, and William Byrd in Virginia a few years later in "The History of the Dividing Line" would write briefly as well. The Reverend Edward Taylor, secluded in the frontier town of Westfield, preserved notebooks filled with poetry which he did not allow published, though it was probably as good as any written anywhere at that time. Not ten years later, the Reverend Jonathan Edwards of Northampton spoke in Boston of theological insights which by midcentury would be set forth in beautifully mannered, precise prose. By then, Franklin had been long absent from New England, and he had taken literature with him, as if he had it in his pocket, neatly stowed, to be used as needed. Not until Ralph Waldo Emerson more than a hundred years later discovered, amid what Franklin had left behind, the materials for revelations of which Franklin could not completely have approved was it to reappear to warm that chill region again.

The fourteen essays which were printed, one every two weeks, in the *Courant* until early in the autumn of 1722 over the signature of Silence Dogood were quizzical commentaries on Boston manners not unlike those which appeared in English periodicals on London manners, except that the Widow Dogood was a New England countrywoman who spoke in native accent of local idiosyncracies. Her name alone—impiously suggestive of Cotton Mather's well-meaning essays—and her state in life were amusing, for Boston seemed overfilled with husbandless women, most of them respectable, but others merry widows, keepers of dram shops or managers of waterfront bordellos. Her given name of Silence was grotesquely inappropriate, for she loved to talk, especially about her neighbors. In the first three essays, however, she spoke mainly of herself, who she was and where she came from, in the manner of Addison in the *Spectator*. She admitted her "natural inclination to observe and reprove the faults of others"[12] and was eager to dedicate this excellent faculty to the good of her countrymen. At sixteen Franklin knew what literature was for: it could mend the manners of men by pointing toward errors; it could admonish and correct, laugh lightly at human frailty, and suggest practical patterns which insured success.

Silence Dogood's first objective observation was on education, in an allegorical dream of Harvard College through whose gates only those approved by Riches might enter. There Learning sat on a high throne, so difficult of access that most of her worshipers "contented themselves to sit at the foot with Madame Idleness and her maid Ignorance," waiting for someone to help them ascend. College men were a worthless crew, "unable to dig and ashamed to beg." The widow spoke for Franklin and his father and all men who worked unashamedly with their hands when she said:

> I reflected in my mind on the extreme Folly of those Parents, who, blind to their children's Dulness and insensible to the Solidity of their Skulls, because they think their Purses can afford it, will needs send them to the Temple of Learning, where, for want of a suitable Genius, they learn little more than how to carry themselves handsomely, and enter a Room genteely (which might as well be acquired at a Dancing-School,) and from whence they return, after Abundance of Trouble and Charge, as great Blockheads as ever, only more proud and self-conceited.

Like any good Bostonian, young Franklin was gallant in defense of women, allowing Mistress Dogood to reply to an attack against female idleness, ignorance, folly, and pride, by asking: Who is less often drunk? Who swears less? Whose work, by tradition and in truth, is never done? Why should women not be proud, when men "will be such *Simpletons* as to humble themselves at their feet, and fill their credulous Ears with extravagant Praises . . . and when Women are by these Means perswaded that they are Something more than human, what Wonder is it that they carry themselves haughtily and live extravagantly?" Whatever was wrong with women was man's fault, especially in not providing them equal opportunities in education. Two weeks later, women were talked of again, this time less gallantly, for the subject now was their pride in dress, especially in absurd, wide skirts: "I would at least desire them to lessen the Circumference of their Hoops, and leave them to consider, whether they, who pay no Rates or Taxes, ought to take up more room on the King's Highway, than the Men, who yearly contribute to the Support of the Government."

The widow also was allowed notions on what poetry should be. "It has been the Complaint of many Ingenious Foreigners who have travell'd amongst us," she wrote, *"that good poetry is not to be expected in New England."* The reason was that New Englanders, in failing sufficiently to praise their own poetry, therefore failed to let the world know of its beauties.

> There has recently appear'd among us a most Excellent Piece of Poetry, entituled, *An Elegy upon the much Lamented Death of Mrs.* Mehitebell Kitel, *Wife of Mr.* John Kitel *of* Salem, *Etc.* It may justly be said in its Praise, without Flattery to the Author, that it is the most *Extraordinary* Piece that was ever wrote in *New-England.* The Language is so soft and Easy, the Expression so moving and pathetick, but above all, the Verse and Numbers so Charming and Natural, that it is almost beyond Comparison.

> > *The* Muse *disdains*
> > *Those Links and Chains,*
> > *Measures and Rules of Vulgar Strains,*
> > *And o'er the Laws of Harmony a Sover-*
> > *eign Queen she reigns.*

> I find no English Author, Ancient or Modern, whose Elegies may be compar'd with this, in respect to the Elegance of Stile, or Smoothness of Rhime; and for the affecting Part, I will leave your Readers to judge, if ever they read any Lines, that would sooner make them *draw their Breath* and Sigh, if not shed Tears, than these following.

> > *Come let us mourn, for we have lost a*
> > *Wife, a Daughter, and a Sister,*
> > *Who has lately taken Flight, and*
> > *greatly have we mist her.*

In another place,

> *Some* little Time *before she yielded up her Breath,*
> *She said, I ne'er shall hear one Sermon more on Earth.*
> *She kist her Husband* some little time *before she expir'd,*
> *Then lean'd her Head the Pillow on, just out of Breath and tir'd.*

She wished she had space for more of this excellent elegy. It seemed to her a new kind of poetry which deserved a name of its own: "seeing it cannot justly be called, either *Epic, Sapphic, Lyric,* or *Pindaric,* nor any other Name yet invented, I presume it may (in Honour and Remembrance of the Dead) be called KITELIC." The appellation stuck—for years bad poetry among New Englanders became Kitelic poetry. To save native poets trouble, Mistress Dogood then set forth "A Receipt to make a New-England Funeral Elegy," even providing samples of useful rhymes: grieve us / leave us; flower / power; physicians / expeditions. "Then season all," she said, "with a Handful or two of Melancholy Expressions, such as Dreadful, Deadly, cruel cold, Death, unhappy Fate, weeping Eyes, Etc." Mark Twain had no more fun when he allowed Huck Finn to comment on the poem which Emmeline Grangerford made "about a boy by the name of Stephen Dowling Bots that fell down a well and was drownded."

The longer they appeared, the more of Benjamin Franklin and the less of his mouthpiece appeared in the Dogood Papers. Echoes of Defoe's ironic voice are heard in two essays which suggest an insurance company for widows and another for aged virgins over thirty, but it is the young Boston apprentice who compares the virtues of moderate drinking with the vices of drunkenness while he painstakingly lists works and phrases from the vocabulary of tippling: "*boozey, cogey, tipsey, fox'd, merry, mellow, fuddl'd, groatable, Confoundedly cut, See two Moons,* are *Among the Philistines, In a very good Humor, See the Sun,* or, *The Sun has shone upon them;* they *Clip the King's English,* are *Almost froze, Feavourish, In their Altitudes, Pretty well enter'd,* etc." Franklin kept his ears open for new rhythms, and his eyes open for local sights, like eagerly amorous sailors arm in arm with their doxies and predatory young ladies who walked darkened streets with "pretty gestures and impertinencies," contributing thereby to "the health and satisfaction of those who have been fatigued with business or study" as well as to the prosperity of shoemakers and dealers in leather.

Almost everything that Franklin would ever say and every tone he later used are foreshadowed in these young essays, the first of their kind in the New World. When he borrowed from Addison, Defoe, Swift, or other men in England or New England, he scrupulously paid interest in native originality of phrase or incident. But not too much originality—nothing too much, neither drinking nor wenching, not even too great a departure from saying things as they had always been said. If Franklin could have had patience or opportunity to read what T. S. Eliot was to write about how individual talent builds on tradition, he would certainly have agreed. If one were to persuade, simple practicality required that he must not seem eccentric or isolated. People responded to what was familiar and homely—the trick was to provide the fillip which convinced without startling. For certainly "an indiscrete Zeal for spreading an Opinion hurts the cause of the Zealot."

More ambitious, the *Dissertation on Liberty and Necessity, Pleasure and Pain* (1725) was less successful. Written in London, where Franklin had gone in what he later recognized as a vain attempt to establish himself all at once as a successful man, the *Dissertation* was a zealous and committed piece, put together from shreds and patches of contemporary thought, a young man's trial at seriously arguing advanced notions about the nature of God and man's responsibilities within limits set by divine law. As a logical deist with no metaphysical tomfoolery about him, young Franklin saw the world as a curious clock with intricate internal workings mutually dependent so that the whole mechanism moved in most exact consistency, its wondrous regularity only disturbed by the eccentric actions of willful men. A creature like any other, man moved in cautious balance between pleasure and pain, an excess of one inevitably requiring an increased visitation of its opposite.

These were philosophic commonplaces, familiar to any alert young man. Nothing is new in Franklin's dogged arrangement, until the final paragraph, dashed off as if in relief to be finished with a brain-taxing exercise. Any Grub Street essayist might have written, "Mankind naturally and generally love to be flatter'd: Whatever soothes our Pride, and tends to exalt our Species over the rest of creation, we are pleas'd with and easily believe, when

ungrateful Truths shall be with the utmost indignation rejected."
A new voice expanded that to say, "But . . . our *Geese* are but
Geese, tho' we may think 'em *Swans;* and Truth will be Truth
tho' it sometimes prove mortifying and distasteful."[13]

People who do not respond to literature often fail to understand that it is not what a writer says but how he says it which is
important. What distinguishes Franklin—or Ralph Waldo Emerson, Henry James, Mark Twain, or T. S. Eliot—is not originality in thought, for they pronounce what all men know. The
hallmark of a man of letters is his competence in devising patterns which seem plain because he has discovered words and
clusters of words which speak directly and freshly. His voice, it
can be said, is his own, like enough to other men's voices to be
recognizable, but with accent and emphasis which allow it to
recall what frazzled words have blurred. Franklin adjusted assiduously to the requirements of literature. When back in Philadelphia, in business for himself, he contributed "The Busy Body"
in 1729 to Andrew Bradford's *American Weekly Mercury,* he
wrote as other periodical essayists wrote, in pretended concern
with the vices and follies of his countrymen: "tho' Reformation
is properly the concern of every Man; that is, Every one ought
to mend One; yet 'tis too true in this Case, that what is every
Body's Business is nobody's Business; and the Business is done
accordingly."[14]

Talent must be fitted to the time, and models carefully chosen.
Franklin curbed his natural bent toward "lampooning and libel-
ling," for which, he had been warned, "I had too much inclination." Men preferred not to be laughed at. Reformation was not
produced by ridicule. "The general tendency there is among us
to this embellishment, which I fear has too often grossly imposed
upon my loving countrymen instead of wit, and the applause it
meets with from a rising generation, fill me with fearful appre-
hensions for the future of my country": deserving young men,
fearful "of being out-laughed . . . continue in restless obscurity." As "The Busy Body" Franklin lashed out at "petty
gentlemen that write satires . . . taking advantage of the ill
taste of the town to make themselves famous for a pack of paltry,
low nonsense, for which they deserve to be kicked rather than ad-

mired." He begged them to control their "overbearing itch for scribbling."

Such words almost certainly were spoken in response to some local situation involving Franklin and his mechanic friends, but it is not necessary to know the incidents which called them forth in order to find the words important. They attacked excess. Successful men were moderate in words and emotion. Using Addison's popular characterization of Cato as a pattern, but remembering other familiar models of morality, the young man of twenty-three made a first sketch of the character which for more than fifty years thereafter would represent to an increasingly admiring public the carefully created personage known as Ben Franklin. Emerson, though capable of more subtle distinctions and placid disinterestedness, added little except depth when a century later he began his quest to discover the marks of human greatness. One of his achievements was the translation to particulars of generalities which Franklin's generation emphasized by writing them with an initial capital letter.

The countenance of the virtuous man, said Franklin,

> is sweetened with Humanity and Benevolence, and at the same Time emboldened with Resolution, equally free from a diffident Bashfulness and an unbecoming Assurance. The Consciousness of his own innate Worth and unshaken Integrity renders him calm and undaunted in the Presence of the most Great and Powerful. His strict Justice and known Impartiality make him the Arbitrator and Decider of all Differences, that arise for many Miles around him. He always speaks the Thing he means, which is never afraid or asham'd to do, because he knows he always means well, and therefore is never oblig'd to blush, and feel the Confusion of finding himself detected in the Meanness of a Falsehood. A mixture of Innocence and Wisdom makes him ever seriously chearful. His generosity to Strangers, according to his Ability; his Courage in the Cause of the Oppressed, his Fidelity, his Friendship, his Humility and Sincerity, his Moderation, and his Loyalty to the Government; his Piety, his Temperance, his Love to Mankind, his Magnanimity, his Publick-Spiritedness, and, in fine, his consumate Virtue, make him justly deserve to be esteem'd the Glory of his Country.

21

SAINT PETER'S COLLEGE LIBRARY
JERSEY CITY, NEW JERSEY 07306

But virtue was not a thing apart, pursued for its own sake: it was a gateway to success. "Almost every Man has a strong Desire of being valu'd and esteem'd by the rest of his Species, but I am concern'd and griev'd to see how few fall into the Right and only infallible Method of becoming so." So Franklin set up, he said in his *Autobiography*, a chart of virtues, and methodically drilled himself in them, one after another. This week he would be temperate—"Eat not to dullness; drink not to elevation." The next week he would avoid trifling conversation, the next he would be orderly, then resolute, then frugal, industrious, sincere, and so on down the list, through justice, moderation, cleanliness, tranquility, to chastity—"Rarely use venery but for health or offspring, never to dullness, weakness, or the injury of your own or another's peace or reputation." At first, he wrote down an even dozen desirable virtues, but a Quaker friend telling him that he was generally thought proud, he added another, humility, and had more trouble with that than all the rest. "I cannot boast of much success in acquiring the reality of this virtue," he confessed years later, "but I had a good deal with regard to the appearance of it."

For, after all, appearance does count. People who dislike Franklin or his kind refer to this attitude as self-serving or cynical. To William Carlos Williams, Franklin is "our wise prophet of chicanery," a man of voluptuous energy, but sly and covert.[15] To some of his contemporaries Franklin seemed a vulgar man who despoiled life of richness and literature of charm: his effect on language, thought Joseph Dennie, was to coarsen it with colloquialism offensive to good taste or refined feelings.[16] Others have found him not in the best sense a dedicated man, because his principal commitment was to himself, whatever he wrote was for a purpose, and words were instruments to persuade other men to attitudes advantageous to the writer.

There was little glitter to Franklin. "An ideal is lacking in this healthy, upright able, frugal, laborious nature of Franklin," said Sainte-Beuve. There is in him no "fine flower of enthusiasm, tenderness, sacrifice. . . . He brings everything down to arithmetic and strict reality, assigning no part to human imagination."[17] When D. H. Lawrence dismissed him as a "snuff-coloured little man" who set up an "unlovely, snuff-coloured ideal, or automaton, or a pattern American," he went on to say that "this pattern-American, this dry, moral, utilitarian little democrat has done more to ruin old Europe than any Russian nihilist."[18] Lawrence must have meant much what Melville meant when he said that Franklin was everything but a poet, or what someone else meant when he said that Franklin was interested in all things about man except his spirit. The Europe which Franklin ruined was the Europe whose perceptions of levels of excellence had hardened to ritual within which men and manners and morals and matters of taste were all enclosed. It was the Europe of loveliness, enthusiasm, tenderness, and grace grounded in tradition which years later, first James Fenimore Cooper, then Henry James attempted to reveal once more to their countrymen.

As a self-made writer, Franklin exhibited almost all the tendencies and attitudes discoverable in succeeding American writers of his kind, and he also shared opinions with others who were in most respects different. When Thoreau in *Walden* spoke of the cost of any thing being the amount of life which must be exchanged for it, he extended what Franklin had said about self-denial in avoiding any action inconsistent with health or fortune "because 'twould cost you more than 'twas worth." Emerson, in asking native writers to turn attention to common things, the meal in the firkin, the milk in the pan, and the song in the street, emphasized in precept what Franklin had established in practice. As much as Whittier or Whitman or Harriet Beecher Stowe, Franklin aimed at an audience of simple people, and his language, more than theirs, reached the working man.

Like Mark Twain, he knew the leavening power of humor and the effective force of the hoax and tall tale. He was as gallant in flirtatious compliments to ladies as he was capable in concocting Rabelaisian anecdotes fit only for masculine ears. America's first successful periodical essayist, he was also her first humorist, in a line which includes Washington Irving (whose image is so mincingly different), Artemus Ward, Mr. Dooley, Will Rogers, and

James Thurber. Laugh but avoid being laughed at: "Pieces of Pleasancy and Mirth have a secret charm in them to allay the Heats and Tumours of our Spirits."

As proprietor for almost forty years after 1729 of the *Pennsylvania Gazette,* as compiler of *Poor Richard's Almanac,* and as editor in 1740 of the *General Magazine,* the first successful periodical of its kind in the colonies, Franklin instructed but also delighted his contemporaries. He informed them with "A Proposal for Promoting Useful Knowledge," "An Account of the New Invented Pennsylvanian Fire-Places," and "Proposals Relating to the Education of Youth." Like his essays advocating paper currency or "On the Causes and Cures of Smokey Chimneys," his "Scheme for a Reformed Alphabet and Reformed Mode of Spelling," his "Art of Swimming," and much of his political writing were matchless examples of well-reasoned exposition, expertly put together, and are of curious interest to the historian as exemplars of the best practical thought of Franklin's time.

In the *Gazette* of 23 June 1730 he argued with himself in Socratic dialogues between Horatio, a man of pleasure, and Philocles, a man of reason who understood that "it behooves us, above all things in this World, to take Care that our Opinions of Things be according to the Nature of Things" because the "Foundation of all Virtue and Happiness is Right Thinking." He set forth a detailed "Apology for Printers," explaining their need to keep a middle course among the variety of opinions, topping it with a familiar fable about a man so plagued with advice on how to manage his ass that he was tempted to do away with the beast entirely. He had great fun reporting on 22 October 1730 "A Witch Trial at Mount Holly," where persons accused of "making their Neighbour's Sheep dance in an uncommon Manner, and with causing Hogs to speak and sing Psalms" were submitted to trial by water: "But being the general Belief of the Populace that the Women's shifts and Garters . . . help'd to support them, it is said they are to be tried again the next warm Weather, naked." "A Meditation on a Quart Mug" on 19 June 1733 provided opportunity for frolicksome, sly instruction. Battered by barmaids, forced into the boisterous company of sots and blamed for their drunkenness, the unfortunate mug lived unhappily, a vehicle of pleasure (like the newspaper, it is presumed), not praised nor condemned for itself, but for its contents —"Shouldst thou produce double Beer, nappy Ale, stallcop Cyder, or Cyder mull'd, fine Punch, or cordial Tiff; yet for all these shouldst thou not be praised, but the rich Liquors themselves."

But it was as Richard Saunders, almanac maker—the Sir Roger de Coverley of the masses—that Franklin reached most readers. Almanacs found their way into almost every home, often furnishing the whole content of family reading. Crops were planted according to their instructions, business deals and love affairs carried out, illnesses cured. They explained how to bake cakes or cure hams and the best time to cut hair, trim cocks, or sow salads.[19] *Poor Richard's Almanac* first appeared late in 1732 and continued to appear at the end of each year for a quarter of a century, its title suggested both by the name of an actual Richard Saunders who published an almanac in England, and by the *Poor Robin* almanac which James Franklin issued in New England.

To fill spaces left blank by more practical matter, Poor Richard purloined wit and wisdom from the finest storehouses of Europe, from Dryden, Pope, Bacon, La Rochefoucauld, Rabelais, and many another, not hesitating to rephrase or reshape when his own words could make a good thing better. "Be not disturbed, O grave and sober reader," he wrote,

> If among the many serious sentences in my book, thou findest me trifling now and then, and talking idly. In all the dishes I have hitherto cooked for thee, there is solid meat enough for thy money. There are scraps from the table of Wisdom that will, if well digested, yield strong nourishment to thy mind. But squeamish stomachs cannot eat without pickles; which, 'tis true, are good for nothing else, but they provoke an appetite.

The scraps made a mixed, but esculent repast. "Not a tenth part of this wisdom is my own," admitted Poor Richard, "but rather the *gleanings* I had made of the sense of all ages and nations." But he seasoned it well with native wit: "Never spare the parson's wine nor the baker's pudding"; "There's more old drunkards than old doctors"; "When there's a marriage without love, there will be love without marriage"; "After three days men grow weary of a wench, a guest, and rainy weather" (or, put another way, "Fish and visitors stink in three days"); "He that lies down with dogs, shall rise with fleas"; "He that takes a wife, takes care"; "Love, smoke, and a cough can't be hid"; "Keep your eyes wide open before marriage, half shut afterwards"; "He that's secure is not safe"; "Most fools think they are only ignorant"; "Clean your finger before you point at my spots."

Poor Richard anticipated Longfellow in advising, "Let us then be up and doing"; and he anticipated Thoreau in advising, "Read much, but not many books." He had no shame in changing Lord Bacon's "Reading maketh a full man; conference a ready man; and writing an exact man" to "Reading makes a full man, meditation a profound man, discourse a clear man." He spoke of plain writing as opposed to "the orator, with his flood of words and his drops of reason." "The learned fool writes his nonsense in better language than the unlearned; but still 'tis nonsense." "Strange! that a man who has enough wit to write a satire should have folly enough to publish it." Poor Richard usually laughed at poets: "Poverty, poetry, and new titles of honour make men ridiculous" or "Great wits jump, says the poet, and hit his head against the post." And critics? "Bad commentators spoil the best of books, / So God sends meat (they say), the Devil cooks."

Best consecutive reading in the almanacs is provided by the introductions. Here Poor Richard quizzically carried on for years the pretense of foretelling the death of Titan Leeds, his principal competitor in the almanac-making business. The gambit was a deliberate steal from Jonathan Swift's hoax on John Partridge twenty-five years before, but most of the matter which Richard Saunders talked about was fresh, or made to seem so. "I might in this place attempt to gain thy Favour," he told readers,

> by declaring that I write Almanacks with no other View than that of the publick Good; but in this I should not be sincere; and Men are now adays too wise to be deceiv'd by Pretenses how specious soever. The plain Truth of the Matter is, I am excessive poor, and my Wife, good Woman, is, I tell her, excessive proud; she cannot bear, she says, to sit spinning in her

Shift of Tow, while I do nothing but gaze at the stars; and has threatened more than once to burn all my Books and Rattling-Traps (as she calls my instruments) if I do not make some profitable Use of them for the Good of my Family.

The next year he reported that he had done well: My Wife has been enabled to get a Pot of her own. . . . She has also got a pair of Shoes, two new Shifts, and a new warm Petticoat."

Genial Poor Richard was overshadowed, however, by Father Abraham who was introduced in the almanac for 1858. His "The Way to Wealth" has been named an "American classic, *par excellence*," sharing with *Uncle Tom's Cabin* the honor of "having passed by translation into more foreign languages than anything else," bearing with it "the mark of our national spirit."[20] More than seventy editions have appeared in English, more than fifty in French, eleven in German, nine in Italian; it has been put into Spanish, Danish, Swedish, Welsh, Polish, Gaelic, Russian, Bohemian, Dutch, Catalan, Chinese, and Greek; it has been done in phonetic writing and in Braille, to become after the *Autobiography* the best and farthest known of Franklin's writings, containing the essence of his homely and practical wisdom.

He had spoken of frugality before, in "Hints for Those Who Would Become Rich" in the *Almanac* for 1737, more explicitly in "Advice to a Young Tradesman" in the *Gazette* in 1748. "Remember," he had said then, "that time is money," and "the way to wealth . . . depends chiefly on two words, *industry* and *frugality; that is, waste neither *time* nor *money*, but make the best use of both." Father Abraham tightened his advice with terse, workaday aphorisms, knowing, he said, that "*a Word to the Wise is enough, and Many Words won't fill a Bushel.*" He reminded readers that "*The sleeping Fox catches no Poultry,*" that "*He that rises late must trot all Day,*" that "*Laziness travels so slowly, that Poverty soon overtakes him,*" that "*Diligence is the Mother of Good Luck,*" and that success comes to him who will "*plough deep while others sleep,*" so that "*Early to bed, and early to rise*" really "*makes a man healthy, wealthy, and wise.*"

Franklin's was the voice of the man in the homespun suit, with all the world before him for his taking. He spoke to apprentices and servant girls and shopkeepers who dreamed of fine houses and carriages and reputation for generosity to the poor; in 1744 he issued as the first novel printed in America Samuel Richardson's popularly didactic *Pamela* which four years before had reminded admiring English readers that a working girl could make good. As a city man he noticed the fields or woods or streams or skies which surrounded Philadelphia, not to remark on their beauty, but their usefulness. Some countrymen complained that "as quacks boast an infallible cure for the itch," so Franklin boasted nostrums "for the preservation of prudence, the cure of poverty." He did that, with no apology: his nostrums worked, he could prove it.

But all work and no play could make Benjamin a dull boy, and Franklin was seldom dull, even when he talked of education (less Latin and more arithmetic) or politics or playing chess. Sometimes he paused to put together convivial verses:

> The antediluvians were all very sober,
> For they had no wine and they brewed no October;
> All wicked bad livers, on mischief still thinking,
> For there can't be good living where there is not
>   good drinking.
>
> Derry-down.

> 'Twas honest old Noah first planted the vine,
> And mended his morals by drinking its wine;
> And thenceforth justly the drinking of water decried;
> For he knew that all mankind by drinking it died.
>
> Derry-down.[21]

He sang the challenge of love, and its failure in competition with companionship:

> Fair Venus calls; her voice obey;
> In beauty's arms spend night and day.
> The joys of love all joys excell,
> And loving's certainly doing well.
>
> Oh! no!
>
> Not so!
> For honest souls know
> Friends and the bottle shall bear the bell.[22]

One evening when Franklin sat with friends in a tavern, some-one remarked how unbefitting it was for honest married men to sing hackneyed songs in praise of some poet's mistress. Return-ing home, where his own Deborah undoubtedly patiently waited him, Franklin composed a more proper song for proper men to sing:

Of their Chloe's and Phyllises poets may prate,
    I sing my plain country Joan,
These twelve years my wife, still the joy of my life;—
    Blest the day that I made her my own.

Not a word of her face, of her shape, of her air,
    Or of flames or of darts, you shall hear;
I beauty admire, but virtue I prize,
    That fades not in seventy year.

. . . .

Some faults have we all, and so has my Joan,
    But then, they're exceedingly small,
And now I've grown used to them, so like my own,
    I scarcely can see them at all.

Were the finest young princess, with millions in purse,
    To be had in exchange for my Joan,
I could not get a better, but might get a worse,
    So I'll stick to my dearest old Joan.[23]

Springtime fancies were perhaps responsible for the Chester-fieldian "Advice to a Young Man in the Choice of a Mistress" which Franklin produced late in June 1745.[24] "I know of no medicine," he confessed,

fit to diminish the violent natural inclinations you mention; and if I did, I think I should not communicate it to you. Marriage is the proper remedy. It is the most natural state of man, and therefore the state in which you are most likely to find solid happiness. . . . It is the man and woman united to make the complete human being. Separate, she wants his force of body and strength of frame; he, her softness, sensibility, and acute discernment. Together they are more likely to suc-ceed in the world. A single man . . . resembles the odd half of a pair of scissors.

But, he continued, if you will not marry

> and persist in thinking a commerce with the sex inevitable, then . . . in all your amours you should prefer old women to young ones. Their conversation is better, and their discretion. Because in every animal that walks upright . . . the face first grows lank and wrinkled; then the neck; then the breast and arms; the lower parts continuing to the last as plump as ever: so that covering all above with a basket . . . it is impossible of two women to know an old from a young one.

And finally, older women "are so grateful."

In 1746 Franklin developed in "Reflections on Courtship and Marriage"[25] an argument which Silence Dogood had begun more than twenty years before, that women might become quite as sensible as men if they could be educated toward reasonableness instead of being pampered and flattered. Marriage was a good thing, beset with problems, but none of which a sensible man could not overcome. Swift never wrote more sharply in disgust than Franklin did when describing how housewives can appear at breakfast

> Downstairs they come, pulling up their ungartered, dirty stockings; slip-shod, with naked heels peeping out; no stays or other decent conveniency, but all flip-flop; a sort of clout thrown about the neck without form or decency; a tumbled, discoloured mob or nightcap, half on and half off, with the frowsy hair hanging in sweaty ringlets, staring like Medusa with her serpents; shrugging up her petticoats, that are sweeping the ground and scarce tied on; hands unwashed, teeth furred, and eyes crusted—but I beg your pardon, I'll go no farther with this sluttish picture.

The *Gentleman's Magazine* of London in its issue of April 1747 contained "The Speech of Polly Baker,"[26] a tale which somehow crossed the Atlantic, no one has discovered how, to take all Europe by storm, reprinted in a score of journals, attracting the attention of Diderot, Voltaire, and Philip Mazzei, and returning to America to reign triumphant, in spite of John Adams's protest against it as "an outrage to morality and decorum," as America's first popularly successful short story. Polly was an honest but unfortunate girl, prosecuted for the fifth time "at Connecticut near Boston in New England" for having born a bastard child. "I cannot conceive," she said with naive lack of precision in choosing words, "what the nature of my offense is. I have brought five fine children into the world at the risk of my life; I have maintained them well by my industry, without burdening the township, and would have done it better, if it had not been for the heavy fines and charges I have paid. Can it be a crime (in the nature of things, I mean) to add to the number of the King's subjects, in a new country that really wants people?" The worst she had done was to deprive some clergyman or justice of peace of wedding fees. Can it be supposed, she asked, "that heaven is angry at my having children, when to the little done by me towards it, God has been pleased to add His divine skill and admirable workmanship in the formation of their bodies and crowned the whole by furnishing them with immortal souls? . . . If you gentlemen must be making laws, do not turn natural and useful actions into crimes by your prohibitions."

She asked them to consider her first seducer, now a magistrate like themselves. She asked them to think of the harm done to society by celibate bachelors who

by their manner of living leave unproduced (which is little better than murder) hundreds of their posterity to the thousandth generation. Is this not a greater offense against the public good than mine? Compel them, then, by law, either to marry or pay double the fine for fornication each year. What must a poor woman do, whom customs and nature forbid to solicit men, and who cannot force themselves upon husbands, when the laws take no care to provide them with any and yet severely punish them if they do their duty without them? The duty of the first and great command of nature and nature's God, increase and multiply; a duty from the steady performance of which nothing has been able to deter me, for its sake I have hazarded the loss of public esteem and have frequently endured public disgrace and punishment: and therefore ought, in my humble opinion, instead of a whipping to have a statue erected in my memory.

No statue was erected—though one of the magistrates who sat in judgment was so impressed that he married her, and together they had fifteen children—but Polly is affectionately remembered by admirers who discover her a cousin to Defoe's Moll Flanders, Polly Peacham of John Gay's *The Beggar's Opera*, and Richardson's Clarissa. Her American descendants from Hester Prynne to Carrie Meeber and Eula Varner have not been more lively nor more likable than she. After Pocahontas, Polly is the first American heroine to triumph before a European audience. She captivated as a sensible female equivalent of practical Ben Franklin, who late in life explained to Madame Brillon that an additional injunction should be added to the Ten Commandments: "*Increase and multiply* and replenish the earth," and who wondered why men who perform all manner of mischief in daylight, lying and scheming and destroying one another, "creep into corners, or cover themselves with the darkness of night, when they mean to beget, as being ashamed of a virtuous action."[27]

Not for several literary generations was another native man of letters to write with equal vigor of doing what comes naturally. Mark Twain, who did not like Franklin because he read only a few of his writings, would have been delighted with the older man's whoppers about American sheep with tails so heavy that carts had to be provided to support them, or his handsomely phrased denial that American streets were "pav'd with half-peck Loaves, the Houses til'd with Pancakes." He might have wished he had written, though secretly, Franklin's letter "To the Royal Academy of Brusselles" which recommended "some Drug wholesome and not disagreeable, to be mix'd with our common Food or Sauces, that shall render the Natural discharges of Wind from our Bodies, not only inoffensive, but agreeable as Perfumes. . . . A pill of Turpentine no bigger than a pea, shall bestow . . . the pleasing Smell of Violets."[28]

From first to last, Franklin was a lusty writer, earthy and with no nonsense about him—not Chloe but plain country Joan, not milady in silks but pretty Polly Baker, not pining and sighing and wasting with care, but action when necessary and under control. However often these are demonstrated as traits common to the sensible eighteenth century or of an emerging, confident middle class, they were characteristics which Franklin set down and established because, in explaining himself, he explained his age. In doing so, he designed a pattern to which many of his successful countrymen would fit. Having made his fortune, the prosperous American dedicates himself to good deeds and public service—Franklin in his mid-forties retired to do precisely that. Comfortably established, he has time to catch up on what he previously had no time for, like the languages Franklin learned. He putters in his workshop over experiments and inventions. He goes abroad as Lambert Strether or Sam Dodsworth did, to discover the riches of European culture. He meets or corresponds with other men whose interests are like his. He discovers and encourages young men of ability, putting them through school, establishing them in business, showering them with advice, and standing as godparent for their children. Secure and with nothing to lose, he enjoys avuncular flirtations, daring compliments which a younger man could only risk if prepared to follow them through.

What separates Franklin from most people like him is that he did all of these, and with such tumultuous energy that he leaves the best-intentioned imitators gaping. His political writings alone could have made his reputation; indeed, during his lifetime, they did. Without abandoning the urbanity learned from Addison, he assumed in his attacks against England in such essays as "Rules by which a Great Empire May Be Reduced to a Small One" and "Edict by the King of Prussia,"[29] the ironic masks of Swift and the straight-faced, outrageous exaggerations of Defoe with such skill that students of satire place him among its masters because of his unerring eye for an opening, his ruthless pressing of every advantage, and his ingenuity in using ironic devices to exploit situations to his advantage. Molded to measures which moved his time, most of Franklin's political essays can thus be relished for their skill in rhetorical organization or their deftness with words, but they are not likely to impress a modern reader with much besides their strong virtuosity. Like yesterday's jokes, they speak clearly only when illumined by knowledge of circumstances which created them or their fortuitous relevance to some similar situation today.

Among the most shockingly successful was "On Humbling Our Rebels," which Franklin published in the friendly London *Public Advertiser* in 1774. Pretending alarm because robust but rebellious American colonials multiplied dangerously fast as a result of early marriages and the amazing fertility of their women, he proposed that all American males be gelded. This done, after "fifty years it is possible we shall not have one rebellious subject in North America." Meanwhile a crop of home-grown tenors might be produced, thus keeping in England the tremendous sums spent each year to acquire them in Italy. "It might likewise be of service to our Levant Trade, as we could supply the Grand Signor's Seraglio, and Harams of the Grandees of the Turkish Dominions with Cargoes of Eunuchs, as also with Handsome Women, for which America is as famous as Circassia."

On hearing reports of British barbarity during the Revolution, Franklin struck off on his press at Passy, near Paris, what purported to be a "Supplement to the Boston *Independent Chronicle*," reporting "eight Pack of Scalps, cured, dried, hooped, and painted with all the Indian triumphal Marks. . . . Containing 43 Scalps of Congress Soldiers, killed in different skirmishes," 62 of farmers killed after surprise attacks at night, 98 of farmers who died fighting to protect their families, 97 of farmers killed in the fields—"only 18 marked with a little yellow Flame to denote their being Prisoners burnt alive, after being scalped, their Nails pulled out by the Roots, and other Torments"; 88 scalps of women, "hair long, braided in the Indian Fashion, to shew they were Mothers. . . . 17 others, Hair very Grey, blacks, hoops, plain brown Colour, no Mark, but the short Club or Cassetête, to shew they were knocked down dead or had their Brains beat out." He proposed to divide the collection "in decent little Packets, seal and direct them; one to the King, containing a Sample of every Sort for his Museum; one to the Queen, with some of Women and little Children; the Rest to be distributed among both Houses of Parliament; a double Quantity to the Bishops."[30]

Franklin was not always so grisly. In "A Parable against Persecution"[31] he spoke in biblical style so adroitly that some readers mistook his words for Scripture. When he described his experi-ments or inventions, he was straightforward and plain, whether the subject was an arrangement of balloons strapped about his shoulders to take weight off his gouty feet or a device by which short men might remove books from high shelves. His letters—on official business, to scientific associates, in friendly discourse, or of admonition and advice—were models, each of its kind. The inexhaustible energy, curiosity, and kindliness of this multiple man are nowhere better revealed than in Franklin's correspond-ence. In an age when epistolary art invited the best talents of men of leisure or ambition, he was among its most adept and versatile practitioners. His letters allow glimpses behind the familiar mask of doughty Ben Franklin to the intelligence and artistry which molded its features so well.

Like many men who glimpse truths which they find it wisest not directly to express, Franklin often spoke most effectively in banter. The indirection of humor was a defense against responsi-bility, making it possible to shrug off the embarrassment of un-manly commitment. Franklin's was the comic view—the world a stage, each man a player, often ridiculous, especially when caught reaching beyond what he could touch. Things not under-stood were to be guarded against, as when one emptied his pockets of all but small coins before listening to a sermon, lest momentary enthusiasm tempt him to put too much into the collection plate. The world of spirit was a pretty fable, useful in playful exchanges, like the one which the comfortably aging Franklin undertook with Madame Helvetius, explaining his visit to the afterworld in dream, where he discovered that her late husband and his deceased Deborah had "formed a new connection which will endure to eternity. . . . Let us revenge ourselves."[32]

One man's myth was as good as another's. Most substantial of the essays which Franklin in his seventies struck off on his private press at Passy[33]—jewelled pieces of precisely patterned prose, like "The Whistle," "The Ephemera," "The Dialogue between Franklin and the Gout," and "The Morals of Chess," any one of which can insure his reputation as a stylist—is the "Remarks concerning the Savages of North-America": "Savages we call them, because their manners differ from ours." Rousseau is again echoed, Chateaubriand anticipated, and Cooper and Melville and Sir James Frazer of *The Golden Bough,* but the voice is Franklin's. White man's training has spoiled young Indians, making them "bad Runners, ignorant of every means of living in the Woods, unable to bear Cold or Hunger," knowing "neither how to build a Cabin, take a Deer, or kill an Enemy." When a missionary preacher attempted to make converts among Indian tribesmen, explaining "the principal historical Facts, on which our Religion is founded, such as the Fall of our first Parents by Eating an Apple, the Coming of Christ to repair the Mischief, his Miracles and Suffering," a spokesman for his listeners politely replied, "It is indeed bad to eat Apples. It is better to make them into Cyder."

"We are much obliged by your Kindness in coming so far to tell us those things which you have heard from your Mothers," continued the Indian.

In Return I will tell you some of those we have heard from ours. In the Beginning our Fathers had only the Flesh of Animals to subsist on, and if their Hunting was unsuccessful, they were starving. Two of our young Hunters having killed a Deer, made a Fire in the Woods to broil some Parts of it. When they were about to satisfy their Hunger, they beheld a beautiful young Woman descend from the Clouds, and seat herself on that Hill which you see yonder among the blue Mountains. They said to each other, it is a Spirit that perhaps has smelt our broiling Venison, and wishes to eat of it: let us offer some to her. They presented her with the Tongue: she was pleased with the Taste of it, and said, your Kindness shall be rewarded. Come to this Place after thirteen Moons, and you shall find something that will be of great Benefit in nourishing your Children to the last Generations. They did so, and to their Surprise found Plants they had never seen before, but which from that ancient time have been constantly cultivated among us to our great Advantage. Where her right Hand touch'd the Ground, they found Maize; where her left Hand touch'd it, they found Kidney-beans; and where her Backside had sat on it, they found Tobacco.

Any explanation of what man could not know was thus an old wives' tale, something heard from one's mother. Men did not bother with such. Religion, spirituality of any kind, was a feminine grace, attractive and worth toying with, just as women were, but must be put aside when work was to be done. Not uniquely an American attitude, nor invented by Franklin, it gained such currency by his presence and words that for generations many among his countrymen could say that writing which searched beneath or above levels of common sense was to be expected only of men or women incapable of more unmistakably productive enterprise. Literature was at best an avocation, to be written surreptitiously under the protective mask of pseudonyms such as Washington Irving and Samuel Clemens would use. When patriotic, or when explaining something—as Cooper explained the inappropriateness of mixing races or classes and as Mrs. Stowe explained cruelty—then it might be understood.

America's promise remained an attractive theme, spilling over from oratory more florid than Franklin would approve. Humor such as his maintained its position as a hedge behind which anyone might hide when he suspected that people laughed at his better intentions. The ventriloquist writer invaded the New World, the mummer behind a masque. Dialect became effective because it spoke in the accents of simple people without the writer taking responsibility on himself for what was spoken. The cracker box, woodland stump, town meeting, lyceum and chautauqua, the quiz show and panel discussion, good things all, became forums from which the plain American spoke, or oracles to which he listened. He became a sturdy, likable, and dependable fellow, this plain American, a good man to have around in almost any emergency, just as Franklin was, who invented him.

He had help. Like any inventor, he took advantage of living at the right time and in the right places, with the right materials at hand. His genes were correctly arranged: he chose his parents wisely. But, all this considered, his achievement was large and lasting. The personage remembered as Ben Franklin is an amalgam of Poor Richard, Father Abraham, the young man who caught electricity with a kite, the sagacious old man in spectacles and fur cap who charmed all Europe, and the boy who was born, it is sometimes said, in Philadelphia at the age of seventeen, trudging its dusty streets with giant loaves of bread under each arm, laughed at then, but probably for the last time—these, and much more: satirist, humorist, storyteller, essayist, letter writer, jokester, precisionist, and punster. What Benjamin Franklin really was is cloaked behind a fabric so expertly woven that no biographer has penetrated it, and so attractively designed that hundreds have been tempted to try. What remains is what he showed of himself, a masked figure playing a part so well that, like Walt Whitman or Mark Twain, he must himself sometimes have had difficulty in distinguishing the poser from the pose.

His *Autobiography* thus becomes the first American book to belong permanently to literature. It created a man. Written, the first part as a moral guide to show his son the way to success, and ensuing parts as a substitute for the treatise on *The Art of Virtue* which Franklin never found time to compose, it offered efficient testimony "that man is not even at present a vicious and detestable animal, and still more . . . that good management may greatly amend him." As much as Rousseau's *Confessions*, the declaration of American independence, or Wordsworth's preface to *Lyrical Ballads*, it announced the emergence of a view of man as good and capable of becoming better. To think of Franklin as a romantic is to stretch the limits of that term, for he combined with his confidence in what Emerson later, more enthusiastically called "the infinitude of the private man," a sense like that of Marcus Aurelius or Hemingway of limits beyond which man may not explore. Taking what was needed from wherever it was found, he made a patchwork of ideas which served him well in warmth and comfort and pleasant dreams.

Composed at various times and in varying moods, the *Autobiography* is not a well-made book. Franklin was sixty-five when he began it in 1771 on a fortnight holiday in Twyford, England, and brought the story of his life through some eighty pages down to 1730. More than ten years passed until, at Passy in 1784, he puttered over new pages which set forth his early methodical plans for "arriving at moral perfection." Returned to America, he took up the task again in 1788, picking up the narrative in 1731 and carrying it industriously forward to 1757. Sometime before his death in the spring of 1790, Franklin added a brief fourth part which ended with events of 1759. In style, the first part is best, written as a letter to his son in leisurely, reminiscent affection for the boy whose adventures it told. By the time he began the second part, Franklin had been convinced by friends that the memoirs should be made public, addressed to young men everywhere. As a result, pictorial narrative is replaced by moral suasion as the industrious but bumbling boy becomes for many pages something of a prig, so intent on self-improvement that he caricatures himself. The third part, still burdened with morality, presses doggedly on, and the brief fourth part breaks off abruptly, as if the narrative might have gone on and one except for the accident that Franklin then stopped writing.

As in *Walden, Moby-Dick,* and *Adventures of Huckleberry Finn,* the story is unfinished, and the hero is off to fresh adventures which an imaginative reader may infer or discover. Without art, except in saying plain things plainly, Franklin thus adventitiously fathered a native literary form and a way of looking at the world which pays less attention to what a person is than to what he becomes or may become. The New World was a land of opportunities, and Franklin demonstrated in his life story how they might be met, through diligence and wise management. If what he said of youthful escapades and young triumphs cannot in every instance be proved true, neither can they be thought false to the legend which his life and his memory of it created. Making drama out of drudgery and a liturgy of service, he authenticated the presumption that with attention to these the least of men might rise and, rising, lift his fellows. "I have always thought," he said, "that one man of tolerable abilities will work great changes and accomplish great affairs among mankind." The lengthening shadow of Ben Franklin is spread over one after another of the institutions he fathered— the fire companies, city watch, schemes for keeping streets clean, for practical education, for justice to the Negro and Indian, for developing a postal system, and helping young men save money by learning to shave themselves.

Ultimately, however, it was that one man, a single and separate person, who must make his way—and Franklin sat for and painted his portrait. As America's first literary masterwork, the *Autobiography* may seem to make a shoddy, poor-relation appearance beside more ambitious and better planned books which follow it. But it holds its own. Badly organized, with hardly a metaphor in all its matter-of-fact pages, but enriched with the power of words as they are really spoken, it presents one character, distinctively, even disruptively American, whom many have attempted to sketch again, but none so well. Looking back over his life, as Mark Twain was later to look back over his, Franklin created an image of the American boy, a more seriously engaged, city-bred Tom Sawyer, who meant well, and who did well by looking out for himself. He learned, perhaps more than Huck Finn, to know the venality of man, but after a few tentative experiments, was too alert and ambitious to let that bother him. Ben Franklin had his eyes open. He knew that men and institutions were often corrupt, but he was confident that they might be improved. Knowing his limitations—that he was not a poet nor a facile conversationalist—he was nonetheless sure that by proper maneuvering of the talents he had, he could move triumphantly ahead, and he did.

"Once in a while I just naturally sit back and size up this Solid American Citizen with a whale of a lot of satisfaction," said Sinclair Lewis's Babbitt. Sidney Smith in England—he who in 1820 asked scornfully, "Who reads an American book?"— once told his daughter, "I will disinherit you, if you do not admire everything written by Franklin."[34] America failed in literary taste, thought the Scottish critic James Jeffrey, because it did not appreciate its best and most renowned author. "Would to God we had in Europe," said Johann von Herder, whose *Letters of Humanity* was largely inspired by the life of Franklin, "a people who could read him and act and live in accordance therewith to their own best well-being! where would we be then!"[35]

To this, as to almost everything else, Mark Twain had an answer. He urged every alert American to "snub those pretentious maxims" which Franklin "worked up out of truisms that had become wearisome platitudes as early as the dispersion from Babel." He scoffed at Franklin's making so much of arriving in Philadelphia "with nothing in the world but two shillings in his pocket and four rolls of bread under his arm. . . . Anybody could have done it." All such "execrable eccentricities," explained Mark Twain, are "only *evidences* of genius, not *creators* of it. I wish I had been the father of my parents long enough to make them comprehend this truth, and thus prepare their son to have an easier time of it. When I was a child I had to boil soap . . . and I had to get up early and study geometry at breakfast, and peddle my own poetry, and do everything just as Franklin did, in the solemn hope that I would be a Franklin some day." Following such an example resulted in "my present state of general debility, indigence, and mental aberration. My parents used to have me up before nine o'clock when I was a boy. If they had let me get my natural rest where would I be now? Keeping store, no doubt, respected by all."[36]

NOTES

1. *Studies in Classic American Literature* (New York, 1923), p. 19.

2. I. Bernard Cohen, *Benjamin Franklin: His Contribution to the American Tradition* (Indianapolis and New York, 1953), p. 38.

3. *The Autobiography of Leigh Hunt, with Reminiscences of Friends and Contemporaries* (New York, 1850), 2: 18–19.

4. *Benjamin Franklin* (New York, 1938), p. 782. Van Doren's is still the best biography of Franklin. More recent, briefer studies include Richard E. Amacher, *Benjamin Franklin* (New York, 1962); Theodore Hornberger, *Benjamin Franklin* (Minneapolis, 1962); and J. A. Leo Lemay, "Benjamin Franklin," in *Major Writers of Early American Literature*, ed. Everett Emerson (Madison, Wis., 1972), pp. 204–244. See also Bruce Ingham Granger, *Benjamin Franklin: An American Man of Letters* (Ithaca, N.Y., 1964) and Alfred Owen Aldridge, *Benjamin Franklin: Philosopher and Man* (Philadelphia, 1965).

5. *Israel Potter: His Fifty Years of Exile* (New York, 1855), p. 81.

6. Charles Francis Adams, ed., *The Works of John Adams* (Boston, 1856), 1: 660, 663–664.

7. William Temple Franklin, ed., *Private Correspondence of Benjamin Franklin* (London, 1833), 1: 38.

8. Adams, *The Works of John Adams*, 1: 660.

9. "Eripuit cœlo fulman sceptrumque tyrannus," the inscription, said to have been composed by the French statesman Anne Robert Jacques Turbot, which appears below the bust of Franklin made in Paris by Jean Antoine Houdon.

10. "What Is an American?" in *Letters from an American Farmer* (New York, 1957), pp. 39–40.

11. This and the unidentified following quotations are from Franklin's *Autobiography*, the best modern editions of which are edited by Max Farrand (Berkeley and Los Angeles, 1949) and by Leonard W. Labaree et al. (New Haven, 1959).

12. Quotations are from those of the "Dogood Papers" collected in Frank Luther Mott and Chester E. Jorgenson, eds., *Benjamin Franklin: Representative Selections, with Introduction, Bibliography, and Notes* (New York, 1936), pp. 96–111. The essays may be found complete in the distinguished new, but yet uncompleted, edition of *The Papers of Benjamin Franklin* (New Haven, 1959–), edited by Leonard W. Labaree, William B. Willcox, and their associates.

13. *A Dissertation on Liberty and Necessity, Pleasure and Pain, 1725*, edited for the Facsimile Text Society by Lawrence C. Wroth (New York, 1930), p. 32.

14. Quotations from "The Busy Body" are from Mott and Jorgenson, *Benjamin Franklin*, pp. 137–186.

15. *In the American Grain* (New York, 1935), p. 156.

16. See Lewis Leary, "Joseph Dennie on Benjamin Franklin: A Note on Early American Literary Criticism," *Pennsylvania Magazine of History and Biography* 72 (July 1948): 240–246.

17. Charles Augustine Sainte-Beuve, *Portraits of the Eighteenth Century* (New York, 1905), 1: 33.

18. *Studies in Classic American Literature*, pp. 30–31.

19. There are many selective reprints of *Poor Richard's Almanac*, among the most useful of which is that edited by Phillips Russell (Garden City, N.Y., 1928) which presents facsimiles of the 1733, 1749, 1756, 1757, and 1758 issues. See also Paul Leicester Ford, *"The Sayings of Poor Richard": The Prefaces, Proverbs, and Poems*

of Benjamin Franklin originally Printed in Poor Richard's Almanacs for 1733–1758 (Brooklyn, 1890).

20. Lindsay Swift, *Benjamin Franklin* (Boston, 1910), pp. 33–34.

21. Paul Leicester Ford, *The Many-Sided Franklin* (New York, 1899), p. 56.

22. Albert Henry Smyth, ed., *The Writings of Benjamin Franklin* (New York, 1907), 7: 434–435.

23. Recorded by John M'Vickar, *A Domestic Narrative of the Life of Samuel Bard* (New York, 1822), pp. 18–19.

24. Paul McPharlin, ed., *Satires and Bagatelles* (Detroit, 1937), pp. 32–34.

25. *Reflections on Courtship and Marriage: In Two Letters to a Friend, Wherein a Practical Plan Is Laid Down for Obtaining and Securing Conjugal Fidelity* (Philadelphia, 1746), pp. 40–41.

26. For a sympathetic and attractive full account of Polly's adventures, in life and in print, see Max Hall, *Benjamin Franklin and Polly Baker: The History of a Literary Deception* (Chapel Hill, N.C., 1960).

27. See Aldridge, *Benjamin Franklin*, p. 283.

28. See Richard E. Amacher, ed., *Franklin's Wit and Folly: The Bagatelles* (New Brunswick, N.J., 1953), p. 68, a delight-filled book to which I am variously and gratefully indebted.

29. *Writings*, 6: 127–137, 146.

30. Ibid., 8: 437–447.

31. Ibid., 6: 254–256.

32. Amacher, *Franklin's Wit and Folly*, p. 56. See also Claude-Anne Lopez, *Mon Cher Papa: Franklin and the Ladies of Paris* (New Haven, Conn., 1966).

33. All most conveniently found in Amacher, *Franklin's Wit and Folly*.

34. Quoted in *Writings*, 1: 33.

35. H. D. Learned, "Herder and America," *German-American Annals*, n.s. 2 (1904): 556.

36. "The Late Benjamin Franklin," *The Writings of Mark Twain* (New York and London, 1903), 19: 213–215.

Nathaniel Tucker

EXPATRIATE PATRIOT

❧ ❧

ATHANIEL TUCKER was a very minor but not unrepresentative poet of the late eighteenth century. Born in Bermuda in 1750, he lived during the early 1770s briefly in South Carolina and visited in Virginia, but then spent the rest of his life abroad, a student at Edinburgh, Leyden, and London, and a physician in Yorkshire until his death in 1807. During the American Revolution, he thought of himself as a patriot marooned in an enemy land, able only to play a spectator poet's part in the struggle of his colonial countrymen for freedom. To their cause he contributed *Columbinus: A Mask*, hoping that it might be adopted in the new United States as a national drama, to be performed each year on some patriotic anniversary and thus, he said, become "the bark in which I am to voyage over the ocean of time to the distant shore of posterity."[1] Instead, it has been hidden away for almost two hundred years in a manuscript copy, unread by almost everyone.

Poor Natty, his brothers called him, for nearly everything that he turned to seemed to fail. Other Tuckers did well. His oldest brother, Henry, was to become president of the colonial council in Bermuda, and Henry's sons would play important roles in the colonization of India. Thomas Tudor, six years older than Nathaniel, received a medical degree from Edinburgh, practiced as a physician in Charleston, South Carolina, became a delegate to the Continental Congress, and during Jefferson's administration was treasurer of the United States. St. George, two years younger than Nathaniel, came to Williamsburg, Virginia, as a student at the College of William and Mary, served with distinction at the battle of Yorktown, and remained in Virginia for the rest of his life, a lawyer, judge, professor, and occasional poet, honored among the state's most prominent citizens. But Nathaniel, whom his family thought blessed with much talent and great goodness of heart, was less successful, largely, it was supposed, because he wanted so badly to be a poet.

During the almost twenty years through which he fed this ambition, he was in idea and expression a weathercock turned successively by prevailing literary winds. He composed first, in the 1770s, after the pattern of Goldsmith and Gray, in regularized couplets, in the spirit of humane rationalism derived from Pope. In the 1780s he discovered the more freely sweeping lines of Milton and Shakespeare better fitted for expressing the enthusiasms of that revolutionary decade. By the 1790s he had given up verse making, fascinated instead by the transcendental revelations of Emanuel Swedenborg which he translated into volumes which would be read by William Blake and Samuel Taylor Coleridge.

As a younger man, he had the unusual notion that poetry in colonial America might be made profitable, that by publishing his verses in small volumes he might, in the phraseology of a later generation, work his way through college. He had been making verses for years, first in Bermuda while he was employed as a clerk with the colonial council, and then in Charleston, where from the autumn of 1771 to the spring of 1775 he intermittently assisted Thomas Tudor Tucker in his medical practice, hoping thereby to put aside enough money to pay for his own medical education. But poetry remained a first love. Nathaniel's first published poem seems to have been a *jeu d'esprit* in the *South-Carolina Gazette* of 9 July 1772 addressed "To Eleazer," a pseudonymous contributor to that newspaper who had been so ungallant as to cast aspersions on the costume and the manners of the young ladies of Charleston: "How cou'd thy sacrilegious Paper dare / To cast such gross Reflections on the Fair?"

Seventy-six lines in couplets streamed from his pen as he turned it upon the "mistaken, vain abuser of the quill" who dared assault, and with such lack of chivalry, the costume and manners of modern maidens. Should they, in these days when men are "no longer by tradition swayed," be bound to fashions inherited from the past?

> Shou'd Fancy, cherish'd by the blooming Maid,
> In new Commodes or Tippets be display'd,
> And the gay Beauties of our modern days,
> Presume to change the fashion of their Stays;
> Consulting Health, Conveniency and Ease,
> Less lightly lac'd, no less expect to please?

Modeled on the more cleanly epigrammatic manner of Pope, in the popular literary fashion of young men of wit who enjoyed the intellectual exercise of wrenching a rhyme into place, Nathaniel's verses were sprightly and skillfully turned, certainly effective, if not as poetry, as argument. There was probably no reader in Charleston who recognized the irony of attacking the tradition-ridden notions of "Eleazer" on modern female fashions through the medium of verses exactly as old-fashioned and conventional as the tightly laced stays they deprecated.

The mood for making verses had settled heavily on Nathaniel since his arrival in Charleston—perhaps because there was so little else for him to do. Study abroad seemed now out of the question, if to attain it he were to depend solely on Thomas Tudor, "from whose tenderness I might expect everything in his power," but who was "at present far from being in a condition to support me in Edinburgh or even himself here." But poetry might help. "I have composed some little things since I have been here," he wrote in November to St. George in Williamsburg, "but none in the amorous style." Among them was a long poem on his native island, over which he had worked lovingly and long and which he called *The Bermudian*. It had been completed by the early part of July and sent to brother Henry in Bermuda for criticism. "I have spent some of my time unprofitably," Nathaniel then apologized, "in a fruitless attention to the Muses."

He wrote again to St. George in February 1773 about plans for the publication of the poem. He urged his younger brother to distribute subscription papers among friends in Virginia, and informed him that Thomas Tudor Tucker would see to the publication of the volume in Edinburgh, or even London. Proceeds from the sale of the two editions, one in Virginia and one abroad, would certainly bring in enough, he thought, to allow him to pursue his education. After those were published, he thought he might venture a second volume which he tentatively planned to call *The Hermit*. Then, if his writings should be well received, he might "turn author and live in a garret" happily for the rest of his life.

His ambition fed hungrily on the praise which the manuscript of *The Bermudian* received in Virginia. The Reverend Samuel Henley, onetime professor of moral philosophy at the college there, wrote a sonnet about it comparing it to Edmund Waller's celebrated poem about Bermuda. James Madison, professor of natural philosophy at the college, wrote four close-filled pages of versified appreciation. Nathaniel sent St. George a packet containing the rest of his writings. "You'll have," he said, "enough poetry to make you sick a month."

Then in the summer of 1773 he went himself to Williamsburg for further planning. Two thousand copies of *The Bermudian* were to be printed there, and two thousand more in Edinburgh where printing was cheap, but with a London imprint because that seemed more respectable. Relatives in Bermuda and friends in Antigua and Saint Eustacia were enlisted for help in securing subscribers.

But matters moved with disappointing slowness. Not until March 1774 did Nathaniel and Thomas Tudor Tucker in Charleston receive copies of the Edinburgh edition, twelve of them, some of which were joyously sent to family and friends, others optimistically offered for sale. The book had been handsomely printed by William Creech in Edinburgh, though the title page, as expected, designated its place of origin as London. Nathaniel was chagrined however that the edition turned out to be of one thousand, not two thousand, copies. Letter after letter went to St. George, urging him to hurry the Williamsburg edition through the press. But not until two months later, in May, did they receive in Charleston copies of that edition, as printed from the press of Alexander Purdie and John Dixon, proprietors of the *Virginia Gazette*. And that was a disappointment also. Four hundred copies were sent to Bermuda. Three hundred dispatched for sale in Charleston. Bookseller James Rivington in New York distressed the brothers by accepting only one hundred and fifty for sale in that city. That left only one hundred and fifty copies for distribution in Virginia, for the Williamsburg edition was also only of one thousand copies.

And even they did not do well. Nathaniel Tucker thought that the fault was with the type which was too small, the margins which were too narrow, and the proofreading which was enexcusably careless, making necessary an unsightly listing of errata. His name was not even on the title page, though its printers in their *Virginia Gazette* advertised it for almost a month in June and July 1774 as "a poem by N. Tucker, Esquire of Bermuda." Perhaps it was overpriced at two shillings and six pence, as compared to the Edinburgh edition which sold for one shilling and six pence. At any rate, it seems to have sold slowly in Virginia. The printers pleaded for several weeks that the "Gentlemen who have subscribed for THE BERMUDIAN" to call for their copies at the post office, "Where they will please lodge the Money" they had promised.

But even without Nathaniel Tucker's name on its title page, the Williamsburg edition was not anonymous. It was prefaced by a dedicatory letter not included in the Edinburgh edition, addressed "To Henry Tucker, Junior, Esq. of Bermuda," and signed "Your most affectionate Brother, N. Tucker." In it Nathaniel defended his "little poem" on four counts. First, it was an initial attempt, for him, in a new literary form, and "written at an early Period of Life." Second, he admitted being "in some Measure, indebted for its plan to Doctor Goldsmith's Deserted Village" so that "several of the Thoughts are . . . borrowed from that pleasing Writer," and others were "suggested by a Similarity of Sentiment." Third, as *The Bermudian* was "an American production, I flatter myself," he wrote, "with some Expectation of Partiality from the Western World."

His fourth defense, hidden in the last sentence of the dedicatory letter, is perhaps most revealing. He had dedicated his poem to the most unliterary of his brothers, but to the one most strategically placed to influence its distribution through the island colonies. Nathaniel expressed a desire "for the Approbation of Men, who, like you, know how to set a proper Value on a good Heart, though its Emotions may not be described in the most classical Language."

But the Western world received *The Bermudian* most casually. Henry Tucker wrote from Bermuda that "not a person of discernment has seen it but is delighted with it and desirous of procuring a copy," but in the mainland colonies sales were slow and public notice was almost nonexistent. In November its Williamsburg printers presented in the *Virginia Gazette* brief notices from transatlantic periodicals, presumably in an effort to create a market for copies which still remained in their shop. A woman poet in Williamsburg wrote lines in its praise, but they apparently circulated only among friends. John Adams in New England later expressed some admiration for *The Bermudian,* but thought it to have been written, not by Nathaniel, but by St. George Tucker. In 1774 people in the American colonies had matters on their minds other than poetry.

The Edinburgh edition, better printed, was also better publicly received. The *Monthly Review* in London found that the poem "indeed, bears the Mark of Juvenility, but it likewise evinces the promising Genius of the Writer; who, if he continues to Cultivate, with Ardour, his poetical powers, will probably soon grow into considerable Favour with the Muses." The *Critical Review* liked it well enough, "notwithstanding a few blemishes which occur in some parts," explaining that "he who is resolved to be displeased at every thing which is not excellent, will find little entertainment in reading," and concluding that if *The Bermudian* was indeed "a juvenile performance," then "we may expect pieces still more finished from the same author." The *Gentleman's Magazine* quoted from the poem at length, with comment that the "happy island of Bermuda . . . has here met with a native to celebrate her praises with all the enthusiasm which the *natale solum* usually inspires, and in numbers not unworthy of a much older son of Apollo." The *Edinburgh Review* spoke of it at length, describing its author as "a Poet in whom the Ardour of Youth, the Love of Nature, and the powerful prepossession for his natural Soil, unite their conspiring Blaze, and animate his Strains with uncommon Force and Tenderness."[2]

But the poem was even to its author not completely satisfactory. The opening apostrophe of seventy-four lines to "Bermuda, parent of my early days" may seem too long and to promise, as Nathaniel Tucker had admitted some months earlier on 5 February 1773 to his brother in Virginia, "more than it was in my power to perform." These lines were a late addition to the poem and shifted its focus from the exile poet to the island, causing St. George Tucker to suggest that its title should be changed to *Bermuda*. Nathaniel explained that his first purpose had been "to write something that would show my attachment to my Bermuda friends." It was only to subserve this purpose that he had taken the conventional liberty, he said "of conveying myself to some hill from whence I might have a view of my native soil and parental seat." For it was not, he insisted, of Bermuda that he wrote, but of his family and friends there and "the domestic happiness I once enjoyed." Other matter was "only thrown in by way of variety." Yet, when a few months after the poem had been published, he sent St. George one hundred and forty-six new lines which could be inserted if a new edition were called for, he wrote then, not of familial matters, but of the devastating effect of a south Atlantic hurricane upon the island.

For though *The Bermudian* is well within the tradition of the English topographical poem, didactic and morally enlightening, its description of a quiet scene mounting in conventional climax to instructive advice, through it also runs another theme, not quite so conventional or, according to classic literary regulations, completely sound. Remembered scenery and family joys are described almost as if necessary items of literary etiquette. At root, the poem is extremely personal, descriptive less of the island or its people than of an exile whose lonely retrospection invites the response, not even of "poor young poet," but of "poor young man"—poor Natty.

Though disappointed at the reception of his poem, "I live in hopes," Nathaniel nonetheless wrote to St. George, of embarking for Europe soon. That failing, he thought of moving north to Virginia, for Charleston seemed now certainly no place for a poet. Everybody there seemed to have turned politician: "The Boston Port Bill makes a great noise here," he told St. George. "Spirited measures are talked of. . . . The storm seems to be gathering over America. God knows what will be the event." He crossed over to Bermuda early in July 1774 for a long holiday with his family, but was again "pestered to death with politics," wishing that Lord North had been damned indeed before his silly methods of plaguing colonists "had entered into his noodle." By the next spring, however, he was back in South Carolina with enough money in pocket—back wages, it has been suggested, long owed to him for his earlier clerkship with the colonial government—to pay his passage to London. In May 1775 he set sail.

Though tempestuous, the voyage was filled with good times which Nathaniel described in doggerel verses which were printed some months late, on 12 September, in the Edinburgh *Weekly Magazine* as "Mr. Clackit to His Brother Abroad." Good times continued in London, and then in Yorkshire with friends from Virginia, as Nathaniel made his way toward Scotland. There, torn between the study of medicine, which he did not like, and the writing of poetry, which he thought his true vocation, he wondered whether he could survive the three years required to obtain a degree at the University of Edinburgh, and thought he probably could not. He wrote something of his discouragement into "The Optimist" which appeared over his initials in the *Weekly Magazine* on 30 November 1775. The vanity of worldly joys and the comfort of resigning one's self to the inevitable were loosely woven into lines imitative of what he had read of Pope, Akenside, and many another, in strands frayed from his own lonely vaunting ambitions.

Medicine, at best, could supply him only respectable security, something to fall back on if poetry should fail. So he worked again over his longer poem, *The Hermit*, which he thought now of calling *The Philosophical Anchoret*, but which appeared sometime in 1776 from the press of William Creech in Edinburgh as *The Anchoret: A Poem*, described discreetly as "By the Author of the Bermudian." Like his earlier volume, it hid provincial origins behind a respectable London imprint. Yet for all such planning, *The Anchoret* seems to have been little noticed. It appeared at just the wrong time for circulation in America, for few books passed then between Britain and her rebellious colonies.

Nor does *The Anchoret* deserve more than passing notice. Its narrative framework does not disguise its conventional didacticism nor its tracings of the young poet's continuing discontent. With it, Nathaniel Tucker takes his place unobtrusively among other minor gloomy egoists of his time who pressed beyond present bewilderment to beat a melancholy retreat to dreams of escape to simplicity. Though St. George Tucker suggested that the poem may derive from a personal experience, the actual death of a young loved one in Bermuda ("Arpasia in The Hermit seems to be the same person with Ardella in the Bermudian"),[3] *The Anchoret* nonetheless presents a conventional pastiche of sentiments often better expressed before, and testifies to its author's familiarity with Milton, with Pope and Thompson certainly, and with others who in the eighteenth century wrote of getting away to some quiet place where nothing can intrude except what is pleasant to the poet.

Apparently finding the medical curriculum at Edinburgh too long or too time-consuming, Nathaniel Tucker completed his degree at Leyden in 1777 with a dissertation in Latin on the successive changes in the human body from one period of life to another. After a tour through Holland and France, he settled briefly in London for further medical studies. There, in the *Morning Post* of 25 February 1778, he published frolicsome complimentary verses addressed "To the Fair Incognita" who some days earlier had sent him Valentine greetings. But he was restless still, an exile, he thought, deprived by the war from immediate possibility of crossing the Atlantic again.

In the spring of 1779 he settled as a practicing physician at Malden in Yorkshire, writing occasionally, but despondent over the war and his inability to take an active part in it. He was overjoyed to receive complimentary verses praising *The Bermudian* from Anna Seward, the celebrated "Swan of Litchfield," who had known Erasmus, Darwin, and Samuel Johnson. In his melancholy versified response to her, he described the war as having produced a "mighty chaos . . . come to confound the world," searing it with "foul contagion." Both of his brothers in America played active patriot parts, while he, virtually a captive, he thought, stood idle. He felt alone and insecure, an alien exile who suffered "On the rough road of life the tilts and jostlings / Of this rude world."

The more he thought of it, the more the American Revolution seemed to him a contemporary instance of the triumph of an ideal such as poets had traditionally fashioned into song. In 1783 as the conflict seemed drawing to a close, he thought that he might contribute a poet's share to American victory by celebrating, not the details, of which he admittedly knew little, but the pulse-quickening promise of which the war in America seemed harbinger, as "British thunder shook, but not subverted," the "throne of Freedom." Neither the quick, probing wit of Pope nor the bludgeon attack of Churchill would suit that task. Turning rather to the more majestic line of Milton, Nathaniel planned an epic which would preserve the memory of the American Revolution in the minds of men forever.

He set himself immediately to the task. Composing rapidly, he completed the first book during the summer of 1783 and started on the second. The composition in its entirety would be called *America Delivered,* "an heroic poem." The first part, consisting of six long books, would have its own title, "The Triumph of Patriotism, or the Defeat of Mammon," an allegory in the grandest style, in which the angels of Heaven and the demons of Hell contended for control of man in America. Nathaniel charted his course in six tight-written pages of prose explanation; then, after thirty-four Miltonic lines of invocation to the Spirit of Liberty, he hastened—the verb is his—to the midst of the action, wherein the reader is introduced to the archangel Michael, "the celestial spirit of Wisdom," as he "shoots like a blazing star" from celestial realms to Philadelphia, to give advice to the American Congress as it meets with British commissioners to consider terms for peace.

At the same time, however, infernal spirits "who occupy the adverse region the other side of Chaos" meet in evil conclave:

> There frightful forms appear'd
> Thronging the ways or riding thro' the air
> On leathern wings, dire hell-engender'd monsters
> Shaggy and vast, or cover'd o'er with scales
> As dragons, breathing fire, with glowing eyes
> That burn'd as lamps; part cloven-footed, arm'd
> With tail of mortal sting, horned and fang'd
> To torture and perplex.

Led by Satan, the spirit of Ambition, they plot the downfall of American liberty: "Princes and potentates, illustrious founders / And sovrans of this newly founded kingdom—." Like his Miltonic predecessor, Nathaniel's Satan is addressing his assembled chief lieutenants, Beelzebub, Belial, Moloch, and Mammon, who speak, each in turn, much in the manner of their speech in *Paradise Lost,* to suggest some evil means of perverting the good colonials. As a result of their deliberations, Mammon is dispatched to earth as Hell's representative best qualified to carry out their corrupt designs.

This is as far as Nathaniel had progressed when that fall he sent a copy of the poem to his sister Bet in Bermuda, asking her opinion of what he had done. Should he continue with it? Or had he attempted something too large for him? She replied in considerate sisterly understatement that the poem seemed to get started very slowly, and was weighted with so much allegorical machinery that, even after a book and a half, the principal action had not yet begun. Nathaniel admitted the fault, but pleaded proudly that he had followed Milton very closely:

I have endeavored to communicate to it and to the characters the goodness and grandeur of my immortal example yet I have sometimes ventured to give up the sublime for the natural which in my opinion makes an agreeable variety and by affording the mind some relaxation prepares it to be more forcibly affected by the next bold passage. Though I have conveyed an allegory under the characters, I have made them very little different from those in Milton, except here and there to mark them (as I thought) more strongly. It was my meaning and intention to make my devils like Milton's but I

54

want to know whether the copy bears any resemblance to the original.

Whether at this stage of composition Nathaniel himself had any more than the most nebulous notion of the direction that his epic would take or even of its contents beyond the portion he had written, there is reason to doubt. "As it would be impossible," he temporized, "for me to give you any idea of the plan and conduct of the poem and of the incidents it is to take in, without writing a volume, I can't now attempt it." But now that the subject, even in vaguest outline, was with him, he wished he might get on with it quickly. "If I was an independent man," he told his sister, "I should take great delight in finishing it, notwithstanding its difficulties."[4]

Again he thought of poetry as potentially profitable. He would solicit or, rather, would have his friends in America solicit, subscriptions for *America Delivered* which would be published in two volumes, six of the proposed twelve books in each volume. He would collect one guinea from each sub- scriber in advance; then he would collect a second guinea at the time the first volume was published. He estimated that "if five thousand subscribers could have been got in America, the interest on that money would have kept me above want and enabled me to proceed without interruption." He earnestly did want to get it done, the subject seemed so worthwhile, filled with such fine poetic promise. He was modest about his pretensions: "Don't suspect me of the affectation of being a Milton," he protested. But the task he had set himself did seem rather more than he could easily accomplish.

Therefore, he put *America Delivered* aside. In the first place, he explained, "the task was arduous and would have taken up the whole of my time for many years." In the second place, it "could not have been proceeded in without a large subscription," which he had no present means of obtaining. And finally, "upon a late revisal of what I did in it, I perceive I had fallen into too close an imitation of Milton, and I believe if I were to under- take the thing again I should execute it in a different way."

But the subject of the Revolution itself was not so readily put aside. If he could not effectively celebrate it in an epic, he would devise some other form better fitted to his talents and his time. "The interest my heart has taken in the American Revolution," he said, "is such as has made me wish not to leave this world without leaving some monument of some sympathy in that truly glorious event in which the obscurity and insignificance of my fortune denied me the happiness of being an actor." Someone would some day recognize its sublime grandeur and write its epic:

> As to the Revolution itself, in which the greatest nations of the now populous earth were engaged both by sea and land, in which one of the noblest privileges of human nature was agitated and contended for with the greatest heroism on one side and the greatest obstinacy and perseverance on the other, in which navies encountered such as the ocean never groaned under before, and armies became vanquished and victorious by the effusion of a deluge of blood: this, I say, I can not but think a more bold and sublime subject and scene for the interference of the turbulent spirits of the dark abyss and their hierarchal Antagonists than the capricious determination of our first mother to rob the orchard of Paradise.

Which, in plainer English means, we suppose, that Nathaniel was sure he had a better subject than Milton had.

During the late summer of 1783 he therefore turned his attention to the composition of "a play or rather a mask, the characters allegorical, representing the origin, progress and termination of the war." He described his plans for it in a letter of 12 July to St. George in Virginia as a "mask or opera" and explained that "as America is represented collectively under the name of Columbinus, I have given that as the title of the performance." The allegorical pattern was suggested by John Dryden's *Albion and Albanius*, though "I hope in point of composition," Nathaniel primly suggested, it is "superior to the mediocrity of that work." The manner was unashamedly Shakespearean, and "judicious friends" in England acknowledged it, said its author, "by far the best thing I ever wrote": they have "made me vain by declaring I had not failed much in attempting the style and spirit of Shakespeare." Lest he sound bumptious, even to his family, Nathaniel provided a more modest declaimer: "Don't think I am fool enough to set up for more than an imitator; far be it from me to pretend to be a rival to that inimitable genius."

New America needed a literature if she were to survive according to the ideals of those who had founded her. A year later, in the summer of 1784, when peace was secure and the young transatlantic nation faced new problems of independence, Nathaniel explained the necessity to St. George, who may have seemed to him too deep in American events to view them properly in perspective:

> How much it is to the interest of a people to give encouragement and protection to those who would hold up to the world a picture of their most noble and exemplary exertions, and build up a monument worthy the admiration of after times, and capable of diffusing and perpetuating the love of public virtue, I leave them to determine. Engaged in more sordid pursuits it has been the crime of nations to neglect their own interest in that of literature, and suffer those men to languish in indigence whose labors might be productive of much benefit to the community. How much have the plays of Shakespeare contributed to diffuse a general knowledge of some parts of the English history and excited the emulation of all orders of men in imitating those acts of heroism which they have seen presented in them. If his noble delineation of the character and fortune of Brutus had been more frequently placed before their eyes, who knows what effect it might have had in preventing the savage war we have lately seen terminated?

America did need a literature if she were to become great. And Nathaniel offered to supply the cornerstone on which it might be erected.

"Actuated by sentiments of this nature," he had begun the composition of the dramatic *Columbinus* as testimony that his own devotion to the cause of American liberty was full-hearted and sincere:

> The agitation, anxieties, emotions of indignation and triumph and sorrow which I have felt as occasion presented through the course of the war I shall not undertake to describe, but leave you to judge of them by your own feeling. Let it suffice to say that it was the subject of all times uppermost in my mind and I return thanks to Providence that the outcome has been answerable to my prayers and wishes. Depressed by sickness and discouraged by various calamities I have nevertheless cherished the love of liberty in a bosom condemned to be chained to the lake of Indigence. By day and by night it has been my favorite theme.

Now, "furnished like Robinson Crusoe, on an unfrequented coast, with excellent materials but miserable tools," he constructed in *Columbinus* the bark in which, he now was sure, he really would "voyage over the ocean of time to the distant shore of posterity."

Columbinus has survived complete, in a beautifully written manuscript which, Nathaniel complained, it had taken him three weeks simply to copy. It is an extended allegory of a type familiar and popular with readers of his time, like, as Nathaniel already had said, Dryden's *Albion and Albanius*, like, also, Arbuthnot's *History of John Bull*, or the American Francis Hopkinson's *A Pretty Story* or Jeremy Belknap's later *The Foresters*, or *The Diverting History of John Bull and Brother Jonathan* by James Kirk Paulding. In order to simplify what he called the "emblematical meaning of the characters," Nathaniel supplied a postscript for the "use of those readers who do not choose to be at the pains of unravelling the allegory themselves." Thus, the character "Albion," he explained, represents the British nation collectively. "Themis," his wife, stands for "the attribute of Justice in general but is frequently introduced as the representative of the democratical or popular party in Britain." Albion's son is "Columbinus," the hero, who is, of course, symbolic of America. Themis's daughter is "Eleutheria" and she "as the name implies can be no other than Liberty for which America contended."

Supporting Columbinus is "Alleghenny," a faithful servant, who stands for "the two great Agents whose resources were so important to America, to wit the Congress and the Army, whereof the latter as a body, may be supposed to have been actuated and directed by the spirit of the former." With him are "Fidellan," faithfulness or trust, and "Mingo," a black boy, devoted to his kindly colonial master. Opposed to Columbinus are "Regan," a courtier, ambitious and scheming, Albion's representative in America (the royal colonial government), and "Bullion," a Caliban-like slave with power to assume fiendish guises at will, who represents "in general inordinate Wealth, but in particular the overgrown influence of the crown of Britain, regarded by her constitution as a dangerous Monster." The latter and the greedy power he represents supply much of the motivation of the action, for to Nathaniel, wealth and the greed for wealth were at the root of all present evil:

> And though princes, viewing it with partial eyes, may hold it an ornament of the court and a proper attendant of the regal state, it may in time appear, as it is here represented, pernicious and fiendlike in its operation. This, at least cannot be denied, that it wears different shapes in different eyes.

Bullion has two daughters, each of whom assists him in his evil designs. "Balliadera," product of the rape of a beautiful Persian maiden, is an enchantress, lovely to look upon but evil, and described in the most lush and oriental phrases Nathaniel could marshal. She is "Luxury or dissolute pleasure . . . not uncommonly the offspring of Bullion, or wealth": "How far Luxury and the spirit of expence, for its own support, may have led to the resource of taxing America," said Nathaniel, "is left for the reader to judge." "Gondola," the second daughter, the misbegotten child of an unwilling Ethiopian mother (herself a symbol of slavery), is a sorceress representing "the favorers of monarchial and arbitrary power, the offspring of Bullion, or crown influence." Other characters, less essential to the plot, but necessary for rounded allegory, are "Darmstadt," the German, and "Gaul," "Iberian," and "Belgias," each representing with less verbal disguise a country which watches or takes part in the conflict.

Greatly simplified, the bare allegorical argument is as follows: Britian (Albion), led on by Wealth (Bullion), has an affair with Luxury (Balliaderia), at which his wife, Justice (Themis), leaves him. Treacherous Regan (his governor in America) convinces Albion that Liberty (Eleutheria) is plotting against him, leading his son, Columbinus, also to revolt. Albion's forces battle Columbinus, until Justice returns with France at her side to turn the tide of battle. As the curtain falls, Columbinus is joined to Eleutheria, the forces of evil having all been routed, and Albion bows in contrite humility to America and to France.

But Nathaniel wove, and with some occasional skill, a tapestry of song and declamation and of intricate development of the allegory until *Columbinus* became under his enthusiastic hand "as long as the longest of Shakespeare's." When the scene opens on the American coast, Albion and Themis appear "seated in a triumphal car drawn by sea-horses; Columbinus, Eleutheria, Tritons and Nereids attending." A chorus of the latter break into welcoming song:

> Let shouts of triumph shake the main
> to mighty Albion's and to Themis' reign!
>
> Victor from the wat'ry plain
> lo! Albion comes with all his train,
> proud monarch of the foaming tide,
> royal Themis by his side;
> over land and over sea
> clarion sound of jubilee,
> and shouts of triumph ring again
> to mighty Albion's and to Themis' reign!

A long first act, unrelieved by action, introduces the principal characters, outlines the ideas which will motivate the development of the plot, and points out the conflict within Albion on which the drama turns. Now, married to Themis, he is both powerful and just. When Regan, his counselor, brings gifts which loyal subjects have sent as token of their love and fealty, the king agrees with his consort that it ill becomes a monarch "with rapacious hand" to despoil his subjects by force,

> to drain the cup
> of patient labour, or like blood-suckers
> to drink up and consume the vital treasure
> that nourishes men's hearts.

He would accept only what was rightly due. If too much were given, let them, he tells his counselor, the overplus be returned:

> O, if kings knew
> to turn the generous current of men's wills
> to good account, not choke up with disdain
> and dry the springs of loyalty when most
> they wish to exceed, how wou'd the prosperous stream
> flow plentiful to drench the thirsty bowels
> of feverish pomp herself, and enough left
> the tender grass to feed and natural plants
> i' the garden of god's earth!

But there was another side to Albion, older than his marriage to Justice, and revealed in his attitude toward the hideous monster-slave Bullion who gathers treasures from all over the world for the king, his master. Like Shakespeare's Caliban in *The Tempest*, whom he in so many respects resembles, Bullion has some of the most effective lines in this play. American literature was soon to become and long to remain so genteel that such words as these which Nathaniel put in the mouth of his monster may have produced something of a shock even to his worldly younger brother in Virginia:

> An he do eat us
> We'll stir up such a turmoil in his guts
> As never colic gendered there.

"Miscreated savage," roars Albion, "where's the gold I sent thee to collect?" And the monster, fawning, replies:

> 'tis all piled up and counted. I have ransack'd
> the greedy ocean's maw for conceal'd treasures;
> search'd all the cavernous deeps, and out o' the
> skulls of fishes cull'd the unown'd gems there hid;

SOME EARLY AMERICAN WRITERS

> from the slug oyster, shrin'd in mother of pearl,
> pluck'd his round precious trap; wedges of gold
> weighed from the sandy bottom; roam'd the shores
> and rocks at ebb'tide after storms for wrecks
> cast thitherward; from the hot bark of trees
> that weep rich gums, gather'd the costly tears;
> swept beds of rivers; rich Pactolus' sands
> sifted; torn up the ponderous ribs of earth
> in fire to torture them, and from smelted ores
> pour'd off the purer metal.

The greed thus fed by fiendish means is to be Albion's downfall. When he and his queen, with Columbinus and Eleutheria, who have talked of nobler things through many pages, leave the stage, then scheming Regan and evil Bullion plot the downfall of the king's better advisors and their own ascendancy to control over his royal purse and power. To reach this end they plan to lure him deep into the forest, where Bullion's treasure-store is hidden, and there confront him with the irresistible Balliadera.

In the second act Albion's downfall is effected against a background of exotic song and prurient chatter from luscious attendant nymphs as the king is led to a sylvan bower by Bullion's beautiful daughter, the queen and all good intentions forgotten completely:

> On couch of roses
> He reposes;
> Love's soft pillow lends his down
> To be prest on
> Let him rest on
> Free from thorns that line the crown.

When Regan then enters to announce that Eleutheria, who we remember is the spirit of Liberty, has roused subjects against Albion, the deluded king orders her banished. But he is troubled in mind and allows his new lover to lead him to her half sister, the soothsayer Gondola, who, like the witches in *Macbeth*, sings evil incantations:

> Thrice, and thrice, and thrice the ground
> with iron wand I circle round,

thrice the mutter'd charm I spread
and utter sounds that wake the dead.
Fires that glare and fiends that rule,
arise from the infernal pool!
arise! arise! arise!

Then the ground opens and flames ascend, in which Gondola reads to Albion this portent concerning Eleutheria: "If she wed with Columbine / this kingdom is no longer thine."

Now we are in the midst of the action, as the third act opens with another weird and Shakespeare-like scene at Bullion's forge, where the fiend is manufacturing a chain to bind Columbinus, until he is discovered by Themis, who steals the chain and departs, she says, for France. Then Columbinus and Eleutheria approach the king in his palace, the young man to plead that the girl be reinstated to her former place of high esteem. Albion, still enthralled by luxury and desire for wealth, orders his guards to seize her, but Columbinus intervenes to allow her escape. Bullion and his hideous daughter set out in pursuit but soon return, Gondola bruised and mangled by Alleghenny, who has rescued the distressed Eleutheria. When Columbinus departs, he meets his sturdy henchman in the forest, who tells him of having come upon Eleutheria, bound to a tree, naked to the waist, while Gondola, the evil child of Bullion, scourged her. Alleghenny presents Columbinus with the bloody cloth with which he had bathed Eleutheria's lacerated back—a cloth of thirteen crimson stripes which Columbinus straightaway vows shall be the banner which will lead him to victory.

The king's noble son addresses his followers as they prepare in the fourth act for battle: "Friends, warriours, countrymen," what is it for which we fight? It is

for liberty; that is, the common benefits of light and air; the privilege to breathe and walk upon God's earth, his free-born creatures, gathering the blessings his bounty hath plac'd in reach, with use and exercise of our opinions to guide our steps: not push'd on by hard taskmasters whither they list, against our wholesome wills; not manacled or fetter'd; not bow'd down with heavy burdens like the brute beasts, whose patience argues defect of reason. Sirs, we fight for the name of human creatures; that distinction which separates man from beast, brave souls from idiots, th' ambitious rider from the horse that carries him.

Spurred by such sentiments, Columbinus's forces are at first triumphant; but later, Albion, joined by German mercenaries, puts them to rout and throws their noble leader into prison.

As Columbinus is being led to the scaffold at the beginning of the last act, in rushes Alleghenny and all his men to rescue him and drive the German scoundrels who guard him from the field. This is no sooner done than Themis enters with the severed head of Regan, "whose hot breath first blew up the coals of war"; and Columbinus joins hands with Eleutheria seated triumphant on her gorgeous throne. The curtain falls as the beautiful, and now reformed, Balliadera sings a new song which Themis has taught her:

> O world, lift up your eyes!
> War's heavy clouds are drift away.
> And in serener skies,
> Bright as the clear star that foreruns the day,
> A new constellation, see
> As the storm dies,
> Begins to rise
> Out of the bosom of the troubled Sea!
> It is the star of Liberty,
> Daughter of the giant War,
> From his dead ashes sprung to blaze afar
> The phoenix of the skies!
> Her light, America, she bends on thee
> And great the nations all that glory to be free!

As we have skipped thus quickly through the one hundred twenty closely written pages of *Columbinus*, taking advantage of shortcuts to avoid the intricacies with which Nathaniel both complicated and explained details of plot and allegory, we find the play, for all its occasional boisterousness, lacking the sustained, swiftly moving action necessary to success in presentation. Instead of progressing straightforwardly, it moves back upon itself more than once, as it painstakingly underlines what Nathaniel called the "emblematical meanings." Almost every incident of dramatic significance takes place off stage, to be recited afterward in detail by characters who posture through long speeches compounded of shreds and patches of worn Elizabethan fustian. The settings alone, ranging from the bosom of the ocean to the bowels of the earth, with forest and palace and hilltop used each in turn, present practical difficulties in stagecraft which, even in our better mechanized days, would be difficult of solution. The business of flames leaping from bare boards at the wave of Gondola's wand, of Bullion rising from the waters of the ocean, or of Eleutheria suddenly materializing for the finale seated in splendor on an elevated throne, though none of them impossible on the eighteenth-century stage, are each perhaps better suited to the magic of modern manipulation.

If *Columbinus* had been printed in 1783 when it was completed, it would have been the first, and perhaps not the worst, of the new nation's patriotic long poems. It would have preceded Timothy Dwight's *The Conquest of Canaän* by two years and Joel Barlow's *The Vision of Columbus* by four. Like them, and like Philip Freneau, John Trumbull, and other young men whose careers were distorted by the American Revolution, Nathaniel Tucker sang the new spirit in old words. But it seems fitting to enroll his small achievement in *Columbinus* as testimony to his right also to a brief paragraph in the history of our literature.

Meanwhile he worked over another play, *The Queen of Jewry*, the subject of which was the death of Marianne as recorded by Flavius Josephus in his *Wars of the Jews*. Equally derivative, it is perhaps better articulated than *Columbinus*, but it is a dull play, without the occasional free-swinging bursts of spirited phrase and action of its predecessor. Nathaniel planned to submit it to the managers of both London theaters, but nothing seems to have come of that. He made a copy for his brother in Williamsburg, and there it remains, a work of painstaking mediocrity, filled with tired imitations of Shakespearean language, scene, and characters. Still in his early thirties, Nathaniel Tucker seems to have been written out.

Early in 1786 he moved to Hull, where he married, fathered seven children, continued the practice of medicine, and became devoutly religious, immersed in Swedenborgianism and pious anonymity. He would not allow his name to be associated with his pioneer translations of the Swedish theologian's treatises on *Divine Wisdom, Divine Providence,* and *The Apocalypse Revealed,* though perhaps his greatest claim to memory is that these translations introduced Swedenborg to such more talented and thoughtful men as Blake and Coleridge. After Nathaniel Tucker's death on 3 December 1807 another edition of *The Bermudian* was issued for the benefit of his wife and surviving children.

NOTES

1. All quotations are from Tucker family correspondence in the Tucker-Coleman Collection in the Earl Gregg Swem Library of the College of William and Mary. For a more fully annotated account of the poet's activities see Lewis Leary, *The Literary Life of Nathaniel Tucker, 1750–1807* (Durham, N.C., 1951); see also *The Complete Published Poems of Nathaniel Tucker together with Columbinus: A Mask,* edited with an introduction by Lewis Leary (Scholars' Facsimiles & Reprints, 1973).

2. Reviews of *The Bermudian* are found in the *Gentleman's Magazine* 44 (July 1774): 230, 327, and in the *Critical Review* 38 (July 1774): 75; for excerpts from other reviews, see the *Virginia Gazette,* 3 November 1774, p. 3.

3. MS copybook of St. George Tucker in the Research Department of the Colonial Williamsburg Foundation, Williamsburg, Virginia.

4. Tucker rambled on at great length about his plans and fears for his poetic drama in a close-written, undated seven-page letter (probably early in 1783) to his sister Elizabeth in Bermuda.

Samuel Low

NEW YORK'S FIRST POET

❦ ❦

S OMETHING should be said for Samuel Low who for more
than fifteen years at the end of the eighteenth century
was persistently a poet in New York, and who was the first
resident of that city to bring his total literary work together in
a collected edition. His first volume appeared when he was
nineteen, his last when he was thirty-five, and in the years between he offered his talent generously on many important public
occasions. Some of his contemporaries seem not to have thought
highly of him as a man or as a man of letters, and there remains
little evidence to prove their judgment incorrect. But in a sense
he was New York's first poet, who celebrated there the return
of peace ("How Freedom fought, and did at last prevail"), who
wrote, sometimes with more ardor than original skill, of its
social and political life, and who, if for that alone, should not
be forgotten.

Only outlines of his life can be reconstructed. He was born
on 12 December 1765 the fourth child and second son of John
and Susannah Bordet Low, and he was baptized at the Reformed
Dutch Church in New York ten days later, his most prominent
kinsman, Nicholas Low, merchant and financier, standing by him
as godfather.[1] His education, probably at the church school, was
sufficiently liberal to allow him early to compose the lively
satirical verses "On Phlebotomus," a ne'er-do-well physician
fond of cadging drinks, and what he later called "Juvenile
Levities" on "The Fool's Friendship" and "The Alehouse."[2]
"The Lover's Complaint," written in 1784, may have been conventionally veiled autobiography: Delia has been away, and
Strephon mourns; but Delia returns, to gladden Strephon's heart:

"So shall my fair my constancy repay / And conjugal endear-
ments crown each day."[3]

But such uxorious expectations would have to wait. Growing
up in a city occupied by British troops, young Samuel Low leaves
no evidence of having had more than a boy-spectator's part in
wartime activities. His relative Isaac Low, extremely wealthy
with an elegant mansion on Dock Street, was active in public
affairs, elected with John Jay and Philip Livingston to the
Continental Congress in 1774, but he later proved to be so
questionable a patriot that he fled to England when Sir Guy
Carleton withdrew his army from the city.[4] Isaac's brother,
Nicholas, also a merchant, though apparently less wealthy, was
more faithfully an adherent to the American cause, and in 1784
became with Alexander Hamilton, Isaac Roosevelt, and John
Vanderbilt one of the first directors of the Bank of the State of
New York.[5]

For young Samuel Low the end of the war was an occasion
for instant celebration in a long poem which was "first published
shortly after the ratification of Peace between America and
Great-Britain." He called the poem simply "Peace,"[6] and in it
gloried that his countrymen, the "painful conflict o'er, could reap
at last / The sweet reward of all their labours past" (p. 124).
Americans now could take comfort in the knowledge that as
"war, and rapine, and oppression cease," their common lot "is
Liberty and Peace" (p. 125). As he surveyed the heroes of the
American Revolution—Washington, Gates, Greene, Sullivan,
Sinclair, and Putnam—the young poet pled that

> never may Columbian's thankless prove,
> But prize the patriots who our cause espous'd
> And bless the impulse which their spirits rous'd. (P. 127)

He spoke ardently of his "Dear, native country," as a

> Land of delight, fair Freedom's fav'rite seat,
> A clime which boasts the growth of ev'ry soil,
> A people virtuous, brave, inur'd to toil,   (P. 130)

where industry, commerce, and science would inevitably flourish,
and where poetry, too long confined to "European climes," would
cross westward to the new United States:

With tuneful numbers here her sons inspire,
Plant in their breasts the true poetic fire,
The fire divine, which lifts th'aspiring thought,
And makes the soul with joy celestial fraught!
Then shall they chant the memorable tale,
How Freedom fought, and did at last prevail;
Then shall their epic strains of battles sing,
And all the horrors which from battles spring:
The deeds atchiev'd by those heroic bands
Who saved their country from Oppression's hands,
In future time with rapture shall be heard,
The fav'rite subject of the Heav'n-taught Bard!
. . . .
When HOMER's genius here sublime shall soar,
And a new VIRGIL grace this western shore.

(Pp. 134–135)

Until such a time might come, Low would supply his countrymen with what he could of native poetry. His forty-page octavo *Winter Display'd, A Poem; Describing the Season in All Its Stages and Vicissitudes,* was modestly identified as "By an American" when it appeared in 1784 from the press of Samuel Loudon.[7] Whatever its shortcomings or its debts to other poets, it is the first long poem to attempt a picture, other than political, of life in the United States. Winter was not a happy season: "this gloomy and vigorous time of the year" was, explained Low, "among the many sad consequences of our common parents' transgression" (p. 4n). It comes "mantled in the gloom of deepest night / In pompous horror shrouded" (p. 3). And while this

horror broods abroad
Dim are the stars, the air a dark profound;
. . . .
Damp is the weather, raw the piercing wind,
Sharp chills thro' man an easy entrance find;
Thick fogs, and rhime, dull, lazy, and impure,
Spead dire diseases, and the air obscure.   (P. 7)

The cruel rigor of winter does not menace the rich, for

In luxury and ease the higher class
Of mortals now the tedious Winter pass;

> Brim-full of choicest liquors, stand the bowls,
> Well-heated, to elate and chear their souls. (P. 16)

But the poor, with "scarce a shelter they can call their home,"

> In vain for pity, they submissive ask;
> For bread in vain they plead; oh! grievous task!
> The churl, the miser, and the powder'd beau
> Alike dismiss the friendless man of woe. (P. 18)

Beyond the city, winter can be less devastating, though it produces perils anywhere, as Low demonstrates with accounts of a peasant perishing in a snowstorm (pp. 19–20), of the menace of a storm at sea (pp. 20–22), of the numbing coldness of Greenland (p. 24), and the hazards encountered by whaling vessels (pp. 26–27). But there are also bright country scenes. The rural milkmaid

> comes to drain the kine; industrious she
> Domestick work to ply; replete with glee
> She treads the virgin snow, she treads and sings
> Joyous and blythe, and hasty with her brings
> The well-used, ample pails, both neat and clean,
> Which seldom void of luscious milk are seen. (P. 13)

There is sledding (p. 30) and skating, as country people "With polished steel adapted to the feet . . . glide adventurous" (p. 29), and there is hunting of small game, of which Low does not approve:

> The peasants oft explore the hills and vales
> For food of pheasant or delicious quails;
> Or lark or quirrels, or the rabbit shy,
> And with strict perquisition, hopeful pry
> In ev'ry lurking cave and hollow tree,
> And slay or take away, whate'er they find,
> Nor one surviving do they leave behind.

If man must do violence to fellow creatures, let him seek, said Low, less helpless game:

> If this emplyment be thy chief delight,
> Devote thy boasted prowess, skill and might,

Upon the prowling Wolf, or tusky Boar;
Or, on the shapeless Bear thy fury pour.   (P. 16)

When snug beside his fire, a man may however find comfort, and even discover some quirky magic in winter, as

Around the room her tricks grimalkin trys;
The crackling faggot up the chimney flies;
The playful vermin through the cieling skips,
And squeak responsive, while the crust they clip:
The merry cricket chirrups on the hearth,
And all conspire to make them harmless mirth.[8]

But, though winter comes, with frigid blasts and brief fireside joys,

Though comfortless the prospect now, and void
All soon shall flourish in Arcadian pride;
The trees shall bud, and every sweet shall spring;
With joyful notes the smiling plains shall ring!
. . . .
And hark! the howling blast is almost o'er,
And spring vouchsafes to visit us once more.   (P. 40)

Late in 1785, twenty-year-old Samuel Low married sixteen-year-old Margaret Kip. A daughter, Judith, was born to them the next September, another daughter, Susannah, in April 1788, a son, Samuel, in December 1789, and another son, Henry Kip, in November 1792.[9] Until 1794 Samuel Low was employed as a clerk in the Treasury Office. He was active in Masonic affairs: in 1789 was treasurer of the Holland Lodge which met then in Fraunces's tavern, in 1792 was elected junior warden, and in 1792 rose to senior warden of that lodge.[10] The first census of the United States listed him in 1790 as a resident of the North Ward, the head of a family consisting then of one free white male over sixteen, one under sixteen, and five free white females.[11] From 1795 to 1803 he was first bookkeeper in the Bank of New York, of which his younger brother, John, during the same period was successively a teller, deputy cashier, and assistant cashier.[12] Low's first wife having died in her late twenties (after "years of suff'ring;—she is now / A sainted Spirit"),[13] he was married a second time on 20 April 1797 to Ann Cregier, to whom a son, Anthony, was born on 12 January 1798.[14]

Meanwhile Samuel Low had become something of an official poet for the city of New York, and especially for the Holland Lodge. His *Ode for the Federal Procession, upon the Adoption of the New Government* appeared on 23 July 1788 as a broadside, "Composed by Mr. L**."[15] In 1789 appeared, again as broadsides, his *Ode on Charity: Composed by Brother Low, of the Holland Lodge; and Sung in St. Paul's Chapel, on the 24th Day of June, 1789, Being the Anniversary of the Festival of St. John the Baptist* and his *Ode to be Sung on the Arrival of the President of the United States*, "Composed by Mr. L**" to the "Tune—'God Save, &c.' "[16] His *Fellow-Craft Hymn, for the Use of Holland Lodge* was distributed as another broadside in 1790, as was his *Ode for St. John's Day, June 24, 5790 [sic], Performed at the Consecration of the New Building for the Use of the Holland Lodge, and the Washington Chapter of Royal-Arch Masons*, both identified as "Composed by Brother Low,"[17] who also produced "Lines Written at the Request of the Members of Holland Lodge, at a Time When a Visit Was Expected from the Grand Master of America."[18] The "Ode, Composed by Mr. Low, for the 12th Day of May, 1790, Being the Anniversary of the Tammany Society or Columbia Order," first published in the *New-York Magazine* for May 1790 was later reprinted as a "Hymn to Liberty."[19] Three years later "An Anthem Sung in Trinity Church at the Celebration of St. John's Day, June 24, 1793, by the Episcopal Children, Accompanied with the Organ" appeared in the *New-York Magazine* as "Composed by Brother Low."[20]

His verses became increasingly mechanical, made to order in borrowed rhythms and tattered clichés. Low may well have been disappointed in expectations of a more than humdrum literary career by the failure of his five-act comedy, *The Politician Outwitted*, written in 1788 and, testified William Dunlap, "rejected by the managers" of the New York theater, "and published for their justification."[21] As issued in 1789, "Printed for the Author, by W. Ross, in Broad-street," it proved to be, if not a good play, not really a bad one either, and it might have been performed with brief success, if only because it was amusingly topical. Its scene is New York, its time the present; unity of time is observed, the first four acts covering one day, the fifth act commencing on the day following. There is good-natured ribbing of local newspapers: the *New-York Journal* opposed to, Francis Child's *Daily Advertiser* enthusiastically in support of, the new Constitution. Old Mr. Loveyet, as ardent in search of a new, young wife as he is in opposition to the new Constitution, is a well-conceived comic character whose political arguments are so ridiculous that they turn upon themselves. Trueman, a schoolmaster, is more wooden, but his arguments in favor of the Constitution are correct: "great and good men," he testifies, have contrived it "for the welfare and happiness of the American nation" (p. 59). So vehemently do the two old gentlemen quarrel that they refuse to allow their children—Loveyet's forthright son and Trueman's pretty daughter—to marry.

Though Charles Loveyet is disowned by his obdurate father, true love finally outwits the politicians, and after a complicated but conventional series of events, Charles marries the fair Harriet, and the fathers are united as Old Loveyet grudgingly admits to some of his error. The action is enlivened by such stock characters as Toupee, the barber, who speaks in an outlandish French accent, and Worthnought, a "beau, a fine gentleman, a smart fellow," but also "a coxcomb, a puppy, a baboon and an ass" (p. 17), whose talk is fashionably clipped and mannered. The dialect of Cuff, a bumbling, carefree Negro servant, is remarkably effective. After the popularity of Jonathan in Royall Tyler's *The Contrast* on the New York stage two years earlier, it was perhaps inevitable that Low would include in his cast a rustic Yankee, Humphrey Cobb, who amusingly misused or manufactured long words. But Royall Tyler had done greatly better, and so had Richard Sheridan before him.[22]

From 1793 to 1800 Low seems to have published nothing. He thought of himself as "obscure and friendless," stultified "Amid a dull, disgusting ceaseless round / Of drudgery, anxiety, and care," bound as a public employee to "A poor, monotonous, insipid task / Mechanical."[23] The world and its suffering was greatly with him as he wrote, sadly now, of the loss of friends:

73

an "Elegy on the Death of Doctor Joseph Youle, Who died February 25, 1795," a poem "Sacred to the Memory of Deceased Friends, written in October, 1798," an "Epitaph on John Frederick Roorbach, Esq., Who Died October 3, 1798, of the Fever Then Prevailing in New York," and "Verses on the Death of Mr. John Loudon . . . Slain by the Accidental Discharge of a Musket during a Military Review."[24] His father had died, and his first wife, a sister and a sister-in-law, several aunts and uncles; his children's teacher was gone, and his "kinsman and friend," John Kip, and friends of his youth were gone also.[25]

The epidemics which ravaged New York at the end of the century apparently ravaged him also. In his "Ode to Health," written in September 1799 he complained that "long and dreary has the period been / Since thy cherubic face I've seen." Once he had known "the life-endearing charms" of health,

> But ne'er, since thy disastrous flight,
> Hath Joy my heart, or Beauty blest my sight.
> . . . .
> And Discontent is daily clouding now
> The dying embers of departed joy.

His description of the plague in New York is graphic and, though generalized in allegorical personification, occasionally eloquent, and deserves remembrance beside the more realistic accounts in Charles Brockden Brown's *Arthur Mervyn*. Though bound by familiar rhetorical phrases, drawn from Alexander Pope, Edward Young, and other transatlantic masters, Low wrote now with power:

> Oh! bear me from this "vale of Tears,"
> That now a lazar-house appears;
> Where mortals, with their air, their food,
> Imbibe the plague which taints their blood.
> And where grim Death his awful standard rears,
> For, lo! just risen from his fetid den,
> Stalks *Pestilence*, invet'rate foe of men!
> In his fell den sepulchral horrors scowl,
> Cadaverous and ghastly to the view:
> Its walls drip exhalations dark and foul,

And baneful hemlock's deepest shades imbue,
Its entrance drear, with noxious weeds o'er shone;
But dreadful vapours dire!
Dread scourge of human kind! with giant force
I see him tread down thousands in his course:
Wan is his visage, squalid his attire,
With labour vast his putrid lungs respire;
His sinewy arms Destruction's besom wield:
  Protect me, Goddess, with thy shield!
For now he whirls contagious blasts abroad;
Tremendous blasts! dread instruments of God!
His sable wings, o'er guilty nations spread,
Make darkness black, and baleful influence shed;
His breath pestiferous infects the air;
His sanguine eyes like midnight torches glare;
Morbific dew his livid lips distill,
And ev'ry pore with subtle poison fill;
Thro' ev'ry nerve of man the deadly juices thrill:
Around him hang the murky fogs of night,
And shudd'ring nature deprecates his blight:—
  Shield me, Goddess, from his sight!

  Oh! bear me far beyond the monster's view;
I see, I see th'envenom'd, haggard crew
Of evils that his fatal steps pursue!—
  Fever first, whose arid heat
  Makes the pulse convulsive beat;
Then *Terror*, mantled in Cimmerian black,
Aghast advances, dreading to look back;
With gaping jaws he comes, and bristling hair,
His eyes, horrific, blast us with their stare.
Next *Silence*, shrouded in profoundest night,
Unheard, flits by, a phantom to the sight;
Reluctant *Lassitude*, with pallid face,
Now slowly lags with faint and feeble pace;
Dejection, sick of his existence grown,
Drags his grief-worn carcase prone;
And *Lethargy*, with soporific dews,
The life-blood curdles, and each sense imbrues;
Lethean drafts the heavy eyelids steep,

Life's almost stagnant functions sluggish creep;
And *Death*, with ghastly smiles, the black procession
   views:
His iron grasp the stoutest heart appals,
And now another, yet another falls:
   Trembling age now drops its crutch—
   Youth quick withers at his touch:
   Horror freezes ev'ry vein,
   To see the thousands he hath slain!
   Hear the sad survivor's moans!
   Hark! what dismal dying groans!
Around them close the shades of Death's long night—
Oh, shield me, Goddess, from the dreadful sight![26]

Low came again to public attention when his "Ode on the Death of General Washington" was read by actor John Hopkinson at the black-draped John Street Theater on 8 January 1800 and for "many successive evenings" thereafter to "public applause."[27] Though apparently not separately printed, excerpts from it appeared in Matthew L. Davis's *An Oration Delivered in St. Paul's Church, on the Fourth of July . . . before the General Society of Mechanics and Tradesmen, Tammany Society or Columbian Order, and Other Associations and Citizens.*[28] Low's *Ode for the Fourth* of July 1800, which was sung in fourteen limpid stanzas and a chorus on that occasion, after the delivery of Davis's oration, was printed as a broadside by John Loudon.[29]

By this time Low's *Poems* had been published in two volumes by T. and J. Swords at their printing shop at 99 Pearl Street, in an edition of just under 400 copies, distributed among 244 subscribers, including John Jacob Astor, James Cooper, William Dunlap, Philip Hone, Peter and William Irving, Dr. David Hosack, and Dr. Samuel Latham Mitchill. In a preface dated 1 May 1800 Low explained that his original intention had been to present, in one volume, only such of his poems "as he deemed best," but that "the partiality of his literary friends" had "induced him to publish, in two volumes, nearly the whole of his poetic writings," some of which, he admitted, "required apology."

> Very few of the Poems were written with a view to publication: several were composed within the last eight months. . . .

Many of the Poems were written at an early age, and most of them under singular disadvantages; among which application to public business, for many years past, was not the least; not only because it allowed little leisure for literary pursuit, but because it is of a nature peculiarly inimical to the cultivation of poetic talent. (1: [5])

Low had reason for apology, for many of the poems are slight indeed, overlaid with sentiment and dulled with echoes from other poets. But, except for Philip Freneau's *Poems* (1786) and *Miscellaneous Works* (1788), no previous gathering of verses published in the United States is more interesting or various. Low experimented with stanzaic forms; he ventured, often cumbersomely, in blank verse; he attempted in "Ellen and Phebe" (2. 137–174) a long, lacrimose pastoral elegy; his songs, however derivative, had lilt and liveliness; his odes were as serious and sincere as the occasions which called them forth. He even experimented with sonnets, a form found seldom among the writings of his native contemporaries. He presented twenty-two of them, usually in three quatrains and a couplet, but with occasional variations in rhyme scheme. He wrote them to his mother, his oldest son, his second wife, and to the memory of his first, to present and departed friends, and on such disparate subjects as a lark, a violet ("Emblem of innocence and modest worth"— 2. 81), a summer cloud, a glass of wine ("Thou who makes the heart of man rejoice"—2. 91), and a "segar" ("Sweet antidote to Sorrow, Toil, and Strife"—2. 92). Peace, happiness, harmony, justice, and the spirit of poetry, each was ceremoniously saluted in fourteen lines which sometimes failed to keep their measure.

Low admired Milton ("The bard divine, the learned sage, / Whose genius glows in ev'ry page"—1. 84) and Kotzebue ("Sweet philosophic poet"—1. 70) whose dramas William Dunlap was adapting for the New York stage. He called on Jean Pierre Florian for a sentimental tale which he versified as "Camira and Angelica," on Matthew G. Lewis's *The Monk* for the plot of "Alphonso and Agnes," and on Isaac Disraeli's romance of *Mejnoun and Leila* for meanings implicit in "Lines on a Spring of Water in King's County, Long-Island."[30] Goldsmith and Gray seem often echoed as he wrote lightly sentimental

77

verses "To a Spider" (2. 145–146), "To an Owl" ("Grave, pensive, musing solitary bird / Who loves to woo the lone and silent night"—2. 146), or "To a Small Fish Caught by Angling" ("Poor little struggling captive wretch, / Ah! not for thee was meant the lure"—2. 152). Native scenes were admired in the "Inscription for Mr. Taylor's North-River Bath . . . Written July 2, 1799" (1. 55) in the lines "On a Spring of Water" beside which urban cares could be forgotten, and, inevitably, in "On the Falls of Passaick" (". . . scarcely less sublime / Than fam'd *Niagara's* tremendous flood"). Low was not particularly original, but he seems sincerely moved as he considered the grandeur and sublimity of the force of falling waters: "Prolific Nature! how august, how grand!— / Thy secret workings how inscrutable" (2. 165).

Charles Brockden Brown, however, in reviewing the collection, expressed higher standards for poetry. Low's volumes contained, he said, examples of versification which could only please readers "whose partiality or courtesy may incline them to praise," and who "require striking instances of poetical deficiency before they consent to be persuaded that the author is not one of the inspired." In occasional compositions such as Low presented, the reader was entitled to expect, said Brown, if not uniformity of excellence, at least neatness and elegance, and these Low did not often display: "Some of the pieces are correct without point or strength; but none of them conspicuous for originality of idea, beauty of simile, ingenuity of description, or harmony of verse. In their greatest efforts they hardly show themselves above the level of mediocrity."[31] Another more generous critic disagreed strenuously: "I have derived much pleasure," he testified, "from the poems of Mr. Low." He thought Brown's comments to have been dictated by pique, because Low's "Ode" on Washington as recited at the theater had been "received with that public applause, which was denied to the frigid and inanimate production of the author of 'Wieland.' " Such a review as Brown had written would "in the days of Pope," he thought, "have inevitably conferred on its author a conspicuous station in the pages of the Dunciad."[32]

But Brown was correct. Though first, Samuel Low did not

maintain his position as foremost among the poets of New York. When he was nineteen, his verses showed promise which he could not fulfill at thirty-five. After 1803 his name no longer appears in the New York directories. Sixteen years later William Dunlap heard at Christ Church in Norfolk, Virginia, a young Episcopal clergyman named Samuel Low who, "though dying of consumption," was "eloquent above mediocrity," who had "studied law, become a player & finally a priest," and who was said to be the son of a clergyman who "resided near Fredericksburg." Dunlap wondered whether the young man's father might not have been the Samuel Low, once a poet in New York, who had "published a volume of bad poems, a bad play, become a drunkard, abandon'd his wife, came South and (as I hope) reformed & become a clergyman of the Church Episcopal." On inquiry he discovered this not to have been the case.[33] Samuel Low, the poet, had disappeared, to exist only in three small volumes of poetry and in a play which was never performed. His shortcomings need not be excused. Though the road he traveled was filled with good intentions, he strode it earnestly and with occasional attractive verve which deserves brief remembering.

NOTES

1. *Baptisms from 1731 to 1800 in the Reformed Dutch Church, Collections, New York Genealogical and Biographical Society* (1902), 3: 28, in which also recorded the baptisms of his, finally, three brothers and two sisters, from 1760 to 1769. The date of his birth is established from a poem entitled "A Card," dated 11 December 1785, in *Poems* (New York, 1800), 2: 3, which invites a friend to join him the next day at a birthday celebration: "twice ten years ago, to-morrow night / Began to breath the rhyming, moon-struck wight!"

2. *Poems*, 2: 100–110.

3. *Poems*, 1: 62. Palemon similarly mourns his Anna in "The Absence," 1: 65, which may also have been written at this time.

4. Thomas Jefferson Wertenbaker, *Father Knickerbocker Rebels: New York City during the Revolution* (New York, 1948), pp. 38–40, 266; Oscar Theodore Barck, Jr., *New York City, 1776–1783* (New York, 1931), pp. 36, 72; and Allan Nevins, *The American*

States during and after the Revolution (New York, 1927), pp. 57, 60.

5. *New-York Packet*, 12 and 23 February 1784, and William Ten Eyck Hardenbrook, *Financial New York* (New York, 1897), pp. 85, 119; see also *Appleton's Cyclopedia of American Biography* (New York, 1888), 4: 38.

6. I have not discovered the poem as published in 1783 or 1784, nor is it listed in Oscar Wegelin's bibliography, *Early American Poetry* (New York, 1930); quotations are from *Poems*, 1: 124–137.

7. As reprinted in *Poems*, 2: 14–75, the poem was substantially "altered," Low then explained, "in such a manner as to render it more fit for the public eye." Not the least unsuccessful of his revisions was the addition of a long, introductory invocation to the ocean, to the muses, and to winter. My quotations are from the more concise and effective first printing.

8. "The author is indebted," said Low in a footnote, "to the inimitable Doctor Goldsmith for these few verses, which the Reader may find among some beautiful stanzas in the Vicar of Wakefield. The transcript is not verbatim; an alteration being absolutely necessary in order to adapt the words to the measure: It must be added, in honour of the above-mentioned Author, that the verses have lost by this; as, indeed, no deviation from the letter of that beautiful Poem, could render the words so admirably descriptive, or express such natural simplicity, and, at the same time, elegancy of diction."

9. *Baptisms from 1731 to 1800 in the Reformed Dutch Church*, 3: 310, 392, 403, 427.

10. *New-York Directory and Register* (1789), pp. 55, 132; (1790), p. 63; (1791), pp. 37, 76; (1792), pp. 74, 200; (1793), p. 90. Other members of the Holland Lodge were John Pintard, DeWitt Clinton, and William Irving, each of whom in his turn rose from senior warden to master; that Low was passed over for this position in 1793 may suggest some lack of confidence in him by his fellow Masons. The changes in his residence—from Partition Street in 1789, to 8 John Street in 1790 and 1791, to Great Dock Street in 1792, to Crown Street in 1793, to Liberty Street in 1794, to 10 Fair Street in 1795, back to Liberty Street in 1797, and, finally, after his second marriage, to 9 Dutch Street from 1798 to 1803, when he moved to 39 Day Street—may indicate that he was not a completely or comfortably settled young man, able to manage well on his salary as a clerk in public office, which was recorded in the *New-York Directory* (1793), p. 185, as from $500 to $800 a year.

11. *Heads of Families at the First Census of the United States in the Year 1790, New York* (Washington, 1908), p. 120.

12. *New-York Directory* (1795), p. 76; (1796), p. 235; (1797), p. 233; (1798), n.p.; (1799), p. 281; *Longworth's American Almanack, New-York Register, and City Directory* (1801), p. 218; (1802), p. 255; (1803), p. 199.

13. "To Samuel, on His Birthday [9 December 1799], *Poems*, 2: 83.

14. *Marriages from 1639 to 1800 in the Reformed Dutch Church, New York, Collections, New York Genealogical and Biographical Society* (1896) 1: 273; *Baptisms from 1731 to 1800 in the Reformed Dutch Church*, 3: 471.

15. A copy of the broadside is in the New York Historical Society Library; the poem is reprinted in *Poems*, 1: 98–103, as "Ode Occasioned by the Adoption of the Present Constitution of the United States and First Published on the Day That Event Was Celebrated in the City of New York by a Procession."

16. Both broadsides are in the New York Historical Society Library; they are reprinted with slight changes in title in *Poems*, 1: 65–66 and 104–105.

17. Copies in the New York Historical Society Library; reprinted, the first as "A Masonic Hymn," *Poems*, 1: 72–73, the second without significant change in title in the *New-York Magazine* 1 (August 1791): 486, and *Poems*, 1: 67–68.

18. *Poems*, 1: 93–94.

19. *New-York Magazine*, 1: 305; *Poems*, 1: 90–93.

20. (June 1793), 4: 377; see *Poems*, 1: 69–71.

21. *History of the American Theatre* (New York, 1832), p. 80.

22. I have found no notices of *The Politician Outwitted* in New York newspapers. An advertisement did however appear on 15 October 1789 in the *State Gazette of North-Carolina* in Edentown, and continued to appear with some regularity for ten months, causing Douglas C. McMurtrie, *Eighteenth-Century North Carolina Imprints, 1784–1800* (Chapel Hill, 1936), p. 109, to list it as a work "of local authorship and manufacture." James Purcell, "Literary Culture in North Carolina to 1820" (Ph.D. diss., Duke University, 1951), p. 210, finds no evidence "to indicate local publication," explains the advertisements there as possibly an attempt by the strongly constitutionalist *State Gazette* to influence public opinion during the turbulent campaign for ratification in North Carolina, and also sug-

gests that the tie between Abraham Hodge of the *State Gazette* and Samuel Low was personal: "Hodge was a former New Yorker and both men were prominent in Masonic circles."

23. *Poems*, 2: 123–124.

24. *Poems*, 1: 31–54.

25. *Poems*, 1: 44–46.

26. *Poems*, 1: 141–144.

27. *Monthly Magazine and American Review*, 3: 179. George C. D. Odell, *Annals of the New York Stage* (New York, 1927), 2: 77, incorrectly assumes that it was Charles Brockden Brown's "Monody" that was recited on this occasion; see n. 32 below.

28. (New York, 1800), pp. 13–14.

29. The *Ode* was printed in Davis's *An Oration*, pp. 24–26; a copy of the broadside is in the New York Historical Society Library; see *Poems*, 2: 9–15.

30. *Poems*, 1: 16–35, 115–122, 2: 154–159.

31. *Monthly Magazine and American Review* 3 (July 1800): 56, 58.

32. "Candidus versus Reviewer," *Monthly Magazine and American Review* 3 (September 1800): 179, 181. Brown's "Monody on the Death of Washington" had been read at the theater on 30 December 1799 by actor Thomas Abthorpe Cooper; see Harry R. Warfel, *Charles Brockden Brown: American Gothic Novelist* (Gainesville, Fla., 1949), p. 183. Cooper had so hesitated in forgetting his lines that, according to the New York *Daily Advertiser*, 1 January 1800, "the Pit groaned aloud, and a small hiss began to issue from the gallery." Further commentary on the merits of Low's verse in the New York *Mercantile Advertiser* on 15 November 1800 did little to increase the poet's reputation.

33. *Diary of William Dunlap* (New York, 1930), 2: 477. Dunlap later identified the young clergyman somewhat ambiguously: "He is the son of John Low, & directed me to his abode in N.Y. at his Uncles at the Union Bank" (p. 528). According to *The Counting House Companion*, a broadside of 1809, Samuel Low's brother John was in that year the cashier of the New Jersey Bank.

Royall Tyler

FIRST GENTLEMAN OF THE
AMERICAN THEATER

❧ ❧

MAJOR ROYALL TYLER had been busy during the early months of 1787. The Treaty of Paris four years before had not in every sense brought peace to the newly united states. Veterans of the Revolution had not been paid. Riots and insurrections threatened good men and true, like the rebellion of Daniel Shays and his followers in Massachusetts. The militia, with roughly the duties of the National Guard today, was often called out to put down disturbances. As a militia officer on the staff of Gen. Benjamin Lincoln who had pursued rebels through northern Massachusetts, Royall Tyler had been dispatched in February to Bennington, in independent Vermont, in an attempt to convince its leaders that activist malcontents who had fled there for safety should be captured and returned to the territory of the United States. Later in that month he was sent by General Lincoln to Boston, and then, on 8 March, he set out for New York for consultations on interstate cooperation in putting down rebellion, taking so long to get there that the assumption must be that he made the trip on horseback, as a soldier should, or that he did some visiting or tavern-hopping on the way. Exactly five weeks after he arrived in New York, his timely patriotic but conciliatory play *The Contrast* opened at the John Street Theater.[1]

The New York which Royall Tyler entered on 12 March 1787 was recovering, though slowly, from the shambles left by Sir Guy Carleton's forces when they had evacuated the city not three years before, looting as they left. As patriot troops had then begun their triumphant march down Bowery Lane toward the little metropolis which nestled at the tip of Manhattan, their elation had changed to anger on discovery of what the British had left: buildings gutted by fire, defaced, or neglected, streets heavy with filth—with, reported Philip Freneau, "dirt and mud, and mouldering walls / Burnt domes, dead dogs, and funerals."[2] Who owned what was a problem, and what to do with property left by Tory citizens who had escaped to Nova Scotia or England. There were also problems of pollution: only two months before Royall Tyler arrived, the Common Council had appointed a commission to control the throwing of waste material into New York's reservoir, its Fresh Water Pond. Slums were being cleared, for poverty-stricken patriots, returning homeless to the city, lived in squalor in neglected and ramshackle former British barracks. Noise abatement programs denied cart men of the city the use of iron-bound wheels which rumbled over and cracked its cobblestone streets. Sewage disposal was on people's minds, and city planning; measures were taken for "preventing the erection of buildings that narrow or encroach upon any streets."

But progress seemed certain. Not ten days before Tyler arrived, the New York legislature had granted John Fitch "the Sole Right and Advantage of making and employing . . . the Steam-Boat by him lately invented," and the gallant sailing ship, *The Empress of China*, had just returned from a round trip to the Orient, opening the wonders and the riches of those lands to Yankee exploitation. While Tyler was in the city, on Easter Sunday, 8 April, the Right Reverend Samuel Provoost was ordained in Saint Paul's Chapel, formerly Anglican, as the first Protestant Episcopal bishop of New York. Just four days before *The Contrast* was performed at the John Street Theater, King's College was officially changed in name to Columbia College.[3] The Old American Company of actors had a month before come overland through ice and snow from Philadelphia, to open the theatrical season in New York on 13 February with the popular sex drama *The Provoked Husband*, following it the next day with Sheridan's uncontested drawing card *The School for Scandal*.[4] Manhattan, then as now, was proud of its cosmopolitan culture. When portrait painter Joseph Wright arrived in the city in April, the *Daily Advertiser* on the thirteenth of that month proudly announced that

"New York bids fair to out vie the sister states in becoming the seat of the arts."

The new country was ready for competence, even competition, in the arts. It had a Benjamin West, president, no less, of the Royal Academy in London; it had a Franklin, though long resident in France, in philosophy; and now it would have a Royall Tyler at home, adept in what his enthusiastic countrymen called "that most difficult of arts." Not even the discouragement which Philip Freneau expressed as he retreated to sea could dampen patriot spirits. "Authors," Freneau suggested, "are at present considered as the dregs of the community: their situation and prospects are truly humiliating." To him literary and political independence were separate entirely: "the first," he explained, "was accomplished in about seven years, the latter will not be completely effected in perhaps as many centuries." He was convinced that the arts can only flourish in an atmosphere "of opulence and refinement," not present "in our age or country." He called on fellow writers to do what he had done, "to graft their talent upon some other calling," for in the United States in the 1780s "it is far more profitable to be a good brick layer . . . than an indifferent poet."[5] And especially with competition from "that damnable place" across the ocean. Even in the theater, what there was of it, foreign voices were heard and foreign ideas set forth.

Royall Tyler, just under thirty, was an unlikely candidate for breaking the hold which imported playwrights had on the American theater, or for giving encouragement, as by his example he did, to other native playwrights, like William Dunlap, who would be even more successful than he. Born in Boston in 1757, the son and later the heir of a wealthy merchant, he attended a Latin school there during exciting times when Liberty Trees were erected on the Commons and great bonfires were lit to celebrate the repeal of the Stamp Act. Boston was then a noisy and provoking town—Samuel Adams and its disruptive tea parties saw to that. British troops patrolled its streets, British officers adorned its more fashionable drawing rooms, and when Tyler was thirteen, bells rang out at night and shots were heard on that

March evening of the Boston Massacre. A year after that, the boy entered Harvard, where he watched grim patriots arm themselves for the siege of Boston, and where, a patriot himself, he refrained from drinking English tea.

He was known as a gay young blade. People spoke of his "brilliant wit," "amusing conversation," and "native talents," but were sometimes dismayed at his escapades. He was briefly expelled—"rusticated" was the term used, which meant that he had to pack his books and spend some time in exile, away from the college, in his case, in Maine—because he and his roommate, dangling a hook from their dormitory window in an attempt to snag a plump piglet that was rooting among the litter in the college yard, snagged instead the wig of Harvard's president, and lifted it quite off his head. Nonetheless when Tyler was graduated, at the age of nineteen, just a few weeks after the Declaration of Independence had been signed, he had done so well that not only did Harvard grant him an A.B., but Yale, which he had never attended, granted him one also.[6]

After graduation, he remained in Cambridge to study law, spending much of his time, however, with John Trumbull, the artist son of the governor of Connecticut whose name was Jonathan and who was a lanky and laconic man, with a generation gap between him and his son and his son's friends, so that he is sometimes thought to have been the model, at least in name, for the ingenuous Yankee countryman in *The Contrast*. There was something humorous about Connecticut in the early United States: it was inhabited by dour deacons who imposed restrictive blue laws, and it produced, said Freneau, the largest pumpkins and onions and epics and families of any state in the union. It was "Terra Vulpina, or the Land of Foxes," where like the "winds that guide [their] wintry reign, / All bow to lucre, all are bent on gain."[7] Fenimore Cooper was later to have great fun with Connecticut, possibly because he had been expelled from Yale. Washington Irving laughed at its dumpling-cheeked maidens and its penny-pinching parsons, and surely the refugee Ichabod Crane was a psalm-singing son of the Nutmeg State.

As an adventuresome and sometimes roistering young bachelor who "entered," said one disapproving contemporary, "with great zeal and zest, into the dissipated habits and manners which characterized the younger men" of his place and time, fond of wine and ladies and long convivial evenings, Royall Tyler was hardly the model of what a pioneering playwright should be—or perhaps he was just the man, for Ben Jonson, we have been told, was also a roisterer in taverns, and poor Edgar Poe, who had troubles also, was to be born in Boston, not many years after Tyler's residence there, as a result of a runaway marriage between a young man from a respectable Baltimore family and an itinerant actress. For the theater and its denizens were not in the new nation universally approved. Young America perhaps had reasons then for believing that it was right in restricting the theater, so that in Charleston one had to go beyond the city limits to see a play, in Philadelphia they were disguised as "concerts" or "lectures" in which, for example, the popular comedy *The Gamesters* was advertised as "A Lecture on the Vice of Gambling," and in Boston they were not allowed to be presented at all. At Harvard, it was ruled, "If any Undergraduate shall presume to be an Actor in, a Spectator at, or in any Ways concerned in Stage Plays, Interludes, or Theatrical Entertainments . . . he shall for the first Offense be degraded—and for repeated Offense shall be rusticated or expelled."[8]

But Royall Tyler seems to have been a young man with a careless regard for rules. Among his college papers has been found "A Prologue" to what must have been a play, or a play in disguise as an exhibition, "intended," he said,

> To shew the vile intentions of the mind
> To paint the real vices of mankind

for since

> Drama first adorned the stage
> Checking the progress of a vicious age
> Here see our crimes and follies all portray'd
> The road to virtue joy and bliss display'd.[9]

He had other avocations also. Rumor has had it that he was quite by accident the father of a son born to a well-known college character, a cleaning woman named Katharine Morse. His later animated courtship of Abigail Adams was interrupted when John Adams, her father, had her shipped off to Europe, away from the charm of so prodigal and, he thought, so frivolous a suitor. After serving briefly in the Continental army under Col. John Hancock, Tyler was admitted to the bar and enjoyed what seems to have been a desultory practice in suburban Braintree. But he was in and out of Boston, at his mother's house and, if later hints are to be believed, at bootlegged plays. A recently published narrative entitled, "The Bay Boy" describes what he calls "The First Theatrical Presentation in Boston," when Addison's *Cato* was played in a tightly closed storefront theater, "every crack and keyhole" of which was "carefully stopped with paper or cotton that no glimmering light might alarm the passing watchman. The entrance was through a bye lane into a door in the backyard, and such was the caution observed that but one person was admitted at a time, while two, one at each end of the lane, were on the watch to see if the person to be admitted had been noticed." When the watchman approached with his staff and whistle, "the lights were extinguished or put under a bushel" until he had passed and, panic abated, "we took new courage and the play proceeded."[10]

It seems possible then that we must discard the traditional account of Royall Tyler coming to New York in the late winter of 1787, to see there his first play and then, so talented was he, so deft and witty, that within a few weeks he had written a play of his own, the first by a citizen of the United States to be performed publicly by professional actors—according to its dedication when published three years later, "the First Essay of *American* Genius in the Dramatic Art." Not all of this seems to be strictly true, no more than is it true that two years later Tyler's Boston neighbor, young Willie Brown, scandalized that city by publishing what has been called, but what is not, the first American novel. Just as other fiction challenges *The Power of Sympathy* for that somewhat dubious honor, so do other plays challenge *The Contrast*. If we are to be concerned with firsts, it is enough perhaps to remember Royall Tyler's comedy, in the words of his biographer, as "the first commercially successful American play" —though the chances are that it failed to bring its author a penny of profit.

Coming when it did, it could not help succeed. The theater in postrevolutionary America became a useful public platform from which to inculcate patriotic adherence to democratic virtues among those who could read and those who could not. Constance Rourke has described this theater as producing "spoken journalism," effective because it underlined those native qualities of which Crèvecoeur had written and of which Franklin was exemplar. Colonel Manly in *The Contrast* is a true blue patriotic American, who neither drinks nor games; he is blunt and honest, the ancestor certainly of James Fenimore Cooper's Edward Effingham or Sinclair Lewis's Sam Dodsworth. His forthright conduct—straight from the shoulder, flat-out, plainspoken, and authentic—contrasts indeed with the Chesterfieldian elegance and shallowness of "that damnable place" from which the new country had won independence. Tyler's prologue explains it well:

> Exult each patriot heart!—this night is shewn
> A piece, which we may fairly call our own;
> Where the proud titles of "My Lord! Your Grace!"
> To humble *Mr.* and plain *Sir* give place.
> Our Author pictures not from foreign climes
> The fashions, or the follies of the times;
> But has confin'd the subject of his work
> To the gay scenes—the circles of New-York.[11]

Apparently at this time New York needed admonition and correction. "If there is a town on the American continent," said a visitor from France, "where English luxury displays its follies, it is New York,"[12] or, as Colonel Manly puts it more politely, "In America, the cry is, what is the fashion? and we follow it" (act 2, scene 1). And Tyler followed fashion assiduously in *The Contrast*, for however timely and patriotic and indigenous, his play leaned hard on foreign models—as did the poems of Barlow, Dwight, and Freneau, the fiction of Brackenridge and Brown, or even the later sketches of Washington Irving. I shall not recite the list of English plays which one commentator or another has suggested that Tyler must have read and been influenced by—I count more than a dozen. For *The Contrast* is entirely within the orthodox tradition of the English drama of sensibility, with frivolous or grasping young women in supporting roles, with comic servants and gossips and headstrong fathers, and with solemn rectitude guaranteed to bind true lovers in happy union. But the proud American audience which first saw *The Contrast* more than a century and a half ago—an audience which we are told included "many of the first characters of the United States"— greeted the performance with "repeated bursts of applause" because of its novelty and timeliness: "nothing," said one of them, "can be more praiseworthy" than its sentiments; it was, said another, a "truly sentimental performance."[13]

Jonathan of course was the hit of the evening: he seemed fresh and new, and so, so American; he was everyone's eccentric neighbor, honestly naive, and it was refreshing and somehow satisfying to be able to laugh at him because the laughter showed Americans to be mature enough to laugh at themselves. Comedian Thomas Wignall played the role so well that some have suspected that the actor-managers of the company, who had leading but less attractive parts, withdrew the play after four performances because he received more applause than they. Whether it really is this Jonathan who is, as has been said, the progenitor of a long line of lanky stage Yankees (and from whom derives the familiar figure of Uncle Sam), or whether it is true, as another has said, that Jonathan not only himself had a progenitor, also named Jonathan, in a comedy played in Dublin almost exactly a year before, but also that in more than one-half of the approximately forty plays written in America before 1787 there were attempts at the creation of a rustic native—whatever may be said of his ancestors or his descendants, Jonathan did now arrive, and for the first time on our stage, as a successfully characterized, or caricatured, native personage shown plain.[14]

His homespun clichés are made to seem of native earth earthy: his mild oaths and expletives—"by the living jingo," "dang it all," "maple-log sieze it," or "swamp it," even his "cursed" and "tarnal" and "Dam'd"; his homely phrases, like "kicking up a cursed dust" or "pretty dumb rich" or even "as thick as mustard"; his explosive oxymorons after kissing (or, as he would have it, "bussing") young Jenny—"Burning rivers! cooling flames! red-hot roses," he shouted, and then, in a supreme delight, "pig-nuts, hasty-pudding, and ambrosia."[15] To a generation nurtured on Gomer Pyle and "Gunsmoke" and *Naked Came the Stranger*, these may seem bland indeed, but not to the 1780s.

For *The Contrast* is a period piece, put together from shreds and pieces of other plays. Its characters are all familiar types except, with some reservations, Jonathan, and even he is largely a Yankee Sancho Panza, just as Colonel Manly is a stiff-backed Don Quixote. If you will be learned with me for a moment, we can recognize the character of Transfer, the broker, as taken from Samuel Foote's *The Minor*, or, if you wish, because a symbolic name is used for a moneylender, from "Premium" in *The School for Scandal*. Maria's situation in relation to her father parallels that of Lydia Lanquish in *The Rivals*, and the same theme was used by George Colman in *Polly Honeycomb*. The relationships of Maria, Manly, and Dimple suggest those found in Hugh Kelly's comedy about *False Delicacy*. And so, with a little time and some stirring about in libraries, we could go on and on.[16]

For, in addition to being derivative, *The Contrast* is among the most literary of American plays, chuck full—in a primerlike way, less learned than T. S. Eliot's *The Waste Land*—with allusions which can delight the well-read reader or confuse an unlearned one. None miss the reference to "grave Spectator" in the first scene, or to Sir Charles Grandison or Clarissa Harlowe, to Shenstone, to *Robinson Crusoe*, and to Sterne's *Sentimental Journey*. Jonathan inadvertently sees "The School for Scandalization" and he makes cryptic allusions to Darby, a comic rustic in *The Poor Soldier*, as played by "Wig—Wag—Wagal," that is, by Wignall, the same comedian who now played the naive American countryman. Jonathan knew psalm tunes, three of them, and one hundred and ninety verses of "Yankee Doodle"; the cosmopolite Dimple knows Milton, and book-wise Charlotte calls Maria and Colonel Manly gloomy "penserosos." Bernard Mandeville's *Fable of the Bees* is mentioned, and Ben Jonson is quoted. The fastidious but pernicious dicta of Lord Chesterfield are central to the action, one of the things that the play is about—for literature is to be used with caution. The commonsense and sensible eighteenth century knew, in England, but especially in America, that literature could lead young girls astray. Love should be governed, says lightheaded Letitia, by the "rule of romance" as found in modern fiction. Not at all, says sensible Charlotte, who makes fun of the "purling streams of sentiment" which flow through modern poetry, and who touches a sensitive spot when she accuses modern criticism of torturing "some harmless expression to a double meaning which the poor author never dreamed of."

As a period piece *The Contrast* is filled with local references and private jokes. Royall Tyler even allows Jonathan to play to the galleries by admitting, though secretly, and hoping that Colonel Manly will not find him out, that he thinks that maybe Daniel Shays had been right to lead an insurrection in Massachusetts. And the colonel is a member of the new American establishment, of the loyal—though aristocratic—Order of the Cincinnati, a name which poor Jonathan cannot pronounce. The colonel is proud to have "humbly imitated our illustrious Washington," he said, "in having exposed his health and life in the service of my country without reaping any other reward than the glory of conquering in so arduous a contest." But he is in New York to urge the Congress to grant pensions to veterans of the Revolution.

New York, and seemingly rightly so, comes in for its share of corrective satire, and so do the very actors who perform the piece. Charlotte Manly thinks her brother so serious and filled so full with patriotic platitude that she dare not introduce him to "polite circles in the city," lest they think you, she tells him, "a player run mad, with your head filled with old scraps of tragedy." She and Letitia, speaking alternately, describe New York society:

> Our ladies are so delicate and dressy.
> And our beaux so dressy and delicate.
> Our ladies chat and flirt so agreeably.
> And our beaux simper and bow so gracefully.
> With their hair so trim and neat.
> And their faces so soft and sleek.
> Their buckles so tonish and bright.
> And their hands so slender and white.

> (Act 2, scene 1)

Compared with people like these, Colonel Manly's "horrid robustness," his "vulgar corn-fed glow of health," would alarm people of high society in New York, who giggle and simper and bow and blush, as well-bred people do. Even his coat looked "as if it were calculated for the vulgar purpose" of keeping him warm and comfortable. But it is a noble coat, a worthy coat, and, surely, he protested "those who have endured . . . winter campaigns in the service of their country, without bread or clothing or pay, at least deserved that the poverty of their appearance should not be difficult." And so, on the colonel talks, protesting against all that is not simple and democratic and native.

To an audience almost two hundred years later, it may seem that the colonel protests too much, and too long. Even contemporary reviewers recognized that the dialogue in *The Contrast*, though "easy, sprightly, and often witty, . . . needed the pruning knife," especially in Manly's long soliloquy in the second scene of act 3. But here the critic was moved by patriotism to admit "the thoughts . . . so just, that I should be sorry . . . were they left out entirely." Another reviewer was so bold as to wonder whether the audience had not "applauded the novelty of the attempt" of producing a native play by a native author "without strictly weighing the merits of its execution." For *The Contrast* was a novelty indeed, and its sentiments "did greatest credit to the author," so that finally "candour must allow its being an extraordinary effort of genius." And so Royall Tyler gained name and fame. His play was thought to rival "the most celebrated productions of the British muse in elegance of invention, correctness and splendor of diction."[17] This may, or may not, have been what he intended.

But his play was effective "spoken journalism" which warned against the dangers of "foreign gold" and "foreign luxury" which Colonel Manly thought had "sapped the vitals" of his countrymen. If America was to succeed, frugality was necessary, and hard work, as Franklin had warned, not "Luxury! which enervates both body and soul, by opening a thousand new sources of enjoyment, opens, alas, also, a thousand new sources of contention and want." Take warning, the colonel advised as he ended his soliloquy in act 3, from the example of ancient Greece, where the "common good was lost in the pursuit of private interest, and that people, who, by uniting, might have stood against the world, by dividing crumbled into ruin. . . . Oh! that America! Oh! that my country, would in this her day, learn the things which belong to her peace!" (act 3). Colonel Manly spoke in the official and the necessary voice of the 1780s, explaining with tie-wig gallantry in the closing lines of the play that "probity, virtue, honour, though they should not have received the polish of Europe, will secure to an honest American the good graces of his countrywomen, and, I hope, the applause of THE PUBLIC." It has not been my observation that many Americans have asked for more.

These final words of Colonel Manly invited applause, and applause was given with tremendous and patriotic gusto, and Royall Tyler—like George M. Cohan in other patriotic days—had his brief time of glory. He wrote other plays—one while he was in New York; others, some of which were produced, even in Boston, have not survived. But Royall Tyler did not live by literature: it was the product, as people said in those days, of his idle hours. As a gentleman might, he wrote light verses—enough to fill a fair-sized volume, most of it frolicsome and convivial, about love and wine and bygone pleasures. During the next twenty years he enjoyed some genteel half-anonymous fame as collaborator with his younger friend Joseph Dennie in a column identified as "from the Shop of Colon and Spondee." He wrote a novel called *The Algerine Captive* which contains much of the best writing he ever did, and he wrote a book called *The Yankey in London*—a city he had never seen—in which he again ridiculed English ways and manners, even attacking such institutions as burly Dr. Samuel Johnson and his James Boswell.

But writing was a sideline, and not entirely a respectable vocation for a well-bred gentleman. Royall Tyler did not publicly put his name to *The Contrast:* it was identified as "by a Citizen of the United States," and that was enough. Even Washington Irving, and many years later, hid his patrician self behind a variety of pseudonyms. Tyler followed Freneau's advice, though I suspect he never read it, by grafting his talent on another calling, which in his case was the law. He became a judge and a professor and, as such, lived to a ripe old age, but he is remembered now

94

for *The Contrast* which he wrote before he was thirty. Most Americans die at thirty, it has been said, but aren't buried until they are seventy. The continuing inconspicuous life of *The Contrast* suggests that Royall Tyler is not completely buried yet.

NOTES

1. After many years of virtual neglect, much has recently been revealed of Royall Tyler. For biographical information I am indebted throughout to G. Thomas Tanselle, *Royall Tyler* (Cambridge, 1967). See also Marcus B. Péladeau, *The Verse of Royall Tyler* (Charlottesville, Va., 1967) and *The Prose of Royall Tyler* (Montpelier and Rutland, Vt., 1972).

2. "New-York," *Philadelphia Freeman's Journal*, 10 September 1783, p. 4; reprinted as "Manhattan City" in Fred Lewis Pattee, ed., *The Poems of Philip Freneau: Poet of the American Revolution* (Princeton, N.J., 1902–1907), 2: 223–224.

3. I. N. Phelps Stokes, *The Iconography of Manhattan Island* (New York, 1926), 5: 1216–1217.

4. George C. D. Odell, *Annals of the New York Stage* (New York, 1927), 1: 255–256.

5. "Advice to Authors," *The Miscellaneous Works of Mr. Philip Freneau, Containing His Essays and Additional Poems* (Philadelphia, 1788), pp. 46–47.

6. Tanselle, *Royall Tyler*, pp. 7–8.

7. "Description of Connecticut," *New York Daily Advertiser*, 10 May 1790, p. 4.

8. Tanselle, *Royall Tyler*, p. 5.

9. Péladeau, *The Verse of Royall Tyler*, pp. 5–6.

10. Péladeau, *The Prose of Royall Tyler*, pp. 144, 146.

11. Péladeau, *The Verse of Royall Tyler*, pp. 7–8.

12. *New York Daily Advertiser*, 23 November 1783, p. 3.

13. See Odell, *Annals of the New York Stage*, 1: 256–257.

14. Discussions of Jonathan and his lineage are found in Marston Balch, "Jonathan the First," *Modern Language Notes* 46 (May 1931): 281–288; Richard M. Dorson, "The Yankee on the Stage," *New England Quarterly* 13 (December 1940): 467–493; and Isaac R. Perley, *The Realistic Presentation of Characters in American Plays Prior to the Eighteen Seventies* (Columbus, Ohio, 1918).

15. Tyler's Americanism in language has been discussed by Marie Killheffer, "A Comparison of the Dialect of the 'Biglow Papers' with the Dialect of Four Yankee Plays," *American Speech* 3 (February 1928): 222–236; George McKnight and Bert Emsley, *Modern English in the Making* (New York, 1928), pp. 479–480; and Roger B. Stein, "Royall Tyler and the Question of Our Speech," *New England Quarterly* 37 (December 1965): 454–474.

16. Excellent discussions of the sources of *The Contrast* are to be found in Arthur H. Nethercot, "The Dramatic Background of Royall Tyler's *The Contrast*," *American Literature* 12 (January 1941): 435–446, and Arthur Hobson Quinn, *A History of the American Drama from the Beginning to the Civil War* (New York, 1927), pp. 294–303.

17. For contemporary and later criticism, see Tanselle, *Royall Tyler*, pp. 78–81.

Charles Crawford

A FORGOTTEN POET OF
EARLY PHILADELPHIA

֍ ֍

IN 1783, as the Revolution drew to a close, only five volumes of poetry were published in the new United States. Four of these were by a gentleman of Philadelphia named Charles Crawford, three from the press of Robert Aitken, at Pope's Head, in Market Street, between Second and Third streets. They were *A Poetical Paraphrase on Our Saviour's Sermon on the Mount, A Poem on the Death of General Montgomery, Liberty: A Pindaric Ode,* and *The Christian: A Poem in Four Books.*

During the next eighteen years, something more than a dozen books by Charles Crawford appeared in Philadelphia, bearing the imprints of some of its best-known eighteenth-century printers: Francis Bailey, Zachariah Poulson, Eleazer Oswald, Thomas Bradford, Asbury Dickens, and James Humphreys. Crawford published *Observations on Negro Slavery* in 1784, a translation of J. P. Brissot de Warville's *Oration* against slavery in 1788, *Observations on the Downfall of Papal Power* and *George Foxe's Looking Glass* in 1790, *Observations on the Revolution in France* in 1793, *An Essay on the Propagation of the Gospel* in 1799, and *An Essay on the Eleventh Chapter of the Revelation of St. John* in 1800. His ode on liberty, which in 1789 had been reprinted in London and criticized in the *Monthly Review* as more commendable for its piety than its poetry, was expanded and renamed *The Progress of Liberty* in 1795; the *Poetical Paraphrase* appeared again, with detailed new annotation, and *The Christian* was expanded from four to six books, both in 1796; *The Dying Prostitute,* one of several poems which had been appended to the 1783 edition of *The Christian,* was issued separately in 1797.

97

In spite of all the literary activity and the evidences of good will which his titles suggest, Charles Crawford presents an enigma. Few traces remain of a man who patronized so many printers, and seldom the same one twice, that suspicion arises of some flaw of irascibility, or perhaps of inability or unwillingness to meet financial obligations. He may have been—though I suspect he was not—the Charles Crawford who in 1785 acquired eight hundred acres of land in Bedford and Northampton counties, and another four hundred acres in Huntington County seven years later.[1] He was an active member of the Pennsylvania Society for Promoting the Abolition of Slavery and the Relief of Free Negroes Unlawfully Held in Bondage.[2] In 1784 he contributed a letter to the *Freeman's Journal* over the signature of "Justice" in which he recommended to Philadelphians the tract recently printed by Isaac Collins in Trenton entitled *A Serious Address to the Rulers of America, on the Inconsistency of Their Conduct Respecting Slavery*.[3] It was undoubtedly he who is listed in the Philadelphia Directory of 1794 as Charles Crawford, gentleman, residing at 163 North Third Street. But these are the only clues which records have been found to disclose.

More hints to his identity are furnished, however, by autograph annotations in several surviving copies of his books. On the title page of *The Christian* in the Huntington Library, for example, someone has described the author as "Charles Crawford of Garnock"; in *Observations on Negro Slavery* as preserved in the New York Public Library, he is named "Viscount Garnock," an attribution which is written also into some of his works in the libraries of the Historical Society of Pennsylvania, the New York Historical Society, and Columbia University. Further evidence is offered by the discovery that the poem "Augustus and Sophronia" which is included in *The Christian* volume is virtually identical with a poem published nine years earlier in London as *Sophronia and Hilario* by Charles Crawford, a fellow commoner of Queens College, Cambridge. Following directions pointed by these clues, something can be reconstructed of the career of Charles Crawford who, if he had no other distinction, might be remembered briefly as responsible for four-fifths of the total number of volumes of poetry produced during what may be thought of as our first national year.

Charles Crawford was born in Antigua, the second son of Alexander Crawford, and was baptized at Saint John's Church on that island on 28 October 1752. His father was a prosperous landowner and member of a family which had come to the West Indies early in the eighteenth century. He had served as provost marshal, had married well, and through industry increased his holdings in plantation land. On his death in 1772, he provided generously for his family: John Francis, the older son, was heir to the estate, but Charles, who was at the time in England, received a legacy of two thousand pounds outright and an annual income of one hundred fifty pounds.

In England, Charles Crawford as a minor had been placed by his father under the temporary guardianship of one Michael Lovell, who seems to have handled the elder Crawford's business affairs in London. "It is well known," explained Mr. Lovell, "to be usual, among the West-India merchants, to have their children consigned to their care." In this instance, however, the responsibility seems to have been enlarged because young Charles Crawford was headstrong and hot-tempered. "When some of these young West Indians first advance to manhood," his guardian further explained, "they are frequently less discrete, and more expansive, than those born in colder climes. Mr. Crawford is a young West-Indian, whose father we offended by our indulgence to the son, whilst the son was offended by our following his father's directions." Relations between Mr. Lovell and his ward were strained to the point that one day, apparently in the summer of 1772, at high noon on a crowded street in Cheapside, the young man publicly caned his merchant protector. "A greater insult to the metropolis could not have been offered," said people who did not like Mr. Lovell and accused him of "making not the least effort to vindicate his honour." The merchant mildly replied: "I bore his impudent anger very patiently, as I dare say any other merchant would have done." The young gentleman, he continued, is now at Cambridge.[5]

99

At the university, at Queens College, where he qualified as among "the younger sons of nobility or young men of fortune" who were known as fellow commoners because of their privilege of dining at the fellows' table, Charles Crawford was soon in trouble again. On 27 September 1773 he was expelled. But the action against him was, he contended, not legal because his expulsion had been the result of an order "made by the Master and two Fellows," and the paper served on him had been signed only by the master; therefore, he disregarded it. Even when the action was confirmed on 13 January 1774 by the signature of the masters and all ten fellows, Crawford still remained recalcitrant. But when not long afterward he "came into the college garden with an intent to take possession of his rooms," he was seized by the porter who conducted him, we suppose with force, out of the premises. Crawford brought immediate suit against the porter, and the porter filed articles of peace against Crawford, which articles were withdrawn, however, "on Mr. Crawford's undertaking not to go in to Queen's College till the disputes between him and that society were legally determined." Litigation dragged on until the spring of 1775, when the Court of King's Bench ruled against the West Indian's contention that his expulsion had been "illegal and unstatutable and consequently the assault . . . not justifiable." As a fellow commoner, Crawford had been "a mere boarder" and had no corporate rights; the expulsion would therefore stand unless set aside by higher university authorities. It stood.[6]

More attention seems always to be paid to the misdemeanors than to the virtues of young men, and so, as Charles Crawford settles down, it becomes more difficult to discover traces of him, except in his writings. Lack of evidence prevents our taking sides in his quarrel with the college, though sympathies may reach out toward a spirited young man who was stubborn in defense of what he supposed his rights. But he could not have been completely pleasant, and whatever good will we admit to, our attitude toward him is soon strained by an examination of *A Dissertation on the Phaedon of Plato; or, a Dialogue of the Immortality of the Soul* which Crawford published during his residence at Cambridge, and of which he was monstrously proud.[7] "My intention," he explained in preface, "was to have given the substance of every thing which has been said in regard to the soul worthy of notice in the Greek, Latin, English, French, Spanish, and Italian languages." If he had not quite done all of that, the present publication might, he said, "be looked upon as the sketch only of a much larger work." He recognized that he opened himself to criticism as "rash and adventurous in the extreme," but was confident of his ability "to pluck some of the laurels which for ages have adorned the tomb of Plato, and from the luxuriant spoil to weave a chaplet for my own brow."

Not only were the ancient philosophers attacked in their arguments in support of the immortality of the soul, but the moderns also—Locke, Hartley, and Malebranche. "There is not one author to be found," he asserted with quick assurance, "who advances one convincing proof of a future state"; what was more, even "the Christian religion plainly denies the immortality of the soul," which was plainly "a quality, and not a distinct substance." The *Dissertation* was just such a forthright pronouncement as many a young man has written, before Crawford's time and since: it shouted loudly of his right independently to reach for truth, and it hedged circumspectly in denying any taint of deism or disregard of fundamental Christian principles. Like most books of its kind, it was not well received. "We find," said a reviewer, "a pompous display of learning and reading, but . . . little of anything original or peculiar to this author (except his licentious manner)." The tract was distorted by "violent partiality toward some, whom he professes to admire and follow, such as *Lucretius, Bolingbroke,* and *Voltaire.*" It was conceded, however, that "the young man is certainly possessed of some parts, more reading, and a tolerable share of classical learning," but his "judgment is borne away by the springtide of his vanity." Because he seemed "far from deficient in natural understanding," the time might well arrive when he would "be sufficiently grown in grace to become ashamed of this unadvised, illiberal, and indecent performance."[8]

But Crawford himself thought well enough of the *Dissertation* to bring out a second, probably revised and expanded, edition before the next year.[9] In 1774 he also had printed in a handsome small volume the poem which he called *Sophronia and Hilario: An Ode*. It tells in hard pressed iambic quatrains the tale of a young man who put the wildness of youth behind him when he met and married the fair Sophronia. Because of the respect for all women which his wife inspired, Hilario vowed never again to boast of his own former conquests among the fair or to allow any other man to soil their reputation by boasting in his presence. When one evening one of his companions did tell all about the women he had seduced, the young husband challenged him immediately to a duel. Hilario is killed, not because he lacked courage or skill, but because his foot slipped on a stone so that he was foully and illegally run through by his wanton antagonist. The villain is immediately struck down by Hilario's loyal friend Horatio, but Sophronia is left alone, dissolved in grief. Floridly sentimental, the poem is as undistinguished in verse as it is elusive in meaning. However, said the *Monthly Review*, "If Mr. Crawford intended this poem as an essay toward discountenancing the foolish and butcherly custom of duelling, he is to be commended for his design."[10]

There was something in the impetuous character or reputation of the young West Indian poet which made reviewers hesitate in criticism, or perhaps in irony pretend hesitation. *Sophronia and Hilario* was admittedly, said one of them, "not the best poem of the kind that we have ever perused," but the critic then paused in mock alarm: "we forbear; not being ambitious of the honour of having our names joined with those venerable ones of antiquity which this sweet-blooded gentleman has treated with such extraordinary marks of *reverence* in his Dissertation on Plato."[11] When three years later, in 1777, Crawford presented another slim quarto, *Richmond Hill: A Poem*, which detailed the influences of nature upon an extremely sensitive but not overly original young man, the reviewer struck out more boldly: "Here is a wonderful poet indeed! he was not made by the hand which made human beings: he was made by—a mountain: 'Hail honour'd Mount! inspirer of my lays! / Thou mad'st the Bard, and merit'st all his praise.' *Ridiculus mus!*"[12]

Crawford's next adventure in verse, more ambitious than any

he had attempted before, was issued in 1781 from Tunbridge Wells, where we may suppose the young man, now almost thirty, lived as a gentleman should, on his patrimony. *The Christian,* published first as "a poem in four books," was to be with him almost all the rest of his life, revised, expanded, and reissued at intervals during the next thirty-five years. It contained not quite a reversal of his attitude as expressed in the *Dissertation,* but a change in emphasis which suggests that the years had brought some calm, or experience some kind of quieting conversion; he may, we think, have married, or wished he had. "I have endeavoured in the poem," he explained in preface to *The Christian,* "to deliver the genuine and unadulterated doctrines of Christianity." The hand of the Enlightment had apparently descended gently upon him; what he had to say, as far as it can be understood, was mildly humane, evangelical, and almost pietistic, but he was not ahead of his time, in sentiment or in verse. His former rash impetuosity was tempered: "If I have failed in any point, and I should be favoured with a future conviction of error, I will ingenuously retract it." Then, in verse hobbled to closed couplets, he recited the vanity and imperfection of all philosophy, from first to last, pointing a barbed pen particularly toward "bewilder'd Hobbes," "Bolingbroke fallacious," "putrid Hume," and the "flimsey, faithless, profligate Voltaire." These offered neither comfort nor light:

> No more by vain Philosophy misled,
> From erring Reason, or from Fancy bred;
> Vague and desultory, no more the Mind,
> In ancient schools Conviction hopes to find.
> . . . .
> From these if no conviction we receive,
> What Comfort less the modern Sceptics give.[13]

He urged others to turn, as he had now turned, to the Gospels, to discover examples of true benevolence revealed in the life of Jesus and the wondrous truth of the Sermon on the Mount. It was avarice which had finally betrayed the Son of God, and love of money was still the lure which tempted men to evil. Like many of his time, ready for the prophetic exhilaration which the influence of Swedenborg was beginning to provide, he dwelt long on those portions of the New Testament which foretold the destruction of Jerusalem and its rebirth as "an important solid argument" for Christian nurture. His old antagonist, the *Monthly Review,* liked the prose preface for its "sensible remarks on the proofs of the truth of Christianity," and found it "much better reading than the poem itself, which is but a moderate performance. . . . Mr. Crawford certainly mistakes his talents when he applies them to poetry."[14]

It must have been soon after the publication of *The Christian* that Crawford somehow crossed the Atlantic during war years, to come to Philadelphia, and there to publish volume after volume designed to enlighten and improve his fellows. How he came, or why he came, there seems now no way of knowing. It may have been trade that lured him, some continuing connection with his planter brother in Antigua. It might even have been that he saw in the new emerging Western nation something of the New Jerusalem which his pious readings foretold. When he presented an expanded version of *The Christian* in Philadelphia in 1783, he told American readers that it was not so necessary for them as for other people "to prove the truth of christianity, before we," he said, counting on the circumstance, we suppose, of his West Indian birth to explain his use of the first person plural as he included himself among them, "expatiate upon its precepts." He congratulated them on their religious liberty, their disavowal of an established church, and he urged them to expand even farther their tolerance and benevolence: "I would recommend to you to open your hearts, in this enlightened and happy aera, to all mankind, to forbear to reproach the Jew, to free the Negro, to tame and to incorporate the Indian, and to invite them all to christianity."[15]

To piece out the volume which was to introduce him to the New World, Crawford added five miscellaneous poems as productions, he hoped, "not altogether unworthy of a Christian." First among them was "Augustus and Sophronia: A Poetical Fiction," a revision of the earlier transatlantic *Sophronia and Hilario,* which Crawford now offered with the hope that it might "have a Tendency, wherever it is read, to decry and to abolish the savage Custom of Duelling." It was followed by "The Dying Prostitute," which was identified—as if to forestall any suggestion that it might be concerned with an American subject—as "originally written in London," then by an equally pathetic and sentimental narrative of "The Forsaken Maiden," by a "Hymn to Spring," and "An Elegy on the Death of Two Young Ladies, Who Died the Same Morning of Inoculation for the Small Pox." Whatever sophisticated sentiment pervaded them, these verses must have seemed to many Philadelphians vapid indeed beside the cleverly devised satire and the pungent, penetrating wit with which Francis Hopkinson and Philip Freneau and others among their patriotic and quarreling citizens were enlivening their newspapers. If the sophistication and the sentiment appealed as imported commodities, no record of it remains, for the city was filled with too many other exciting things to leave much time for public discussion of poetry.

Nor could the other volumes which Crawford published in Philadelphia in 1783 have fared greatly better. *A Poem on the Death of Montgomery* was a pedestrian salute to the brave ideals of men who helped make the New World free, but it limped in spirit and sentiment behind the undistinguished verse on much the same kind of subject which was at just this time pouring from the prolific pen of Col. David Humphreys of New England. *Liberty*, which in title might have been expected to find public response, was principally a humanitarian's account of the evils of slavery in the West Indies, a sedate subject which danced incongruously to the pindaric measure which Crawford attempted to impose. *A Poetical Paraphrase on Our Saviour's Sermon on the Mount* was a reminder to freethinkers everywhere "that the Person who delivered such wise and good precepts could not have been an imposter." In each, good intention was a feebly inadequate cloak for malformed verse. The Beatitudes, for example, have probably seldom been more unimaginatively mangled:

> Blessed are they, in spirit who are poor,
> For they the kingdom shall of heav'n procure;
> Blessed are they, who innocently grieve,
> For they celestial comfort shall receive;

Blessed the meek, for they full long shall stand
In well earn'd honours in the plenteous land.[16]

Crawford's prose is better because it pretends less. *The Observations upon Negro Slavery* in 1784 warrants brief attention from students of our early literature because of a lengthy footnote on Phillis Wheatley, whose career as poet, Crawford said, offered evidence that Negroes are not by nature inferior. The *Observations upon the Downfall on Papal Power*, which may have appeared as early as 1785, is dedicated "To the Emperor of Germany. Most Noble Joseph!" and praises him for "unlimited toleration of the Jews," and *George Foxe's Looking Glass* a few years later is prefaced with a plea for the same toleration.[17] Though his writings do not seem to have been noticed in the Philadelphia press, Crawford apparently grew in reputation among fellow humanitarians. In September 1788 he hurriedly translated Brissot de Warville's *Oration* urging cooperation among abolitionists everywhere, explaining that he undertook the task in order to save the Pennsylvania Society for Promoting the Abolition of Slavery "the expense of hiring a translator," not at all because of "overweening conceit of my own knowledge of the French language."

Yet for all his benevolent good will, Crawford seems to have remained a man with intense pride of birth, an aristocrat as loyal to British institutions as to Christian morality. "I can safely say," he averred, "though I have known many Deists, that I scarcely know one moral character among them."[18] Thomas Paine was a case in point: "It is common for infidelity and sedition to be united; but Paine, though ignorant and absurd, seems to have done more mischief than almost any man in the propagation of both" as he scattered " 'firebrands, arrows, and death' through the world." Crawford called on divine justice to bring retribution to so vile an offender, so *"putrid* and *offensive* when alive"* that his inevitable damnation is clearly manifest: "Let those who have raised the works of this detestable enemy of God and man, by a false praise, beware the law . . . here, and the punishments hereafter." Every student of history, he said, should remember "that some of the Roman emperors who persecuted Christians, died in as horrible a manner as it is possible Tom Paine will die."[19] For himself, Crawford stated his position without equivocation: "I am no Democrat, no contender for the wild and mischievous doctrine that all men are equal; for reason and Christianity teach us that a king is above a subject, a governor above a citizen, and the master above his servant."[20]

Nor did he approve of rebellions, even when they were called revolutions: "There is nothing," he said, "in any part of the scriptures which is favourable to the wanton murder of kings and nobility, from an erroneous idea of equality." His *Essay on the Eleventh Chapter of the Revelation of St. John* was dedicated to the thesis that, although the great earthquake mentioned in that part of the Bible was prophetic, its prophecy was not fulfilled with the fall of France. He warned Americans to beware, to listen carefully to the advice of John Adams which was, said Crawford, that "there is better chance of the interests of the United States being promoted by the establishment of a limited monarchy, than by a republic." He decried the atheism of Mirabeau and Robespierre and "the execrable and nonsensical writings" of Thomas Paine. He seems to have been frightened by the upsurge of sentiment toward Jefferson, and he may have been disturbed by the essays which Freneau at just this end-of-a-century time was contributing to the *Aurora* over the pseudonym of "Robert Slender, One of the Swinish Multitude." Perhaps, Crawford admitted, some few of these "modern anarchists are misguided enthusiasts," but not all of them; they rather "resemble the infidel atheists, who existed in the time of the apostle," and who must be attacked as Saint John had attacked them. This "republican delusion," the "most mischievous that ever afflicted society," rose through a "perversion of the scripture by ignorant or designing men," or by enthusiastic partiality to such Roman authors as Tacitus, Livy, Lucan, and Ovid, rather than to the holy word of God.[21]

"The titles of duke, marquis, earl, count, and baron," said Crawford, "have nothing absurd in them." Indeed, "the title duke is used by Moses, who was a great advocate for subordination and order." How important, then, it is "to expose the aim of those fanatical democrats, who have wished to bring the nobility of England, after that of France, into contempt." After all, he temporized, "though some things may be wrong, there are many right in the English government."[22]

Soon thereafter Charles Crawford returned to England, probably in 1800, certainly by 1803. It may have been the death of his older brother in Scotland, in April 1800,[23] and the necessity for helping settle his brother's estate which sent him back over the Atlantic again. It may have been that the New Jerusalem of America seemed doomed because of its infidel democracy. It may have been that his brother's death seemed to open opportunities for inheritance of something more valuable than estate by bringing Charles Crawford, he must have thought, one step nearer to the titles which for generations had been held by members of the Lindsay and Crawford families, to which he by tradition if not by record belonged. The present twenty-second Earl of Crawford, fourth Viscount Garnock, was a little younger than he, but he had led a rugged life as an officer of the British army; he was unmarried, and without heirs.[24]

Only one volume with Crawford's name on the title page appeared in Philadelphia after 1800, and that was a "second edition," perhaps pirated, of *An Essay on the Propagation of the Gospel*, in 1801. Two years later, in 1803, his *Poems on Several Occasions* was published in London in two handsome volumes, the first volume containing *The Christian* in six books, the second, the shorter poems. "In proportion to our approbation of the virtuous and amiable tendency of Mr. Crawford's writings," said the still critical *Monthly Review*, "must be our regret in being restrained . . . from paying any high compliment to his Muse. . . . Good meaning is not sufficient atonement for bad poetry."[25] But Crawford, no more now in England than he had been in America, was not easily shut off. He began to issue a series of *Letters to the Hebrew Nation* which stirred up enough controversy to require an answer from a German apologist more than twenty years later.[26] And then, in 1814, he published as his last book a fine, fat quarto of *The Poetical Works of Charles Earl of Crawford and Lindsay, Viscount Garnock*, in which he printed again, and for the last time, the poems over which he had been working for almost forty years.

Little more is discovered of Charles Crawford, and even less of his pretentions to nobility. When George, earl of Crawford, Viscount Garnock, did die, in Ayrshire, in 1808, still without heir, and "the dignities of Lindsay and Garnock developed on the heirs male of the Lords Lindsays of the Byres,"[27] several rivals for the title put forth their claims, some persisting in attempting to restore what the *Gentleman's Magazine* called their "dormant dignity" even fourteen years later, but with no success.[28] Among them, though his case never seemed to have reached high enough to become matter of record, was Charles Crawford, formerly of Philadelphia, who may have based his claim on descent from a collateral line or perhaps even from one of the natural children which one or another of the earls of Crawford were said to have produced.[29] When the history of rightful holders of the titles after which he aspired was written, Charles Crawford was dismissed as simply another unsuccessful claimant, but one who stubbornly and without any legal grounds whatever "assumed the title of Earl of Crawford and Lindsay." He was remembered as having "lived for many years at Cheltenham," an increasingly strange old gentleman who "distinguished himself by his liberal subscriptions to charities," especially missionary societies, and who "published several poems, for the most part . . . very indifferent."[30]

NOTES

1. *Pennsylvania Archives, Third Series*, 25: 479.

2. See Crawford's preface to his translation of J. P. Brissot de Warville's *An Oration upon the Necessity of Establishing at Paris, a Society to Co-operate with Those of America and London, towards the Abolition of the Trade and Slavery of Negroes*, appended to T. Clarkson, *An Essay on the Impolicy of the Slave Trade* (Philadelphia, 1788), p. 137.

3. Reprinted in *Observations on Negro Slavery*, pp. 21–24.

4. Vera Langford Oliver, *The History of the Island of Antigua* (London, 1896), 2: 182; also 2: 288; 3: 418.

5. *Gentleman's Magazine* 43 (October 1773): 517.

6. J. A. Venn, *Alumni Cantabrigiensis* (Cambridge, 1944), 2: 169; Charles Henry Conyer, *The Annals of Cambridge* (Cambridge, 1852), 4: 378.

7. *A Dissertation on the Phaedon of Plato; or, a Dialogue of the Immortality of the Soul, with Some General Observations on Writings of that Philosopher, to Which Is Annexed, a Psychology; or, an Abstract Investigation of the Nature of the Soul; in Which the Questions of All the Celebrated Metaphysicians on That Subject Are Discussed.* By Charles Crawford, Esq., Fellow Commoner of Queens College, Cambridge (London, 1773).

8. *Monthly Review* 49 (December 1773): 437–443.

9. No copy of the second edition has been discovered. It is mentioned in the *Monthly Review,* above, as "recently received," and is advertised as "lately published" in *Sophronia and Hilario: An Ode* (London, 1774), [p. 28].

10. *Monthly Review* 50 (May 1774): 407; see also *Gentleman's Magazine* 44 (May 1774): 230.

11. *Monthly Review* 50 (May 1774): 407.

12. Ibid., 57 (October 1777): 328.

13. *The Christian,* pp. 4–5.

14. *Monthly Review* 69 (September 1783): 259–260.

15. *The Christian: A Poem; in Four Books, to Which Is Prefixed a Preface in Prose in Defense of Christianity, with an Address to the People of America* (Philadelphia, 1783), pp. iii, v–vi.

16. *A Poetical Paraphrase,* p. 12.

17. I have found the *Observations upon the Downfall of Papal Power* only in "A new edition" of 1790; the preface, however, is dated November 1785. No copy of *George Foxe's Looking Glass for the Jews* has been discovered; it is advertised in 1790 in the above *Observations,* p. 44, as "lately published," with "a Preface, by this Author, in which he contends for the unlimited Toleration of the Jews."

18. *The Dying Prostitute* (Philadelphia, 1797), p. iv.

19. *An Essay on the Eleventh Chapter of the Revelation of St. John* (Philadelphia, 1800), p. 62n.

20. *An Essay on the Propagation of the Gospel* (Philadelphia, 1799), p. 5.

21. *Essay on the Eleventh Chapter of the Revelation of St. John,* pp. 12, 34–57 passim.

22. Ibid., pp. 48, 72.

23. Oliver, *History of the Island,* 1: 182.

24. See Sir James Balfour Paul, *The Scots Peerage* (Edinburgh, 1906), 3: 40–41.

25. *Monthly Review*, n.s. 45 (September 1804): 94.

26. *A Second Letter to the Hebrew Nation* was published in London in 1807; *The First and Second Letters to the Hebrew Nation* was advertised as "lately published" in the *Poetical Works* (London, 1814), p. 211; *Three Letters to the Hebrew Nation* appeared in 1817; it may be assumed that a *First Letter* and perhaps a *Third Letter* were also issued separately, though they seem not to have survived. Evidence of controversy is supplied by the listing in the British Museum *Catalog of Printed Books* which lists *Bennett(s) Israels Beständigkeit. Eine . . . Beleuchtung mehrerer Bibelstellen, insbesondere sogenannter messianischer Weissagungen; in kritischer Erwiederung auf das von Lord Crawford erschienene öffentliche Sendschreiben an die hebräische Nation* (1835).

27. Paul, *The Scots Peerage*, 3: 40–41.

28. *Gentleman's Magazine* 92 (February 1822): 172; see also *Journals of the House of Lords* 55: 214–215.

29. Paul, *The Scots Peerage*, 2: 42. There had been an earlier Charles Crawford in the family, a younger son of John, first Viscount Garnock, who died in 1746 "without legitimate issue." The administration of his estate "occasioned a family dispute" which just may have caused Alexander Crawford in Antigua to have named his second and next-born son after him, as he may also be supposed to have named his first son after the deceased's titled father. But no more than could researchers in the early nineteenth century can I today discover the links between Alexander Crawford of Belfast who settled as a planter in Antigua early in the eighteenth century and the titled family in Ayrshire from which our Charles Crawford claimed descent.

30. A. W. C. L. Crawford, *Lives of the Lindsays* (London, 1849), 2: 294n.

Joseph Brown Ladd

OF CHARLESTON

❧ ❧

WHEN Mathew Carey established the monthly *American Museum* in Philadelphia in 1787, he presented in the Poets' Corner of that periodical what amounted to a representative anthology of contemporary American poets. By the end of eighteen months five poems by Timothy Dwight had appeared, six by John Trumbull, eight by Francis Hopkinson, eleven by David Humphreys, seventeen by Philip Freneau, and thirty-five by Joseph Brown Ladd. The literary strivings of the first decade of postrevolutionary America were fairly represented by these six poets. And each of them has been remembered by scholars and biographers; each has been fitted into his own small niche in our histories of the development of American letters, except the last, who was, on the count of popularity, at this time most representative of them all.

Joseph Brown Ladd was born in Newport, Rhode Island, in 1764. He had little formal schooling, for "his father's circumstances," we are told, were "moderate." Yet we dare say that there was none among the poets of late eighteenth-century America who displayed, at least on the surface, more of what eighteenth-century America was pleased to denominate culture. As a boy Ladd soon tired of farming, at which occupation his father had set him at the age of eleven. He would rather, we are informed, retire with a pleasant book to some hidden and rustic retreat than work in the fields. He had already, at the age of ten, produced his first poem, an "Invocation to the Almighty," and soon was to see it published in Solomon Southwick's weekly *Newport Mercury*. Among his other accomplishments, he—like many another New England boy of his time—is said to have been able to repeat great chunks of the Bible from memory. At fourteen he was bound apprentice in a local mercantile establishment, only to find that shopkeeping and poetry did not mix. More congenial employment was soon found for him as a printer's devil in the office of the *Mercury*. But here the boy's facility at satirical balladry and his willingness to have his lucubrations circulated as broadsides brought him into conflict with some of the victims of his satire, among whom is said to have been no less a personage than the eminent theologian Samuel Hopkins. The reverend clergyman went to Father Ladd; Father Ladd with punishment in his eye went to young Joseph; young Joseph retired from the printing business in disgrace.

What to do with the boy? He seemed to fit nowhere. At fifteen he was placed under the tuition of Dr. Isaac Senter, a scholarly young man and one of the most promising physicians of Rhode Island. The boy now "entered upon his studies as though sitting down to a banquet with an appetite sharpened by long fasting." He laid out a curriculum for himself, not in science and medicine alone, but in philosophy and rhetoric (Locke and Blair), in Greek and Latin and Hebrew, in French, and "in his hours of relaxation" in the English poets and essayists. He continued to write poetry himself. He fell in love romantically, with a wealthy young lady whose avaricious foster parents broke the match and the young lovers' hearts in order to retain a guardian's share in the girl's income. In 1783, at nineteen, he had completed his studies, had received a license to practice medicine, and was ready to start out on his own.

Up to this point, up indeed to the age of twenty, Joseph Brown Ladd is a nebulous and legendary figure, his youth almost too exactly like the romantic concept of the youth of almost any romantic young poet. We depend for our knowledge of his first twenty years on the biographical sketch which W. B. Chittenden prefixed to *The Literary Remains* of her brother which Mrs. Elizabeth [Ladd] Haskins published in 1832, almost fifty years after Ladd's death. Rhode Island records, even the *Newport Mercury*, with which the young man is said to have been associated, tell us little more. We are not even sure exactly why he came to South Carolina in 1784. The legend is that in Newport he made the acquaintance and secured the friendship of Gen. Nathanael Greene, who suggested the move and supplied the doctor with letters of recommendation. We may be fairly certain that he settled in Charleston for much the same reason that both Philip Freneau and Joel Barlow considered settling there at about this time—because in turbulent postwar America there was probably no better place for a footloose young man of ability to establish himself now that the British had evacuated the city and most of the Tories did not dare return. At any rate, we do know that Dr. Joseph Brown Ladd did arrive in Charleston in 1784, and that he remained there, an active, admired, and much quoted young man until his death two years later.

Now we are on solid ground. "On Wednesday last," announced the *South-Carolina Gazette* on Saturday, 20 November, "the sloop 'Dove,' Capt. Phillips, arrived here from Rhode-Island, with whom came passengers, Mrs. Quash, Mrs. Shubrick, Lambert Lance, Esq. . . . [and, at the end of the list] Dr. Ladd." This may not have been the first trip the young physician made to Charleston. Indeed, we are led to believe by the memoir mentioned above that he had arrived in South Carolina earlier in the year. Perhaps he had made a first exploratory visit to investigate prospects, and then had returned to Newport to settle his affairs there. But now he was in South Carolina to stay.

He was captivated by the people he met, "their affability, their courteous manners, and the polite attention by which strangers are treated by them." Every house, he found, was "a caravansary where the wearied traveller is sure of a welcome reception, refreshment, and repose." Except for the danger of autumnal fevers, South Carolina seemed to him "the most agreeable country perhaps in the universe." It was gay and cultured, without the harshness of New England in either climate or manners. "Plays, concerts, and assemblies amuse the town; visiting, entertainments, and parties of amusement are the pleasures of the country."[1] Ladd did notice, he believed, a certain reprehensible tendency toward occasional excess in "dissolute Pleasures and luxury." "Bacchus is a deity," he said, "much respected in this country." Yet, "no objection can be made to the sway of so amiable, mirth-inspiring a divinity, when limited by prudence and moderation." After all, the young man temporized, "without the assistance of wine, in all warm climates the mind is enervated, the spirits become languid, and the imagination effete." He knew, furthermore, as a physician that "wine by its tonic quality obviates the debility induced by climate." At any rate, it was pleasant so to believe. And it was pleasant to be in South Carolina. Surrounded by slaves and accustomed to command, the Charlestonians might at first meeting seem haughty, even dictatorial. But Ladd soon learned to know them better. "Courtesty, affability, and politeness," he found, "form their distinguishing characteristics." For social virtues, "I venture to assert," he said, "that no country on earth has equalled Carolina."[2]

In this society the young physician seems soon to have made a place for himself. On 4 July 1785 he was chosen to deliver an Independence Day address, the second ever to have been made in the state, before Governor Moultrie and other leaders and officials of South Carolina. Seven years before, another and more famous physician, Dr. David Ramsay, had delivered in Charleston the first Fourth of July oration ever spoken in the new nation. Now, at twenty-one, Ladd must have felt keenly the responsibility which rested on him as successor. He spoke manfully to the occasion. "Succeeding ages," he promised, "shall turn the historic page and catch inspiration from the era of 1776. They shall bow to the rising glory of America; and Rome, once mistress of the world, shall fade in their remembrance." As he warmed to his subject, Ladd opened wide every patriotic stop: Lexington ("Oh, Britain! write that page of thy history in crimson, and margin it with black, for thy troops fled! routed with stones, with clubs, and every ignominious weapon; they fled from our women, they were defeated by our children"), the brave American soldier ("When the historic leaf shall shiver in the blaze, when all human works, the great Iliad itself, receive their finish from the fire, the soldier's memory must survive, for it is registered in heaven!"), George Washington ("Oh! that upon this day ye would join your friendly vows with mine to eternize the name of Washington"), our military heroes ("Men whose names shall descend to posterity with coeternal honor!"), and God

("The great Generalissimo of our army from whom all honors flow"). The oration ended in a crescendo of rhetoric and patriotism. A young man in a young country spoke in glowing hyperbole. And he seemed to believe everything he said. The oration was a success. Long extracts from it were printed in the Charleston papers.[3]

Ladd was now on his way to at least a local fame. On 15 July over the signature "Arouet" he published in the *Columbian Herald* an "Ode for the Anniversary of American Independence," to be sung to the tune of "That power who form'd the unmeasur'd seas." Eight stanzas there were, calculated to "swell each patriot breast," make "generous tears flow round" for all American "martyrs in the glorious cause" of liberty:

> Sons of Columbia! all attend
> And give the genius of your land,
>   The tribute of a song;
> For now eight summers passed away
> Again returns the glorious day,
>   When freedom made us strong.

From this time until Ladd's death in November a year later, more than seventy contributions, in prose and in verse, signed "Arouet" are to be found in the Charleston *Columbian Herald.*[4] Hardly an issue of the newspaper appeared without one, sometimes two poems or articles over his soon very familiar signature. He wrote tearful epitaphs, rousing patriotic songs, and soulful addresses to a maiden named Amanda. He translated Homer, and he corrected Alexander Pope for mistakes he had made at the same task. He wrote under the influence of Ossian, Goethe, Collins, Milton, and the Old Testament prophets. No such public parade of learning had appeared in Charleston before. The young man seemed at ease with Fénelon and Voltaire; he knew Thomas Paine and Socrates; he bandied about the names of Locke, Blair, Newton, Bacon, Plato, Statius, and ever so many others. His readers were to understand that their poet translated with equal ease from Hebrew, Greek, Latin, German, and French. He published a war song "long sought for in vain among the remnants of antiquity; and . . . now first restored." He attempted a modernization of one of Thomas Chatterton's spurious Rowley poems, from the language of "Owlde Inglonde." In his innocence and his desire to appear a cultured young man of the world, he even went so far as to pretend that some of his poems were "translated from the Gaulic of the celebrated Ossian."

And his readers apparently thought his poems splendid. "Phocion" wrote the editors of the *Columbian Herald* on 12 October to demand more of them. When "Cato" in the *Charleston Evening Post* had the ill grace to scoff at "Arouet's" wordy imitativeness, "Crito" immediately took the scoffer seriously to task.[5] "Philomela" wrote charmingly "To Arouet"[6] that she unworthy knew indeed that his lines would live to all eternity. And an anonymous admirer found in Ladd the successor to Vergil, Voltaire, Pope, and Dryden as heir to the mantle of Homer:

> Again he lives, and what was *Homer's,* now
> With common voice on *Arouet* we bestow;
> The high sublime of the divine old bard
> Breathes in thy numbers, in thy song is heard;
> No more we *Homer's* imitator see,
> For thou, sweet bard, thou thyself art he.[7]

Soon Ladd announced that he had prepared a "New American Version" of the Book of Psalms, "to be Published when a sufficient Number of Subscribers Present."[8] Then, on 21 October 1785 Messrs. Bowen and Markland, who, in addition to printing the *Columbian Herald,* had for sale in their shop on Church Street, opposite the City Tavern, stationery, Irish wafers, quills, Morocco pocketbooks, Dutch sealing wax, and Watts' psalms and hymns, were proud to announce "Proposals for publishing by Subscription The Poems of Arouet." The volume would be a "new miscellany, entirely American," of one hundred thirty pages, priced at one dollar, and would be "put to the press as soon as a sufficient number have subscribed to pay the expence." Five days later a larger advertisement appeared, filling one-third of a column—larger, indeed, than any advertisement in the *Columbian Herald* before. It ran irregularly for four months, until 16 January 1786, announcing proudly of the projected volume:

This work produced by one of the earliest of American bards cannot fail to excite the attention of a patriotic public. Every American must wish to possess one of the first productions of his country in poetry, which has appeared in a miscellaneous form: And those acquainted with the beauties of AROUET will pleasingly anticipate their publication. The author's character it were needless to illustrate, we shall only observe that he has many admirers, and seems to be growing daily in reputation.

The publishers were authorized to say that the volume would contain the author's "best pieces only, corrected and refined; together with a number of original poems, excluding such trivial pieces as obtain their *only* value from the favourite signature of AROUET." Furthermore, "animated with the best of motives," the publishers solicited particularly "the patronage of the *Fair*." It is not to be presumed, they said, that the ladies of this country will "suffer their favourite poet to slumber in oblivion." The response to these proposals was apparently not immediately overwhelming. One hundred ninety-five citizens of South Carolina, "generously inclined to encourage the effusions of genius in this production of our youthful *American Bard*," had subscribed for 284 copies when the edition finally appeared, "the obstacles which hitherto delayed the publication being removed," in August of 1786.[9] The company of subscribers included many of the first names of South Carolina. The Honorable Aedanus Burke, the Honorable David Ramsay, and Peter Freneau, Esq., were on the list. The Moultrie family signed for eighteen copies, the Draytons for eleven, the Pinckneys for nine, the Rutledges for four. The volume, if not a financial, was a social success.

Yet poetry, though it must have been taken very seriously by the young physician, was at best only a sideline. One helped oneself to social reputation perhaps through graceful verses, but even in Charleston they could not have passed in lieu of cash. We may suspect that Ladd helped in some practical manner—setting type, composing paragraphs, or reading proof—in the printshop of Bowen and Markland: we are told that he had been trained in Newport for such work, though we cannot just be sure that it might not have been beneath the dignity of even a hungry young doctor. Of the extent of Ladd's medical practice in Charleston there is little evidence. His later biographer tells us that it was splendid, but we may perhaps be justified in being wary of the eulogistic exuberances of early nineteenth-century biography. By midsummer of 1786, however, he advertised:

> The poor families in the city of Charleston, who may at any time stand in need of medical assistance, and are so distressingly circumstanced that they are unable to purchase it, are hereby informed, that by calling on Dr. Ladd, at the house of Mrs. Theus, No. 87, Churchstreet, the really poor man will find a medical friend—ready to assist him with prescriptions, advice, and in particular cases with medicine gratis.
>
> The Doctor will devote two hours in a day to this purpose, from 7 to 9 o'clock in the morning; at other times the nature of his engagements will render it difficult for him to attend. He cannot, however, at any time, be deaf to the distressed invalid. *The pleasure of doing good is the most elevated and refined of all the pleasures, and the only enjoyment that can reconcile us to the woes and miseries inseparably annexed to human life.* Of this the Doctor is convinced, and yielding to the impulses of a feeling heart, it will ever be his pride and happiness, so far as it is in his power, to
>
> > "Still distress's soul-afflicting cry,
> > And wipe the bursting tear from sorrow's eye."[10]

Projects other than either a medical practice or poetry, however, engaged the young physician at this time. He was apparently casting about for some means surer than these for gaining a livelihood. He published in the *Columbian Herald* in three parts "An Essay on Primitive, and Regenerative Light,"[11] which was so well received that Bowen and Markland soon issued it as a volume.[12] It was an ambitious undertaking, written with verve and some display of knowledge, an essay "in which," Ladd said, "it is attempted, upon original principles, to account for every luminous phenomenom—the light of flame, the phosphoric glow, and the sparkling of the blue ocean."

But a more ambitious undertaking was already projected. The Charleston newspapers announced that "to ornament and expand the human mind, by the rays of liberal, soul-illuminating knowledge, the public are presented with Proposals for a course of Philosophical Lectures by Dr. Ladd." At twelve public meetings he would "consider all the modern discoveries and improvements in natural and experimental philosophy." Revealed would be "the sublime knowledge of that grand and stupendous fabric, the Universe . . . upon the principles of the immortal Newton." Moreover, ventured the same daring young man whom we have seen correcting Alexander Pope and whom we shall soon see chiding Dr. Samuel Johnson, "many deficiencies of that Prince of Philosophers will be supplied from the discoveries of modern times." Yet it would not be drudgery to his listeners: "In treating of the sun, the moon, the starry heavens, and the earth on which we tread, a new world opens on the mind, and many a beautiful avenue of knowledge will be explored." As a modern young scientist, versed in newest methods, Ladd could assure prospective subscribers that "the causes of night and day . . . and other phenomena, will be explained and demonstrated—not by mathematical reasoning, but by a series of experiments, obvious to every eye and fitted to every capacity."

He promised to explain the causes of the winds, the flow and reflow of the sea. Tornadoes, whirlwinds, waterspouts, volcanoes, earthquakes, burning mountains, meteors, "with many other entertaining, wonderful and sublime phenomena" would be amply discussed and "presented to the mind by a method new, curious and striking." Nature would be stripped of her mystery by a variety of beautiful experiments, "at once sufficient to astonish and convince"; her most hidden operations, which "the superstitious vulgar have supposed . . . produced by magic," would be exposed as part of universal law. Even the flaming comet "will appear divested of all the terrors with which ignorance and superstition have cloathed it; the milder sun-beam of truth will discover it to be a habitable earth like that on which we tread." And the sun and "those innumerable other suns which illuminate an infinity of space, will no longer appear to be frightful gulphs of fire, but inhabitable worlds."

Such would be the "sentimental feast" prepared for the ladies and gentlemen of Charleston. Nor need they fear that their lecturer would be pedantic; rather, he assured them "as he conducts them o'er the ample field of science," they would find "fresh flowers to adorn the path, and new beauties at every step . . . *pressing on the eye and twining round the heart.*" The soul would "expand itself with discoveries of sublime truth," as a new world opened to "the mental eye and the beauty of surrounding prospects" more than amply compensated for the "fatigues of the little journey."[13]

The first lecture was announced for five o'clock on the evening of 22 September 1786 at the statehouse; but at the last moment was postponed to three days later. Tickets would be twenty-one shillings nine pence for the course or five shillings a pair for a single lecture—just half what one would pay to enter the pit of Charleston's Harmony Hall, its theater just outside the city limits at Louisburg.[14] But there seems to have been little response from the public. It was a shame, thought the editor of the *Charleston Morning Post,* in a country where foreigners were so well received, and so well rewarded for their merit, that Dr. Ladd, an American, "be less successful in the prosecution of his plan, which he offers for public approbation and encouragement." None could conduct such a series of lectures better than he, for "perhaps no subject requires a more cultivated style, or a greater nicety of arrangement than disquisitions of the nature of these in question." Ladd's popularity is indicated again as the editor concluded, "When such a person as the doctor gratifies the public with his labours, we wish and may expect to meet with something as well in style as in matter as near perfection as the subject to be discussed will allow of."[15]

All the fine plans came, however, to nothing. The second lecture was never given. "Dr. Ladd being recovered from his late indisposition," the *Morning Post* announced on 7 October, "he intends, we hear, to continue his philosophical lectures next week." But by the next week Dr. Ladd was embroiled in a controversy of which he did not live to see the end.

Meanwhile the individual poems of "Arouet" had continued to grace the pages of the *Columbian Herald.* Imitative, pretentious, sentimental, they indicate to us, nevertheless, the popular literary fare on which our ancestors fattened at the end of the eighteenth century. One sighed then without a self-conscious and superior smile when the poet wrote "To Amanda"[16] thus: "Ah! how I listened when your silence broke / And kissed the air which trembled as you spoke." One had the good sense to see solid and sentimental eighteenth-century philosophy behind such lines from an "Epitaph on an Old Horse"[17] as these:

> Let no facetious mortal laugh,
> To see a horse's epitaph;
> Lest some old steed, with saucy phiz,
> Should have the sense to laugh at his.

One gloried in an attempt at Homeric metaphor, and one's pleasure was not one whit dampened by knowledge of "pathetic fallacy," when Ladd in an "Elegy, Sacred to the Manes of Philander,"[18] wrote:

> When the tall oak, amidst tempestuous gloom,
> From heaven's own thunder shades the lowly broom;
> If o'er its head the vivid lightnings burst,
> Rive the big trunk, and level it with dust,
> Each shrub laments the fall: and full in view,
> A mournful chasm tells them where it grew.
> So fell Philander; and where once he stood,
> We long shall mourn the generous and the good.

One could turn from "The Terribly Sublime Description of Jehovah"[19] ("Midst pealing thunders, fire, and smoke, / Jehovah's awful silence broke") to the doggerel "What Is Happiness?"[20] ("'Tis an empty fleeting shade") or the lugubrious "Sorrows of Charlotte at the Tomb of Werter"[21] or the pretentious "Remonstrance of Almasa, Wife of Almas Ali Cawn, to General Hastings"[22] to such a burlesque "Epitaph"[23] as

> Here lies entomb'd the Boy divine,
> Who whilom shone the God of Wine.
> O let the sad Madeira pour—
> Ye full decanters weep a shower—
> Ye glades speak his wondrous works—
> Ye bottles mourn—lament ye corks;—
> And let each soul who call'd him friend
> In flowing bumpers mourn his end.

This was all popular newspaper verse. It was interlarded, to be sure, with erudite references to the classics and to the accepted literary great of Europe, yet even this hardly raised it high above a level of poetic mediocrity. Meanwhile Ladd worked seriously on another, a longer poem. Nothing he published was to be more popular than the "Prospect of America." Two extracts from it appeared in the *Columbian Herald* on 31 August and 2 September. When it later appeared complete in *The Poems of Arouet,* it was excerpted with approval in Philadelphia and Boston.[24] Two years after Ladd's death an itinerant phrenologist announced at Edentown, North Carolina, "a moral, serious 'Lecture on Heads' and exhibitions of transparent Paintings from Dr. Ladd's poem."[25] The "Prospect of America" is of a type with John Trumbull's *Prospect of the Future Glory of America* (1770) and with Philip Freneau's *The Rising Glory of America* (1772). It shares in the patriotic optimism of David Humphreys's *A Poem on the Happiness of America* (1781), Timothy Dwight's *The Conquest of Canaän* (1785), and Joel Barlow's *The Vision of Columbus* (1787). Young American poets wrote fervidly of the development of the new nation in which they found themselves. Epics were in the air, and Ladd snatched eagerly for his share in the poetic celebration. In the "Prospect of America," Benjamin Franklin, John Hancock, Samuel Adams, and, especially, George Washington, each received unstinted praise. John Dickinson and Thomas Paine ("Immortal Payne! whose pen . . . Could fashion empires while it kindled awe!") were eulogized for their parts in the American Revolution. Nor were rival American poets forgotten: Phillis Wheatley ("Afric's heir to fame"), John Maylem ("Untaught he sung by all the muse inspired"), Joel Barlow, and Philip Freneau were each noticed with generous brief praise.

Ladd was not so generous when he contributed in prose his "Critical Remarks on Dr. Johnson" to the *Columbian Herald* of 2 September. It is difficult to understand how the young Charlestonian, guilty himself on almost every count, could charge the English writer with "swelled, pompous, bombastical language, an affected structure, and verbosity of style." Yet he did, a young American David peppering hard at a literary Goliath. And by doing so he anticipated the romantic writers of England by many years.[26] Ladd, at the peak of his popularity, wrote:

The swelled bombastic style succeeds with the lower class of readers, who are by far the most numerous. Hence, every writer who is deficient in real genius, will affect pomposity, and magnificence in language. It gives him popularity; and popularity is the food of authors. It is that for which every writer from the heroic poet to the critical scribbler, is eagerly contending; and the influence of this popularity upon the herd of imitators, is almost beyond conception.

Did Ladd thus sign his own literary death warrant? Did he, too, only succeed with the "lower class of readers," and for the same reasons? Can he who criticized most tellingly in Johnson those faults which were most evident in himself claim from us today any remembrance as an American poet? In charity, we recall that many of Ladd's poems are said to have been written when he was in his teens, before he came to Charleston.[27] Many that he wrote in South Carolina were the slightest sort of ephemera, written hurriedly for an occasion, apologized for by his publishers. When his collected *Poems* did appear after many delays in August 1786, the printers announced that "a long indisposition of the author had not only retarded publication, but deprived the readers of many pieces which would have made no invaluable addition to this miscellany."[28] Yet, even in charity, we may not linger over what Ladd might have done. His faults are obvious: imitativeness, pretentiousness, sentimentality, insipidity. But, with all, he was sensitive to new currents in literature, perhaps as much so as any American poet of his generation.

With Philip Freneau and Timothy Dwight he is to be remembered as one of the earliest native writers to be influenced by the preromantic poets of England. Echoes of Gray, Goldsmith, and Collins are heard in his lines. Turning away in spirit, if not always in form, from the mechanized couplets of Pope, he listened with care to the more vigorous music of Milton. He broke from the couplet, though only occasionally and tentatively, to the freer forms which would characterize the nineteenth century. More specifically, he was the first in America to write versified adaptations of the prose poems of Ossian.[29] He composed in the Della Cruscan manner before the amazing popularity of Robert Merry and his imitators in England and America. He reacted articulately to Goethe's *The Sorrows of Young Werther* less than a year after the first American edition of that international best seller appeared in 1784,[30] and was thus harbinger of the sentimental epidemic which was seriously to affect many early American novels. Finally, Ladd was self-consciously American, adapting his poems to an American audience, often writing on American themes, reworking the Psalms into what he proudly designated a "new American version."

The young man was in poor health for the greater part of the late summer and early autumn of 1786. His illness interfered with the speedy publication of his *Poems* and with the immediate continuance of his philosophic lectures. It may be kindest to believe that it was also in some measure responsible for the letter addressed "To Ralph Isaacs," which he published in the *Charleston Morning Post* on 14 October 1786, and in which he charged:

> The wanton, unprovoked attempts you have made by circulating a number of scandalous reports to injure the only man whom in this country you might have called a friend, completes so black a system of infamous behavior—that I am under the necessity of publishing you to the world as a base, ungrateful villain.
>
> While yet a stranger, I took you by the hand, and admitted you to the friendship of an honest, unsuspecting heart. Like the despicable Viper, you have attempted to gnaw that heart from my bosom, and have at once discovered the dangerous subtlety of the serpent, with all a serpent's venom.
>
> I account it as one of the greatest misfortunes of my life that I ever became intimate with such a man, and as I move in a sphere of life and character far superior to you, I, from this time, not only renounce the whole circle of your acquaintance, but disdain to speak to any man who hereafter takes you by the hand.
>
> This is the first time that ever Dr. Ladd's name was prostituted to an address of such insignificance, and it shall be the last. I leave you to your own reflections. I leave you to your insignificance. May the infamy of your conduct continually haunt your imagination, and may every past incident prove to you a lesson of wisdom, which shall admonish you in terms far

more energetic than those of my pen. Go, rash boy—lay aside your insolence—forbear to be ungrateful, and beware, never to call forth the just resentment of any man to publish you as I have done.

The identity of Ralph Isaacs, thus published to the world as an ingrate, has not been discovered.[31] He was evidently a young man no older than Ladd, and as quick tongued. On 16 October he addressed his spirited reply "To the Public":

In answer to a late address under the signature of Dr. Ladd, a production replete with falsity and abuse, and fraught with circumstances of unexampled turpitude; I am reduced to the necessity of requesting a few moments of the public attention.

This publication, the pure result of a maddened brain, grown desperate by infamy, now worthy soever of silent indignity, requires notwithstanding a lash of reprobation.—A sacred regard for the opinion of the world, and an ardent desire of vindicating my honor, with the honest intention of frustrating the insidious machinations of a designing rascal, are the motive by which I am actuated.

The *self-created Doctor* impeaches me with having injured his character—brands me with the sin of ingratitude—is lavish in conferring on me the most approbrious appellations, and finally boasts of the essential services I received at his hands. Sensible, in the first place, that he had no reputation to lose— that ignorance and folly were the sole springs of his conduct, there would have been a manifest insanity in my attempting to injure the character of a man whose fame was already blasted, I confidently assert that Dr. Ladd is a dangerous imposter— that he is at this moment under pecuniary obligations to me, and should consequently be considered as an object of detestation and abhorrence.

The Doctor presumes much on his superior station in life; and of the services he rendered me in this country; but I shall never envy the condition of a wretch, nor acknowledge any services from a man, whose notorious indigence must make him incapable of assisting a beggar.

Not many days have elapsed since he attempted to assasinate me; he attacked me with a pistol in one hand, and a stick in the other; I immediately disarmed him of his stick, which I now retain for the inspection of the curious.—Hence his cowardice is equally conspicuous with his infamy.—The meanness of his origin, and his daily misery, would have remained unnoticed; charity would suggest the idea, had he not contrasted my situation in life with his own.—He lately made an inefficient effort to be united in matrimony to a ———. But what a compliment does he pay to the numerous train of gentlemen with whom I have the happiness to be connected in this City, when he exclaims, "I from this time not only renounce the whole circle of acquaintance, but disdain to speak to any man who hereafter takes you by the hand." I now appeal to my acquaintances in particular, and the public in general, to decide between us.

I dare boldly affirm, that the event of a little time will convince the world, that the self-created Doctor is as blasted a scoundrel as ever disgraced humanity.

This could not pass unnoticed. But two days later the editor of the newspaper declined to allow the quarrel to continue in his columns: "The Animadversions on a pending dispute," he said, "are written in a strain of acrimony and ill-nature, that renders a publication of them extremely improper." Young men of Carolina, however, had recourse to other expedients than words. On 21 October the *Post* informed its readers: "Yesterday morning Dr. Ladd and Mr. Ralph Isaacs met behind the barracks, and after taking ground at about 20 feet distance, the latter gentlemen fired and wounded the former in both legs, near the knees." Ladd, suggests his biographer, purposely fired wide of his mark. He was carried from the field, the fibula of one leg badly shattered. "Both gentlemen," reported the *Post*, "behaved with bravery and resolution, Dr. Ladd in particular, made an offer of firing hand to hand, which was refused by the seconds."

And on 2 November 1786 Joseph Brown Ladd died, aged twenty-two, as a result of his wounds. Of Dr. Ladd's character, said the *Post* on the next morning, "a few words will suffice. He was modest, unassuming, candid and humane, extremely grateful for favors received and very ready to acknowledge and return obligations." Of his poetry, which the obituary found to bear "evident marks of genius and exalted imagination," it was admitted, " 'Tis true it may not entirely please the rigid critic, yet the fire of youth which often oversteps the bounds of cold correctness, will be an excuse."

Ladd was, in short, a young man sensitive to the reaction of his readers, and he wrote what his contemporaries wanted. In a period of change he was neither of the past nor wholly of the future. Taste was altering rapidly amid the intellectual and political revolutions at the end of the eighteenth century, and Joseph Brown Ladd, who anticipated many innovations, did not live to share completely in any of them. His period of maturity was brief: two years filled with more than seventy newspaper contributions, a medical practice, preparation for a series of public lectures, and two volumes issued from the press left little room for authentic literary development. As firmer voices rose, his chameleon style became lost in a welter in which it had no distinguishable part. Too much like those who had gone before, too faintly suggestive of what developed from him, he shares the fate of many transitional figures—oblivion.

What he might have been, then, is beside the point. At best, Ladd can live but obscurely today, a poet of his time, by ours forgotten. A few who search reverently through the past for clues to the secret of American cultural tradition will find him significant for the trends he represents. Most of us, however, will pause over him briefly, and then go on to matters pertinent to our own day, with only a memory, foggy perhaps and in the backs of our minds, that once in Charleston there did live a versifier who in the late eighteenth century was very popular, but whose name for the life of us we cannot remember.[32]

NOTES

1. "View of the Society and Manners in South Carolina. Letter I," *Columbian Herald*, 26 October 1785; reprinted in *The Literary Remains of Joseph Brown Ladd* (New York, 1832), pp. 220–224; facsimile ed., with foreword by Lewis Leary (New York: Garret Press, 1970).

2. "View of the Society and Manners in South Carolina. Letter II," *Columbian Herald*, 4 November 1785; reprinted in *Remains*, pp. 224–228.

3. See *Columbian Herald,* 22 July 1785.

4. For a checklist of Ladd's contributions to periodicals, see Lewis Leary, "The Writings of Joseph Brown," *Bulletin of Bibliography* 18 (January–April, 1945): 131–133.

5. 28 and 30 August 1785.

6. *Columbian Herald,* 18 May 1786.

7. "To Arouet, the Bard," *Columbian Herald,* 25 May 1786.

8. *Columbian Herald,* 2 October 1785. The volume was never published.

9. *Columbian Herald,* 29 May and 14 August 1786.

10. *Columbian Herald,* 14 August 1786.

11. 10, 14, and 17 August 1786.

12. See *Columbian Herald,* 24 August 1786.

13. *Columbian Herald,* 14 August 1786.

14. See *Columbian Herald,* 22 and 25 September 1786.

15. *Charleston Morning Post,* 9 October 1786.

16. 8 August 1785.

17. 10 August 1785.

18. 12 August 1785.

19. 15 August 1785.

20. 24 August 1785.

21. 7 September 1785.

22. 9 February 1786.

23. 26 December 1785.

24. See *American Museum,* May 1787, and *Herald of Freedom,* 27 October 1789.

25. *State Gazette of North Carolina,* 3 November 1788.

26. See Bernard Smith, *Forces in American Criticism* (New York, 1929), p. 10.

27. W. B. Chittenden in *Remains,* pp. xvii–xix.

28. *The Poems of Arouet* (Charleston, 1786), p. v.

29. Frederic I. Carpenter, "The Vogue for Ossian in America: A Study in Taste," *American Literature* 2 (January 1931): 409.

30. See F. W. Lieder, "Goethe in England and America," *Journal of English and Germanic Philology* 10 (December 1910): 550.

31. We infer that he was, like Ladd, from Rhode Island, and we may guess that he was related to Jacob Isaacs, a prominent merchant and broker of Newport, with whom there is reason to believe Ladd had laid the foundation for a quarrel some months before: when it was advertised in the *Newport Mercury* of 6 February 1786 that one Jethro Allen would "exhibit an experiment of extracting fresh

water out of salt water, without fire," and that tickets for the performance were to be purchased from Jacob Isaacs, Ladd (in Newport apparently on a visit to his parents) responded in the next issue of the paper with a forthright exposure of the scheme as a hoax. The implication that Isaacs was party to the imposture could not have been accepted with tranquillity by any of the merchant's family.

32. And in this lapse we shall find ourselves in the company of men who might have been later contemporaries of the poet: Samuel L. Knapp, in *Lectures on American Literature* (New York, 1829), p. 104, called him Josiah Ladd; Samuel Kettell, in *Specimens of American Poetry* (New York, 1829), 1: 334, called him William Ladd.

Philip Freneau

A REASSESSMENT

❧ ☙

PHILIP FRENEAU remains inconspicuously with us, dutifully anthologized and unavoidably, though often casually, described in most literary histories. He wrote much that was bad, hurried, or useless, but he wrote also a few brief lyrics which in almost any other country or any other situation would identify him as a poet. The United States has not been consistently kind to its minor writers, preferring those most massively visible who propose substantial surveys of man's confrontation with himself or nature or with demands of a democratic society. Literary commentators among us have been most likely to praise that which seemed to them most consistently and substantially American, the new voice, new native insights, comprehensive and prophetic, satisfying because suggestive of the largeness and the newness which is America. Necessary, even inevitable, this view has shunted aside or dismissed many fine poets who responding to the requirements of their time wrote more than they should have written, hurriedly and in imitation even of themselves. The schoolroom poets of the nineteenth century have had, we are accustomed to hear our friends say, their portraits turned to the wall, their gentility inappropriate to the commodious capacity of the New World. But they are being found out now, as masters, not in many modes nor in largeness or consistent depth, but in a few poems which time and a fresh look have rediscovered. It is not necessary, I think, to ask how many poems a poet must write, but whether among the mass of his work there are a dozen, or even two, or one, which can continue to speak.

Only the most generous of readers will discover among the three large, but incomplete, volumes of Freneau's collected verse more than a handful to which he can respond with more than patriotic or antiquarian pride. But Freneau's continuing presence suggests that he too may be entitled to more generous critical attention than he has yet publicly received. Often overpraised for what he intended or for his not always completely selfless devotion to democratic ideals, and sometimes undervalued, often, I think, because he has been overpraised, he has occupied a convenient place in literary history as a somewhat stunted native talent, important to mention as attention passes from the engaging imagery of Edward Taylor to the Wordsworthian echoes in Bryant and the deft, dark imaginings of Poe. Harry Hayden Clark has explained in generous detail Freneau's literary ancestry, his debt to the classics and to one or another of the poets of eighteenth-century England, and Nelson Adkins has explored Freneau's honest, though finally indecisive, fumblings toward explaining the "cosmic enigma" with which he found himself confronted. Philip Marsh has been assiduous in the collection of Freneaueana.[1]

But Freneau as a poet who sought to capture in words the fragile substance of his vision has been overshadowed by attention, sometimes lingering sentimentally too long, on Freneau the patriotic poet of the American Revolution, who laid waste his talent in defense of political democracy or, more simply, in necessary defiant ridicule directed against people who, it seemed to him, opposed it. His way with words and his honest anger and extraordinary talent allowed him to overwhelm almost every opponent, but he was a sensitive man who could not take as good as he gave, so that his life was a series of public advances and private retreats. He did not stand up well under the reciprocal abuse of partisan political controversy in which almost every contestant spoke with devastatingly frank and sometimes scatological force.

Freneau first withdrew from public debate in 1775, when he was twenty-three—not quite four years after he had been graduated from Nassau Hall at Princeton—with hotheaded valedictory verses patched and expanded from a collegiate satire. He recalled his earlier literary ambitions and his onetime wish to leave America for Europe where "Poets may flourish, or, perhaps they may," but he expressed also his continuing conviction that the New World, its mountains, streams, and forests (all the "charms . . . that nature yields"), could together "conspire / To raise the poet's fancy and his fire." Those last five words are worth pausing over, for fancy and fire became hallmarks of the young Freneau. At nineteen, he had written of "The Power of Fancy" ("Ever let the fancy roam!"). Now he spoke of "the flame that in my bosom glows" as "gall'd and slander'd," he stood alone against "foul-mouthed" opponents. "Sick of all feuds" ("wars of paper . . . wars of steel"), he would flee "the rude contest" and "to the sea with weary steps descend":

> In distant isles some happier scene I'll choose,
> And court in softer shades the unwilling Muse,
> . . . .
> Safe from the miscreants that my peace molest,
> Miscreants, with dullness and with rage opprest.
>
> (Pp. 264–265)

The lines rhymed, their meter was correct, but Freneau recognized these satires of 1775 which seemed to flow so easily on call as "flighty lays," not in any sense the measure of a poet. At twenty-three, he looked confidently forward to poems in "more exalted rhime, / By labour polish'd, and matur'd by time." During two years in the Caribbean, he continued to court the muse, but she continued to be mostly unwilling. He wrote laboriously of "The Beauties of Santa Cruze" (which I have elsewhere described as "a museum piece of baroque landscape,"[2] the technique of the miniature painter uneasily adapted to the gigantic canvas of the muralist), with humorous good fun of "The Jamaica Funeral," and haltingly, with occasional power, of "The House of Night." But then he was caught up in combat again, and the fire of anger burned as during the next four years he produced his sharpest, most vitriolic satire. As in the early 1780s he became involved in internecine quarreling, the heat of his often personalized attacks drew returning fire from opponents, less skilled and less unrestrained than he, so that in 1784 he fled again to the sea and to visions of poetry.

Much of the give and take of Freneau's wartime newspaper quarreling can be followed in Fred Lewis Pattee's large edition of the *Poems*. The virulence of the attacks against him, to which Freneau finally responded by again simply withdrawing, can be gauged by lines which Pattee in 1902 (2: 180n) found "too vile to reproduce," and which may or may not record an actual, but unsubstantiated, unfortunate, but unforgettable incident. After accusing Freneau of "vile abuse, and low scurrility," his unidentified opponent directed against him, he said, weapons such as "you yourself have used" against those "you've dirtily abused" by stating:

> Cannon, well pointed, may a coward hit,
> And leave him sprawling with his breeches sh—;
> Your mem'ry sure, some few years can review,
> What dire misfortune then attended you.
> A slave undaunted, laid his stripes so well,
> Your fears, how great, the consequence did tell;
> For as your hide the flagellation feels,
> The *yellow* filth came trickling to your heels.
> The people crouded, soon began to stare.
> The foremost cry'd—Lord what a stink is there;
> It is not *Skunk,* another soon reply'd,
> See how the cowskin penetrates his hide;
> At ev'ry stroke the dread *effluvia* flies,
> With stink the nose, with filth attends his eyes;
> While on the ground lay sprawling *this great wit,*
> And there we leave him, wallowing all besh——.[3]

No wonder Freneau quit the contest in outrage, incapable of a reply as unrestrained. But he was an effective satirist, as deft and truculent perhaps as any of his generation. When he was re-called to public duty again, as editor of the *National Gazette* in 1791, he resharpened his weapons, to wield them, though with less recklessness now, against new opponents. To remember him, however, only as "the Poet of the American Revolution" or as—*mea culpa*—"that rascal, Freneau" is to do him disservice. He deserves a prominent and permanent place in any history of political satire in English: as a practical propagandist he cleverly adapted the lines of other literary scolds—Horace, Pope, Church-ill—so adroitly that what he said was the more effective because readers were allowed the pleasure of a small shock of gratifying recognition of familiar rhythms and phrases used to ridicule contemporary crotchets. But fires of indignation or partisanship burned with less heat in the later satires, though there may have been an inward burning of self-reproach as Freneau in his forties became increasingly uncertain that he could ever keep the promises which as a younger man he had made to himself.

The later propaganda, in verse or prose, seems to me less commendable than his wartime satire. Whatever his success in support of Jeffersonian policies, in the early 1790s or at the turn of the next century, what he wrote then only occasionally scorched with angry flame. He gives the impression of being tired; he had said many of the same things before, and said them better. Conditions during these later times, when he was joined by or joined with an active and articulate organized political group, did conspire to make his words briefly persuasive. Freneau may indeed, as Jefferson once said, have saved our Constitution when it was galloping fast toward monarchy, but, if he did, it was as a journalist, skilled in that trade, not as a poet. As a journalist, he was dedicated and sincere; if a hireling, he was a willing servant to the now tattered vision of his early years. For, though what Freneau dreamed of, for himself or for his country, may have finally proved chimerical, he never allowed that vision utterly to escape.

I shall say little of his writings in prose, which seem to me workaday and somehow shoddy when examined beside the prose of more articulate contemporaries. On public matters, Hamilton did better, as did John Adams, James Monroe, and many another; Franklin achieved a manner of his own, homespun and plausibly native, but Freneau's essays seldom conceal the patchwork of convention which inspired them. The personae through whom he often spoke, though native in name or residence, are too often familiar to almost any admirer of Addison or Goldsmith. Hezekiah Salem speaks briefly with winning wit or slapstick tomfoolery, but he smirks and mumbles like almost any clownish countryman from almost any country. Priscilla Tripstreet or Christopher Clodhopper are better in name than in person.

The historian of what might be called the Americanization of the essay may, however, find something to say about progression of personae in Freneau's periodical prose. Early in his newspaper career he speaks in the character of a world-traveled hermit, first designated as "The Pilgrim," then as "The Philosopher of the Forest"; then later as the observant Greek Indian Tomo Cheeki, native and uncorrupted, who visited and commented on the strange habits of the white man in Philadelphia; and still later as the shrewd countryman Robert Slender, whose ingenious observations on policy and custom might have reserved for him a more respectworthy place among indigenous characters if he had spoken more plainly in his own voice. For whatever mask Freneau assumed in prose, the voice which speaks from behind it seems to me monotonously the same and does not carry well across the years. Some of his essays contain passages which are usefully quotable, but I find none which in entirety will stand alone, praiseworthy rather than representative.

For I see Freneau as a poet, and as a poet caught between the beckoning of his fancy and the fervor of his patriotic fire, a victim to both, neither of which he could often effectively control. He wrote too much, too rapidly, and too long. Given a subject, he was likely to take it in his teeth like a terrier, shaking it and worrying it, then letting it drop, to slink away, neither quick nor conquered. Classic in form, his verses often lack classic restraint and concision: more often than not they go on too long in roundabout repetitiveness, the focus shifting, backing away and then returning, not quite under control, inconsecutive but sometimes charming.

What certifies him as a poet is not his thought, which he shared with many of his generation, nor his subjects, most of which were those of almost any contemporary, but his occasional adroitness with word or phrase, his brief insights which seem sometimes quite aside from what he is talking about. Many of them seem to me almost Keatsian, like "Here drowsy bats enjoy a dull repose" (p. 206) or "So glide ye streams in hollow chambers pent, / Forever wasting, yet not ever spent" (p. 213). With Plato as persona, he can quietly advise that "The little god within thy breast / Is weary of his mansion here" (p. 321). Sometimes he packs a line with sounds which link to sense with fearful impact as he describes the "grief in ecstasy of woe run mad" (p. 270) in the chamber where death lies dying. At other times he achieves an almost synesthetic quality in verses such as "Steep me, steep me some poppies deep / In beechen bowl to bring on sleep" (p. 228). Byron's translation a literary generation later of "Adrian's Address to the Soul" is not more deftly musical than Freneau's at twenty-two:

> Little pleasing wand'ring mind
> Guest companion soft and kind
> Now to what regions do you go
> All pale and stiff and naked too
> And jest no more as you were wont to do.[4]

Many of these happier combinations of sound and sense appear among his earliest poems, before his voice was coarsened by anger or despair. And much that remains central to his thinking is found in the early poems: life is short, death is certain, and of afterlife no mortal mind can know. Thus at sixteen in "The History of the Prophet Jonah" he could have Jehovah declare:

> Enjoy thy gifts while yet the seasons run
> True to their course and social with the sun;
> When to the dust my mandate bids thee fall,
> All these are lost, for death conceals them all—
> No more the sun illumes the sprightly day,
> The seasons vanish, and the stars decay:
> The trees, the flowers, no more thy sense delight,
> Death shades them all in ever-during night.   (P. 202)

A year later in "The Pyramids of Egypt" he said much the same again: those "piles of wonder" which were the pyramids "scorn to bend beneath the weight of years," though the palaces and temples of Egyptian kings which once surrounded them

> all, all are gone,
> And like the phantom snows of a May morning,
> Left not a vestige to remember them!   (P. 205)

Yet even these must vanish. Though "the pride of art," they also were erected "to the pride of man" as "the sleeping place of death." Within their sturdy walls " 'Tis darkness all, with hateful silence join'd." There "marble coffins vacant of their bones, / Shew where the royal dead in ruin lay!" (p. 206). For death finally claims all, workman and ruler, and even art (this Freneau seems on the brink of saying directly, but backs away as if in confusion), and even time which is "but a viewless point on the vast circle of eternity (p. 207). And when at eighteen Freneau gave himself over to "The Power of Fancy" ("Come, O come— perceived by none, / You and I will walk alone"), he asked himself,

> What is this *globe*, these *lands*, and *seas*,
> And *heat*, and *cold*, and *flowers*, and *trees*,
> And *life*, and *death*, and *beast*, and *man*,
> And *time*,—that with the *sun* began—
> But thoughts on reason's scale combin'd,
> Ideas of the Almighty mind? (P. 208)

The sources from which Freneau drew these familiar notions of the awesome inevitability of death, the fleeting inconsequence of man and of his creations, and the power of illusion are less important than the manner in which Freneau expressed them and the mood, mixed of resignation to what man must endure and fitful visions of what man regenerated might become. The holding of these two attitudes side by side was attempted in "The American Village" and is the reason perhaps for the insertion of the tearful tale of doomed Indian lovers into that celebration of possibilities for excellence in a village undisturbed by the troubles which plagued Goldsmith's degenerating Auburn. When Caffaro and Colma die, as even lovers must, young Freneau dismisses them with wistful but somewhat cynical agnosticism:

> FAREWELL, lamented pair, and whate'er state
> Now clasps you round, and sinks you deep in fate;
> Whether the fiery kingdom of the sun,
> Or the slow silent wave of Acheron,
> Or Christian's heaven, or planetary sphere,
> Or the third region of the cloudless air;
> Or if return'd to dread nihility,
> You'll still be happy, for you will not be. (P. 223)

Man's life on earth, or anywhere, is fleeting; his noblest monuments fall to ruin; time itself (that "viewless point / On the vast circle of eternity") passes to dream existence ("Ideas of the Almighty mind"), recalled only by imperfect fancy; even death is not immortal ("You'll . . . be happy, for you will not be"). Moving into his twenties, Freneau attempted to snare in words these elusive certainties which had been filtered through his training in the classics, his reading in the poets of England, and his apparently only partially directed studies in theology. They never settled to a formula, as perhaps they never could, and as Freneau's conviction of the elusiveness even of a poet's vision would not allow them to, but they remained with him, providing an ambience beyond which his finer poetry seldom moved. As he attempted an ambitious ordering in "The House of Night," he warned:

> Poetic dreams are of a finer cast
> Than those which o'er the sober brain diffused
> Are but a repetition.

For its place in the story of Freneau's groping toward expression "The House of Night" must be read in the 75 stanzas in which it first appeared in 1779,[5] which (though several seasonable stanzas may have been added just prior to publication) is nearer to that toward which a young Freneau had groped two or three years before than are the 136 stanzas into which it was expanded in the *Poems* of 1786, where it is more rationally discursive, less subjective, and less revealing of personal turmoil than when Freneau, ten years before, had cut his unwieldy argument short by exclaiming,

> Enough—when God and nature give the word
>   I'll tempt the dusky shore and narrow sea:
> Content to die, just as it is decreed,
>   At four score years, or now at twenty-three.

At twenty-three, rather than versifying an argument, Freneau created a nightmare vision which he did not have the skill fully to communicate. The elements are there: a lonely midnight ("Mist sate upon the woods, and darkness rode, / In her black chariot, with a wild career"), a "black sip travelling thro' the noisy gale," dim buildings seen through darkness and surrounded by rank weeds and drooping blossoms ("nought but unhappy plants or trees were seen; / The yew, the willow, and the church-yard elm, / The cypress with its melancholy green"), and from these buildings the confused murmur of voices ("Much did they talk of death, and much of life; / Of coffins, shrouds, and horrors of the tomb"), and high above in a dim-lit lonely chamber death lay dying ("Death, dreary death"). And dying death demanded life—"Some cordial potion or some pleasing draught" as succor; yet he was tired also of his long continued, quite too easy victory ("What glory can there be to vanquish those / Who all beneath his strokes are sure to die"). With a final dramatic gesture he

> Gave his last groans in horror and despair,
> "All hell demands me hence," he said, and threw
> The red lamp hissing thro' the midnight air.

Death's kinsmen ("Each horrid face a grizly mask conceal'd") placed his body in a tomb, and as the poet stooped to write death's epitaph, the light of morning came, revealing to the poet that his "weary night" of fearsome imagining had been a dream. And as a dream, and only a dream, though dreams "are perhaps forebodings of the soul," too much must not be made of it: "Stranger, whoe'er thou art," the poet continues, "Say does thy fancy rove like mine; / Transport thee o'er wide lands and wider seas?" "Perhaps," he said, "in future years,/ At awful distance you and I may roam." At any rate, he temporized four years later, "the rude irregularity of nature pleases me more than the completed strokes of art." As Leslie Fiedler and Arthur Zeiger have suggested, "Freneau is finally too well-behaved and conventional to achieve full frenetic horror."[6] But he did in "The House of Night" come close, closer than he ever would again, and as close as any countryman would come for half a century.

For Freneau never ventured so far again. These early verses reveal promise of a poet, but a poet fated never to roam another time at such "awful distance." He would continue, and increasingly, to find small relevance between what was and what should be. The world he inherited was soiled by errors made by people who had gone before him, and he cherished visions of a better world, like that which had existed, in fancy only perhaps, before the cruelty and greed and coarse insensitiveness of man had spoiled it. Young Freneau dreamed that his new Western world might exhibit opportunities for riches other than of gold, for unconfused decency and individual self-reliance. Like young men everywhere at almost any time, Freneau dreamed the good dream which subtle men call primitivist or Edenic, beyond the reach of men confused by progress.

Freneau did not share Joel Barlow's vision of a New World made rich by commerce and invention. Expansion of commerce, he explained in "The Rising Glory of America," depended on the development of science. But science in turn depended on freedom for free men to work among free ideas:

> This is a land of ev'ry joyous sound
> Of liberty and life; sweet liberty!
> Without whose aid the noblest genius fails,
> And science irretrievably must die.　　(Pp. 12–13)

This "sweet haunt of peace" had been invaded by men of avarice who sought "New seas to vanquish, and new worlds to find" ("How few have sail'd in virtue's nobler plan, / How few with notions worthy of a man"). Thus at twenty in "Discovery," the most successfully compact of his early poems, Freneau affirms again the theme set forth in "The American Village," but addresses himself now to England as the miscreant who despoiled his dream, even usurping religion as a means of bending "nations to her own belief":

> Ah race to justice, truth, and honour blind,
> Are thy convictions to convert mankind—!
> ·　·　·　·　·　·　·　·　·　·　·　·
> If wealth, or war, or science bid thee roam,
> Ah, leave religion and thy laws at home,
> Leave the free native to enjoy his store,
> Nor teach destructive arts, unknown before. (Pp. 18–19)

The American Revolution then allowed the young poet to focus his anger at an identifiable opponent, a nation, a force, a way of life which could be made responsible for corruption bred of mismanagement. An enemy had appeared, tangible and palpable, against which he could direct his cries of hatred and dissent, could express directly and without the subterfuge of poetry his disappointing discovery of the basic irrelevance of things as they were. No longer need there be vague disquiet about mismanagement in general; a people was there to be confronted, and idea to be defended, not just talked about:

> When God from chaos gave this world to be,
> Man then he formed, and formed him to be free,
> In his own image stampt the favourite race—
> How darest thou, tyrant, the fair stamp efface! (P. 24)

And after he became a participant in the war and was captured and imprisoned, he vowed in "The British Prison-Ship," which has been called, though I think it is not, America's first successful long poem:

> WEAK as I am, I'll try my strength to-day
> And my best arrows at these hell-hounds play,
> To future years the scene of death prolong,
> And hang them up to infamy in song. (P. 46)

What power his wartime verses have is the lyric power of anger or power of vicious taunting as he swung with bludgeon or pierced with rapier. He became quotable because timely. His rhythms were right, his rhymes simple, his arguments unswerving. The proper word was the effectively wrathful word, and there were few occasions for delicacy as statement subdued poetry.

Yet not always. He was to write joyfully "On the Memorable Victory Obtained by the Gallant John Paul Jones" and gleefully "On the Fall of General Earl Cornwallis," useful occasional presentations, workmanlike and appropriate. Among his battle pieces, however, only "To the Memory of the Brave Americans" survives as a poem complete, not only for such lines as "'Tis not the beauty of the morn / That proves the evening shall be clear—" or the quatrain from which Walter Scott borrowed a line for *Marmion:*

> They saw their injur'd country's woes,
> The flaming tower, the wasted field;
> They rushed to meet the insulting foe,
> They took the spear—but left the shield, (P. 69)

but also for its consistent and restrained gravity in which grief balances pride as the valor of ragged Americans is told in lines which evoke classical memories. Freneau's fancy and his fire are here, and I think for the first time, effectively conjoined, producing a poem which for its time and purpose seems exactly right.

For even amid the din of party warfare in Philadelphia and the alarums of enemy activity both to north and south, poetry could fleetingly survive. On 24 October 1781 Freneau inserted into the *Freeman's Journal,* wedged between verses of bitterness and calls for patriotic courage, a small and almost perfect poem, less distinctive in idea than in image. He called it then "A Moral Thought," though he changed the title later to "The Vanity of Existence," and it is one of the few of his writings which he did not putter over to alter for later printings. Beginning conventionally with a well-worn but well-phrased observation on what time can do to youthful vision, it calls to question and suggests depths of unannounced meaning to the apparently commonplace last two lines of the second stanza in the stark, controlled image with which the poem closes:

> In youth, gay scenes attract our eyes,
>   And not suspecting their decay
> Life's flowery fields before us rise,
>   Regardless of its winter day.
>
> But vain pursuits, and joys as vain,
>   Convince us life is but a dream,
> Death is to wake, to rise again
>   To that true state you best esteem.
>
> So nightly on some shallow tide,
>   Oft have I seen a splendid show,
> Reflected stars on either side,
>   And glittering moons were seen below.
>
> But when the tide had ebbed away,
>   The scene fantastic with it fled,
> A bank of mud around me lay,
>   And sea-weed on the river's bed.   (P. 318)

But poetry was most often put aside for argument. A year later Freneau's anger and despair, never long submerged, rose again to the surface. "Curs'd be the day," he said,

how bright soe'er it shined
That first made kings the masters of mankind,
And cursed the wretch who first with regal pride
Their equal rights to equal men denied.   (P. 85)

Freneau's critics were correct when they accused him of building a reputation on mere "newspaper verse." And Freneau recognized it for what it was: deft and timely, more polished than most, metronomic in rhythm, repetitive in thought. Like Whittier and many another, he offered what he could of his talent in defense of what he thought, at that time and for that time, to be most important. But he seems to have been often distraught, uncertain, anxious about the vanishing of his vision: "Thou happiness! still sought but never found, / We, in a circle, chace thy shadow round" (p. 86).

When the Revolution was over, he got away, again to the lush quiet of the West Indies and a life at sea. Was it escape from turmoil, escape to poetry, or, as Roy Harvey Pearce has suggested, a withdrawal like that of Melville's Bartleby: "I prefer not to"?[7] Not long before in "Advice to Authors," which internal evidence identifies as another valedictory to political skirmishing, he had advised: "graft your authorship on some other calling. . . . Poets are . . . at present considered as the dregs of the community . . . lampooning each other for the amusement of the illiberal vulgar." It is, he said, "far more honourable to be a good bricklayer or a skilful weaver than an indifferent poet." And then, like Bartleby: "If fortune seems absolutely determined to starve you, . . . retire to some uninhabited island, or desert, and there, at your leisure end your life with decency."[8]

What he wrote during the six years before 1790, during most of which time he guided coastal vessels between New York and Charleston, dropping off verse for instant publication at either port, was lighter and brighter than much that he had done before, tinged with good humor as he caricatured "The Newsmonger," "The Drunken Soldier," "The Roguish Shoemaker," and other native types chosen from among the strange but simple people who in a democracy might be supposed to have an increasingly important voice. The genre was familiar—the kind of character sketch which Freneau would have been familiar with, if not in

Theophrastus, in almost any of the eighteenth-century essayists, in England or America, the kind which in prose Washington Irving, and after him Charles Dickens and Bret Harte, would make popular. Nor was Freneau the first among his countrymen in comic caricature. Franklin, for one, had preceded him in prose, and John Trumbull in verse. But Freneau during this period did it consistently well, and knew brief popularity greater than he had known before or would know again. Verses of this order were reprinted in newspapers from Boston to Savannah where he became affectionally known as Captain Sinbat or Sinbat the Sailor, unpretentious, good-natured, and utterly nonpolitical.

These homely verses represented not a new departure, only a new emphasis. Even as a very young man, Freneau had an eye, if not an ear, for winsome human frailties. "The Expedition of Timothy Tauris, Astrologer,"[9] which is said to have been first printed in New York in 1775, recounts in a long, and finally tedious, burlesque narrative what seems to have been a collegiate pilgrimage to the Falls of Passaic, where, the narrator said, he

> enjoyed a regale
> Of victuals three times every day, without fail:
> There was poultry, and pyes, and a dozen things more
> That the damnable college had never in store.

There he met and described in pliant anapests a whole cast of native characters, for a goodly crowd was there: "Here were Nellies, and Nancies, and Netties, by dozens / With their neighbours, and nephews, and nieces, and cousins." Among them was Mammon the merchant, Japhet the Jew, Slyboots the Quaker, Dullman the broker, Samuel the deacon, Nimrod the soldier who attracted all girls, Dr. Sangrado who "was vexed to the soul / To see so much health in this horrible hole," a tedious lawyer named Ludwig, a belle named Miss Kitty who has sometimes been thought to have been drawn from life, a boisterous farmer, Milhollan, who every morning "tippled three glasses of gin / With as many, at least, of three devils within," and Pedro the Parson who

> Talked of his wine, and he talked of his beer,
> And he talked of his texts, that were not very clear;
> And many suggested he talked very queer.

The "Expedition" is jaunty good fun, buoyantly inconsequential. Like John Trumbull's earlier "The Progress of Dullness" and Fitz-Greene Halleck's later "Fanny," it is crammed with local reference and private joking which in a more quiet time might have gained it mild applause. Freneau was fond of that kind of verse, deftly colloquial and broadly humorous, with some flick of satire in it. He was to venture it again, with more feeling, in "The New-England Sabbath-Day Chase" which poked fun at that natural enemy of any man from the middle states, through Irving and Cooper to Harold Frederic—the dour but self-filled man from Connecticut, which produced, Freneau said elsewhere, the largest pumpkins and poems and families of any state in the union. He used the humorous travel motif again in *A Journey from Philadelphia to New York*,[10] written in the person of Robert Slender, stocking weaver. "The style," said an advertisement in the *Freeman's Journal* on 25 April 1787, "is smooth and easy, and the pleasurable air that is diffused over the whole piece will certainly render the whole poem acceptable to such as choose to read it."

Evidence does not exist that many, then or now, have chosen to read this, which Freneau later called "A Laughable Poem," to test its acceptability. In lines of lilting whimsy Freneau touched again on his distaste for city life, even in Philadelphia, that

> gravest of towns on the face of the earth;
> Where saints of all orders their freedom may claim,
> And poets, and painters, and girls of the game.
> . . . .
> Our citizens think, when they sit themselves down
> In the gardens that grow on the skirts of the town,
> They think they have got in some rural retreat,
> Where nymphs of the grove, and the singing birds meet
> When only a fence shuts them out from the street;
> With the smoke of the city beclouding their eyes
> They sit in their boxes, and look very wise
> Take a sip of bad punch, or a glass of sour wine;
> Conceiting their pleasures are equal to mine.

With Robert Slender traveled William Snip, a merchant tailor, and Susanna Snipinda, his frivolous wife; bold Captain O'Keefe, a "killer of man and a lover of beef"; Touppee, a simpering French hairdresser; Billy O'Bluster, a seaman, who was "always in taverns, or always in love"; Ezekiel, a pettifogger from New England; and, not least, poor Bob, a young poet, who "Had sung for the great and rhym'd for the small, / But scarcely a shilling had got by them all." The journey to Burlington by boat was stormy, but "we stowed away snug, / Some link'd with a lady, and some with a jug." Proceeding then overland to Perth Amboy, the traveler's stage tumbled off the road, was raised, and repaired, and the journey continued, the travelers bruised and quarrelsome. A final leg was again by boat, which after further misadventures and much facile rhyming brought the party to New York as fatigued as a reader who had followed them. Late in life, Freneau tried the long humorous poem again in "Elijah, the New England Emigrant,"[11] in which Deacon Hezekiah Salem of that state of large pumpkins and families attempts to explain to his son-in-law the disadvantages of setting out for western territories, telling him that

> A farm on Alabama's streams
> Might do in JOEL BARLOW's dreams . . .
> Such rhyming dealers in romance
> See nature only in a trance.

But Freneau was not good at narrative. He had a flair for character, but not for character in action. In "The Pictures of Columbus," written, he said, in 1774, but not published until twelve years later (predated then, I have thought, in order to establish precedence over Barlow's *The Vision of Columbus* of 1787), he reached more closely toward success with a variety of meter in what may be considered a closet drama on his familiar theme of the New World, once filled with "sweet sylvan themes of innocence and ease," despoiled by greed and cruelty. The most lively of the eighteen "Pictures," however are not those which develop the argument, but those which present characters in dialogue: the "Discontents at Sea" and the exchange between an irascible couple named Thomas and Susan in "A Sailor's Hut, Near the Shore" (which was later to be presented separately as "An Irish-Town Dialogue") in which the husband complains:

> I wish I was over the water again!
> 'Tis a pity we cannot agree;
> When I try to be merry 'tis labour in vain,
> You always are scolding at me;

to which she replies

> If I was a maid as I now am a wife
> With a sot and a brat to maintain,
> I think it would be the first care of my life,
> To shun such a drunkard again.   (P. 245)

Other verses which Freneau wrote in the later 1780s are personal, even plaintive, as he told of hardships and storms at sea. He must have recognized that most of the rhymes which he turned out with quick facility were workaday and derivative: "Poetic dreams," he had earlier recognized, "are of a finer caste." A mood of discouraged resignation appears in new poems on death or desolation: "The Dying Indian" ("Vigour, and youth, and active days are past" [p. 328]) and "The Seasons Moralized" ("Winter, alas! shall spring restore, / But youth returns to man no more" [p. 335]). He mourned "The Vicissitude of Things" and in "The Poetaster" spoke of the folly of writing poetry. In "Verses Made at Sea in a Heavy Gale" he dolorously complained that "ruin is the lot of all," and he marred three fine lines of showing rather than telling with a fourth line of quizzical lamentation:

> Now to their haunts the birds retreat,
> The squirrel seeks the hollow tree,
> Wolves in their shaded caverns meet,
> All, all are blest but wretched we.   (P. 330)

For as he moved through his thirties, Freneau's fires of enthusiasm did not burn brightly. His fancy was walled by despondency in "The Vernal Ague":

> Where the pheasant roost at night,
> Lonely, drowsy, out of sight.
> Where the evening breezes sigh
> Solitary, there stray I.
>
> Close along a shaded stream,
> Source of many a youthful dream,

Where branchy cedars dim the day
There I muse, and there I stray.
. . . .
Great guardian of our feeble kind!—
Restoring Nature, lend thine aid!
And o'er the features of the mind
Renew those colours, that must fade.
    When vernal suns forbear to roll.
    And endless winter chills the soul.
(Pp. 260–261)

Restoring nature did come briefly to his aid when early in the summer of 1786 he came upon the Azalea Viscosa (the white, the wild, or the swamp honeysuckle) in bloom along the riverbanks of South Carolina: the flower that was also doomed, which would have its little day, and die. Moving momentarily beyond himself to observation and contemplation, in muted tones he created in "The Wild Honeysuckle" the one succinct lyric meditation on which much of his reputation has since then depended. And perhaps rightly, for none certainly in the New World had done better, in restrained power or delicacy. If not a great poem, it is an almost flawless evocation of mood, deepened perhaps from its earlier expressions by realization of opportunities lost, Freneau's own brief flowering unrecognized and wasted. As in "A Moral Thought," he discovered what Emerson would explain as a spiritual truth gained through observation of a natural fact, and Freneau revealed it now with a simplicity which poetry in English would wait a dozen years for Wordsworth to surpass. Placed beside Bryant's "To a Fringed Gentian" or even his better "The Yellow Violet," Freneau's lines read freshly clear, graced with wonder and some awe:

Fair flower, that doth so comely grow,
Hid in this dreary dark retreat,
Untouch'd thy little blossoms blow,
Unseen thy little branches meet;
    No roving foot shall find thee here,
    No busy hand provoke a tear.

By Nature's self in white arrayed,
She bade thee shun the vulgar eye

149

And planted here the guardian shade,
And sent soft waters murmuring by—
  Thus quietly thy summer goes,
  Thy life reclining to repose.

Smit with these charms that must decay,
I grieve to see thy future doom—
(They died—nor were those flowers less gay,
The flowers that did in Eden bloom)
  Unpitying frosts, and autumn's power
  Shall leave no vestige of this flower!

From morning suns and evening dews
At first thy little being came—
If nothing once—you nothing lose,
For when you die you are the same—
  The space between is but an hour
  The empty image of a flower.[12]

His more popular verses continued to be such things as "The
Virtue of Tobacco":

  Unhappy those, whom choice or fate
  Inclines to prize this bitter weed;
  Perpetual source of female hate;
  Of which no beast but man will feed,   (P. 382)

the lilting lines on "The Dish of Tea":

  LET some in beer place their delight,
  O'er bottled porter waste the night,
    Or sip the rosy wine:
  A dish of TEA more pleases me,
  Yields softer joys, provokes less noise,
    And breeds no base design,   (P. 391)

and "The Jug of Rum" ("Within these Prison-walls repose /
The seeds of many a bloody nose").[13] These doggerel lines were
reprinted more than any of the others; they were imitated and
parodied. Freneau was less successful when serious in "May to
April," in which May dolefully reports that "Month after month
must find its doom," so that, when she is gone, then "Summer
dances on her tomb" (p. 352), creating a decently grotesque

image which does not quite compensate for the stumbling lines which precede it.

Of Freneau's three poems on the American Indian written during this period—"The Dying Indian," "The Indian Student, or Force of Nature," and "Lines Occasioned by a Visit to an Old Indian Burying Ground"—I find the first, though less often anthologized, most impressive, mainly, I think, because it contains fewer lines which seem to me might better have been omitted or amended. The second is too long; it contains too many shady banks and woody wilds and dewy lawns. By what seems to be common consent, the best lines are the last when, disappointed at what Harvard cannot teach him,

> to western springs
> (His gown discharged, his money spent,
> His blanket tied with yellow strings.)
> The shepherd of the forest went.   (P. 359)

But, in spite of the incomparable yellow strings and the nice periodicity of that final sentence, how commonplace it is, dramatic however and with a farewell flourish which is anticipatory perhaps of Huck's lighting out for the territory, but without matter to sustain it or shimmering of suggestion to hold it in a reader's memory.

"The Indian Burying Ground" (pp. 355–356), widely admired then and now, is greatly superior, its first two stanzas and its last two stanzas as movingly affective as any which Freneau wrote. But the space between seems to me labored, and inadequate in carrying out the transition from "the soul's eternal sleep" of the first stanza to the "shadows and delusions" to which "Reason's self shall bow the knee" in the last. Here again is evidence of Freneau's lifelong adherence to the kind of Platonism ("What is this *globe*, these *lands*, and *seas*" but "Ideas of the Almighty Mind") which was to find surer voice in Emerson half a century later. But Freneau was a poet, not a thinker: "And long shall timorous fancy see / The painted chief, and painted spear." Even if somewhat rudely forced, his familiar musings on transience, on the soul's eternal sleep, on the power of art (the "imaged birds, and painted bowls") to simulate truth, and the power of fancy to recreate what reason cannot, are here set forth again, more maturely, with better economy, and less as statement than as suggestion secured by imagery: "The hunter and the deer a shade."

More diffuse, more musical, "The Dying Indian," in attempting less, achieves more. Shalum (in later versions Tomo-Cheeki) speaks in dramatic monologue as he prepares for the long, lonely journey he must go "Without a partner, and without a guide." What echoes the poem contains of other poems by other poets are good echoes. Freneau here combines his questionings of futurity with his skill in establishing a character through what the character is allowed to say. The freer rhymes of his popular verse are now seriously engaged in expression of Freneau's central concern, expressed more lightly, with memorable economy: "What mischiefs on the dead attend!"

> On yonder lake I spread the sail no more!
> Vigour, and youth, and active days are past—
> Relentless demons urge me to that shore
> On whose black forests all the dead are cast:—
> Ye solemn train, prepare the funeral song,
> For I must go to shades below,
> Where all is strange and all is new:
> Companion to the airy throng!—
> > What solitary streams,
> > In dull and dreary dreams,
> All melancholy, must I rove along.   (P. 328)

Freneau has freed himself here from easy conventions of rhythm which makes much of his verse seem quite too facilely adept. An atmosphere of sadness surrounds this poem, of resignation and courage also, and trust that

> Nature at last these ruins may repair,
> When fate's long dream is o'er, and she forgets to weep
> Some real world once more may be assigned,
> Some newborn mansion for the immortal mind!
> > > (P. 330)

A pastiche perhaps of what other men had often pondered, Freneau's long musings on evanescence are here most poignantly expressed, and as foreboding dramatized rather than as allegation or protest.

As he left the sea, for marriage and, he hoped, retirement to his Monmouth countryside, Freneau spoke again of quiet and seclusion. The "Stanzas Written on the Hills of Neversink" is not often reported among his more pleasing poems, but it seems to me of its kind superior. A meditation on landscape not unsimilar to Richard Lewis's lines on Patapsco or Bryant's hymns to the American forest, it speaks with simple directness as Freneau, perhaps on one of his final voyages, approaches the New Jersey highlands:

> These heights, the pride of all the coast,
> What happy genius plann'd,
> Aspiring o'er the distant wave,
> That sinks the neighbouring land:
> These hills for solitude design'd,
> This bold and broken shore;
> These haunts impervious to the wind,
> Tall oaks, that to the tempest bend,
> Half Druid, I adore.
> . . . .
> Proud heights! with pain so often seen,
> I quit your view no more;
> And see, unmov'd, the passing sail,
> Tenacious of the shore:—
> Let those, who pant for wealth or fame,
> Pursue the wat'ry road;
> Let sleep and ease—blest days and nights,
> And health attend these favorite heights,
> Retirement's blest abode.[14]

But retirement remained elusive for almost fifteen years. Drawn again to political wars until 1793, Freneau lived uneasily then for a few years in Monmouth as a country printer, rural newspaper editor, and almanac maker, until in 1797 he ventured again to New York to edit a periodical which he hoped would be strictly literary but which turned out to be political indeed, and when that failed he returned to New Jersey to fulminate, mainly in prose, against people who did not approve of Thomas

Jefferson. During the first years of the nineteenth century he was again at sea, until in his mid-fifties he finally returned to his New Jersey home, to live on inconspicuously for a quarter of a century, remembered, when remembered at all, as a gaffer more contentious and bibulous than a man of his age should be. Experience had taught him to view his country as "a *tasteless land,*" unfriendly to poets: "The home-made *nobles* of our times, / . . . Hate the bard and spurn his rhymes." Follow Washington Irving's example, he counseled: "Lo! he has kissed a monarch's—hand" and found thereby success:

> Why pause?—like IRVING, haste away.
> To England your addresses pay!
>
> . . . .
>
> In England what you write and print,
> Republished here in shop, or stall,
> Will perfectly enchant us all.[15]

As for himself: "My little is enough for me, / Content with mediocrity."

Whether Freneau had grounds for disenchantment can be argued by others, who may find him to have been poorly repaid for years of versatile agitation. What he wrote during the last decade of the eighteenth century seems not to have been unsuccessful in stirring people to action or anger, gaining for him reputation as an American Charles Churchill, a Juvenal in smallclothes, embodying, as Henry Wells has said, the genius of a robust society in a youthful and stirring land. Launched as he was on an ocean of news and special pleading and satire, he had mainly time only for lighter verse: he wrote with a workman's precise knowledge of "The Country Printer"; he gave rhymed "Advice to Ladies Not to Neglect the Dentist"; he chuckled over graffiti found in a tavern at Log-town in the pine barrens of North Carolina. His apparently unfinished long poem on "The Rising Empire" contains occasional amusing descriptions of a sturdy and strong-ribbed Dutch maiden from Long Island, unmoved by idle passions or "frail ideas of romantic love," who "heeds not valour, learning, wit or birth, / Minds not the swain—but asks him what he's worth," and pokes fun again at Connecticut where "Bards of huge frame in every hamlet rise" and rhymes "Come rattling down on Greenfield's reverend son."[16] All these are done with learned facility, as by a repetitive village scold, with something of quaint fancy, but little fire.

What may survive from these important years when a new nation was establishing itself are smaller things apparently done in days of rural relaxation. The awkward care with which Freneau revised and reworked the verses "On a Bee Drinking from a Glass of Water" and "On a Fly Fluttering around a Candle" suggests a decline in the spontaniety of his lyric power, but "To a Caty-Did," first printed in 1815, survives with gay abandon which recalls earlier evocations to the power of fancy. Avoiding the whimsical sentimentality of Joseph Rodman Drake's "The Culprit Fay" which Poe was to find distasteful, it moves with winsome inevitability toward what Harry Hayden Clark has identified as Freneau's "indwelling master-thought," his "pensiveness on the brevity . . . of life and the certainty of death." No apology is needed for reproducing so complete a poem complete. It brings together almost every poetic trait that had separately at other times been praiseworthy in Freneau: his competence in form, his attraction to native nature, his adroitness with word or phrase, his mood of wonder and auspicious awe; it guarantees, if no other did, his title as poet.

> In a branch of willow hid
> Sings the evening Caty-Did:
> From the lofty locust bough
> Feeding on a drop of dew,
> In her suit of green array'd
> Hear her singing in the shade
>   Caty-did, Caty-did, Caty-did!
>
> While upon a leaf you tread,
> Or repose your little head,
> On your sheet of shadows laid,
> All the day you nothing said:
> Half the night your cheery tongue
> Revell'd out its little song,
>   Nothing else but Caty-did.

From your lodgings on the leaf
Did you utter joy or grief—?
Did you only mean to say,
I have had my summer's day,
And am passing, soon, away
To the grave of Caty-did:—
  Poor, unhappy Caty-did!

But you would have uttered more
Had you known of nature's power—
From the world when you retreat,
And a leaf's your winding sheet,
Long before your spirit fled,
Who can tell but nature said,
Live again, my Caty-did!
  Live, and chatter, Caty-did.

Tell me, what did Caty do?
Did she mean to trouble you?—
Why was Caty not forbid
To trouble little Caty-did?—
Wrong, indeed at you to fling,
Hurting no one while you sing
  Caty-did! Caty-did! Caty-did!

Why continue to complain?
Caty tells me, she again
Will not give you plague or pain:—
Caty says you may be hid
Caty will not go to bed
While you sing us Caty-did.
  Caty-did! Caty-did! Caty-did!

But, while singing, you forgot
To tell us what did Caty not:
Caty did not think of cold,
Flocks retiring to the fold,
Winter, with his wrinkles old,
Winter, that yourself foretold
  When you gave us caty-did.

Stay securely in your nest;
Caty now, will do her best,

All she can, to make you blest;
But, you want no human aid—
Nature when she form'd you, said,
"Independent you are made,
My dear little Caty-did:
Soon yourself must disappear
With the verdure of the year,"—
And to go, we know not where,
    With your song of Caty-did.   (Pp. 410–412)

It sounds almost like a lullaby, doesn't it?—soothingly sung at bedtime to someone who is very young and very sleepy, an early nineteenth-century Christopher Robin perhaps, or Freneau's own daughter Katey who was in her teens when the poem appeared.

More serious but less impressive are Freneau's late musings on "Belief and Unbelief," "On the Universality and Other Attributes of the God of Nature," "On the Religion of Nature," and "On the Uniformity and Perfection of Nature" which fumbles toward restatement of a familiar conviction: "All, nature made, in reason's sight / Is order all, and *all is right*" (p. 423). Deism, pantheism, and stoic faith rub shoulders here in decent workaday stanza when in "Science Favourable to Virtue" Freneau reminds himself again that "The mind, though perch'd on eagle's wings, / With pain surmounts the scum of things" (p. 416). During the War of 1812 he was again a patriot poet with verses on battles and blockades and British depredations. Weary of war and man's inconstancy, his plaint was gentler now as in "The Brook in the Valley" he found another analogue in nature:

The world has wrangled half an age,
And we again in war engage,
While this sweet, sequestered rill
Murmurs through the valley still.
   .   .   .   .
Emblem thou of restless man;
What a sketch of nature's plan!
Now at peace, and now at war,
Now you murmur, now you roar;

> Muddy now, and limpid next,
> Now with icy shackles vext—
> What a likeness here we find!
> What a picture of mankind! (Pp. 417–419)

Too much must not be made of Freneau. As a talented man he responded to the impulses of his time in the voice of his time, borrowing whatever was found useful in content or form. He argued in verse against the cutting down of trees in cities, against the encroachment of commercial wharves; he pled the cause of the Negro, the American Indian, the debtor, the drunkard, and the abused army veteran; he championed Thomas Paine as well as Thomas Jefferson; he joined deistic societies and he welcomed the writings of Swedenborg and, though cautiously, the advent of unitarianism. Wavering between extremes of passionate involvement and classical restraint, he has been found to be a primitivist sturdily convinced of the values of sympathy and national self-reliance, a patriot endowed with idealistic fervor and generous compassion, a brooding man dogged by personal adversity but serenely stoical in rational acceptance of his world, a humorist whose touch was not always light, a satirist of wide range and sharp-toothed striking power, but above all a lyricist haunted by a sense of the evanescence of beauty and the vacantness of death. To the historical scholar he becomes a convenient and quotable gauge. The convergence in him of familiar ideas and modes of expression render him a useful exemplar of the liberal or humane or democratic or patriotic convictions of an important time. The student of literature recognizes him as a transitional figure, grounded securely in the past and reaching tentatively toward the rewakening of sensibility called romanticism. Read carefully he may be discovered a poet who wrote a single poem in a variety of forms.

If Freneau did have but one effective note, and it of sadness at the frail duration of mortality, he sometimes struck it remarkably well. His legacy may be four poems, or five, or perhaps six: each must make his own count. He was not, I think, "the father of American poetry,"[17] for in a strict sense he had no descendants. Poets who came after him looked to other models, and usually from abroad, so that it can be doubted whether the direction of literature in the United States would be in any important respect different without him. But he was there, isolated by war and his own limitations, a victim to his fancy and his fire: "To write was my sad destiny, / The worst of trades, we all agree." As a voice of his time, he shares the fate of time, but as a person who approached a mystery with wonder and stoic resignation he will survive until that mystery is explained.

NOTES

1. The standard biography of Freneau is Lewis Leary, *That Rascal Freneau: A Study in Literary Failure* (New Brunswick, N.J., 1941; reprint ed., New York, 1964, 1971). Important critical commentary is found in Nelson F. Adkins, *Philip Freneau and the Cosmic Enigma: The Religious and Philosophical Speculations of an American Poet* (New York, 1949) and in the introduction to Harry Hayden Clark, ed., *Poems of Freneau* (New York, 1929). Fred Lewis Pattee, ed., *The Poems of Philip Freneau: Poet of the American Revolution* (Princeton, N.J., 1902–1907), 3 vols., and Philip Marsh, ed., *The Prose Works of Philip Freneau* (New Brunswick N.J., 1956), are useful, but textually inexact. Unless otherwise indicated, all quotations from Freneau's verse in the present essay are from Clark, ed., *Poems of Freneau,* their location in that volume indicated within parentheses in the text.

2. *That Rascal Freneau,* p. 70.

3. *Philadelphia Independent Gazetteer,* 7 September 1782, p. 3.

4. Written in the margin of Freneau's copy of *The Works of Alexander Pope,* now in the Princeton University Library; see Leary, *That Rascal Freneau,* p. 46.

5. *United States Magazine* 1 (August 1779): 355–362. The poem as later expanded is in Clark, ed., *Poems of Freneau,* pp. 266–288.

6. *O Brave New World: American Literature from 1600 to 1840* (New York, 1968), p. 512.

7. *The Continuity of American Poetry* (Princeton, N.J., 1961), p. 202.

8. *The Miscellaneous Works of Mr. Philip Freneau, Containing His Essays and Additional Poems* (Philadelphia, 1788), pp. 46–47.

9. Pattee, ed., *The Poems of Philip Freneau*, 1: 123–136.

10. Ibid., 2: 338–358.

11. Lewis Leary, ed., *The Last Poems of Philip Freneau* (New Brunswick, N.J., 1945), pp. 33–52.

12. I have used the text of the first printing in the *Charleston Columbian Herald*, 6 July 1786. When Freneau reprinted the poem in *Miscellaneous Works* (1788), the second line was changed to "Hid in this silent dull retreat," the last line of the second stanza to "Thy days declining to repose," and the last line of the fourth stanza to "The mere idea of a flower." In *Poems* (1795) the final line became "The frail duration of a flower" (for the poem in its apparently final state, see Clark, ed., *Poems of Freneau*, pp. 340–341). The changes seem to me significant and, with alterations made in others of his poems and in his prose, invite someone to take on the difficult and lengthy task of preparing a complete and annotated text of Freneau's writing.

13. See Leary, *That Rascal Freneau*, p. 179; another version is in Pattee, ed., *The Poems of Philip Freneau*, 3: 66–67.

14. *New York Daily Advertiser*, 26 January 1791; a somewhat different version is in Clark, ed., *Poems of Freneau*, pp. 374–376.

15. Leary, ed., *The Last Poems of Philip Freneau*, p. 112.

16. Pattee, ed., *The Poems of Philip Freneau*, 3: 8–9.

17. But see Harry Hayden Clark, "What Made Freneau the Father of American Poetry?" *Studies in Philology* 26 (January 1929): 1–22.

Hugh Henry Brackenridge's
Modern Chivalry

꧁ ꧂

I<small>N</small> its more than one hundred and fifty years of existence, *Modern Chivalry* has become, according to Mark Twain's definition, a classic—a book which many people have talked about, but which not many people read. This, as its whimsical author might have explained, may not be entirely the book's fault, for *Modern Chivalry* has long been out of print and thus inaccessible to all but the most assiduously curious. It is, however, worth reexamining in order that a new generation may determine whether this old book deserves to be remembered among native minor classics, and on what shelf it should be placed—whether with books of humor, satire, or honest social commentary, with ordinary fiction, or only set aside as collateral reading for the student of history. Hugh Henry Brackenridge himself called it "a book without thought, or the smallest degree of sense." His "business," he said, was "to speak nonsense; this being the only way to keep out of the reach of criticism."[1] During his lifetime and for many years afterwards, readers responded with delight to his comic discernment and uncommon good sense. It will not be surprising if, reintroduced, they continue to do so.

Like many humorists, Brackenridge was a person of extremely serious purpose. He was a self-made man, a very model of the versatile early American—lawyer, politician, editor, teacher, essayist, preacher, rhymester, and novelist. Born in 1748 at Kintyre, near Campbeltown, in Scotland, the son of William Brackenridge, who in 1753 emigrated to Pennsylvania, to York County on the frontier, there to settle in a district known as "The Barrens" in Peach Bottom Township, the boy was early hardened by plow and ax as he joined other Scotch-Irish pioneers in hewing farm acres from tracts of virgin forest.[2] The new land, its perils and hardships, matured young Brackenridge early. Indian raids were a constant menace, rocky fields a backbreaking challenge; but there was time also for education. Before he was thirteen, the boy had exhausted the resources of nearby Slate Ridge School and continued his studies in Latin and Greek with a local clergyman who encouraged his pupil's faculty for making versified adaptations of Horace and for composing humorous lines in Scottish dialect. Sometimes he would trudge thirty miles through backcountry roads to Fagg's Manor in Chester County, to borrow books and receive hardheaded Presbyterian advice from the Rev. John Blair, soon to become a professor at Princeton. By the time he was fifteen, Brackenridge had a school of his own at Gunpowder Falls in Maryland, where he is said to have ruled with a strong arm over students, many of whom were older than he, once impressing his authority by snatching a burning brand from the fire to brandish as a club before recalcitrant charges.

Five years later, in 1768, he entered Princeton, a classmate of Philip Freneau and James Madison. Older than his friends, he became a leader among them, active in the formation of the Whig Society, a literary club which engaged sometimes in more than verbal warfare with its rival Cliosophic Society. Tales are told of heads broken in taverns and of dormitory riots so serious that the authorities considered abolishing both groups. Relics of collegiate skirmishes are preserved in a manuscript notebook of versified "Satires Against the Tories," in which Brackenridge, Freneau, and Madison wrote with scurrilous, bright vigor of the "compleat Victory" which they presumed to have gained over their adversaries. In 1770 Brackenridge collaborated with Freneau in the writing of "Father Bombo's Pilgrimage to Mecca in Arabia," which, if it really were completed and if the whole of it could be discovered, would challenge for place as the first novel written in America. The few chapters which survive identify it as a lighthearted hodgepodge of Gulliver, Laurence Sterne, and geography, filled with good fun and with traces of the Irish brogue which Brackenridge was later to use more successfully in *Modern Chivalry*. On graduation in 1771 he collaborated again with

Freneau on a Commencement Day poem called *The Rising Glory of America,* which celebrated in sonorous, Miltonic lines the promise of expansion, development, and inevitable greatness of the new land and which, when published the next year in Philadelphia, introduced two of America's earliest and most promising young writers to a public which was too busy with other things to pay much attention to them.[3]

After graduation, Brackenridge remained at Princeton as master of the preparatory school, before returning to Maryland to take charge of an academy at Back Creek, near Princess Ann, in Somersot County. There he was joined in the fall of 1772 by Freneau, and the two friends planned literary projects together and read in theology for ministerial careers which neither achieved. "We have about thirty students in this academy," Freneau wrote Madison, "who prey on us like leeches."[4] In 1774 Brackenridge had a breakdown from which he never completely recovered—for the rest of his life he confessed himself subject to nervous agitation under pressure. Later in that year, he received an M.A. degree from Princeton, for which occasion he prepared and read a *Poem on Divine Revelation* (Philadelphia, 1774), which demonstrated that Christianity, spreading from Palestine to Europe and then westward, achieved its purest form in the New World. Again he admitted debts to Milton, but critical friends thought he had not paid them well, for the poem stumbled and gestured through lines which speak more clearly of a young man's good intentions than of his success in expressing himself in the grand style.

During the first year of the American Revolution, Brackenridge remained at the academy in Maryland, where he wrote for student production two heroic plays, *The Battle of Bunker's Hill* (Philadelphia, 1776) and *The Death of General Montgomery* (Philadelphia, 1777), in high-sounding verse meant to stimulate patriotic ardor. Soon after the Declaration of Independence, he left schoolteaching to become—though not ordained as a clergyman—a chaplain with the Continental army. "There are two ways," he apologized to Washington's troops at Morristown after the Battle of Princeton, "in which a man can contribute to the defense of his country, by the tongue to speak, or by the hand to act. . . . The talent of speech is mine, and that alone is my province."[5] But in 1778 Brackenridge left the army and set out for Philadelphia with a thousand pounds in his pocket and a quixotic literary scheme in his head. In a city torn apart by war, where patriotism and profiteering vied tumultuously, he planned a monthly magazine—a "literary coffee-house of public conversation"—which might convince all enemies that Americans "are able to cultivate the *belles lettres*, even disconnected from Great Britain; and that liberty is of so noble and energetic a quality, as even from the bosom of war to call forth the powers of human genius."[6]

But in spite of high hopes, the *United States Magazine* (and its editor's money) lasted only one year. Some assistance was received from Freneau, who submitted contributions in verse or prose to almost every issue—among them, bucolic descriptions of quiet tropical islands, a versified celebration of "The Beauties of Santa Cruz," and the chillingly portentous poem on "The House of Night." Brackenridge presented his pioneer short story of "The Cave of Vanhest," the first native tale set against a realistic background and the first fiction to use the realities of the American Revolution as a theme. Except for things like these, however, the magazine was a mishmash of political and patriotic scraps. Meanwhile Freneau went off briefly to war, and Brackenridge turned to the study of law, preparatory to being admitted to practice in Philadelphia, in December 1780.

But, he said, "I saw no chance of being anything in that city, [where] there were so many great men before me." Perhaps elsewhere, a man of his disposition and talents might find competition less distracting. Therefore, he continued, "I pushed my way to these woods where I thought I might emerge one day, and get forward."[7]

The "woods" to which Brackenridge went in 1781, at the age of thirty-three, were on the frontier beyond the Alleghenies, in the newly established town of Pittsburgh (which until recently had been an Indian trading outpost): "If town it might be call'd that town was none / Distinguishable by house nor street."[8] There he practiced as an attorney, grew with the community, wrote accounts of Indian raids for Freneau's *Freeman's Journal* in Philadelphia, and became active in turbulent frontier politics as a member of the state assembly. In 1786 he established the *Pittsburgh Gazette;* three years later he opened the first bookstore in that city; not long afterward he became one of the founders of Pittsburgh Academy, which later became a university.

As a legislator he made himself unpopular by supporting the proposed Constitution of the United States against the wishes of shirt-sleeved frontier constituents who preferred few regulations of any kind. An unfortunate remark that he could vote as he pleased and then write a piece for his paper to appease the people, for the people were fools—whether he really made it or not—did Brackenridge great harm. So severe was the reaction against him that his law business dropped off, and he was forced to withdraw from politics and thereafter to speak his mind guardedly in order to reestablish his private affairs.

Particularly bitter was his disappointment at being defeated as a representative from his district to the Constitutional Convention in 1787, and by an Irishman who was unfit, Brackenridge thought, for public office. He ridiculed the people's choice in a rhymed satire in the *Pittsburgh Gazette* for 14 November 1787, in which he characterized his opponent as a mere Teague O'Regan, the popular generic name (like Pat or Mike of a later day) for the immigrant Irish laborer, or bogtrotter, as he was often called:

> Whence comes it that a thing like this,
> Of mind no bigger than a fly's,
> Should yet attract the popular favor
> Be of his country thought the saviour?

He made fun of his opponent as "Traddle," a workingman elevated beyond his natural place and unequipped for the business of government; better by far that he had been left to ply his humble trade as weaver, like any other "Paddy just out of Cork." His election seemed characteristic of a time when men of brawn and brass, experienced in the rough practice but not in the subtle science of politics, were entrusted with the future safety of their land; "and yet," Brackenridge charged in the *Gazette* of 1 March

1788, "there is not a word said with regard to the ancestry of any of them; whether they should be altogether Irish or only Scotch Irish. If any of them have been in the war of the White Boys, Hearts of Oak, or the like, they may overturn all authority, and make the shilelah the law of the land." Unlearned, vulgar, and rapacious people—tradesmen, weavers, barbers, bargemen, dancing masters, and tailors—had the presumption to oppose measures put forward by men like the cosmopolitan John Jay and Brackenridge's collegemate, James Madison:

> I would submit it to any candid man, if in this constitution there is any provision for shaving a beard? or is there any mode laid down to take the measure of a pair of breeches? Whence then is it that men of learning seem so much to approve, while the ignorant are against it? the cause is perfectly apparent, *viz.* that reason is an erring guide, while instinct, which is the guiding principle of the untaught, is certain.

No wonder, he said in the *Gazette* a week later, with such representatives at the Constitutional Convention, that Pittsburgh and all Pennsylvania west of the mountains must "submit to stubborn fate / And be the backside of the state."

"All our misfortunes," he told his backcountry readers on 29 March, result from the "simplicity of those we send to represent us in the public bodies." When in June the Constitution was finally ratified and adopted, he spoke again of that "inferior race . . . which croak among the bog," like "animals which live by the credulity, the want of discernment, and the changing temper of the populace." Now that they seemed defeated, "O, frogs of the marsh, local demagogues, insidious declaimers, your pond is about to be dried up," he challenged in the *Gazette* of 28 June: "no more amongst the weeds and in the muddy fluid shall you lift your harsh voice. The marsh is drained; the dome aspires, and bright tinges of the rising day, gild its summits." But was it really drained? Was corruption and mediocrity driven from politics and the minds of the people? Brackenridge thought not.

Considered a Federalist—that is, according to the common notion, an eastern man and a friend to money and privilege—by frontier Democrats, Brackenridge found himself extremely unpopular: "My character," he complained, "was totally gone. . . . My practice was lost." He thought it necessary thereafter "to be silent, and add nothing more to the popular odium."[9] His young wife had died after not more than three years of marriage, leaving him with an infant son. In the late summer of 1790 he was married again—a "Maud Muller" or, perhaps more accurately, a "Pygmalion" match—to "a young girl of obscure German parents on the banks of the Ohio," reported the *Pennsylvania Mercury* in Philadelphia on 4 September, whom he "has brought to this city to spend the ensuing winter, and receive the advantage of some education."

As he turned his attention now to his family and to the restoration of his legal practice, Brackenridge kept his hand in literature also. A satirical "Memoir of the Philosophical Society," in which he made great fun (as he would later in *Modern Chivalry*) of vulgar pretensions to scientific knowledge, was said—probably erroneously—by the archdemocratic *Independent Gazetteer* of 22 February 1787 to have been written in pique as a result of having been blackballed by the society, but "An Ode for the Celebration of St. Andrew's Day" in the *New-York Magazine* for February 1791 was a loyal Scot's contribution to perpetuating traditions of his homeland; and his "Thoughts on the Present Indian War," which appeared in three installments in Freneau's *National Gazette* in Philadelphia in February 1792 was widely reprinted in other periodicals as the testimony of a patriotic native expert who knew the Indians, their haunts, and their wiles.

While he worked to regain his status as a lawyer, much of his extracurricular literary attention was turned, however, to a long satiric poem, written in the meter of Samuel Butler's *Hudibras*, like John Trumbull's *M'Fingal* which had so popular a vogue during and just after the Revolution. Brackenridge called it "The Modern Chevalier," and in it he ridiculed again the misadventures of Traddle the weaver, elected to public office for which he had no training. But the attack was now turned not only against demagogues who led people about by the nose, but also against people who thoughtlessly allowed themselves to be led. The doggerel verses recorded the disillusionment of a modern knight-errant who traveled about the countryside watching democracy at work. A benevolent friend persuades the chevalier to make his observations public:

> It would do service to the state,
> If such a noble Knight as you
> Would teach them what they ought to do,
> And give them seasonable lessons
> Respecting such their crude creations,
> That on the one hand while they pass
> The ignorant though monied ass,
> So on the other should avoid
> The chusing such amongst the crowd
> As are unqualified, though less,
> They may in property possess.[10]

Wealthy fools and ignorant fools both must be avoided. Brackenridge sought simple phrases and witty rhymes (*lessons, creations; avoid, crowd*) which might catch and tantalize the ear. The grand Miltonic manner of his patriotic poems, the classical precision of his martial dramas—these were put behind him as Brackenridge fumbled now toward a means of expression which could reach people, and make them smile, and think, written in language simple and direct and bluntly colloquial. But this verse was poor stuff indeed, limping in syntax and meaning, and the truth was that people, particularly frontier people, did not read or understand verse as much as people in Butler's England or John Trumbull's New England used to. After puttering over "The Modern Chevalier" for many months (probably through much of 1788 and 1789), Brackenridge put the verses aside and turned instead to prose. The result was *Modern Chivalry*, the first two volumes of which appeared in Philadelphia, deposited for purposes of copyright with the clerk of that district on 14 February 1792.

Like Whitman with *Leaves of Grass* many years later, Brackenridge was to spend the rest of his life expanding and "improving" this formless tale of the wanderings and adventures of quixotic Captain Farrago and his bogtrotting Sancho Panza, Teague O'Regan. A third volume was published a year later—this time in Pittsburgh, where it is remembered by historians as the first literary work both written and printed west of the Alleghenies. A fourth volume appeared in Philadelphia in 1797, many of its incidents inspired by the Whiskey Rebellion of a few years before. Brackenridge, whose eyewitness account of *Incidents of the Insurrection in the Western Parts of Pennsylvania* (Philadelphia, 1795) had increased his reputation as an intelligent observer and commentator, meanwhile had done well as a lawyer. He built himself a fine house, and in 1799 was appointed to the Supreme Court of Pennsylvania. Some wealth came to him, and much fame; but he still had things to say, though he cannily disguised them with satiric humor which he called "nonsense"— "this being," he explained, "the only way to keep out of the reach of criticism." Sedition laws made plain speech dangerous—a truth known also to his friend Freneau, who wrote his own satirical observations in the person of an imagined Robert Slender, a weaver, who knew nothing of politics or anything else, except what he read in the newspapers.

In 1804 and 1805 two new volumes of *Modern Chivalry, Part II*, appeared in Carlisle, Pennsylvania, where Judge Brackenridge now sat in court; it attacked skunk-scented journalism, the economic programs of Jefferson and Gallatin, and popular prejudices (shared by Brackenridge's old friend Freneau) against everything British. In 1815 an edition of all six volumes appeared (in Philadelphia and Richmond), to which were added new materials in which Brackenridge ridiculed Erasmus Darwin's theories of evolution and the folly of allowing untrained men to attain positions of command during the War of 1812. Further additions were planned, which would see Teague O'Regan finally becoming the United States ambassador to the Court of St. James; but Brackenridge died on 25 June 1816, without carrying them to completion. Three years later a revised final edition of *Modern Chivalry* was issued by his son, containing all parts previously published, "with corrections and alterations made by the author."

Like *Don Quixote*, Sterne's *Tristram Shandy*, and Fielding's *Tom Jones*, all of which must often have been in Brackenridge's mind as he wrote, *Modern Chivalry* is a tale of adventuring, episodic and repetitive—what is generally known, perhaps with not too much discrimination, as a picaresque novel. But whatever

169

its European antecedents, it is distinctively an American book, not just because of its homespun, native characters and its often slapstick, broad humor which links it casually to Irving's "Legend of Sleepy Hollow" (1820), to Augustus B. Longstreet's *Georgia Scenes* (1835), and to Seba Smith's accounts of the escapades of Jack Downing during the 1830s and 1840s; but also because it is a narrative of journeying and questing, like *The Adventures of Huckleberry Finn* or, at farther remove, *Moby Dick*—another of those tales, loosely strung, which it seems might go on and on, without plotted ending. There is no central story to *Modern Chivalry*, except the journeying and the adventures met on the way: it contains one elastically adaptable situation and a single theme. Like Cooper's *Home As Found* (1838) and H. L. Mencken's bellicose jocosities a century later, it stands firm on its premise that democracy as practiced in America is a good thing ("beyond all question," said Brackenridge, "the freest government"); [11] but that it is subject to amazing malfunctionings when tinkered with by bumbling, ignorant, or conscienceless men.

It is not necessary to study Brackenridge's biography nor to follow his public career as politician and occasional writer in newspapers of his time to understand that he was a loyal American democrat who thought his own thoughts, unencumbered by what other people supposed that he should think, for *Modern Chivalry* makes that plain. A Jeffersonian Democrat who was rewarded with a judgeship for his contributions to politics, he recognized the shortcomings of his own party as candidly as he did those of the opposition. The enemy was not narrowly political; it was human greed and human stupidity, and man's failure to recognize the place which his talents have prepared for him.

Captain Farrago is a good-natured caricature of the Jeffersonian agrarian ideal—a small farmer, well-read and well-mannered, who had patriotically enlisted for the defense of his country (stumbling his way through the army with a commission which he was not always sure that he knew how to use), and who then returned to cultivate his lands and observe his countrymen, quick to correct and admonish. If his first thought was always of himself, his comfort and his persistent concern that, by whatever means, he must keep his servant with him, to curry his horse and shine his boots, the captain is nonetheless an honest republican, whose second and longer thoughts are deviously humane and generous. That he rides while his servant walks, that he sips wine in the parlor while Teague eats in the kitchen or pigs it in the stable with the hostlers, that Farrago is a gentleman and the bog-trotter certainly is not—these things are intentional and subtle commentaries on democracy in Brackenridge's time, which even small stretching of imagination can make apply to other times as well.

Only the most matter-of-fact reader will accept verbatim everything which Brackenridge has to say, even in those chapters "Containing Observations" or "Containing Reflections," in which he seems to step aside from the narrative, as Fielding did in *Tom Jones*, to comment in his own voice. He is a wily and unreliable witness, whether talking of his purpose in writing, the books which have influenced him—and what an impressive listing it is: Rabelais, Le Sage, Cervantes, Swift, and all the rest, the plainness of his style, or his attitudes toward the American Philosophical Society, the American Indian, or the aristocratic Order of the Cincinnati. As a humorist he can stand aside, recognizing that serious advocates for any single aspect of a question are likely to appear ridiculous, but also that his own mediating attitudes are often ridiculous. The sensible man, he seems to say, will recognize that intelligent, informed, disinterested reasoning is necessary for the solution of every problem—whether it is concerned with dueling or voting or meddling with servant girls; but that even so rational a man as Captain Farrago or the narrator himself is finally caught up in the inevitable, human, lovable, laughable trap of self-interest.

To find ridiculous only what Brackenridge seems repetitively to attack is to lose much of the finer flavor of his satire. Physicians, lawyers, clergymen, army veterans, strong-armed and strong-voiced politicians, makers of treaties with underprivileged people, mob violence, and lovesickness all come under his bantering, double-edged observations. Most people, by and large, are foolish. Brackenridge, to be sure, is serious about the dangers of popular suffrage; he manifestly distrusts the Indian and says some scurrilous things about the Negro—though many readers will agree with his quizzical logic which explains that, of course, Eve was black; he cared little for the Order of the Cincinnati, and spoke of that tediously at length in bad verse which he cannily pretends was someone else's, but he indubitably would not have liked later democratic veterans' groups either. Whatever historians may say of his attitudes as being representative, either of the best thought or of the most ill-considered judgments of his time, most readers will not pause long over them, nor worry much about them,[12] but will accept Brackenridge's "playful satire," not in the manner of "weak brethren, who might be offended," but for "the pleasure that a little mirth gives."[13]

For it is not Brackenridge's ideas which can give continuing life to *Modern Chivalry*, nor even his assurance that "the people are a sovereign, and greatly despotic; but, in the main, just": these only reserve it a place on the historian's shelf as a quaint and curious volume, valuable in explaining how strangely people sometimes used to think, one more testimony to be added to other books which do the same thing as well. It is the episodes, humorous and humane, and the lively, plainspoken words which Brackenridge finds for talking about them, which can certify the book as still alive. Sometimes they will produce only the kind of thoughtless guffaw which slapstick usually elicits; but at another time, they coax a quiet smile. Some readers, when presented with Teague befeathered and caged, will recall Melville's later presentation in *Israel Potter* of a manacled Ethan Allen who was also made the sport of curious, well-meaning people, or, fiction submitting to fact, Ezra Pound caged on the parade ground at Pisa. Brackenridge's language, particularly in the early versions, before he cleaned it up for respectable presentation in the revised posthumous edition of 1819, is simple, direct, colloquial, and sometimes coarse. He calls a hussy a hussy, speaks with natural familiarity of bodily functions, and does not feel that he needs to use dashes or asterisks when it is necessary to have a character described as a son of a bitch. Many years would pass, and much public and private censorship, before everyday speech was more faithfully recorded, or the activities of ordinary people presented with such unblushing candor.

Not all of *Modern Chivalry* will please all palates. Some of it is riotously vulgar, its humor too broad, its dialect exaggerated. Some of its stories will be dismissed as old chestnuts, often cracked open before. Brackenridge's straight-faced suggestions about what to do to the Indians or about Negroes or Irishmen may seem bluntly inhumane, offensive to readers of strong opinion. Many will find the book uneven, with too many pages devoted to too little matter or to chattering irrelevancies. Others will inevitably regard it as a quaint artifact, revelatory of idiosyncrasies among their forebears and proof of their own advance. Many more, however, may accept it for what it is—perhaps, as Brackenridge said of it, "a book without thought, or the smallest degree of sense"; certainly not as a testimony to man's tragic plight, but as a stalwart but stumbling ancestor of other American books which have dared the sacrilegious, comic view that man is queer and crotchety and that he strays often from the path of righteousness, but that he is about the best that can be had or enjoyed or scolded. Teaque O'Regan had less good sense than Huckleberry Finn, and fewer moments of grace—unlike Huck, he yearned to be "civilized," and all at once; but as much as Huck, he was his own worst enemy, and, as an observer and commentator or as a person to be observed and commented on, he is every reader's good friend. Captain Farrago never did cut him down completely; not even Brackenridge could laugh him off the stage. He was sturdy, sometimes honest, and not always bright; but he prevailed. We recall that he eventually was nominated as an ambassador—and to the Court of Saint James. What followed after that, we are not told.

NOTES

1. *Modern Chivalry*, ed. Lewis Leary (New York, 1965), p. 26.

2. The standard biography of Brackenridge is Claude Milton Newlin, *The Life and Writings of Hugh Henry Brackenridge* (Princeton, N.J., 1932) to which I am greatly indebted; see also Daniel Marder, *Hugh Henry Brackenridge* (New York, 1967).

3. For a model of modern textual scholarship, see J. F. S. Smeall, "The Roles of Brackenridge and Freneau in Composing 'The Rising Glory of America,'" *Papers of the Bibliographical Society of America* 67 (3rd Quarter 1973): 263–282.

4. Lewis Leary, *That Rascal Freneau: A Study in Literary Failure* (New Brunswick, N.J., 1941), p. 45.

5. Newlin, *Life and Works,* p. 59.

6. *United States Magazine* 1 (January 1779): 3–4.

7. Newlin, *Life and Works,* p. 51.

8. Ibid., p. 59.

9. Ibid., p. 106.

10. Ibid., p. 114.

11. *Modern Chivalry,* p. 42.

12. Brackenridge's political and social views are set forth in Newlin, *Life and Works,* pp. 112–123, 251–266, and 300–304, and in his edition of *Modern Chivalry* (New York, 1937), pp. xxviii–xl.

13. *Modern Chivalry,* p. 184.

John Blair Linn

1777–1805

❦ ❦

THE literary generation in America which produced the novels of Charles Brockden Brown, the essays of Joseph Dennie, and the plays of William Dunlap brought forth no poet whose product could stand against even the small measure of excellence set by these three—unless it was John Blair Linn. Yet he and his verse made small impact on his own times and have made hardly any at all on ours. His contemporaries explained away his failure by admitting that, "though unquestionably a man of genius," Linn "experienced no extraordinary vicissitudes, achieved no romantic adventures, visited no distant regions, and died at a juvenile age."[1] Our century, in excess perhaps of masculinity, has been content to list him among America's early "cooing and whimpering weaklings"—too puny for work and therefore sent to college, decadents nourished only on decay.[2]

In tolerance, John Blair Linn deserves a better epitaph. He did die at twenty-seven of consumption. But he left behind him, in addition to five volumes of verse, three volumes of prose, a play which had been presented on the New York stage, an impressive list of periodical publications, and a large local reputation as an orator. Few men of his time, at his age, had done more. But for all this, John Blair Linn is without any doubt a very minor, though not, therefore, necessarily an unimportant transitional poet. No line that he wrote is significant today, except as it helps explain the sterile and, on the whole, neglected literary period in which he lived. He apparently influenced no one, and he never quite solved, even for himself, the problems which confronted a young man born to the traditions of the eighteenth century and growing toward maturity amid the freer, sometimes it must have seemed deteriorating, influences of the early nineteenth century. As he fumbled through the confusion of his time, he inevitably recognized its hesitation between law and license as symptomatic of the social and religious dilemma which also confronted his countrymen. Though his gropings came to no good or convincing end, for him or for his contemporaries, they may suggest some few of the reasons why, amid the intellectual and emotional turmoils of the nineteenth century, America did not produce a poet.

John Blair Linn inherited good Scotch-Irish blood both from his mother and his father. William Linn, born in backcountry Pennsylvania in 1752 of emigrant parents, probably met Rebecca Blair first at Princeton, where her father was professor of divinity and where William Linn attended college in company with Aaron Burr, Philip Freneau, and James Madison.[3] After graduation and a short term of conducting school in Philadelphia,[4] William Linn was ordained a minister of the Presbyterian church, served as a chaplain in the Continental army, and married Rebecca Blair, before settling as pastor at Big Spring (now Newville) in Pennsylvania. There he remained for seven years, and there on 14 March 1777 his oldest son was born and named for his maternal grandfather.

When the boy was seven his father left Pennsylvania to become president of Washington College in Maryland. Two years later he answered a call to the Presbyterian Church in Elizabethtown, New Jersey, but remained there only a few months before receiving, in November 1786, an invitation to become copastor of the Collegiate Dutch Reformed Church in New York. From this point onward William Linn's life was filled with activity and honors. He became, successively, a regent of the University of the State of New York, first chaplain of the House of Representatives and an intimate in the household of General and Mrs. Washington, acting president for three years of Queens College (Rutgers), and, just before his death in 1808, was elected president of Union College in Schenectady. He was famed as an orator, a liberal theologian, an active ecclesiastical politician, a great writer of pamphlets, and an ardent advocate of church unity—a fighter, said one of his contemporaries, who did his best to "break down the disgraceful barriers of useless distinctions between Protestant sects."[5] "Christians," he insisted, "require only to know and understand one another better in order to be united in love."[6] Even in the fact of the onrushing menace of Methodism, he preserved equanimity: "The only way to counteract them is to outpray and outpreach them. . . . I love to see zeal in religious matters even if a little wild."[7]

His only son early showed zeal which, though not for many years abundantly religious, must have been heartening to his father. When, at the age of nine, John Blair Linn was put into the hands of the "several respectable" but now anonymous teachers which New York afforded, he was already advanced in the study of Latin and was reputed—as are most young men who later become writers—to have even then "exhibited a strong attachment to books."[8] At fourteen he was ready for Columbia College. Here in addition to the regular courses in the classics, mathematics, and natural and moral philosophy, he must have attended with more than compulsory interest the lectures in rhetoric and belles lettres delivered each week by Pres. William Samuel Johnson. Here he received "a complete course of instruction . . . in the art of writing and speaking . . . with propriety, elegance and force—the rules and principles of true taste and the rules of just criticism." Each Saturday, he, like every other student in the college, submitted to the president an original composition, for correction in spelling, grammar, style, and sentiment.[9]

As a student, John Blair Linn seems to have been thoroughly normal, a lively and popular young man, not particularly conscientious, and fond of innocent roistering. At seventeen he certainly had no intention of following his learned father's profession: "Hard is the solitary parson's lot, / Wrapt in the gloom of poverty and care."[10] He had, one of his classmates remembered, "a bias for pleasure, a taste for it; so much so, that I have often . . . wondered how he escaped its pollution as he did."[11] His college days were apparently carefree and easy so that he could later look back with some nostalgia to the time "When Academic bell, which called to pray'r / Rous'd us from couches undisturb'd by care."[12]

By the end of his junior year at Columbia, seventeen-year-old John Blair Linn had established some local reputation as a young man of letters. His verse and prose had been appearing in the *New-York Magazine* since February 1794 over the fashionable pseudonym of "Æmulus," side by side with writings from such eminent New Yorkers as William Dunlap, Samuel Latham Mitchill, James Kent, and Josiah Ogden Hoffman. His first contribution to the *New-York Magazine*—and, so far as is presently discovered, his first published writing—was an essay in prose entitled "The Young Compositor," which was "Designed to expose the errors of youth" and was composed, Linn later tells us, "at a much earlier period of his life than any other performance" which he cared to preserve.[13] In spite of his apologies for it, the essay is not without merit, and is significant in our study of Linn because it strikes for the first time a note which he was often to repeat. "The chief end of writing," he insists, "is to be understood, and simplicity in stile must then be best." He attacks with youthful recklessness both the turgidity of the great Samuel Johnson and the excesses of "flowery writers . . . who delight in pleasing the ear more than improving the mind."[14] Such commonsense pronouncements were drawn straight from Scotch Hugh Blair's *Lectures in Rhetoric and Belles Lettres*, the textbook from which President Johnson hammered home principles of composition to his students at the college.

As a young poet, however, Linn already allowed himself the young poet's right to inconsistency as he developed his thesis. "To the imagination," he rhapsodized:

> man owes some of the most pleasing moments of his life; it wafts him to celestial regions, unseen, untrod, and brings to his contemplative view, those beautiful and captivating scenes which none but she herself can paint. It is she that paints the lovely grottoes, the verdant vallies and spreading lawns, the retreats of muses, and the gentle streams which meander through them; she brings to the view of the youthful lover, the charming form of his Amelia, and dwells with the pleasing prospect, when she shall be his. She [we are not quite sure whether the antecedent is "Imagination" or the charming "Amelia"] presents to youth honor, fame, reward.

Linn's contemporaries must have recognized this as nothing at all new. The same thing had been better said half a century before by Joseph Warton in his "Ode to Fancy," and again almost within Linn's lifetime by his father's classmate, young Philip Freneau, when he, too, was an undergraduate. Coleridge would soon state it with more discrimination and more effective finality. But it was a pleasing thought, always popular and apparently well received. As to shackling the imagination, Linn—perhaps smarting as a student under the necessity of revising his weekly themes—spoke feelingly: "When it flows naturally," he said, "[it] is an evidence of genius," and no writer endowed with this heaven-given gift ought ever "to mend the language in which the idea presents itself," for then, though "the language is raised, the thought is fallen."[15] This in America in 1794 is either youth or romanticism, or both.

But if in his critical theory Linn seemed to face even tentatively toward the future, he certainly in his poetry looked directly into the pages of current literary periodicals which featured solid, eighteenth-century sentimentalism. There is lilt to his verse as he pictures the sorrows of a shepherd lad who mourns for his rustic companion:

> Eliza! ah, who can describe?
> Who her beauty and charms can unfold?
> Who can paint great Sol in his pride
> When he mounts his bright chariot of gold?[16]

But there are echoes here of many other charming songs. And so there are still further echoes when, in another issue of the magazine, Linn describes the misery of an American captive with the gentle but anachronistic name of "Almeran," who wastes away in a melancholy Algerian prison, "far from the voice of Julia and of Love," far from Columbia's "happy cultur'd fields" where "Freedom's charms" are known to all.[17] As a sophisticated young man of his time, Linn joined other magazinists in paying graceful poetical tribute to the sentimental bluestockings whose snippets in verse were popular in the "Poet's Corner" of so many American periodicals, when in his third contribution to the *New-York Magazine*, he attested: "When beauteous Adeline atunes her lyre, / Each poet-bosom thrills with genial fire."[18]

Apparently encouraged by the reception of his periodical contributions, Linn soon planned to publish a whole volume of his own. It was to be a surreptitious undertaking, known only to his most intimate companions. By the end of June 1794 not much more than a month after his seventeenth birthday, he distributed proposals among his classmates, his friends in the city, and acquaintances up the Hudson, in Albany. He self-consciously admitted nervous anxiety as a "youth about to enter the field of criticism," but was at the same time hardheaded enough to warn his agents not to allow any volume out of their hands "without having first received the cash."[19] Though the work seems to have been ready for the printer by the end of September, it did not appear until six months later, in the late spring of 1795. One hundred and seventy-two subscribers had been procurred for 194 copies of *The Miscellaneous Works, Prose and Poetical,* issued from the press of Thomas Greenleaf anonymously as "By a Young Gentleman of New York." Livingstons, Roosevelts, Schuylers, Van Dorens, Pauldings, and Irvings were all represented among Linn's patrons. It was backing of which any young man of his time might have been proud.

The Miscellaneous Works is a curious melange of the didactic and the sentimental, in verse, critical essays, and prose fiction. It bears the stamp of its time and of its author's youth. It was "sent into the world without apologies," though Linn did in candor admit that "the Author has many to offer." In it we find the inevitable plaintive address to that thoroughly un-American bird, the nightingale; in it, also, the equally inevitable, plaintive elegy to a deceased fair maiden, and odes to melancholy, to the sorrows of reflection, and to solitude: "Thy haunts, O Solitude! I love to rove, / Along thy lawns, beneath thy shady grove." In solitude the poet might soft indulge his "bosom's secret thought" and "bid the tear of dubious sorrow flow." Linn admired "flow'ry dales" and "murmuring streams," by which one might listen quietly to the "songster's plaintive song," and where the "voice of noisy man," the "clam'rous discord of the town" never intruded. Here the "brownish thrush" (his one native reference) tunes his "clear mellifluous lay" while "Philomela resumes her evening tale." Here "music and silence hold their tranquil reign" and trembling moonbeams consecrate the scene. Here alone, while evening shadows remind the contemplative wanderer of sad "humanity's appointed lot," may the poet's "bleeding heart" find solace.[20] Readers of poetry at the end of the eighteenth century in America admired such sentiments. They were sad enough to make one feel good, and they stimulated memory of many other sad songs about tombs and tears and solitude and death. Yet these lines were not entirely imitative. John Blair Linn simply looked into his sensitive adolescent heart and wrote. He tells us a great deal, both of his own fine poetic frenzy and of the writers who in his reading fed it, in his portrait of "The Poet":

> Musing he sits upon a limping chair
> And on his hand reclines his thoughtful head;
> His rolling eye-balls on the ceiling stare,
> And a slow tribute to reflection shed.
>
> His ragged floor, neglected papers spread,
> Some dirty books display their grief worn forms,
> There Richard Blackmore rears his *epic* head,
> And Richard Savage, dauntless bard of storms.
>
> Sad Otway, Dryden, Butler, Swift, arise,
> Sweet Pope, smooth Thompson, Nature's fav'rite son,
> There youthful Chatterton salutes the eyes,
> And *he* who Rome's Augustine laurels won.   (P. 97)

Young Linn was an apprentice, learning his trade from many popular masters, from Gray, Shenstone, even from Robert Merry, who "breathes in many lines the pure strain of poetry" (p. 124). He read into Chatterton gloomy portents of each young poet's doom. Gray's "Elegy" was clearly before him as he wrote:

> Serene the eve, the sun's withdrawn his light,
> Luna has risen with her twinkling train,
> The whirring bat, now wheels in rapid flight,
> Hush'd is the breeze that whispered o'er the plain.
>   (P. 125)

Later he must have opened beside it something from Blair or Thomson to give dark and funereal overtones to such lines as

> The dusky raven sends its mournful cry,
> The distant thunder repercussive roars,
> The fading light faint glimmers on my eye
> Now sable night his frightful curtain lowers.
>
> (P. 147)

He versified Ossian into conventionally rhyming iambic pentameters and turned "David's Elegy over Saul and Jonathan" into equally conventional couplets. Even when he attempted an American theme, in "The Discovery of Tobacco," and knew that neither the "grandeur of Homer's epic song" nor the "music of Barlow's lay" was suitable to his subject, his English models were with him. Gray is again heard in "The precious plant with greenish hue serene, / Here breath'd its fragrance, here it blushed unseen" (p. 162). And Shakespeare's "The man that hath not music in himself" is also heard:

> The man who not in pouch tobacco keeps,
> Nor hath not pipes laid up in numerous trays,
> Is led by rapine and by wrath's control.   (P. 166)

As a writer of fictional prose narrative Linn also faithfully imitated popular standards. The achievement of Washington Irving, Hawthorne, and Poe seems infinitely remote when viewed against the background of such a tale as, for example, Linn's "History of Elvira." The scene is a country seat near London (a locale of which Linn, of course, knew nothing at first hand). The heroine, beautiful, pale, and sad, is the only daughter and sole consolation of her widowed father, a retired army officer. She meets and, in innocence, falls in love with Charles Harmer, a handsome but an evil young man. "When guarded by the most accurate hypocrisy," Linn moralizes, "how could an unsuspicious female penetrate into the real character of a lover, especially when that hypocrisy is connected with beauty, and manners the most refined and engaging?" Then a good young man enters the story, Capt. George Dormer, formerly an officer under Elvira's father, who is now searching for his lost sister, the beautiful, the wronged Isabella. His search seems in vain, until one day Elvira, musing alone in her favorite woodland retreat, sees lying on the forest floor the figure of a girl whose clothes are in disarray, whose hair is wild, and whose eyes are red with weeping. It is, of course, Isabella, and even distraught with misery she is beautiful. She, too, had loved handsome Charles Harmer, had allowed her affectionate and trusting heart to rule her reason until now, alas, deserted, she is forever ruined. Elvira then so effectively charges the errant young man with his guilt that he repents, and marries Isabella. And Captain George? "Need we add," Linn concludes, "that he did conduct himself in such a manner, as to win the affections of Elvira, and to bestow on her the name of Dormer, as well as that of a mother" (pp. 177–201).

Linn's early critical essays are scarcely more original than his verse or his narrative prose. His remarks "On Poetry," "On Descriptive Poetry," "On Elegiac Poetry," "Of Hope and Reflection" are little more than free paraphrases or extensions of the solidly reasoned conclusions which he found in his college book of Blair's *Rhetoric*. "Blair has taught us," the young man confessed a year later, "all the critic's rage."[21] Yet it is perhaps worth our while to pause for a moment to consider with this young collegian of 1795 exactly what he thought of the art to which he aspired. "Poetry," he tells us, "is the language of passion and fancy." For instruction one may seek the philosophical writer, but "when we seek amusement blended with instruction, we explore the beautiful walks of the muses, where the senses are more captivating, and where nature promiscuously rises to our view." Poetry "harmonizes the soul, and animates it. . . . The breast of sensibility is touched by its pensive strain." Solitude is the poet's best delight: "he counts her the parent of reflection." Like Pope at Twickenham, the poet reclines "beneath her cooling shade, where naught can disturb his meditation: he listens to the music of the grove, and the distant fall of some running stream— "It is there he receives the inspiration of the Muse." Yet, as he stumbles through rhapsodic and overadjectived descriptions of the wild and lonely loveliness of nature, he reminds himself that simple phrasing is best. "Pedantry," he said, "is unamiable in youth." One ought to "adorn his style with the garb of neatness, but ought not to deck it with too many flowers."[22] Linn clearly

did not know where he stood amid the confusion of what his readings told him should be written and the frantic promptings of his
own adolescent sensibility.

Meanwhile, this young poet had to make a living. In casting
about for a profession, Linn first turned to law and read for
several months under the supervision of his father's friend,
Alexander Hamilton, who had recently retired from public office
and resumed practice in New York. But legal studies did not suit
his errant fancy: "his favourite authors continued to engage most
of his attention; and his attachment to poetry acquired new
force."[23] And well it might, for extracts in verse and prose from
The Miscellaneous Works were appearing with gratifying regularity and heartwarming approbation in some of the best local
periodicals. The editor of the new and fashionable *Lady and
Gentleman's Pocket Magazine* suggested "that the friends to the
profession of science and Belles Lettres in America, will look
with favourable eye" on the productions of so young a man. "The
catalogue of American poets, though small is respectable—and we
anticipate its augmentation by the addition of a Linn to the names
already high on the list of fame."[24]

Soon subscription papers were distributed for another volume.
Only 150 individuals—including, however, Alexander Hamilton,
David Ramsey, and James Kirk Paulding—signed for the work.
When it appeared early in 1796 as *The Poetical Wanderer*, this
second book must have been a disappointment to its young author.
It was only roughly stitched into a cheap, blue cover: "complete
binding," the printers explained, "could not be performed without loss, calculated from the . . . number of subscribers." In
content it exhibited little advance over the first volume of a year
before. The same type of derivative essay was to be found: "The
Early Poetry of Greece," "On Tragic Poetry," "On the Power
of Noble Actions on the Mind." One fictional narrative was included—"Rinaldo: A Gothic Fragment," a melancholy episode
in a moldering castle at midnight. As an apprentice, Linn still
experimented, groping a little more boldly for an idiom of his
own. "Oscar: A Poem" is in rhythmic and alliterative prose, "in
imitation of the manner of Ossian." "Oenone: The Distressed
Shepherdess" is "imitated from Ovid"; the "Ode to Supersti-

tion" is "in imitation of Collins"; and "Hope: An Irregular Ode" is an exercise with the meters of Pindar. Linn was still reading widely, in Milton now, in Otway and Schiller, and in the Greek poets. He tried his hand at blank verse, very regular and sedate: "When will the world resume its wonted state? / When will those Grecian days again return?"[25]

In spite of inevitable discouragement at the lack of interest in his second volume, Linn continued to toy with literary projects. He enjoyed the cultural opportunities of New York, and the theater, we are told, became his chief passion. By the end of the year, Linn had himself written a play—"a serious drama, interspersed with songs"[26]—which was accepted by John Hodgkinson and William Dunlap, joint managers of the Old American Company. *Bourville Castle; or, The Gallic Orphan,* it was called, and Hodgkinson himself was to play the title role. How much of the drama as presented at the John Street Theatre on the evening of 16 January 1797 was in the form Linn had originally written it, however, we do not know. Both William Dunlap and Charles Brockden Brown, who was visiting in New York at the time, had some hand in revising it and preparing copy for the performers.[27] But even with their expert assistance, *Bourville Castle* was not considered successful enough on its debut ever to be presented a second time. No copy of the manuscript has survived, and what seems to have been the only press notice of the performance appeared two days later in the New York *Minerva*—written probably by Brockden Brown himself.[28]

Linn's distaste for legal studies increased as the year wore on. "The distrust which I contracted for the law," he later admitted to his father, "might perhaps chiefly arise from a sickly and over delicate taste. The pages of Coke and Blackstone contained to my apprehension, nothing but horrid jargon." He could not bear the "tricks and artifices" of law, the "enlisting of all one's wit and wisdom in the service of any one that could pay for them." None of his friends, then, could have been greatly surprised that, in this frame of mind, Linn turned to the ministry. Nor, remembering the young man's predilection for pleasure, could they have been surprised that he was removed from distractions of city life, with its playhouses, its bookshops, and its minor convivialities, to Schenectady, where his father's friend, the Reverend Dirck Romeyn, one of the founders of Union College, had recently been appointed a professor of theology by the Reformed Dutch Church.

His mind had been "restless and uneasy, and continually on the wing," but in the "state of comparative solitude" which he found in his new, more rural surroundings, Linn discovered a new, "sober and quiet peace," where he might "abstract himself from the world, and, with the least interruption possible prepare himself for the solemn employment in view."[29] John Romeyn, a Columbia classmate, and Alexander McLeod, a serious young Scotchman, were his fellow students, both of them also literary and both, like Linn, eager to see their productions in print. They wrote essays and little poems for the local papers,[30] and spent hours together in discussions of life and literature. John Romeyn remembered Linn as a student "capable of deep research, though constitutionally indisposed to it. His genius was poetic. He always preferred a poem, or criticisms of polite literature, to any other species of composition."[31] But in these surroundings and in this company, the young poet seems to have been happy. "I regret not," he wrote his father, "the gay objects of New-York which I have exchanged for the now dreary scenes of Schenectady. The pleasures of my former life were too often pleasures of an hour, leaving behind them the anxiety of days and years." He was very young, very sincere and pious: "The applause of men I no longer prize, and self approbation becomes every day of greater value."[32]

After almost two years at Schenectady, Linn in the late autumn of 1798 was licensed to preach by the Chassis of Albany. He had received an M.A. from Union College the year before, and another *in absentia* from Columbia that spring. His studies completed, he set out again for New York. On 11 November 1798 his father wrote to Romeyn: "My son is not yet returned. I have heard of his preaching in several places up the North River. I expect him shortly, & that he will agreeably to your recommendation, spend this winter in close application to his studies."[33] We suspect that the younger Linn's tour of preaching was so planned as to allow him to tarry as long as possible in the vicinity of

Poughkeepsie, where lived Col. John Bailey and his daughter, Hester, who is remembered as a "young lady of beauty and merit," and with whom Linn is said to have been carrying on for some time a very serious and, we may be sure, a very poetic courtship.[34]

In February of the next year Linn was recipient of an extremely flattering call from the First Presbyterian Church at Elizabeth in New Jersey. Formal notice from the elders, deacons, and trustees, promising him "proper respect, encouragement and obedience," together with a salary of three hundred pounds a year, was sent to him on 24 February.[35] But at just this time he was also offered the position of assistant to the venerable John Ewing at the more fashionable First Presbyterian Church at Philadelphia. He preached for five weeks on trial, until on 1 April the congregation unanimously voted to elect him copastor, at thirteen hundred dollars a year and with a manse at 165 Walnut Street. In New York again on 18 May he married Hester Bailey,[36] but then returned to settle in Philadelphia, where on 13 June he was ordained and two weeks later installed in his office.[37]

The young clergyman liked his new surroundings. "I still grow more and more pleased with my situation in life," he wrote six months later, "and I hope that God may make me the instrument of some good." He fell readily into the religious activities of the community, and did his best to get his two friends, McLeod and Romeyn, placed there in the same city with him.[38] The Reverend John Ewing, who served in double capacity, both as senior minister of the First Church and as provost of the University of Pennsylvania, was almost seventy, and much of the burden of preaching and of pastoral duties must have fallen on the younger man. But Linn enjoyed both. "Few persons in America," one of his associates tells us, "ever attained so great a popularity as a pulpit orator." His manner was found "peculiarly attractive" by another, who praised his public discourses: "Chaste, impassioned and energetic, they irresistibly seize upon the mind and fix the attention. His figures are bold, varied and not infrequently sublime." Contemporaries were impressed by his "strain of ardent and unaffected piety."[39] He spoke as a poet, divinely inspired.

Philadelphia was full of people important for a young man to

know. Pres. John Adams was a member of the Presbyterian congregation, and "was pleased," said Linn, "to give me the freedom of his house at all times."[40] Members of Congress and
equally distinguished members of the American Philosophical
Society were to be met on every hand. At the bookshop of Asbury
Dickens on Second Street, the literati of the city met almost every
morning. They formed a "constellation of American genius,"
said the English traveler, John Davis, "in whose blaze I was
almost consumed."[41] Here were to be found Charles Brockden
Brown who was becoming better and better known as a novelist
of native distinction, Joseph Dennie who was setting the city
straight on all literary matters in his weekly *Port Folio*, Charles
Jared Ingersoll whose tragedy of *Edwy and Elgiva* had recently
been produced with success, and a group of other young men,
none of whom would ever be as famous as their more worthy
fathers—Richard, son of Dr. Benjamin Rush; Philip, son of
Alexander Hamilton; and Samuel Ewing, who wrote graceful
verses over the pseudonym of "Jacques." From this group was
recruited the Tuesday Club which held its weekly meetings often
at the home of Joseph Hopkinson, and in whose programs John
Blair Linn soon apparently took an active part.[42] Nowhere in
America was there at this time a more active or a more stimulating literary society.

Spurred by these associations, Linn again turned actively to
writing. When the death of Washington in December 1799 presented him with a subject worthy of his most serious effort, he
composed a prose poem of some twenty pages "in imitation of
the manner of Ossian." It was a form of which he was particularly fond, in which he had experimented at length in both his
earlier volumes. His present subject demanded freedom, he
thought, for "when great grief or joy affects the soul, our expressions cannot be subjected to the rules of art. A sudden exclama-
tion, in seeming irregularity and incoherent sentences, evidences
that the speaker feels more than he expresses."[43] This was very
romantic, very modern, and very true, but the sorrowful meanderings which Linn produced were not popular among his contemporaries. And, for the first time, he had signed his name to a
publication! Reviewers found *The Death of Washington* un-

couth, grotesque, even debasing. "We should be pleased to see Mr. Linn select a different pattern for his imitation," suggested the New York *Monthly Magazine*, "he has talents which might be successfully employed in a manner more conducive to a lasting reputation."[44]

By December 1800 Linn had a more ambitious literary production in hand. It was not to be, he said "with my former wanton brood the offspring of haste." It was something over which he had worked a long time, had passed around among his friends in Philadelphia. Even his family, who could not always have been pleased with his earlier writings, advised him to publish it.[45] Subscription papers were distributed in New York and Philadelphia; they were sent to his friends in Schenectady and to his father's friend, Jedidiah Morse, in Massachusetts.[46]

Perhaps no serious poetical work in America had ever been greeted with such critical acclaim as *The Powers of Genius* when it appeared in the spring of 1801. Months before its publication, anticipatory notices began to appear in leading American literary periodicals. It should receive, said the *Philadelphia Repository*, the ready patronage of "every gentleman of taste in this country."[47] Joseph Dennie in the *Port Folio* announced that the forthcoming poem "deserved the notice and encouragement of every American";[48] he printed fifty-four lines from it as a preview of what the reader might expect;[49] and he encouraged an exchange of critical remarks from his subscribers on the poet's distinction between taste and genius.[50] Charles Brockden Brown's *Monthly Magazine* in New York was inspired by announcement of Linn's poem to present a trenchant essay on the lack of significant American poetry in the past.[51]

When *The Powers of Genius* finally appeared in April, over the imprint of Asbury Dickens of Philadelphia, notices were equally flattering. The *Port Folio* did chide Linn for the occasional irregularity of his meter,[52] and the *American Review* in New York took him lightly to task for having chosen a firth in Scotland rather than some native stream for the setting of narrative portions: "Are there no love-lorn swains on the banks of the *Schuylkill*, or the Lehi? and do not the *Hudson* and *Dela-*

ware afford scenes equally suitable to the American poet?"[53] But
the volume was popular, and it sold rapidly. More important, it
was noticed with respect in England.[54] A second edition was necessary within a year, "a pleasing proof," said American reviewers,
"of growing attention of our countrymen to native genius."[55]
And when two years later a third edition appeared, published in
London and printed in the "most ornamental manner, with the
smoothest paper, the brightest types," it was understood as a be-
lated acknowledgement by Englishmen that literary genius was
"not wholly unknown on this side of the Atlantic."[56] Americans
were proud to find Linn's poem

> The harbinger of that effulgent blaze,
> Which shall, ere long, with wide diffusive rays,
> Pour on *Columbia's* plains the golden day,
> And *"Powers of Genius"* to a world display.[57]

The Powers of Genius is a disquisition in verse which attempts
a reconciliation between the eighteenth-century "school of taste"
as mirrored through the commonsense exposition of the Scotch
rhetoricians, particularly Hugh Blair and Lord Kames, with
whose works Linn was familiar to the point of unconscious
plagiarism, and the new and growing interest which young men
of letters found in the writings of Ossian and Robert Burns, and
their recent new discoveries of Ariosto and Shakespeare. These
latter, who fit into few of the patterns presented by traditional
criticism of the earlier eighteenth century, represented genius,
free and unrestrained; they were masters of impassioned utterance and divinely inspired insight. "If we examine," said Linn,
"the greatest works of genius that have appeared in the world,
we will find that they were all written without attention to the
rules or directions of any critic": "Taste is confin'd to rules, it
moves in chains, / Genius those fetters and those rules disdains."[58]
The man of genius is the lord of literary creation, servant to no
compulsion except his own invention. Much the same thing Linn
had said before, when he was a boy of seventeen. He reinforced
his statement now with impassioned apostrophe.

It was his purpose, first, to describe genius, then to "describe
its progress, to ascertain the marks by which it may be known,

and to give the prominent features of those writers who have excelled in its different departments" (p. 10), for "Judgement to all in every state is given, / But genius is the rarest boon of heaven" (p. 18). "Genius," he explained, "is the highest power of the soul," yet has seldom been examined with care by critics. Even "uncorrected" by study, it "still overcomes every difficulty and . . . stoops not to the smaller niceties of taste, but, heedless of them, pours along its irresistible course." In America, it was true, there had been few evidences of the power of genius. Linn knew and had faintly praised the writings of his countrymen, Joel Barlow, Timothy Dwight, John Trumbull, and Philip Freneau;[59] but no one of them seemed heaven inspired. Therefore, Linn pleaded:

> Genius! awaken in this new-born land;
> Hold o'er these chimes thy sceptre of command;
> Here wave thy banners; sound thy trump of fame,
> And give to glory the Columbian name!
> Drive darkness far before thy golden ray,
> And let us live beneath thy noon of day! (P. 25)

At root, as we have already seen in his early writings, Linn was unconditionally on the side of active and unrestricted invention. It was a young man's proper domain. In 1800 he was still in temperament particularly sensitive to imaginative suggestion. But he was also bred an eighteenth-century American and a Presbyterian, one who had become a popular young clergymen whose reputation as a churchman depended on his continued advocacy of uncompromising religious and ethical standards. Religion, he explained, is a structure complete, in which there can be no change. It depended on its tradition and on the control which tradition exercised over the sinful passions of men. And literature was second only to religion as "the fountain of our greatest consolation and delight" (p. 8). *The Powers of Genius* was thus written with honest intention of promoting both literature and morals (p. 10).

Religious thought and moral conduct depended on the observance of unequivocal rules, standards, dogmas. So, almost as if in spite of himself, Linn admitted of literature: "The greatest incorrectness is frequently connected with genius. Numerous errors spring up in the most fruitful mind. The rich soil which gave birth to the oak, also produced weeds and sickly flowers" (p. 7). Taste, then, admittedly inferior to genius and admittedly derivative, must impose restrictions on the imagination through exercise of judgment and sensibility. Genius, in short, is not enough. It must be at once strengthened and modified by standards which are superimposed from without. Linn does not pursue the subject as far or as explicitly as many critics before his time and since have done. "Definitions," he temporized, "often rather confuse than enlighten the mind." He quoted Lord Kames, Beattie, Longinus, Hugh Blair, and drew his own poetic conclusion, that "taste is the willing umpire of the soul" (p. 16).

A glance at the writers Linn then most admired explains more than does his own tortuous exposition. Shakespeare, Ariosto, Ossian, and Burns, hampered by no restrictions, were his delight. Outdistancing all was Shakespeare, whose "soul was kindled by no borrowed fire," who "was visited by no beams except those of the sun of nature" (p. 20). Ariosto also "delighted in the sublimity of irregularity" (p. 22). Ossian's "wizard strain" (p. 65) was matched by the simpler but no less "exquisite . . . wild genius" of Burns (p. 24). Below them were ranked many more, Cowley, Cowper, Chatterton. On the other hand, Milton's writings were "mines of intellectual gold," containing many burning thoughts of genius (p. 92), and it was to men like Milton and to writers of "polished genius"—such as Virgil, Petrarch, Tasso, Beattie, Cowper, and Gray—that Linn was to give his final, though less enthusiastic approval. Alexander Pope, whom Linn dismissed as with little to recommend him but smoothness of versification (p. 31), is conspicuously absent.

Linn did his best to think through the tangle of evidence which he presented, to resolve his own expressed contradictions. But his loyalties were divided: on the one side was Shakespeare ("this wonderful man"), Ossian, Burns, and Fielding; on the other, Milton, Gray, and Richardson, who were certainly more consistently respectable. What conclusions do appear in *The Powers of Genius* are so hedged about with reservations and restrictions that they are logically meaningless. But, beyond logic, the argument which Linn carries on with himself in this poem is significant, both as an index to his own personality and as a mirror of the American audience for which he wrote. "The fervour of poetry decreases as refinement and learning increase," he said. "Nature loses her simplicity, and assumes the vestment of Art" (p. 68).

Here, clearly, was a respectable young man who examined and, with certain large and conventional reservations, found worthy of approval the rhapsodic or melancholy flights of unrestricted imagination which were beginning to characterize much modern writing. He knew and admired them all—again with respectable reservations—Ossian, Burns, Rousseau, and Mrs. Radcliffe. He championed fiction, which "thrills the fancy of enraptur'd youth," at the same time temporizing with a cautious footnote warning against the dangers of novel reading.[60] Essentially, Linn lacked robustness, in thought and in expression. His allegiance to the new was tentative and timid, retreating every time it was faced with the solid, uncompromising dogma of moral or religious standards. He never solved within himself the conflict between what he seemed intuitively to believe and what his social training and his theological studies taught him. From one point of view, of course, he simply never grew up; from another, he never had the strength to remain young.

Linn's health, which from boyhood had never been robust, by the summer of 1802 had taken a serious turn for the worse. A sunstroke contracted on an overland journey to New York left him with days of violent fever and subsequent addiction to recurrent, unpredictable spells of nausea and dizziness which seriously interfered with his clerical duties. More than once he is said to have conducted services when only the support of the pulpit rails kept him from falling. Each attack brought with it fits of despondency and gloom. He worried about his duty to his family, about his duty to his congregation. He seemed to know with melancholy certainty that the hand of death was on him. Prescience of his own doom must have led him, in the funeral sermon which he preached in September on the death of his elder colleague, John Ewing, to warn his listeners and, perhaps with his own poetic ambitions in mind, to remind himself that "the giddy children of an hour, we on the very brink of the grave indulge in the luxury of a vain imagination, start the phantoms of hope and the objects of pursuit. . . . The iron scythe of time is ever in motion, and men are the grass which falls beneath its sweep."[61]

But for a clergyman of twenty-five, Linn was doing very well. He succeeded Dr. Ewing as senior pastor of the most prominent Presbyterian congregation in Philadelphia. He was active in the formation of a city-wide ministerial association. He moved in the best of social and literary circles. He received the degree of doctor of divinity from the University of Pennsylvania, the youngest man so honored in its history.[62] He had already one son, would have two more, though one of them would not outlive him. Mortality aside, he might look forward to a long career, crowded with many other honors.

When in October 1803 Charles Brockden Brown began the monthly *Literary Magazine and American Register,* Linn became one of its principal contributors, with verse or prose in every issue, signed with the pseudonym "I. O." His lyric style had become more subdued now, and his melancholy chastened to somberness. Thus, in "Lines to Olinda," he mourned pensively:

> Sad echo, from thy mossy hall
>   Didst thou the wanderer see;
> And didst thou answer to her call,
>   And did she speak of me?
> Soft gales of evening, bath'd in dew,
> O! have you seen her as you flew?[63]

He submitted extracts from a long, blank-verse poem which he was writing at the time.[64] His tone was somber, even when he wrote of the "Village Maid,"[65] especially when he pondered sentimentally on "Youth."[66] His own frailty seemed to increase his melancholy as he considered the subject of "Ruins." Only Freneau, and he only occasionally, had in America written better blank verse.

> I like to look upon the waste of time,
> To stand 'mid ruins, while the ruthless wind
> Shakes the old column, and through battered walls

194

Pours his long sullen howl. From such a scene
The mind takes thought, and sadly ponders on
The flight of years, on man, unstable man,
Who walks the earth, and breathes a fitful life,
And falls before the blast that levels all.[67]

Linn's contributions in prose consisted of a series of "Critical Notices" in which he reasserted his literary preferences—but now, for Milton, for Gray and Young.[68] The clergyman's liking for Milton was growing. Appreciation of the author of *Paradise Lost* had become, in fact, a "criterion of the taste and mental elevation" of any reader: "None can fully admire him, but those who are raised above the *profanum vulgus.*" Linn was clearly settling to a maturity in which he no longer see-sawed between the merits of genius uncontrolled and the restrained niceties of taste. Milton's genius was divinely guided, was spoiled by none of the extravagancies of Ossian, of Tasso. His "heavenward flight" made the "bat-wing wheelings" of the modern Wordsworth seem pathetically ludicrous. "I know few performances which have assumed the name of poetry . . . so truly worthless as Wordsworth's *Lyrical Ballads.* . . . His pretended simplicity resembles the vacant-headed girl, who in order to appear interesting and discover more infantile sweetness, hangs her head on her shoulders, points forward a coral lip, and rolls backward and forward a dark eye-ball devoid of speculation."[69]

Growing up or sickness, Presbyterianism or simply the fact that he happened to live in early nineteenth-century America had done something to the brave literary speculation of the younger John Blair Linn. Poetry was divinely inspired, and it had little to do with the fresh, new American scene around him. It was not to be measured in the exact beat of Popean rhyme, nor was it, on the other hand, to be allowed the license of ordinary speech or the subject matter of ordinary events. It was sublime divination, through which earth-bound man caught quick and breathtaking glimpses of God's will. It dealt in superlatives and generalities, because the particular and the commonplace were vulgar. Simplicity of expression which had been Linn's earlier literary ideal was incapable of coping with the close-pressing mysteries of death and immortality which now beset him. His had become

195

the sick man's dramatic certainty that his illness was the world's illness, and that the nostrum needed for the soothing of his own sick spirit was solace for all men.

By April 1803 Linn had sufficiently recovered from his illness to enter a brave and impassioned controversy with Dr. Joseph Priestley, who from his retirement in Northumberland had recently issued a provocative liberal pamphlet entitled *Socrates and Jesus Compared*. A courageous young David setting out in confidence to combat one of the most respected theological giants of the day, Linn based his rebuttal piously on the infallibility of the "word of God which teaches that no one except Jesus Christ ever appeared on this earth in the form of a man who was without sin." "I was nursed,"he explained significantly, "with the strongest prejudices in favour of genius and learning, but there is a voice from Heaven to which I owe a more implicit, a more awful respect."[70] As the controversy developed, each antagonist played carefully with the words by which he would affirm either the humanity or the divinity of Jesus. Priestley had erred, Linn insisted, by elevating the pagan Socrates to such eminence that the Son of God was debased.

Like most theological arguments, it must have seemed to the layman rather pointless. But Linn, girded in obstinate orthodoxy, lashed out hotly—some of his more tolerant contemporaries thought with too much warmth—against the implicit Socinian heresies of the older man. He matched Priestley authority for authority in an impressive display of clerical erudition. Xenophon, Strabo, and Plato were quoted in turn as witnesses against the essential immorality of Socrates and his failure to look beyond the limits of mortality to the grave. Priestley defended himself in a reasoned reply. Then Linn attacked again, this time rebuking with well-documented piety what seemed to him an attack on the absolute divinity of his Lord. From his deathbed Priestley dictated a second reply, in which he again defended his doctrine of the humanity of Jesus and explained, with humility such as Linn never approximated, his admittedly tentative conception of the manner in which God might make his will effective through the persons of many men of different temperaments.[71]

Meanwhile Linn had engaged his leisure hours in the composition of a long narrative poem, "suitable," he protested, "to the profession of a minister of God." It was to be "an attempt to describe some of those persecutions which Christians suffered under the tyrants of Rome, and to exhibit . . . the blessed effects of the light of the gospel, when carried into heathen lands." It was humbly to be offered to the public "as the recreation of one, who, next to the religion of his Saviour, would most zealously endeavour to promote the literature of his country."[72] Early in 1804 he drafted a flattering letter to Bielby Porteus, bishop of London, whose popular poem on death and whose theological writings Linn had found both instructive and delightful, asking permission to dedicate the new poem to his lordship, for whom the American protested admiration "higher than that which I entertain for any Prelate in England."[73]

But, in spite of lip service to orthodoxy, Linn's romantic and fundamentally profane imagination often led him astray as he composed the story of *Valerian*. He does what he said he would do—recount the adventures of a faithful Christian martyr, shipwrecked on a pagan shore, who wins a barbarous, native chieftain and his people to Christianity by manly means, which include the winning of the chieftain's comely daughter for his bride. But the narrative on the whole is poorly handled and the didactic portions are unimpressive. Though in *Valerian*, as in his earlier poems, Linn is greatly derivative, it is in rhapsodic and descriptive passages, in which his imaginative flights are hampered by no control of plot or characterization, that he achieves his greatest success. He breaks away in *Valerian* from the couplet form which had made some portions of *The Powers of Genius* hard and jingling, to an irregular blank verse which he often handles with skill.

Valerian was not published during the poet's lifetime. It appeared in 1805, with an introduction by Charles Brockden Brown, who shortly after Linn's death had married the latter's sister Elizabeth. The poem was to have been Linn's monument: on it he intended, Brown tells us, to entrust his future fame as a man of letters.[74] Joseph Dennie greeted it with mild praise. "The design," he said, "was obviously pious, and the execution, in many instances, perfectly poetical." One needed, however, to plead tolerance for its obvious imperfections: "When it is remembered that it was an unfinished and unrevised work, instead of provoking the severity of criticism, it ought to experience much of the warmth of applause."[75]

During the winter and spring of 1804 Linn had been attacked several times with symptoms which seemed to mark his ailment unmistakably as consumption. Obtaining a leave of absence from his congregation, he had gone for a long holiday to New England to recuperate. Discouraged, he had written from Boston to his father:

> I cannot discover that I have received the least benefit from my voyage or travel, nor have my spirits ascended the smallest degree above their customary pitch. . . . I feel the ruin of an intellect, which, with health, would not have dishonoured you, my family, or my country. I feel the ruin of a heart, which I trust was never deficient in gratitude towards my God, or my worldly benefactors. This heart has always fervently cherished the social affections, but now broods over the images of dispair, and wars ineffectually with the pang which speaks my dissolution.

Returning to Philadelphia in July, he submitted his resignation to the elders of his church. It was not accepted. Through the hot summer months his illness seemed progressively to grow worse, and his spirits lower. In despair, he wrote again to his father. Might he not lead a useful life in some activity less strenuous than that of a clergyman? Should he not resign? "May not a righteous Providence point out this conduct as the only road to health?"

These questions were never answered, for that evening—the evening of 30 August—at 10:30 young Dr. Linn in agony called his wife to his bedside. "I feel something burst within me. Call the family together: I am dying." His sister's fiancé Charles Brockden Brown completes the story: "He had scarcely time to pronounce these words, when his utterance was choked by a stream of blood. After a short interval, he recovered strength and sensibility sufficient to exclaim with fervency, clasping his hands and lifting his eyes, 'Lord Jesus, pardon my transgressions, and receive my soul!' "[76]

So died John Blair Linn at twenty-seven of consumption. What he had wanted to do far exceeded what he was able to accomplish.

He had never been strong, and the kind of poetry he wrote, even the type of religion he defended, may well be attributed to his lack of robustness, what some of his older contemporaries would have called the "morbidity of his constitution," and what one of his classmates helps explain by informing us that Linn "was much under the influence of the fear of death, and a reluctance to dying."[7] Even Brockden Brown in candor was forced to admit that the young clergyman's compositions could be regarded only as "preludes to future exertions, and indications of future excellance." It is futile, then, to speculate today on what Linn might have written. Accepting him as he is, he represents with Joseph Dennie in criticism, William Dunlap in the drama, and Brockden Brown in the novel, more certainly than any other poet of his immediate generation the struggle of American men of letters to catch up all at one jump with the literature of England, to create by imitation a literary culture which would be at once full-blown and distinctively American. He, with his perhaps greater contemporaries, was neither of the quarrelsome and energetic generation of Philip Freneau, Timothy Dwight, and Joel Barlow, nor of the more confident, energetic generation of Washington Irving and Fenimore Cooper.

As we look back over the almost 200 years separating his time from ours, it is easy to be condescending and with aftersight to tell Linn's failures. Torn between such different stylistic masters as Shakespeare, Milton, Gray, Ossian, and Burns, he never did develop an idiom of his own, or—what is perhaps another way of saying much the same thing—never resolved even for himself the social, religious, and literary dilemmas of his changing age by the creation of a single new pattern of thought. We can underline the words of others by pointing out the "cultural lag" demonstrated in Linn's disapproval of Wordsworth and his too languid adherence to Gray. We can suggest that he praised the wrong things in Milton. We can explain that he threw aside the precise correctness of the English neoclassicists, but lacked the artistic imagination (or the experience) of a Poe or even a Lanier which would allow him to fashion new concepts of form or manner. If we wish, we can emphasize his confusion of poetry with religion, which made the voice of the poet a distillation of the voice of God, and the end of poetry uncompromisingly moral. Linn so shared all these faults with his time that we are tempted to put him aside as simply a transitional poet, in a transitional age, caught between the impetus of tradition and the dazzling, revolutionary ideas of the turn of that century.

Yet we cannot quite put him aside. We can blame him for disregarding the example of Philip Freneau, who had found among the simple facts of American life the materials for simple American songs, until we remember that Freneau also when he was a young man aimed at loftier things. Almost alone among his contemporaries Linn applied himself seriously to the problem of determining what we in our day would call "the function of the poet," as an artist and as a member of society. Temporizing and timid as he sometimes was, he did seek, as all poets must, an explanation of the poet's purpose. Shackled by self and environment, he never found it, but he wrought well in giving expression to attitudes of a generation which remembered enough of its schooling in Pope to deliberate cautiously both in relinquishing old convictions and in accepting the brave new ideas which were bursting about them at the beginning of the nineteenth century. Linn never discovered how these stimulating and "American" ideas of all kinds of freedom could be fitted to forms which tradition had taught him would endure. But—like other men before him and since—he called on his countrymen to do what, tied to his time, he found himself unable to do:

> Like Hercules in his cradle, she [America] has manifested a gigantic grasp, and discovered that she will be great. . . . Beneath our skies, Fancy never sickens, nor dies. The fire of poetry is kindled by our storms. Amid our plains, on the banks of our waters, and on our mountains, dwells the spirit of inventive enthusiasm. These regions were not formed, only to echo the voice of Europe: but from them shall yet sound a lyre which shall be the admiration of the world.[78]

NOTES

1. *Port Folio*, n.s. 1 (January 1809): 21.
2. Fred Lewis Pattee, *The First Century of American Literature* (New York, 1935), pp. 363–364.

3. William Linn received his first degree on 12 October 1772 when he delivered a graduating address on "independence of Thought," and his second degree in October 1775; see *New Jersey Archives*, 1st ser. 28 (1899): 273, and *New-York Gazetteer*, 12 October 1775.

4. *Pennsylvania Journal*, 19 May 1773; see Robert Francis Seybolt, "Schoolmasters of Colonial Philadelphia," *Pennsylvania Magazine of History and Biography* 52 (1928): 363, 371.

5. "View of Linn's Sermons," *New-York Magazine* 6 (January 1795): 16.

6. "An Address, Delivered September 25, 1792, at the Annual Commencement at Queens College (New Jersey) to the Young Gentlemen Who Took Their Degrees on That Occasion," *New-York Magazine* 3 (October 1792): 617.

7. MS letter, William Linn to———, 16 April 1793, New York Historical Society.

8. Charles Brockden Brown, "A Sketch of the Life and Character of John Blair Linn," *Port Folio*, n.s. 1 (January 1809): 21–23. See also Linn's "Youth," *Literary Magazine and American Register* 1 (March 1804): 424–425.

9. "The Present State of Columbia College, in New-York," *New-York Magazine* 5 (May 1794): 291.

10. "The Parson: An Elegy," *The Miscellaneous Works, Prose and Poetical*. "By a Young Gentleman of New-York" (New York, 1795), p. 35. The poem is dated "1st October, 1794."

11. John Romeyn, quoted by Charles Brockden Brown in the introduction to *Valerian* (Philadelphia, 1805), p. xxii.

12. "An Epistle to a Friend," *The Powers of Genius* (Philadelphia, 1801), p. 124.

13. 5 (February 1794): 83–86; reprinted in *Miscellaneous Works*, p. 130.

14. Ibid., p. 16.

15. Ibid., pp. 14–16.

16. "Eliza: A Pastoral Song," *New-York Magazine* 5 (March 1794): 186–187. For a complete listing of Linn's periodical and separate publications, see Lewis Leary, "The Writings of John Blair Linn," *Bulletin of Bibliography* 19 (September–December 1946): 18–19.

17. "The American Captive—An Elegy," *New-York Magazine* 5 (September 1794): 577.

18. "To Adeline," *New-York Magazine* 5 (September 1794): 577.

19. MS, John Blair Linn to Abraham Hun, Jr., of Albany, dated 1 July 1794, in the Historical Society of Pennsylvania, and MS, Linn to Hun, 23 September 1794, in New York Historical Society; see also [Samuel Blair], "Biographical Sketch of the Reverend John Blair Linn," *Literary Magazine and American Register* 2 (October 1804): 556.

20. "To Solitude, An Ode," *Miscellaneous Works*, pp. 9–11. Further quotations from this volume will be identified within parentheses in the text.

21. *The Poetical Wanderer: Containing, Dissertations on the Early Poetry of Greece, on Tragic Poetry, of Nobles Actions on the Mind. To Which Are Added, Several Poems. By the Author of Miscellaneous Works* (New York, 1796), p. 16.

22. "On Juvenile Institutions," *Poetical Wanderer*, pp. 42–44.

23. Brown, "Sketch," pp. 25–26.

24. 1 (November 1795): 218. Linn's writings appeared in the *New-York Magazine:* "Genius.—A Poem," 5 (June 1795): 379–381; "Lines on the Death of Cuthullin," 5 (August 1795): 504–506; "Elegy,—Supposed to Have Been Delivered by Chatterton, Just before His Death, after He Had Taken a Portion of Arsenic," 5 (September 1795): 571–573; "The Effects of Moderation," 5 (September 1795): 530–533; "On History," 5 (October 1795): 597–600; in the *New-York Weekly Magazine:* "On Hope and Reflection," 1 (9 September 1795): 81; "On Elegiac Poetry," which ran as the leading article for four weeks, 1 (16, 23 September, 7, 14 October 1795): 97–98, 105, 113, 121; and in the *Lady and Gentleman's Pocket Magazine:* "On Elegiac Poetry," 1 (15 September 1796): 104–110, and (from *The Poetical Wanderer*) "Oscar: A Poem, in Imitation of Ossian," 1 (1 November 1796): 218–221.

25. "Orlando: The Melancholy Shepherd," *Poetical Wanderer*, p. 8.

26. *New-York Weekly Museum*, 14 January 1797.

27. William Dunlap, *A History of the American Theatre* (New York, 1832), 1: 652.

28. See Evert A. and George L. Duyckinck, *Cyclopaedia of American Literature* (New York, 1856), 1:652.

29. Undated letter to William Linn, in Brown, "Sketch," p. 28. See also "Biographical Sketch of the Reverend John Blair Linn," *Literary Magazine and American Register* 2 (October 1804): 555.

30. Brown, "Sketch," p. 28, states that, while in Schenectady, Linn "indulged himself in some poetical effusions and wrote occasionally

some essays in prose, which were published in a newspaper of that place." Theodore Romeyn Peck, in a memoir of John Romeyn in W. B. Sprague, *Annals of the American Pulpit* (New York, 1857), 4: 221, says that Linn, Romeyn, and McLeod "joined in several literary undertakings which met the public notice." Only a few scattered numbers of the *Mohawk Mercury* and the *Schenectady Gazette*, published at this time, are to be found in the American Antiquarian Society and the Harvard University libraries, and in none of them are found contributions which with any assurance can be assigned to Linn or his fellow students.

31. Quoted by Brown, introduction to *Valerian*, p. xxii.

32. Brown, "Sketch," pp. 28–29.

33. MS letter, William Linn to John Romeyn, 12 November 1798, New York Historical Society.

34. Brown, "Sketch," p. 29.

35. The call to Linn, signed by Aaron Ogden, clerk, is among the MS collections of the Historical Society of Pennsylvania.

36. *Records of the Reformed Dutch Church in New Amsterdam and New York* (New York, 1890), p. 276. Mrs. Linn's name is subsequently spelled variously Hetty, Esther, Hester.

37. MS "Minutes of the Corporation," Presbyterian Historical Society, p. 41; Brown, "Sketch," p. 29, and "Biographical Sketch," p. 555. Ewing's salary at this time was $800 a year.

38. MS, John Blair Linn to John Romeyn, 3 December 1799, and ibid., 19 August 1800, *Historical Society of Pennsylvania*.

39. Quoted by Brown, introduction to *Valerian*, p. xxxi.

40. MS, John Blair Linn to John Romeyn, 3 December 1799.

41. *Travels of Four Years and a Half in the United States of America during 1798, 1799, 1800, and 1802* (New York, 1909), p. 204.

42. Milton Ellis, *Joseph Dennie and His Circle* (Austin, 1915), p. 157; Ellis Paxson Oberholtzer, *The Literary History of Philadelphia* (Philadelphia, 1906), p. 176, and Davis, *Travels*, pp. 203–205.

43. *The Death of Washington: A Poem in Imitation of Ossian* (Philadelphia, 1801), p. iii.

44. 2 (April 1800): 309.

45. MS, John Blair Linn to John Romeyn, 6 December 1800, Historical Society of Pennsylvania.

46. MS, John Blair Linn to Jedidiah Morse, 26 March 1801, Historical Society of Pennsylvania.

47. 1 (13 December 1900): 39.
48. 1 (17 January 1801): 21.
49. 1 (24 January 1801): 31.
50. 1 (1 March 1801): 83, and 1 (21 March 1801): 92–93.
51. 3 (December 1800): 472.
52. 1 (4 April 1801): 105–106.
53. 1 (April–June 1801): 208.
54. "It is honourable and complimentary both to the author and to his country," said the *Port Folio* (1 [12 December 1800]: 399), "that the English reviewers speak in kindly terms of his work." This apparently refers to some now undiscovered commendation either of *The Miscellaneous Works* or *The Poetical Wanderer*. I find no review of the first edition of *The Powers of Genius* in English periodicals of the time, nor any notices of it mentioned in William B. Cairns, *British Criticism of American Writers, 1783–1815* (*University of Wisconsin Studies in Language and Literature*, no. 1, 1917). The *Monthly Magazine* (11 [July 1801]: 62) simply notes that the book "has just made its appearance." On publication of the second edition, the same London periodical (15 [July 1803]: 695) remarks: "We fear the general charge of deficiency of *genius* in American poetry will not be cancelled by Mr. Linn's 'Powers of Genius,' a second edition of which has recently appeared. Nor do we find that the want of this quality is compensated by any remarkable harmony of versification, or by any thing excellent in the notes which are pretty thickly strewn throughout the poem." The English edition of 1804 was reviewed judiciously and, in the whole, favorably in the *Eclectic Review* (1 [January 1805]: 54–59): "Dr. Linn certainly possesses a respectable talent for poetry. . . . His versification, however, bears many marks of haste, and is often deficient either of spirit, or of melody." Other notices of this edition are found in *Annual Review* 3 (1804): 571; *Antijacobin Review* 18 (July 1804): 306–307; *British Critic* 25 (March 1805): 316–317; *Critical Review*, 3rd ser. 5 (May 1805): 29–30; *Evangelical Magazine* 12 (August 1804): 273–274; *Monthly Magazine* 19 (28 July 1805): 658; *Monthly Review* 45 (November 1804): 319–320; *Monthly Visitor*, n.s. 7 (May, June, July, and August 1804): 13–15, 113–114, 221–227, 333–336; *Poetical Register* 4 (1804): 490–491; *Universal Magazine*, n.s. 1 (June 1804): 608–610.
55. *American Review* 1 (April–June 1801): 208.
56. *Port Folio* 4 (1 September 1804): 277.
57. "To the Rev. John Blair Linn, A.M. Minister of the First

Presbyterian Congregation, of Philadelphia—on His Poem, Entitled "The Powers of Genius,' as Also on His Pulpit Eloquence," *Port Folio* 1 (2 May 1801): 144; forty-four lines of rhymed praise, signed "G——B——."

58. *The Powers of Genius* (Philadelphia, 1801), p. 19. Further quotations from this volume will be identified within parentheses in the text.

59. "A True Account of the Life and Writings of Pegasus Helicon," *Miscellaneous Works*, pp. 90–91. Barlow's *Vision of Columbus* was "one of the first productions of the age"; Trumbull "far surpassed Peter Pindar the great wit of Britannia"; Dwight overwrote but was sometimes sublime; and Freneau, seeking simplicity, turned out lines which "seem to flow without labour."

60. As an up-to-date young man, Linn knew and criticized the novelists: Mrs. Radcliffe was "cloth'd in the robes of terror and of night"—"in her department of genius, in the present day, none can approach her" (*The Powers of Genius*, p. 39). Richardson "wrote with good intention, for he was a man of virtue and piety." On the other hand, Fielding was without any doubt the man of greatest genius among the novelists: he could not therefore be passed over, "but," Linn explained, "the truth must not be withheld—that his works contain many scenes of indecency!" Fielding, then, could not be wholeheartedly recommended. As a matter of fact—again it is Linn the clergyman speaking—"there are few novels I would recommend unconditionally: and I would recommend that all of them be read sparingly" (ibid., pp. 37–38).

61. *A Discourse Occasioned by the Death of the Reverend John Ewing, D. D., Late Senior Pastor of the First Presbyterian Congregation, of the City of Philadelphia, and Provost of the University of Pennsylvania* (Philadelphia, 1802), pp. 21, 26.

62. Records, Office of the Secretary, University of Pennsylvania.

63. 1 (October 1803): 47. This poem was later used as a song in *Valerian*, pp. 94–96.

64. Each of these subsequently appeared with very little change in *Valerian*: "Artaban the Robber," 1 (November 1803): 111–112; "Extract from a Narrative Poem in M.S. Exordium. Alcestis and Azora," 1 (December 1803): 192–193; "The Boar Hunt. From a Manuscript Poem," 1 (January 1804): 268–270; and "Extracts from an Original Poem in MS. Night-Song of Azora," 2 (April 1804): 376–377.

65. 1 (December 1803): 191–192.

66. 1 (March 1804): 424–425, and 2 (April 1804): 18.

67. 2 (May 1804): 117.

68. The "Critical Notices," numbered in series from 1 to 8, appeared in each issue but one from October 1803 to June 1804. All but numbers 3, 5, and 8 were signed with Linn's pseudonym "I. O." Internal evidence seems to suggest that he did not write number 5 (on Goldsmith) nor number 8 (on the poetic treatment of death).

69. 1 (February 1804): 336–341.

70. *A Letter to Joseph Priestley, L.L.D.F.R.S.&c.&c. In Answer to His Performance Entitled Socrates and Jesus Compared* (Philadelphia, 1803), pp. 30, 5–6.

71. See Thomas Belsham, *Zeal and Fortitude in the Christian Ministry Illustrated and Exemplified* (London, 1804), p. 36, and *A Short Account of the Last Illness of the Rev. Dr. Priestley, in a Letter from His Son Mr. Joseph Priestley* (London, 1804), pp. 55, 61. As one rereads the controversy today, Linn seems certainly not to have the best of it. His first *Letter* was dated 3 April 1803. Priestley replied moderately in *A Letter to the Reverend John Blair Linn, A.M. Pastor of the First Presbyterian Congregation in the City of Philadelphia. In Defense of the Pamphlet, Intitled Socrates and Jesus Compared.* Then in a second pamphlet, written in August, but not published till the autumn of 1803, Linn replied with some temper with *A Letter to Joseph Priestley L.L.D.F.R.S. In Answer to His Letter in Defense of His Pamphlet Entitled Socrates and Jesus Compared.* Priestley's *A Second Letter to the Revd. John Blair Linn D.D. Pastor of the First Presbyterian Congregation in the City of Philadelphia in Reply to His Defense of the Doctrines of the Divinity of Christ and Atonement* was dated 11 November 1803, and ended with "every good wish" that Linn might "soon come to the knowledge of the great truth" that Linn now opposed, a truth, wrote Priestley, "which (owing to early and deep rooted prejudices) cost me much labour to acquire." Samuel Blair, "Biographical Sketch," p. 558, reports that Linn later regretted "some expressions, which, on reflection, he perceived to be too acrimonious, and rather unbecoming his years; and what greatly added to his regret, was that the doctor departed his life before he received a letter of apology, which had been prepared for conveyance."

72. Preface to *Valerian*, p. xxv.

73. Draft of a letter from John Blair Linn to Bishop Porteus, 18 January 1804, Historical Society of Pennsylvania. The permission for dedication was apparently not granted, if, indeed, the letter to

Bishop Porteus was ever sent, for *Valerian* appeared with no dedication.

74. Introduction to *Valerian*, pp. xv–xvi.

75. *Port Folio*, n.s. 1 (January 1809): 21.

76. Brown, "Sketch," pp. 16–21. A more realistic and perhaps more matter-of-fact account of Linn's last moments is found in the *United States Gazette*, 1 September 1804. After Linn's death, the congregation of his church ordered "to have the pulpit and the clerk's desk covered with black [for a period of one year] in testimony of their respect for their deceased pastor": the church treasurer was directed to pay all funeral expenses, to pay full salary and manse rent to his widow for two months, and thereafter for five years to pay her $200 a year (see "Minutes of the Congregation," p. 87). Linn's funeral sermon was preached by the Reverend Dr. Samuel Blair; before the funeral on 31 August, the Reverend Ashbel Green delivered an address to the congregation (see *United States Gazette*, 1 September 1804, and *Literary Magazine* 2 [October 1804]: 554).

77. Alexander McLeod, quoted in introduction to *Valerian*, p. xxiii.

78. *Powers of Genius*, pp. 63, 65.

The Education of
William Dunlap

❧❧

EW Americans have been more versatile than William Dunlap. A portrait painter who studied in London under Benjamin West, a dramatist responsible for some of the more popular of our early plays, a poet whose work appeared in the first anthology of native verse, an aspirant in fiction whose early attempts inspired Charles Brockden Brown, a biographer, a pioneer historian of American art and of the American theater, dramatic entrepreneur, diarist, friend and patron of men of letters, art, and the stage, William Dunlap wrought earnestly in a career of more than fifty years—from his first crayon portrait of George Washington in 1783 to his history of the New Netherlands in 1839. It spanned a period which began with the aspiring first generation of writers in the new republic, like his brother-in-law Timothy Dwight and his fellow dramatist Royall Tyler, and ended with the triumphant generation of the 1820s and 1830s when Dunlap corresponded familiarly with James Fenimore Cooper, gave avuncular advice to Washington Irving, was clubman with William Cullen Bryant, and vied for popular favor with John Howard Payne. Never for long quite at the center of things, his activities nonetheless touched upon and overlapped that of almost every American man of letters, every American painter, every American person of the theater of his time.

In all, he was the most generous of men, with great talent for friendship. His heart, it can be said, was in the right place. He housed, fed, and encouraged impecunious young writers. He befriended indigent actors. He was active in manumission societies. Hardly any humane or cultural enterprise of his time failed to find him its supporter. He was a man fated to be used and to be useful, to improvident actors, aspiring poets, and friends who sought recuperation at his hospitable country place in Perth Amboy, as well as to historians and biographers of a later time who have rewritten or revised what he so assiduously chronicled. If only a shadow, he is a luminous shadow whose destiny seems to have been to be often among the first but never among the foremost.

His life and multifarious activities have been well recorded, perhaps never so interestingly as by himself. Scattered among his histories of place, theater, and art are reminiscent accounts of his own career which, when supplemented or annotated by entries from his diaries, could be gathered into a substantial volume entitled The Autobiography of William Dunlap.[1] Its first chapter would certainly detail his education and how it had failed him, a person perhaps born at the wrong place at the wrong time whose desultory schooling was interrupted or misdirected by war and illness and the doting parents of an only child, but was supplemented by a zest for self-improvement which testimony from his diaries reveals coming to a climax in his early thirties when he doggedly began to read and record his reading of every entry in his encyclopedia, from cover to cover, from A to Z. Because what Dunlap says of himself and his schooling in war-torn America seems fairly to represent much of what must have been the experience of many other young literary aspirants of his time, and may therefore suggest something of some of the reasons why literature lagged in the new United States, it is recorded below, boldly paraphrased or quoted from his own reminiscences, supplemented only slightly from other sources. It is his story, and he tells it well.

He was born on 19 February 1766 in Perth Amboy in the colony of New Jersey, the only child of Samuel Dunlap, a retired British army officer from Londonderry in northern Ireland who had served with distinction under General Wolfe at Quebec, had later been assigned with the Forty-seventh Regiment to Perth Amboy, where he met and married Margaret Sargent, sold his commission, and settled into the not unprosperous life of a country storekeeper, a merchant importing goods from England and the West

Indies (*A*, 2: 288). William was apparently not a sturdy boy; indeed what portraits of him survive reveal him as probably not a very sturdy man, though he lived beyond four score and ten. Among his earliest recollections were those connected with sickness, and the relief derived from being carried in the arms of his father, who told him stories of soldierly adventure (*T*, 2: 40).

His "first school" was among the slaves of his father's household: "Every house in my native place, where servants were to be seen, swarmed with black slaves. . . . My father's kitchen had several families of them of all ages." There, he said, his taste was formed, "in the mirth and games of the negroes, and the variety of visitors of the black race who frequented that place." Among slaves, "the child is taught to tyrannize—the boy is taught to despise labor—the mind of the child is contaminated by hearing and seeing that which perhaps is not understood at the time, but remains with the memory." More than fifty years later, he protested, "Such is the school of many a one even now, in those States where the evil of slavery continues" (*A*, 2: 288–289).

When old enough, he was sent to a local dame school, moving from that to the elementary classes of an Irishman named McNaughton, and at the age of eight studied briefly with Thomas Johnston, an Oxonian who had been engaged to oversee the schooling of the youth of Perth Amboy. When he complained, "Education I had none, according to the usual acceptation of that word, . . . and much of what is to the child most essential education, was essentially bad," he seems to have been remembering principally his "medley of kitchen associates": "To be petted, indulged, spoiled, and have their example before his eyes was the lot of the only child of the master of the family" (*T*, 2: 41), an influence which was increased when the Revolution began "by soldiers who found their mess fare improved by visiting the negroes, and by servants of officers billeted in the house" (*A*, 1: 288–289).

"But, on the other and brighter side," he remembered, "it was my happiness to be the favorite of a being of a very different kind, and to become attached in early childhood, to an aged man who lived almost the life of a hermit, having neither wife nor child." How vividly Dunlap remembered Thomas Bartow, once prominent in colonial politics, but now "a small thin old man, with straight gray hair, pale face, plain dark-coloured clothes, and stockings to suit—his well-polished, square-toed shoes were ornamented with little silver buckles, and his white cambric stock, neatly plaited, was fastened with a silver clasp. When he walked, a cane with an ivory head aided his steps, which halted through age and rheumatism. . . . By some arrangement with my indulgent parents," Dunlap explained, "I was permitted to go every Sunday to this still more indulgent old gentleman who read the Bible regularly but who never went to church" (*T*, 2: 41–42), who alone among the gentlemen of the village kept no slaves, and whose house was filled with books and pictures (*A*, 1: 289–290).

"The boy was his companion at home, and his only companion when he rode or walked abroad. In winter, he gambolled about the room while the old man read: or was sent into the garret to bring down dried grapes, which hung on frames, carefully preserved after ripening on the vines in his garden; or took the key to his library and selected books to place on the table before him, that he might explain the pictures or tell the stories." When war threatened the village, Bartow packed his goods and moved westward, and Dunlap never saw him again, "except in my dreams. Through a long life his image has visited my hours of sleep—always changed—generally sick—or insane—or confined to his chamber and forbidding my approach to him" (*T*, 2: 42). And from these dreams Dunlap would awake, he said, "like Caliban, with the disposition to weep for the renewal of my dreams" (*A*, 1: 291).

Seemingly a surrogate for Dunlap's busy merchant father, Bartow quickened the mind of a nine-year-old boy whose later writings would often contain accounts of sons separated from fathers, real or deputy.[2] "Patiently he turned over pages of Homer and Virgil in the translations of Pope and Dryden, and of Milton's poems, and explained the pictures, until I was familiar with the stories of Troy and Latium—of heaven and

hell, as poets tell them. . . . Thus commenced a love of reading," Dunlap testified, "which has been my blessing" (*A*, 1:
290).

By this time, war was unsettling the colonies. The boy recalled
a visit with his father during the summer of 1775 to New York,
where "Horsemen's helmets, swords and belts, with other equip-
ments, were displayed at shop doors and windows," and where
he saw "a company of gentlemen practicing, with an instructor,
the small-sword salute" (*A*, 1: 292). Perth Amboy also prepared
for war. A militia company was formed, and the boys of the
village, young Dunlap included, paraded with wooden swords
and guns in imitation. Before withdrawn for combat duty at
Boston, officers of his father's former regiment visited often at
the Dunlap home, and the boy, apparently a favorite among
them, was in and out of their quarters and barracks. He liked to
play with his father's sword, gorget, and sash: "Familiarity with
military pomp and revelry, guns, drums, and all the allurements
which such an artificial state presents, formed another part of
my education" (*T*, 2: 44; *A*, 1: 294).
The British garrison gone, militia from the surrounding
countryside thronged into Perth Amboy, a ragtag conglomeration, he thought, "an almost unarmed rabble of every age and
class." Dunlap was better impressed by a troop of Continentals
which passed through on its way to Canada. In appearance and
discipline these soldiers presented a contrast to the militia, and
also to the red-coated veterans to whom he had been accustomed.
"Some in rifle frocks of brown linen, with trousers of the same—
but well equipped, though more like hunters than soldiers—
others in blue and red uniforms with white trousers, a black
cap on the head, the cartouch-box and bayonet slung in black
belts, and a round canteen for water, which, with a bright musket,
formed the equipment of these fine young men, now marching
to the north to be placed under Montgomery" (*T*, 2: 45).
When later in 1775 British troops massed on Staten Island
threatening Perth Amboy and a conflict seemed imminent, the
Dunlap family moved to Piscataway on the banks of the Raritan
River not far from New Brunswick. No schooling now for the

nine-year-old boy, only informal lessons in arithmetic and pen-
manship from his father, and some desultory reading in what
books he could find, with swimming and fishing and sailing
providing, he admitted, better "delights of liberty and idleness":
"The Declaration of Independence caused a sensation which I
distinctly remember, but my sports and rambles had more interest for *me*" (*A*, 1: 292). During the summer of 1776 he
"rambled about the fields, caught perch in the brooks, or sun-fish
in the mill-ponds, and was as happy as liberty from school and
nearly all restraint" allowed. But, he boasted, "I read the whole
of Shakespeare," lingering longest over the historical plays in
which battles abounded (*T*, 2: 45–46).

For war was now his schoolroom. He watched British troops
marching through Piscataway, plundering as they went, in
"promiscuous pillage." He heard the lamentations of women
and children as soldiers carried off their belongings (*A*, 1: 292):
"Here a soldier was seen issuing from a house armed with a
frying-pan and gridiron, and hastening to deposit them with
the store over which his helpmate kept watch. The women who
followed the army assisted . . . in bringing the furniture from
the houses, or stood as sentinels to guard the pile of kitchen
utensils or other articles already secured and claimed by right
of war. Here was seen a woman bearing a looking-glass, and
here a soldier with a feather-bed—but as this was rather an in-
convenient article to carry on the march, the ticking was soon
ripped open, and a shower of goose feathers were seen taking
higher flights than their original owners ever soared to." Schooling aside, this scene, said Dunlap, was itself "a lesson" (*T*, 2:
46).

The boy accompanied his father when he walked to meet the
British commander on the highroad in order to reveal himself
as a loyal subject of the king, and the Dunlaps followed the
army back to Perth Amboy which had become an armed camp
where were gathered "the flower and pick of the army, English
Scotch, and German, who at this time had been brought in from
Rhode Island. Here was to be seen a party of the 52d Highlanders, in national costume, and there a regiment of Hessians,
their dress and arms a perfect contrast to the first. The slaves of

Anspach and Waldeck were there—the first as sombre as night, the second as gaudy as noon. Here dashed a party of the 17th Dragoons, and there scampered a party of *Yagers*. The trim, neat and graceful English grenadier, the careless and half-savage Highlander, with his flowing robes and naked knees, and the immovable stiff German, could hardly be taken as parts of one army" (*A*, 1: 293).

But beyond the "pride, pomp, and circumstance of war," there was misery also, plundering, and cruelty: "Here might be seen soldiers driving in cattle, others guarding wagons loaded with household furniture, instead of hay and oats they had been sent for." The boy watched disciplinary "flogging of English heroes, and thumping and caning of German; the brutal licentiousness, which even my tender years could not avoid seeing in all around, and the increased disorders among my father's negroes, from mingling with the servants of officers" (*A*, 1: 293–294). He remembered hearing at night the heavy tred of troops and the rumbling of wagons filled with wretched wounded. He especially remembered one conspicuously tall and handsome grenadier whom he followed with admiration a short distance down the highroad, and then not long later saw him again, returned from battle, wounded, and "no longer . . . the hero I had admired" (*T*, 2: 48). "These lessons and others more disgusting . . . were my source of instruction in the winter of 1776–7" (*A*, 1: 294).

When war pressed more perilously on Perth Amboy in the spring of 1777, the Dunlaps took refuge in British-occupied New York, leaving many of their possessions behind them. New York was then even more an armed camp, a poorly administered despotism, crowded with soldiers and with people like the Dunlaps who sought protection from rebellious neighbors. Food was scarce, prices soared, and fuel was in short supply. Redcoats, tars, and privateers rubbed elbows with rowdy refugees in waterfront dramshops. Drunkenness, brawling, gambling, and the looting of public and private buildings were so inadequately controlled that it was said to be "dangerous to walk the streets at night or to be in a crowd in the day." The army was billeted in public buildings, warehouses, private homes, stores, and even churches. Rough barracks were thrown up to accommodate the hordes of loyalists who streamed into the city. Rebel incendiaries were a constant threat. Hardly six months before the Dunlaps arrived, almost one-fourth of the city had been destroyed by a fire which people suspected had been purposely started.[3] "Over the ruins of this fire," said Dunlap, "I wandered, when a boy, in every direction. . . . The ruins . . . were converted into dwelling places by using the chimneys and parts of walls which were firm, and adding pieces of spars, with old canvas from the ships, forming hovels—part hut and part tent. This was called 'Canvasstown'; and was the receptacle and resort of the vilest dregs brought by the army and navy of Britain, with the filthiest of those who fled to them for refuge" (*H*, 2: 79).

New York provided excitement in plenty for a boy, and edifying contrasts. He could watch the military parade each morning on the Mall in front of the ruins of Trinity Church. The havoc of war and the bustle of martial splendor were to be seen on every side. Again there were the massive and moustached ponderous Hessians, the kilted Highlanders, the gaudy Waldeckers, dashing Yagers, and splendid grenadiers "glittering," he remembered, with "gallant pomp." There were new streets to explore, and a waterfront and harbor filled with heavy cargo vessels and sleek privateers; there were cricket matches among the officers to be watched, and band concerts to be heard almost every evening on the Mall; there was horse racing even, until prohibited as a public menace, on the city streets; and there was the theater on John Street where British officers presented plays.

Dunlap's dedication to the stage began when at twelve he was taken to a performance of George Farquhar's *Beaux' Stratagem*. He marveled at "the crowd of well-dressed people, tier on tier, . . . the lights, the music, the drop-curtain, the mysterious anticipation of the wonders behind it, . . . then the magic and moving pictures, . . . the creatures of another world, or of ages gone by." After that, he was "occasionally indulged in going to the theatre . . . and enjoyed the delights of reading over the plays after seeing them acted, and recalling the actors" and how they had interpreted each part (*T*, 2: 49).

Not for long, however. On coming to New York, the boy was enrolled briefly in a Latin school, but then was transferred for some reason which he never completely understood to the tutelage of Thomas Steele, a former artilleryman and a Quaker, who "gave me," said Dunlap, "all the instruction I ever received from such institutions." Meanwhile, he read widely, everything he could lay his hands on, Shakespeare again, and Pope's Homer for the first time, nostalgically recalling happier days with Samuel Bartow as he read it (*T*, 2: 48). But war impinged even on such fugitive delights. From his schoolroom window he looked out toward Livingston's sugarhouse on the corner of Crown and Nassau streets, used now as a prison where captive patriots "pined, sickened, and died. During the suffocating heat of summer, when . . . I could not catch a cooling breeze, I saw opposite to me every narrow aperture of those stone walls filled with human heads, face above face, seeking a portion of the external air. What," he wondered, "must have been the atmosphere within. Child as I was, the spectacle sank deep into my heart" (*H*, 2: 141–142).

But more than war cut into Dunlap's education. He was twelve years old when in June 1778 he played in a woodyard with boy companions in a boisterous, perhaps warlike, game of peppering one another with wood chips. "In this sport," he later recorded,

> my right eye was cut longitudinally, by a heavier piece of firewood than was in general use by the combatants, and, deprived of its use, I was led into the house, accompanied by all my affrighted associates. A carriage was prepared, and I was delivered to my distressed parents. After many weeks of confinement to my bed, and more to the house, I slowly regained health; but never the sight of the organ. By degrees I recovered the full use of the remaining eye, but the accident prevented all further regular schooling." (*A*, 1: 295)

It may have been some comfort that the surgeon who attended him was also one of the principal actors at the John Street theater, and was remembered by the boy for his spirited portrayal of Scrub in Farquhar's *Beaux' Stratagem*.

For his injury also prevented, at least for a time, his "visiting the theatre, as the glare of light was painful and injurious." And his "application to drawing," for the first time mentioned by Dunlap as "one of my sources of pleasure," was also suspended. For the next five years he worked in his father's store on Queen Street, where the elder Dunlap dealt in glassware and china and, when it could be obtained, tea (*T*, 2: 49–50). But events took place in New York which even a partially sighted, convalescent boy could not miss. One hot night in August 1778, when he had left his bed to lie "panting on the floor near a window," he was roused from fitful sleep "by the cry of fire, and the ringing of alarm bells," and, looking out, saw "everything illuminated by the blaze" which had sprung up on the waterfront, to spread devastation over great portions of the city. The next morning, as he joined a boy companion in standing guard over rescued furniture, he looked with awe and wonder at what he saw before him: even the face of the sun seemed "disfigured by the curling masses of black and red smoke, as they mounted from the half burned buildings" (*H*, 2: 164–165).

The next day brought more wonder, and terror also. Summer heat continued intolerable, and the spirits of the people of New York were depressed by the thought of further conflagration. About one o'clock that afternoon "masses of black clouds over-shadowed us from the west," said Dunlap, "and a thunderstorm commenced with violence; but the flashes of lightning, or the deafening peals of thunder did not prevent my father's family from setting down to dinner, for it was while thus engaged that a crash," which later investigation discovered to have been the explosion of a powder ship in the harbor, "startled every one out of his seat; the houses appeared to shake; papers which had been left near an open chamber window came fluttering down in fantastic gyrations." Suspicion that the house had been struck by lightning "seemed to be confirmed, as the tiled roof on the front rattled to the pavement, and torrents of rain poured in without impediment." Running to the street, Dunlap found "all the houses with tiled roofs in the same condition. Consternation was general, and the cause unknown of so violent and extensive a conclusion. . . . Every house facing the river was uncovered in front, exposed to pelting rain, and every face that was seen looked horrour struck," It was a day to be remembered, a day "of gloom and darkness" (*H*, 2: 165).

Heat and fire were not the only inflictions suffered by the people of the beleaguered city. During the winter of 1779–1780, a "long continuance of severe cold closed the bay of New York, with solid ice, so that I remember," said Dunlap, "to have seen a troop of horse and artillery crossing to Staten Island on this immense bridge, which connected all our islands, one with another, and with the main land." The British army suffered greatly, but the civilian inhabitants of New York suffered even more. "Wood was cut . . . by the military, and few trees escaped the ax that winter. But fuel and provisions were scarcely to be purchased by the citizens, even those who had the means of paying exorbitant prices. In many instances household furniture was broken up to supply the fire necessary to support life. I well remember," he said, "the beaten tracks for sleighs and waggons, winding occasionally around, and between the walls of ice; and a similar road in use to Hoboken, from whence some wood was procured by a party of soldiers" (*H*, 2: 165–166).

Amidst such perils of war and nature, Dunlap recalled that books and pictures "became the companions of my leisure, and as I had as much time to bestow on them as I pleased. I had acquired the use of India ink and became attached to copying prints. I was encouraged by admiration—good engravings were lent to me, and by degrees my copies might almost pass for the original prints. . . . Seeing that I aspired to be a painter, and talked of West and Copley, and read books on art, my father looked out for an instructor for me." But the instructor who was found paid slight and only temporary attention to his young pupil: "I went to his room in the suburbs, now Mott Street, and he placed a drawing book before me, such as I had possessed for years: after a few visits the teacher was not to be found. I examined his portraits—tried his crayons, and soon acquiring a set, commenced painting portraits, beginning with my father's. From painting my relations I proceeded to painting my young companions, and, having applications from strangers, I fixed a price of three guineas a head. I thus commenced portrait painter in the year 1782, by no means looking to it for subsistence, but living as the only and indulged child of my parents, . . . and doing as seemed best to me. Thus passed my life to the age of seventeen" (*A*, 1: 295–296).

"I was now," he continued, "at the period of full animal enjoyment. . . . Books did not at that period attract me as they had done." His first venture in oils was a tavern sign meant to attract the patronage of sailors. Meanwhile, he attended evening classes in French, and dancing classes which earned him "the reputation of one learned in that valuable mystery," which was more, he confessed "than my French master could say for my grammar." He also "began two dramas: one on the story of Abou Hassan, in the Arabian Nights, and the other on some incidents of Persian history" (*T*, 2: 50). And, he admitted, "Another branch of my education which will throw further light on my fitness for self government," was introduction "to the billiard tables of New York, not, he protested, "as a gambler, but an idler." As he turned eighteen, his "evenings were divided between a billiard room on Crane Wharf and sleigh rides out of town, with cards and dancing" (*A*, 2: 301–302).

In the summer of 1783, after six years "shut up in a garrison town," Dunlap took advantage of the preliminary treaty of peace to return briefly to Perth Amboy, to visit Princeton where the Congress was in session, to visit with friends at Rocky Hill, and for the first time to visit Philadelphia, where he admired, as an aspiring fellow professional, the paintings of James Willson Peale. One summer day, during "a solitary walk, on the road between Princeton and Trenton, a party of military horsemen appeared. . . . They were all dressed in the well-known staff uniform of the United States, blue and buff, with the black and white cockade, marking the union with France, in their cocked hats, . . . and at first view all appeared equal, and all above the average height. But the centre figure was the tallest of the group, and I knew that I saw in him the man on whom every thing centred." In awe, Dunlap removed his own cocked hat in a salute which was instantly "returned in the same manner by the chief, and every hat in the company was lowered with its waving plume to me. . . . It was a precious moment. I had seen Washington" (*T*, 2: 51–52).

"For eight years of my life," he said, "the name of Washington had been familiar to my ears, though surrounded by his enemies." When first heard, "his name was coupled with sarcasm and taunts," but "his name grew with my growth," challenging and surpassing that of General Howe or General Clinton of the British armies, and greatly surpassing the names of British officers who patronized the young painter's studio or acted for his pleasure in the New York stage, until as the war ended "even Englishmen spoke of him with respect" (*T*, 2: 50–51). As the American hero passed by that day on the road, "I turned," said Dunlap, "and gazed as at a passing vision. . . . Although all my life used to . . . the gay and gallant Englishman, the tartan'd Scot, and the embroidered German of every military grade, I still think the old blue and buff of Washington and his aides, their cocked hats worn sidelong, with the union cockade, . . . was the most martial of anything I ever saw" (*A*, 1: 298).

Not long afterward, the friend with whom he was staying at Rocky Hill, "amusing myself with my flute, my music books, and my crayons" (T, 2: 50), introduced the young man to George Washington, whose headquarters were scarcely a mile away and who, "on his daily rides, . . . usually stopped, and passed an hour" with Dunlap's host (*T*, 2: 52). It was a thrilling experience which left the young man breathless with awe. He was even more thrilled a few days later, while practicing on his flute, to hear the general in the next room remark that "love of music and painting are frequently found in the same person." But the greatest thrill of all was to be invited to Washington's headquarters to do a crayon portrait of the great man, and then another of his wife: "This was a triumphant moment for a boy of seventeen." And as days went on, his visits to Washington's billet became more frequent: to be saluted by the soldiers who were deceived by his fine clothes into thinking him important, to "breakfast and dine day after day with the General and Mrs. Washington, and members of Congress, and noticed as the young painter," this, said the enraptured young man, "was delicious" (*A*, 1: 300).

In November he was back in New York in time to witness the arrival there of Washington and his entourage, "accompanied by the citizens on horseback and on foot who went out to meet him and accompany his triumphant entry; while the English fleet sailed from the no longer hostile harbor." Soon Dunlap also would sail from New York to England, for "it had now been decided," he said, "that I should go to London in the spring, and the winter was passed in painting and making preparations for the voyage." He experimented further with oils on another picture of Washington, this time done from memory. The general "in full uniform, booted and spurred," stood "heroically alone" at the battle of Princeton beside the fallen body of General Mercer who was "dying in precisely the same attitude that West," with whom Dunlap hoped to study in England, "had devised to picture the dying of General Wolfe." For Dunlap was even as an artist still unformed. His education, he confessed, had prepared him shabbily "for entering the labyrinth of London, alone and unguided, at the age of eighteen" (*A*, 1: 200–201).

The brig *Betsey* on which he sailed from New York on 8 May 1784 did not arrive at Gravesend on the Thames until the middle of June. Immediately on landing, carrying letters for John Singleton Copley and pictures to be presented for the approval of Benjamin West, Dunlap proceeded to London, where he bought new clothes, in the English style, and saw to it that the samples of his work, two drawings and the painting of Washington at Princeton, were safely forwarded. A few days later he was escorted by a Quaker friend of his father to the painter's establishment on Newman Street. "The impression made upon an American youth of eighteen by the long gallery leading from the dwelling-house, to the lofty suite of painting rooms—a gallery filled with sketches and designs for large paintings—the spacious room through which I passed to the more retired *atelier*—the works of his pencil surrounding me on every side— his own figure seated at his easel, and the beautiful composition at which he was employed, as if in sport; not labor; are all recalled," wrote Dunlap, half a century later, "with a vividness which doubtless proceeds, in part, from repeated visits to, and examination of, many of the same objects during a residence of more than three years in London" (*A*, 1: 79).

Though Quaker-born and Quaker-educated, West impressed his young visitor as being as "un-Quaker-like . . . as any man in London" in manner, conversation, and conduct (*A*, 1: 79): his "powdered hair, side curls, and silk stockings . . . gave no indications of Quakerism." After greeting his visitors, the painter, Dunlap remembered, "took us back to the room we had passed through, and where my specimens were deposited." When on examining one of Dunlap's drawings West remarked that, though well enough executed, it indicated only a talent for engraving, then, said Dunlap, "I sunk from summer heat to the freezing point." But when the picture of Washington was unrolled, the "artist smiled—the temperature rose." West agreed to take Dunlap on as a pupil, and found him rooms in the house of another artist who would provide preliminary instruction. "Before leaving the house of the great painter, it may be supposed," said Dunlap, "that I gazed with all the wonder of ignorance and the enthusiasm of youth, upon the paintings then in the rooms."

"I was now left master of my own actions, he continued,

> and of two rooms in the house of Robert Davy, Esq. I was put in possession of a painting room on the first floor, or second story, and a furnished bed-chamber immediately above it: and for these, and for my board, fire, etc., I was to pay a guinea a week. After seeing the lions of the Tower, and other parts of London, I sat down to draw in black and white chalks from the bust of Cicero; and having mastered that, in every point of view, I draw from the Fighting Gladiator (so called),—and my drawing gained me permission to enter the Academy at Somerset House. I know not why—perhaps because I was too timid to ask Mr. West to introduce me, or too bashful and awkward to introduce myself: but I never made use of the permission.

Instead, "I went with my portfolio, port-crayon, chalks and paper, and delivered them to the porter, made some excuse for not going in, and walked off: I never entered the school or saw my portfolio again." And "these drawings above-mentioned, and a few pictures in oil, executed under the direction of Mr. Davy, who taught me to set a palette as he had been taught in Rome, were all the records that remained of my exertions to become a painter, which the year 1784 produced" (*A*, 1: 303–304).

For not many months after his arrival, Dunlap became ill. "At the time I left my portfolio at Somerset House (a wet autumn evening)," he explained, "I suffered from what terminated in an abscess, and confined me to my bed or bed-chamber during the winter." By May of the next year, his health had improved enough to allow him to attend an exhibition at the Academy, but that was all. "Thus passed," he said, "a year in London—lost to all improvement" (*A*, 1:304–305). During the summer of 1785 he did some desultory drawing and daubed at a few portraits of friends. He seldom saw Benjamin West "except when invited to dine, which was generally when he had Americans at his table." He was shy in his presence, and wondered whether the painter's apparent lack of interest in him resulted from reports by Davy of lack of talent or lack of application. He worried that his loss of an eye was an irremediable handicap. He accused himself of excessive timidity. He thought himself certainly ill-prepared for life or for art. He was conscious of being only an undisciplined youth, to whom "the wonders of art . . . communicated no instruction because of lack of previous education" (*A*, 1: 305–307).

"I look back," he later said, "with astonishment at the activity of my idleness, and the thoughtlessness of consequences with which I acted." At nineteen, his return to health came to him, he confessed, "as a torrent of delight": "The enjoyment of the present was never interrupted by remembrance of the past or anticipation of the future." He spoke of "mirth and midnight revelry" in which "every source of information was neglected. I thought," he said, "only of the present that was full of delight, and that was full of delight to my empty mind. . . . Many a day was wasted in walking to the New York Coffee House, near the Royal Exchange, under pretence of looking for letters from home. The morning lounged away, I dined at the Cock eating house. . . . Dining and port wine over, there was 'no use going home,' the theatres stood midway; and when the play was over, I might rest from a lost day, and not dream that I had been doing wrong or neglecting right. Many a day was spent in pedestrian expeditions to Richmond Hill, Hampton Court and Greenwich; or in rides to more distant places. . . . Sometimes it was an excuse that pictures were to be seen—but I looked upon pictures without the necessary knowledge that would have made them instructive" (*A*, 1: 305–308).

After two years in London, Dunlap left his rooms with Davy and moved to a furnished first floor flat on Broad Street in Soho. "My establishment," he wrote, "was elegant and increased my expenses. I breakfasted in the house, and for dinner made one of a mess, principally half-pay officers who had served in America. This eating and drinking club was established at a porter house in Oxford Street" where a "course of meat was followed by a dessert of pudding or pies, and each man was allowed a pint of porter as table drink. However scarcely a day passed but brandy punch followed the dessert, and sometimes wine." In all, he admitted, "I was a favorite with my companions—I was always full of life and gaiety; and moved by a desire to please" (*A*, 1: 301). He remembered that once "having learned a new song & sung it with the applause of my companions, I after singing it at a club in the Strand, near Charing-cross, went, tho' pretty late, to the Bucks-lodge at the pewter platter near Holborn in the hopes of being asked to sing. And many a time I sate & listen'd to stupidity & ribaldry in the shape of song or story in the impatient hope that my turn would soon come, or that the person now exhibiting would call up on me to perform next" (*Diary*, 1: 51).

Little serious painting seems to have been done during this period, and those examples which he took to West for comment were received, he thought, coldly, as if the painter had given up interest in him. Dunlap now, as he had been in the presence of Washington and would often be again, was awed by human greatness: "my habit of silence in the presence of those whom I considered my superiors," he said of this meeting with West, "was very detrimental to me. . . . I stood in the presence of the artist and wondered at his skill, but stood silent, abashed, hesitating—and withdrew unenlightened;—discouraged by the consciousness of ignorance and the monomaniacal want of courage to elicit the information I eagerly desired" (A, 1: 310). Among convivial companions, however, "I was," he said, "supposed to possess humor or wit. I had some knowledge of music and could sing to satisfy my associates; but I did nothing to satisfy the man who had it in his power to serve me. My follies and faults were reported, and exaggerated to Mr. West, and as he saw no appearance of the better self which resided in me (for there was a better self), he left me to my fate" (*A*, 1: 208–209).

Outside the studio, Dunlap's "inexhaustibly good spirits, frankness, and unweariable cheerfulness," his quickness at song or story, attracted pleasant companions. With one, he traveled by stage, riding proudly on top with the armed guard, to Scotland, where at the castle at Stamford he looked casually at paintings—"Madonnas and Bambinos, and Magdalens, and Crucifixions, but I believe," he admitted, "all did not advance me one step in my profession." In November 1784 with Samuel Latham Mitchill, a friend from New York who had recently taken a medical degree at Edinburgh, he set out on a walking tour of Oxford and its vicinity. At Blenheim, they saw the Duke of Marlborough's collection of pictures "with some pleasure and little profit." At Windsor, they saw the royal family (*A*, 1: 311–314).

Meanwhile word had apparently reached New York, perhaps indirectly from Benjamin West, that Dunlap was paying more attention to other things than he was to painting. In the summer of 1787 his "life of unprofitable idleness was terminated by a summons to return home." Passage had been arranged by his parents. His canvases and paints were packed in preparation for embarkation in August. "Thus ended," he said, "a residence in London of sufficient length to have made a man of abilities feebler than mine a painter. . . . I was . . . led astray and gave up the pursuits of my profession for the pursuits which youth, health, and a disposition to please and be pleased, presented me" (*A*, 1: 314–315).

After a passage of seven weeks, Dunlap arrived in New York early in October. During the voyage he had done some painting, two portraits of the captain, and had assisted in refurbishing the figurehead of the vessel. On landing, "I found myself," he said, "in my mother's arms, and surrounded by the black faces, white teeth, and staring eyes of the negroes of the family." He installed himself as a painter with a studio in his father's house, "but with little success as to emolument. By degrees my employers became fewer, my efforts were unsatisfactory to myself, and after a year or two abandoned painting, and joined my father in the mercantile business" (*A*, 1: 315).

Meanwhile, he had joined his friend Mitchill and Noah Webster as a member of the Philological Society, a literary group formed by the young men of New York for mutual improvement and instruction, and this, he recorded "led to a more regular course of study than I had ever known. I sought assiduously to gain knowledge, but unfortunately could not be content without exposing my ignorance by writing and publishing." Urged on by the success of Royall Tyler's *The Contrast* which had appeared on the New York stage only a few months before his arrival from London, Dunlap wrote a play of his own which was accepted by the managers but never staged. He began composition of an epic poem based on the story of Aristomenes. But mainly he seems to have remained a genial man about town, "drawn," he admitted, "into some societies called convivial" (*A*, 1: 315–316).

His education may be thought, if not to have ended, to have come to a turning point when just before his twenty-third birthday "William Dunlap, an eminent Portrait Painter, and a member of the Philological Society, only son of Mr. Samuel Dunlap, Merchant," was married to "the amiable and accomplished Miss Nabby Woolsey, of Fairfield, in Connecticut."[4] A second play, apparently written before his marriage, was accepted for production, advertised during the later summer as by "a gentleman of this place, much celebrated for his wit and humour," and who "besides great ability in the Dramatick, . . . has a peculiar talent in the Lyrick way of writing, and that in a manner new and unknown." Even before *The Father, or American Shandyism* was played for the first time at the theater on John Street early in September, announcement had been made, "As soon as three hundred Shandean subscribers are obtained, the work will be put to press."[5] Dunlap was proud to remember that it was the first native play performed by professional actors to be published by an American press (*T*, 2: 152).

During that fall he wrote further for the theater, two prologues and an interlude, but he was head of a household now, with responsibilities which increased when in December his son John was born, the first of three children and the only one of them to survive him. More time was spent now in his father's mercantile business which by early 1790 was advertised as that of Samuel Dunlap and Son, dealers in fine glassware, china, and tea. He contributed occasionally to the *New York Magazine*,[6] and kept his hand in by sometimes painting portraits of his friends. After his father's death in 1791, the business was all his own, requiring fatiguing trips to Boston and Philadelphia. He took in partners then to help him, for Dunlap had much business of other kinds, meetings of the Friendly Club, an expanded continuation of the Philological Society, and of the Manumission Society in which he played an increasingly active part. He was doing more writing now than painting. But mainly he remained an active man about town, less convivial perhaps than he had been, but a fine fellow still to be with. In 1796 he left the store in other hands to become a theatrical entrepreneur and, ten years later, a bankrupt. His professional career had begun, and his professional friendships which extended over forty years more.

He had talent for almost everything except success, and for this, late in life, he blamed his education which was cut into by war and illness and irresponsibility. He had neither the confidence in himself nor the canny ingenuity of a Benjamin Franklin, nor the supreme confidence of a Henry Adams who was sure that his time and his place were responsible for his not having been sufficiently capable of making the kind of life he thought he should have made. Dunlap, a more humble man, placed the blame upon himself, with quite too little recognition that he, like many of his war-bred generation, attempted to build ambitious edifices on foundations too flimsily prepared to support them.

NOTES

1. Dunlap does title chap. 13 of *The History of the Rise and Progress of the Arts of Design in the United States* (New York, 1834), the "Autobiography of the Author. William Dunlap." I have used the edition edited by William Wyckoff (New York, 1965), quotations or paraphrasing from which will be identified within parentheses in the text as *A* followed by volume and page designation. For his *History of the American Theatre* (New York, 1832), I have used the reprint of the second edition (New York, 1963), which will be similarly identified as *T*. For his *History of the New Netherlands* (New York, 1839–1840), I have used the reprint (New York, 1970), which will be designated as *H*.

2. This circumstance was first pointed out, I think, by Robert H. Canary in *William Dunlap* (New York, 1970), p. 17.

3. See Oscar Theodore Barck, Jr., *New York, 1776–1783* (New York, 1931), pp. 57–84 passim.

4. *New-York Daily Gazette*, 16 February 1789.

5. Ibid., 26 August 1789.

6. Lewis Leary, "Unrecorded Early Verse of William Dunlap," *American Literature* 39 (1967): 87–88.

Thomas Branagan

REPUBLICAN RHETORIC AND ROMANTICISM

IN AMERICA

❧ ❧

THOMAS BRANAGAN was one of America's most prolific authors during the first two decades of the nineteenth century. He published something more than twenty separate volumes in verse and prose, some of them running through at least five editions within as many years, all of them read and most of them apparently popular. His occasional verse appeared in broadsides and copiously in the newspapers, and his book-length narrative of *Avenia* in 1805 was the first poem of any considerable length devoted in this country to the subject of Negro slavery.

Yet Thomas Branagan appears in none of our literary histories, is mentioned in none of our biographical dictionaries, is not even given a line in the detailed local histories in which loyal Philadelphians have chronicled their cultural past. He is one of a score of forgotten men who wrote before Irving, Cooper, Longfellow, and Poe, who anticipated Emerson and Whitman, and who—if we are to understand what we do or do not have of cultural heritage—should not be passed over.

Thomas Branagan, thus neglected, could be here introduced from several points of view: as an early American literary adventurer; as a representative of the impact of unruly Irish manners on polite American culture; as a murky mirror of early nineteenth-century ideas—something in the manner of Thomas Paine or Robert Ingersoll; as an early reformer—disciple of Howard, Godwin, Day; as a literary Lorenzo Dow who wrote Methodism and evangelism and popular religion enthusiastically into tracts, much as Norman Vincent Peale does today. Instead, perhaps we can glance at him briefly as—in addition to all these —a coincidental representative of certain aspects of English romanticism which we are sometimes taught did not appear in nineteenth-century America until many years later.

Thomas Branagan was born in Dublin, of a respectable, reasonably well-to-do Roman Catholic family on 28 December 1774. His boyhood, he says, was unhappy. His mother died when he was five, and he was brought up by a father who seemed to the boy "destitute of parental tenderness." His schoolmasters were unfeeling and cruel, so that his whole life in Dublin until he was fourteen was remembered as "a continual scene of misery." This in spite of the fact that "my father . . . took pains to give me a good education, but in vain; for, though he gave me in charge of the best teachers, I continued what is generally called a dunce."[1]

Dunce or not, Branagan seems to have been a sensitive, devout young man who particularized his sins in a pocket diary, "in order to relate them," he explained, "with more facility to my confessor."[2] The beggars of Dublin moved him to such pity that he vowed to devote half his earnings to the poor forever.[3] "Truly," he said, "I was a little zealous devotee."[4] In school meanwhile he experienced continuing difficulties: "I was flagellated until I was all in a gore of blood. . . . I do believe that a child of common capacity, could have learned as much in nine months as I did in nine years."[5]

So, when he was fourteen, Thomas Branagan went to sea, first with his father's consent on short voyages across to England, then to Spain on "a boisterous passage through the Bay of Biscay," and later to Russia, Denmark, and Norway, to Prussia, and Poland. Homesick then, after months away, he jumped ship when British soil was reached again, and beat his way back to Dublin again, where, instead of happy paternal greeting, he was met with reprimand—for the captain was a friend of the elder Branagan and word of the runaway boy reached home before he did. "I was so irritated at the reproval," said Branagan, "that, in a few days after, I left my relatives and friends, without their knowledge and consent," and he went to Liverpool, "having heard that a smart lad of moderate knowledge and industrious habits might get an eligible situation and good wages, to sail out of that port."[6] The year was 1790, Thomas Branagan was sixteen, and now on his own.

He sailed from Liverpool on a slaver bound for West Africa, where he remained for some six months, exploring inland, trading with the natives, buying slaves, and once, Melville-like, deserting his shipmates for an idyllic few weeks among the simply hospitable and happy noble savages of the Gold Coast, who made him "as welcome in their rural abode," he said, "as if I had been a dear friend or relative." Though they knew him as a slave trader and "had not sufficient food for themselves, yet they divided it without my solicitation, and gave me a part without ever reproaching me." He could have filled a folio volume with his adventures there among the primitive blacks, with whom he found more kindness, more hospitality than among the Christians of Europe or America.[7]

After sharing in profits when the cargo of slaves was sold in Granada, Branagan set out for the West Indies, where he sailed from Saint Eustatia for Savannah, "escaping many alarming dangers on the American coast." Then he signed in the service of the Dutch on vessels which supplied garrisons throughout the Caribbean. Finally he joined an English privateer, until his conscience got the better of him and he left this nefarious business to become instead an overseer on a sugar plantation in Antigua.[8] There he remained four years, experiencing "a variety of adventures," and would "in all likelihood have been advanced to what the world calls *a gentleman:* but I preferred virtue in rags, to vice arrayed in costly clothing."[9]

It seems to have been at about this time or earlier—at any rate, by the time he was twenty-one—that Branagan succumbed to a new, very severe and lasting religious experience. He was converted to Protestantism, probably by the Moravians, possibly by the Methodists—or, as he put it, "the gracious Redeemer had compassion upon me, and blessed me with a sense of his pardoning love and regenerating grace." And soon "I got convinced," he continued, "of the great evil of slavery and saw that those who took any act or part thereof, were guilty of oppression in the sight of God." Therefore, "although religious friends and even the Methodist preachers who generally kept slaves, all advised me to continue my employment, I was necessitated by conscience to give it up."[10] Not long afterward, "I voluntarily relinquished . . . [my] lucrative situation in Antigua, and threw myself on that all-beneficient providence, which hitherto has provided for me, and, I trust, will provide for me in all time coming."[11]

Or, interpreted from another point of view, he left Antigua for Dublin, to see to the settling of his father's estate. His relatives in Ireland greeted him cordially after his eight years of absence. But, "when they understood that I had forsaken the church of Rome, they persecuted me as a heretic, and defrauded me of my rights with impunity." Then it was that Branagan determined to seek his way to America. He laid out what funds he had in certain unidentified "valuable articles" which he shipped on board a schooner bound for Philadelphia; and he himself took passage on the same vessel.[12]

His arrival in the New World was not propitious. Let him tell the story:

> The vessel on which my property was shipped, was caste away, at the Capes of Delaware, and I lost it all, my clothes excepted, and I was robbed of them by one of the passengers, who also robbed me of two silver watches, one of which I detected on his fob, and my apparel on his back; of course I recovered a part of my clothes, and one watch, and advised the man, who was a Friend by profession, not to do so any more, as in a strange land, by acting in this manner, he would ruin his character and come to nothing.

But even misfortune had its bright side:

> I can not but admire the infinite goodness and wisdom of my God, in this afflictive dispensation of his gracious providence: while chief-overseer, I became exceeding proud, having an elegant horse to ride upon, a servant to follow me, being cloathed in gay even foppish apparel, and having every accommodation to make life agreeable, and no labour, it was absolutely necessary in order to crucify my proud spirit, to reduce me to poverty in a strange land.[13]

There seems to be no record existing of how Thomas Branagan, thus humbled, made his way in the Quaker city. "About three years after my arrival," that is, in 1801, "it was in my mind," he tells us, "to preach the gospel; which I did with the approbation and consent of one of the most pious sects in America, to which I then belonged." The sect, we suppose, was Methodist, perhaps Moravian. "I used to visit and preach to the poor and the needy, the halt, the maimed and the blind, in the Bettering-house, and scarcely missed one Sabbath in about two years."[14] Meanwhile he had married, and fathered one son, who died, "a new saint," on 22 October 1802, at the age of twenty-one months. A second son, born in 1803, died five years later. A third, born in 1812, lived only one week.[15]

Then, some six years after his arrival in Philadelphia, Thomas Branagan began to break into print. "It was in my mind to bear testimony against slavery, from the press, as well as the pulpit; and it was astounding how my good God qualified me for this service." He admitted himself "assuredly destitute of every natural qualification, necessary to appear before the public as an author." He had "little school learning, less natural capacity, and scarcely common sense; but the Almighty," he explained, "generally makes us of such poor, ignorant, destitute creatures, to confound the wisdom of the wise . . . and mighty."[16] Within two years, in 1804 and 1805, four separate books surged from his pen, two in verse, two in prose, each devoted to a full-hearted humanitarian argument against traffic in human beings.

The first was in prose—*A Preliminary Essay, on the Oppression of the Exiled Sons of Africa: Consisting of Animadversions on the Impolicy and Barbarity of the Deleterious Commerce and Subsequent Slavery of the Human Species.* It was presented as "by Thomas Branagan, late a slave-trader from Africa, and planter in Antigua, who, from conscientious motives, relinquished a lucrative situation in that island; and now from a deep sense of duty, publishes to the world the tragical scenes, of which he was a daily spectator, and in which he was unhappily concerned." The volume was dedicated to "all friends of humanity, particularly the president and members of the Abolition Society, and the people commonly called Quakers, who, by their distinguished exertions for the suppression of slavery and the relief of the oppressed Africans, have done immortal honour to themselves—to humanity, and the Christian name."[17]

Thomas Branagan was a plain man. "To novelty of sentiment, or to refinement of composition," he said, "he does not pretend." Neither could be expected from a slave trader or a West Indian planter. His was a labor of pious love, and he defied "logicious cavellers and snarling critics" to find fault as they would, either with his matter or his manner. He was no weaver of fancy dreams, no romancer, no novelist. The merits of his cause would plead excuse, even for his literary inaccuracies. He wrote plain sense, as a plain man, for plain people. He wrote not for fame or gain, but for the good of mankind. He knew that of which he wrote. He had been there.[18]

Yet what, he asked, might he expect to be the fate of his "humble, but well-meant endeavours" for the good of his contemporaries? "While the phantom dreams of the romancers and novelists are read with assiduity, my performances will, doubtless be by many treated with great neglect." How slothful, negligent of every good thing was his age! "To every serious strain the heart is shut and the heart inpenetrable," while at the same time "the idle fopperies and the foolish dreams" of the romancer "find the readiest access and the fondest entertainment." The reader of fiction, he charged,

> is amused, he is delighted, he is in raptures. Delusory prospects, fancied scenes open to him, with which he is, at once astonished and delighted. Every thing he sees is marvelous. Every house is a palace or a cottage; every man an angel or a fiend; every woman a goddess or a fury. Here the scene momentarily varies; and assumes new appearances. Now it is a dreary castle full of spectres and ghosts, robbers and murderers. Next moment it is a beautiful villa or a splendid palace, resounding with the notes of festivity or joy. Now it exhibits the appearance of a loathesome dungeon, with rattling chains and chilly damps. Suddenly it is changed into a beautiful garden with fragrant flowers, blushing partners, inviting fruits, and melodious songs; by which the juvenile mind is entangled and infatuated. Then succeed adventures, intrigues,

rapes, duels, elopements, darts, sighs, groans, armies, murders. Debauchery in this way assumes the form and name of gallantry.—Revenge is termed honour. . . . Thus the destruction of the human soul is accomplished; the arts of seduction are practised, and female innocence is ruined. Thus libertines endeavour, too successfully endeavour, to emancipate mankind from the shackles of religion and humanity. This they call freedom. Fatal freedom! . . . They debase themselves to a level with the brutes; and, like them, abandon themselves to every species of sensuality.[19]

With no such perverting vagaries would Thomas Branagan concern himself. He would write only of what he knew, of simple moral truths which would touch and uplift the human heart. Not only was the African oppressed, but what shocking barbarities were practised against him! Branagan wrote at length then on the beauty and the fertility of the green hills of Africa, the humanity and hospitality he had experienced there among the natives. "After all my travels, in both the old and new worlds, I do not hesitate to say, this is the most beautiful and fertile country I ever beheld." Its happy inhabitants reclining under lofty palms! "What simplicity in their dress, and in their manners! How innocent, benevolent, and hospitable! Yet how the white man has tricked them."

Again Branagan bears testimony also to his own unhappy part in this treachery: "In the midst of remonstrances, and lamentations, and shrieks, sufficient to pierce the mountains and rocks, I have torn and dragged from their happy country these once happy people." Now is he haunted by the memory:

> See them collected in flocks, and like a herd of swine, driven to the ships. They cry, they struggle, they resist, but all in vain. No eye pities; no hand helps. Into the hold of the vessel they are forced. Their limbs, already wounded and lacerated, and bloody, are loaded with heavy chains. Such numbers are compressed within so small a space, that the air almost immediately becomes pestilential, from the putrid effluvia of which they contract diseases.

Exposed to "every insult and abuse . . . men and women entirely naked" are examined "more minutely than the butcher does the cattle he intends to purchase. The poor female slaves, innocent and unaccustomed to debauchery, are ready to sink with grief and shame." Husbands are parted from wives, children from mothers, each to undergo miseries in the sugar fields. How merciless the driver's whip! How wretched the huts in which they rest their bleeding bodies! How poor and scant the food they are allowed to eat! On some estates they are not even permitted to wear clothes! They are subject to whippings on every occasion, to rape on almost every.[20]

This, as he had said, was no romancer's dream. It was realistic, and sensational. Branagan had been there. He knew. He recorded fact. "I write not what I have read or heard, but what I saw, and, to my shame, I must add, what I did; for in the tragical sense I was an actor."[21] His was a confession, written, we must suppose, with intention no less sincere than that of Jean Jacques Rousseau or Benjamin Franklin. And yet, at the same time, he satisfied his readers with all the trappings of Gothic thrill—the chains, the whip, the sadistic, the sexual titillation. He wrote of colorful and mysterious regions far away. He played on the sure knowledge of his contemporaries that primitive man, untainted by civilization, was fine and pure and happy. He touched strongly on the quivering string of humanitarian sympathy which made men of sense and of sensibility equally aware of the advantages to be derived from applying the Golden Rule. More than this, it was exhibitionism, realism, gothicism, primitivism, and humanitarianism written for the common man, leveled to a set of responses of which the simple reader was capable.

For Branagan's intention throughout was rhetorical: he wanted to persuade. He had something important to say, and he wanted to reach as many people as possible. *The Preliminary Essay* was exactly what its title suggested, a prologue to later publications, particularly to a work in verse of "considerable magnitude on which he had been employed for some years." It was Branagan's conviction "that many will read a performance in poetry, who will not be induced to peruse the same materials, however well arranged and digested in prose." Poetry was more elevated, more serious, more inspirational: readers in the early nineteenth century were accustomed to find their own highest aspirations mirrored there. The "younger set," Branagan thought, were especially "fond of poetical compositions," because it was easier for them "to retain in their memories a metrical, than a prosaic" argument. It was for these reasons, then, that in his second book Thomas Branagan as a practical man turned, he said, to verse. Admitting his manifest inadequacies, he set his argument, and "with no small labour," within the "form of a tragical poem. May it accomplish the salutary purposes for which I composed it."[22]

The poem appeared early in 1805 as *Avenia; or, A Tragical Poem on the Oppression of the Human Species, and Infringement of the Rights of Man*. It was put together in six books, and admittedly in imitation of Homer's *Iliad*. "Perspecuity instead of elegance, utility instead of method, the development of truth"—these, "instead of flowers of rhetoric," he insisted, "have been my primary objects in the prosecution of the work." He sought no personal gain. His object was "the happiness not the applause of mankind, to be useful rather than systematical." Above all, he would be plain: "The attempt to adorn truth . . . is like painting a diamond, in order to beautify it."[23] Perhaps nowhere in our literature of the early nineteenth century is there clearer, more succinct statement of literature as a tool for the shaping of moral virtues than in those simply naive, sincere, admittedly plagiaristic platitudes of Thomas Branagan. More plainly than Hawthorne or Longfellow or any of the more sophisticated, artful writers of the midcentury, he represents the climate of popular opinion on things literary against which Poe protested.

Avenia, among the most useful, remained Branagan's favorite among his works. It was his first, apparently begun before *The Preliminary Essay*. It was undertaken "from the most generous motives; namely to vindicate injured innocence and advocate the rights of man." And in composing it Branagan was assisted, he was sure, "by some supernatural power, for no person saw the MSS, much less corrected it, till it was sent to the press."[24]

> When I remember my profound ignorance at the time I commenced writing . . . and that I did not know what a semicolon, a note of admiration, or a quotation mark meant, I

237

cannot help but believing that the Almighty ordered it so, that he might confound the wisdom of the wise, the scientific, the philosophic advocates of moral corruption, by the simple statement of an illiterate child of nature.

The "plan, the design, the arrangement of the poem," he said, "are original." Only the versification was imitated, from Homer, as he admitted on the title page. And from more than Homer: "I availed myself of similitudes I had seen and copied pieces I had read." But it was all for good cause. "And where," he protested disarmingly, "is the author the most profound, who does not do the same? though, no doubt, more careful in their transposition than I was. Even Virgil . . . copied Homer."[25]

It seems perfectly clear that in imitating Homer, even talking about Homer, Branagan copied Pope. And in spite of protestations that incidents of the poem were founded on fact and represented scenes which he himself had witnessed, it seems equally clear that Branagan's experience was transformed to familiar patterns of antecedent English verse:

> Awake my muse, the sweet Columbian strain,
> Depict the wars on Afric's crimson plain.
> Sing how the poor, unhappy sable dames
> Are violated at their rural games;
> How Afric's sons surrounded with alarms,
> Die in the cause of liberty, in arms;
> How with their bloody scourge the Christians go
> To Africa, dread ministers of woe;
> How big with war their tilting dungeons ride,
> Like floating castles o'er the yielding tide.
> What pen can half their villainies record?
> What tongue can count the slaughters of their sword?[26]

Which is exactly what Branagen sets out to recount. He tells of the princess Avenia, first seen in circumstances of idyllic, bucolic pleasure, attended by dusky nymphs who dance with her through the forest green—Avenia, in love with and loved by the faithful Angola, idolized by her brave big brother Louverture. Then, as her nuptials are being celebrated with dance and song, the cruel Christians come, and they carry her off to captivity. Through five books there is a medley of pursuit and escape,

of battle and retreat, as loyal African hosts turn in bloody conflict against the white marauders. The gallant Louverture dies
bravely in heroic single combat; the prince Mondingo almost
triumphs, until superior, efficient, civilized Christian weapons—
of the kind Mark Twain was later to talk about—drive him also
to defeat. In the end, the white men triumphantly slaughter their
courageous dark opponents. Avenia is carried to a West Indian
plantation, where she is sold and soon after ravished by her base
new master, so that she flees from his lustful arms to a high rock
which overhangs the sea and flings herself therewith to the more
pure embrace of a watery grave.

> No mortal eloquence can paint their woes,
> Depict their wrongs, and malice of their foes:
> Not MILTON's pen, nor SHAKESPEARE's tragic lyre,
> Nor HOMER's flame, nor POPE's poetic fire.[27]

Yet Thomas Branagan would try. And later in the same year,
timed to reach the public just when the Missouri question of
whether new states should be slave or free was being debated in
Congress—in 1805, he tried again, with the publication of a
second poem, *The Penitential Tyrant; or, Slave Trader Reformed,* described as "a pathetic poem, in four cantos." It seems
to be an earlier writing of *Avenia,* though it may be, as Branagan
himself says, that its imperfections are due to the fact that it
"was prepared hastily for the press, merely as a work that might
do some good, and which at any rate do no harm." It is less
vigorous than *Avenia,* filled with generalized flights on the rural
happiness of the African, the cruel designs of the white man,
with bright descriptions of blood streaming from lacerated backs,
of limbs festering in chains, of heartbreak as black families were
torn apart, and of the sense of penitence which the writer felt
for having had part in these things—the whole recounted without identification of particularized characters (such as Avenia or
Louverture) or of particularized battles or braveries. The verse
seems not so tied to eighteenth-century models, but is, if anything, less competent than the verse of the earlier poem: "the
unsystematical arrangement of my writings, the simplicity of my
style, and the desultory plainness of my phraseology" are all,

explained the author, "convincing circumstances . . . that I am far from aspiring to the reputation of an author."[28] His aim was simple truth, unadorned, unadulterated.

Still later in that year he produced another pamphlet in prose, which he called *Serious Remonstrances Addressed to the Citizens of the Northern States, and Their Representatives: Being an Appeal to Their Natural Feelings & Common Sense: Consisting of Speculations and Animadversions, on the Recent Revival of the Slave Trade, in the American Republic: with an Investigation Relative to the Consequent Evils Resulting to the Citizens of the Northern States from that Event. Interspersed with a Simplified Plan for Colonizing Free Negroes of the Northern, in Conjunction with Those of the Southern Free States, in a Distant Part of the National Territory: Considered as the Only Possible Means of Avoiding the Deleterious Evils Attendant on Slavery in a Republic.* The title generously presents his argument almost complete. Branagan was one of those humanitarians to whom the opening of the west, particularly the Southwest, seemed to offer an opportunity for guilt-ridden American slave owners to hide their sins on the expanding frontier. His argument throughout was for colonization—and that is perhaps one reason why Branagan is not better remembered among historians of abolition movements in America.

But, that aside, as matter for the sociological historian, we find in this polemic volume another of Branagan's heightened, richly adorned pleas for simplicity. He postures almost like Whitman, and suggests again that writing with an eye on the proletariat was no invention of 1855, or of the 1930s:

> That pedantic style, and systematical arrangement peculiar to many writers, must not be expected of this work. The writer has made it his particular object to digress from the common mode of composition in this respect, because he wishes not to please the learned, but to profit the illiterate, to convince the understandings, and not to gratify the literary taste of his fellow citizens; and he flatters himself his plain arrangements will be as well received by the patriotic, the independent citizens of America, as if they were embellished with flowery emblems of fancy, the profound flourishes of

rhetoric, the superfluous disquisitions of criticism, the majestic brilliancy of diction, and the fascinating flippancy of language . . . all of which in fact have no other tendency, than to demonstrate the pride and vanity of man's degenerate heart, and lull the unguarded patriot, the industrious plebian, the virtuous farmer, and the honest mechanic asleep in the cradle of political sensibility.[29]

Indeed, the "fascinating flippancy" of his time engaged some of Branagan's most headlong diatribe:

> The sable crimes of this licentious age,
> Condemn my silence past—demand my rage!
>
> . . . .
>
> Such blasphemy, and systematic swearing;
> Such bawding, drinking, stealing, lying, gaming;
> Such cold religion, warm incontinence;
> Such bare-fac'd treach'ry, and profuse expense;
> Such languid charity, and such daring crimes;
> Such shameless fashions, and such impious times.[30]

Especially, such shameless fashions. In *Avenia* he launches out on one parenthetical passage addressed to the "fair, half naked to the solar ray":

> the dresses now by women wore,
> Would make a harlot blush in days of yore.
> Such fashions have I seen in open day,
> Which decency forbids me to display;
> Their swelling breasts, their necks and elbows bare,
> With eyes enticing, and with curling hair,
> Their robes so fashion'd that degen'rate men
> May fancy all the wond'rous charms within.[31]

"When I view the obscene, the indecent manner in which too many mothers dress their daughters," he submitted in a footnote to *The Penitential Tyrant,*

> I tremble, I tremble for their chastity; It is virtually tempting the debauchee to tempt them, and to lay a snare for their destruction. Nay, it is even inviting the lawless ruffian to acts of open violence; and, while female fashions continue to be so immodest, I think in point of common justice, the law ap-

plicable to such outrages [as rape] ought not to be so strict and severe. . . . How cruel . . . for a lascivious female . . . to dress in such a manner as not only to entice, but almost to force the male of ardent passions to acts of violence, and the law to condemn him to death, while she is suffered to pass with impunity.[32]

But this, sincere and fervent as it may have been, was aside from his main point. Branagan looked with compassion on even the potentiality of what he called the injured innocence of what he also called the American fair: "By dire example ruin'd, thus wretched lies / Millions of youthful dames with streaming eyes."[33] So, as a well-meaning and impressionable man of his times, a rational and therefore a practical man, Branagan dealt in his next two books with just that subject, and offered forthright, practical advice. It seemed perfectly clear that young girls were seduced because young girls were ignorant, or—to put it another way—that women were enslaved by men in this and in other matters because women were not properly educated. Many people, including Branagan's fellow Philadelphian Brockden Brown and Mary Woolstonecraft had said, were saying just that.

Branagan, however, eschewed, he said, generalities, and came to grips with the realities of his own day. The principal reason, he submitted, why so many "ignoramusses abound in the country parts of the American Republic, is . . . that parents are so parsimonious or . . . avaricious, that they too often neglect to send their children to school.[34] I would ask, he challenged, "what makes the distinction between the savage and the sage? The answer is obvious, INFORMATION. And yet forsooth thousands in this free country are indifferent with respect to obtaining information as if it was of no utility whatever." It is not knowledge for its own sake with which Branagan is concerned, but with useful knowledge, something which works to immediate practical advantage. And, he continued,

it is not only the plebeian who is thus blinded by local prejudices and sentimental ignorance, but even persons who are distinguished by their commercial intercourse and consequent riches, who are notwithstanding sometimes as destitute of polite information as the wild Indians on the banks of the

Ohio; the reason is obvious, they are so immured in the tumult of business, and perhaps the vicissitudes of folly, that they cannot be prevailed upon to forgo either.[35]

Branagan rang no challenge to his countrymen to look out from under their iron lids as Emerson did. He did not suggest that they come out from behind their gigantic counter which Leigh Hunt saw stretching along the Atlantic coast from Florida to Maine. He was a practical man, who, within limits, fitted his cloth to the disagreeable pattern which mankind in its folly had made. So he put together an early nineteenth-century digest for busy readers, a capsule catchall of knowledge, which he called *The Flowers of Literature: Being a Compendious Collection of the Most Interesting Geographical, Historical, Miscellaneous Subjects in Miniature.* It was "intended to facilitate the improvement of youth in particular, and adults in general, whose pecuniary resources will not admit them to purchase, nor relative avocations allow time to peruse voluminous productions on these important heads." Put together so that he who ran busily and he who could not afford fine books might read, his compilation was, Branagan boasted, if not original, at least "more comprehensive and embraces a greater number of subjects than any other of the kind that has appeared in this, or perhaps in any other country."[36]

A year later, in 1807, he carried his crusade farther with a volume entitled *The Excellency of the Female Character Vindicated,* which he described as "an investigation relative to the cause and effects of the enroachments of men upon the rights of women, and the too frequent and consequent misfortunes of the fair sex." It was intended "as a counterpoise to those vile and vulgar publications which are continually teeming from our presses, and which frequently instill the most destructive poison into the mind of the rising generation, and eventually prove the destruction of the giddy, the volatile, and the gay." Specifically, he purposed,

> to inform the mind and establish the virtue of women; to erect barriers in order to stop seduction in its mad, and too successful career; shut the floodgates of temptation which

modern fashions have opened; shelter female innocence from the innovations of libertinism; and, finally, nurture the smallest bud of their juvenile virtue to its full blossom, and thereby promote individual tranquility, domestic felicity, national prosperity, and the honour and happiness of posterity.[37]

All the catchwords were there—they had to be, for they made up the facile language of a time when Washington Benevolent Societies, sons of Cincinnatus or of Tammany, patriotic and philanthropic groups of all kinds enjoyed mild orgasms of such hortatory banalities.

The Excellency of the Female Character makes excellently good reading, inevitably invocative of a kind of supercilious pleasure. The temptation is to quote from it at length, what Branagan further says of the "spurious, futile, and pernicious publications . . . teaming from our presses," perverting the innocent, yet rewarded with popularity; or what he has to say of the menace of the debauchee, of the indecency of worsted pantaloons, or—in fascinating detail—of the new, clinging, and plunging French fashions. He quotes Pope, the Bible, William Livingston's *Philosophic Solitude*, Mrs. Rowson's *Charlotte Temple*, and most frequently, himself. He suggests the establishment of a female university,[38] and the isolation of syphilitic cases in almshouses and jails. He wonders what modern young men are coming to as he sees "young Master Tommy . . . with his pantaloons up to his chin, his waistcoat about six inches long, his half boots with tassels, a watch on his fob, a club under his arm, and a seegar in his mouth, strutting along with his arms a-kembo, with all the self-consequence of a nabob."[39] Young Master Tommy is a person we recognize, a cousin certainly of the attractive young fops Washington Irving and his friends were writing at just this time into *Salmagundi,* with which they kept New York in an uproar.

And here again Branagan vaunts what we are perhaps justified in calling his Republican Rhetoric: his insistence on his own simplicity, the simple commonsense utility of his message, and the simple language (or what he can approximate in his prolixity of simple language) in which he clothes it for simple people like himself:

My primary object is to be useful, without paying the least regard to the critic's malicious sneers, the debauchee's vindictive frowns, or the fashionable dame's consequential declamations . . . I conceive it to be the duty of an author, who writes for the good, not for the praise of man, to make his readers reflect, not laugh; to study utility more than elegance; brevity more than redundance; to forego prolixity and exhibit variety. A well-poised sentiment, a simplified argument, supported by reason and common sense, an instantaneous exhibition of the common fact, have a better tendency to convince the understanding, inform the mind, and reform the heart, than volumes of elegant, refined, but futile composition.[40]

Caught up by the infectuous flow of his own words and the intensity of his convictions, Thomas Branagan wrote on and on, repeating the few simple ideas which he put forth in his first volumes. His books came regularly from the press. *The Beauties of Philanthropy* and *The Excellency of Virtue* both appeared in 1808, *The Intellectual Telescope* and *The Pleasures of Death* in 1809. *The Rights of God* in 1812 and *The Charms of Benevolence* in 1813 seem to have been the most popular, and they ran through five editions each. He followed them with *A Beam of Celestial Light in a Dark, Deluded, and Degenerate Age* in 1814, *The Pleasures of Contemplation* and *A Glimpse of the Beauties of Eternal Truth* in 1817, and *The Pleasures of Paradise* in 1832. Less toothsome in title, but equally forceful were his *Political Disquisitions on the Signs of the Times* in 1807, his *A Concise View of the Principle Religious Denominations in the United States* in 1811, his *The Pride of Britannia Humbled, or the Queen of the Ocean Unqueened*, put together in 1815 as a triumphant catcall at the end of the second war with England, and his compendious *The Guardian Genius of the Federal Union*, in which in 1839, and again in 1840, he brought together the most tellingly rhetorical of his writings into what amounts to a two-volume anthology.

After *Avenia* and *The Penitential Tyrant* he published no separate volumes of verse, except the pamphlet entitled *The Poetical Apotheosis of General George Washington*, written in

1811 to convince citizens of Philadelphia of the propriety of erecting a statue to the father of their country on Chestnut Street, opposite the statehouse. But dozens of Branagan's shorter poems, on virtue, on almshouses, on slavery, on the amelioration of conditions in American jails, on the virtue of young ladies, appear scattered through his prose tracts and also in the newspapers of his time—for, to put it mildly, he had a genius for getting into print.

Except for this however he seems to have been a very modest man, so that his personal career is extremely difficult to follow. In 1811 he broke from sectarian religious affiliations, to become a stridently nonsectarian itinerate preacher who traveled through all the middle and northern states spreading his philanthropic gospel. He had no use for well-fed, smug, fashionable clergymen, who were hypocrites, little better than panders. His mission was to the poor, "the sons and daughters of affliction," he called them: "I did attempt to preach to them in their wretched lanes and alleys."[41] Sometimes they turned on him with hooting and garbage and stones. "I used to deliver my message, on horseback, in the streets, in the highways, in private houses, school houses, and meeting houses." Once, he remembered,

> when passing through Princeton, New-Jersey, I felt it my duty to address the collegians relative to the true Christian divinity. . . . I therefore posted by bill on the market-house, and rode up the street till I was nearly opposite the college, when with palpitating heart, quivering voice, and eyes fast closed, I sung a hymn, still on horseback—a crowd of collegians and others soon gathered, and some began to laugh and geer, when I began my discourse, but soon were all attention, and continued so till I ended it.

"Thus," he went on, "I delivered either a written, printed or verbal address in every hamlet, town, and city I passed through between Philadelphia and the District of Maine."[42]

He planned to extend his mission among all the "cities and seaport towns between . . . Maine and Georgia, through which I expect to travel for truth's sake."[43] Indeed, "were I possessed," he said, "with the voice of a trumpet, and adamantine lungs, methinks I would make all America reverberate with my remonstrances."[44] He traveled some seven hundred miles, on foot, on horseback, entreating his listeners: "Seek Christ in your hearts. . . . Turn from all men to the light within." And he sought earnestly within himself for the truths which he knew were there. A journal which he kept of his travelings was "so tainted with enthusiasm," which seemed to him a worldly thing, that he later burned it.[45]

After 1818 little is discovered of Branagan's activities, except for an occasional glimpse as he continues to speak and write valiantly: "to please, to honour, to glorify God, and be a benefit and consolation to his intelligent but unfortunate creatures . . . to cure them of inordinate love of earthly objects, and to stimulate them to seek their happiness in contemplating his sovereign beauty."[46] As he became older, even more humble, and less active, he offered his writings without charge to the public: "I intend," he said in 1817, "to deposit a collection of my minor works, in nineteen volumes, in the Franklin Philosophical Library . . . with the request that if any respectable person or persons, disposed to republish them . . . they should be accommodated with a copy."[47] He seems to have retired then to simple living and continued occasional preaching, we suppose, until 1843, when the records of Saint George's Methodist Episcopal Church in Philadelphia inform us that he died in that city of the palsy on 12 June of that year, aged 69.[48]

We have skipped very quickly over only a portion of Thomas Branagan's long career. Perhaps enough has been revealed of him and his philanthropic intention to enable us to write him down as—among other things—something more than tentatively what better people than we have called a romantic. He had no patience with rules; he looked into his own heart, his own experience, and wrote; he used the first person confessional; he celebrated the goodness of primitive people and of unsophisticated ideas; the faraway and the horrible were favorite themes; he melted at the suffering of the poor; he yearned toward a good which transcended sense; he mixed rudely as a reformer into other people's business; he was concerned with the education of children, of women, of the underprivileged; he did his best to write for the common people in what he could approximate of their language. If these, or any combination of these, are symptoms of the romantic fever, then Thomas Branagan had it badly—and here, in this country whose inhabitants are often said to have been immune to its ravages until many years later.

He was a radical, a devout Christian, a friend of the downtrodden. Like Philip Freneau, he signed himself proudly "one of the swinish multitude." He believed with fervor that truth, as he saw it in his own heart, would make all men free, and that men were infinitely capable of progressing toward a more perfect state. Yet he was, like Freneau again, self-consciously an American, an outspoken literary nationalist, even a little petulant on the subject:

> I do not expect that any thing I can produce, tho' I was blessed with the astonishing talents of a Homer, and judgment of a Virgil, will command general attention in America, unless it was previously published and eulogized in England, and introduced as European manufacture. For I am morally certain that if Burns or Bloomfield had made their literary appearance in this commonwealth, neither of them would have found a single patron, or perhaps a book-seller to publish their poems.[49]

As a Christian, he had little good to say of the later writings of Thomas Paine, yet he agreed that "man, in certain parts of the United States, by the cunning craft of selfish priests, is reduced to a poor, dependent, bigotted, distorted, prejudiced superstitious man." He thundered against "college manufactured" ministers who "let the poor go to hell by the thousands." Yet this, nor any other evil need not be, for modern man, enlightened man, man freed of bonds of bigotry is "capable of a degree of intellectual improvement bordering on the celestial."[50]

It was Thomas Branagan's mission, thus echoing and anticipating, to awaken his fellows to the possibility and the practicability of the recognition of avenues within themselves which led toward truth. He reworded many of the ideas which stimulated better men than he as they moved toward the intellectual and literary renaissance of the midcentury. A simple man, a good man, a man of intense feeling, of profound concern with himself and his fellows, he caught at many notions which enlivened his time, and he rewrote them as best he could for all men to read. The trouble with Thomas Branagan and his admirable intention is that, though he wrote fervently, he did not write well. He admitted himself "desultory and inelegant." He grieved later in life that he had once "attended too much to the jungle of words."[51]

But, even admitting his literary inadequacies, he disarms us. "Alas!" he said, "the world is too full of books, replete with golden lies, in support of despotism; and embellished with the flowers of rhetoric, in defense of vile and vulgar sensuality."[52] And what is literary fame? "What is the approbation of poor perishing mortals who will shortly be the food of worms? . . . What are the plaudits of those depraved and partial critics, who eulogize and render popular those intellectual murderers (who deserve the gibbet more than the highway robber who only kills the body, while they destroy the soul)? . . . What are the vociferated praises of millions of 'stupid starers' to one self-approving thought, begotten by conscious rectitude?"[53] And whatever else we take away from Thomas Branagan, we cannot deny him his "self-approving thought."

NOTES

1. *The Penitential Tyrant* (New York, 1807), pp. 2–3. Young Branagan's chief affections went out to his old nurse, the wife of one of his father's domestics, with whom he lived in the country until he was almost four. "My parents had adopted, and uniformly practised the unnatural custom, of sending their children at our birth, from under their inspection, and giving us in charge of nurses in their homes; and I recollect one of my sisters who was almost starved before it was found out by my father, who instantly had her taken home"—*The Excellency of Female Virtue* (New York, 1807), p. 136. "This unnatural mode of educating children, I consider one of the greatest misfortunes of civilized society, and pregnant with a thousand evils to both parents and children"—*The Pleasures of Contemplation* (Philadelphia, 1818), p. 39.

2. *The Charms of Benevolence* (Philadelphia, 1813), p. 292.

249

3. *Avenia: or, A Tragical Poem* (Philadelphia, 1805), p. 333.

4. *The Penitential Tyrant*, pp. 3–4.

5. *The Pleasures of Contemplation*, p. 39.

6. *The Penitential Tyrant*, p. 4.

7. Ibid., pp. 7–8; see also *The Pleasures of Contemplation*, pp. 17–18.

8. Ibid., pp. 11–12. "We cruised off the harbours of Cape Francoise and Port-au-Prince, from whence the rich planters were making their escape, with all their wealth, in American vessels, from the fury of the negroes, who were at this time in a state of insurrection. And while these unfortunate persons were thus sailing for American ports, we constantly captured and robbed them of all their property. . . . While I was on board of this privateer, however, I was enabled to see, by the light of the good spirit of Grace . . . that privateering was as wicked in the sight of Heaven, as high-way robbery, hence I relinquished all my prize money, which would have amounted to several thousand dollars"—*The Charms of Benevolence*, pp. 293–294.

9. Ibid., p. 16; see also *The Penitential Tyrant*, p. 295.

10. *The Charms of Benevolence*, p. 294.

11. *A Preliminary Essay, on the Oppression of the Exiled Sons of Africa* (Philadelphia, 1804), pp. 30–31.

12. Ibid., pp. 20–21.

13. *The Charms of Benevolence*, pp. 295–296.

14. Ibid., p. 296.

15. See *Avenia*, p. 171n, and also Burial Records, Board of Health, Philadelphia, 1807–1814. His wife, Ann Branagan, died on 28 April 1830, at the age of 47—see Record of Saint George's M.E. Church, Philadelphia, 1785–1856, 1: 346.

16. *The Charms of Benevolence*, p. 296.

17. *A Preliminary Essay*, p. 2.

18. Ibid., p. 5.

19. Ibid., pp. 19, 23–24.

20. Ibid., pp. 32–33, 35.

21. Ibid., p. 26.

22. Ibid., pp. 4, 26–27.

23. *Avenia*, pp. ix, 311. "I have voluntarily delivered the manuscript to the printer for publication gratis . . . if any bookseller should wish to publish another edition . . . he shall be . . . at liberty [to do so]"—pp. 310n–311n.

24. *The Pleasures of Contemplation*, p. 18. When a second edition was prepared in 1810, then Branagan however did seek aid, from a benevolent, "respectable and amiable physician of Philadelphia [a certain Dr. (Thomas?) Atlec, of whom I have been able to discover little]; whose urbanity is only commensurate with his erudition," and who corrected and revised the sometimes halting meter.

25. *Avenia*, pp. 18–19.

26. Ibid., pp. 15–16.

27. Ibid., p. 256.

28. Ibid., p. 3.

29. Ibid., p. v.

30. *The Penitential Tyrant*, p. 57.

31. Ibid., p. 260.

32. Ibid., p. 182.

33. *The Penitential Tyrant*, p. 262.

34. *The Flowers of Literature* (Philadelphia, 1806), p. 233.

35. Ibid., p. 7.

36. Ibid., p. 5.

37. Ibid., pp. iii, xii.

38. Elsewhere, in order to counteract the influence of aristocratic American colleges, he suggests the establishment of state universities "to be supported at public expence," manned by "republican teachers . . . chosen by the legislature." They should be large, "sufficiently extensive for the accommodation of at least 3000 boys." A student's total expenses should be between $52 and $104 dollars a year, and "the male orphans of veterans" should be admitted gratis. Here all American boys, even the sons "of indigent citizens, may be taught all the useful branches of science; such as reading, writing, arithmetic, surveying, navigation, mensuration, anatomy, botany, law, physic, etc."—*The Charms of Benevolence*, p. 24.

39. *The Excellency of the Female Character*, p. 29.

40. Ibid., pp. 35, 52.

41. *The Charms of Contemplation*, p. 298.

42. *A Glimpse of the Beauties of Eternal Truth* (Philadelphia, 1817), pp. 4–5, 9.

43. Ibid., p. 9.

44. *Political Disquisitions* (Philadelphia, 1807), p. 61.

45. *A Glimpse of the Beauties of Eternal Truth*, pp. 5, 7.

46. *The Pleasures of Contemplation*. 5th ed. (Philadelphia, 1815), p. 14.

47. *A Glimpse of the Beauties of Eternal Truth*, p. 3.
48. 1: 486; see also the Philadelphia Board of Health Records, Register of Deaths, 1 June 1842–30 March 1847.
49. *Political Disquisitions*, p. 12.
50. *The Charms of Benevolence*, p. 10.
51. *Avenia.* 2d ed. (Philadelphia, 1810), p. 10.
52. *The Charms of Benevolence*, p. 5.
53. *A Preliminary Essay*, p. 4.

THE LITERARY OPINIONS OF
Joseph Dennie

If Dennie had not that intellectual vigor which crushes to obtain an essence, or dissolves to develop a principle; he had judgment and taste to arrange a sentence, and polish a period. His imagination was rich and excursive; it knew no thralldom and spurned at no narrow bounds. It had that which the country wanted more than anything else, *a refined taste.*

Samuel L. Knapp (*Lectures on American Literature,* 1829)

THERE is no question about it, Joseph Dennie was opinionated, egotistical, autocratic, and high-handed. He suffered no fools gladly, was bigoted, snobbish, and sycophantic. Yet there are compelling reasons to accept the testimony offered on his tombstone in the Burying Ground of Saint Peter's Church in Philadelphia, that he "devoted his life to the Literature of his Country," and "contributed to chasten the morals, and refine the taste of the nation." If he had not existed, someone else could have risen in his place as the inevitable, necessary man. But Dennie arrived, and because he was there, truculently assertive, the literature of his country retained inherited attitudes which revolution and enthusiastic patriotic nationalism might otherwise have put aside. Admirers were not mistaken when they called him the Columbus of polite literature in the United States.

He was a Massachusetts man, the most successful in letters from that state of his generation. He was born in Boston in 1768, but when the British took over that city seven years later, he was taken with his family to Lexington, where he passed his boyhood until 1783 when, the revolt of colonials against the mother country having ended in victory, he returned at fifteen to Boston to enroll in a commercial school. A year of study there and another year as an apprentice in a counting house convinced him that checking invoices and bills of lading was not what he wanted most to do. So, after boarding for a year in Needham with a clergyman who prepared him for college, he entered Harvard, at nineteen older than many of his classmates, "buried" for three years, he said, "in that rubbish of a school," that "sink of vice, that temple of dulness, that roost of owls."[1] Suspended once for impertinence, he was graduated in 1790, and then read law for four years in Charlestown, New Hampshire. There his literary career began, with contributions to *The Morning Ray* in nearby Windsor, Vermont, and to *The Eagle, or Dartmouth Centinel* in Hanover, of an essay series which he called "The Farrago," light, bright, and lively, intended to amuse and instruct in the manner of Franklin and Addison and the irrepressible Laurence Sterne.

For a brief period he served as a lay reader in the village church at Charleston, and then at another village some five miles to the north. During the summer of 1794 he began what would become a long literary association with Royall Tyler who had been a collegian in Cambridge when Dennie was a schoolboy there and who now practiced law across the Connecticut River in the village of Guilford, Vermont, as they put together a periodical column called "from the Shop of Colon as Spondee," Dennie writing in prose as Colon and Tyler in verse and Spondee. He had himself been admitted to the bar that summer, but confided to his parents, "I never shall be a silent unenterprizing lawyer. My talents . . . are *superficial,* but they are *showy,* & the deficiencies of Judgment in the thought are in *vulgar* opinion compensated by the boldness & glitter of fancy in the expression." He was a confident young man, boldly dogmatic and certain that he knew the way to success: "Let the hair brained enthusiasts prate . . . as loudly as they please to the contrary, a young adventurer in any walk of life must take advantage of the wants & weaknesses of his fellow mortals, or be content to munch turnips in a cell amidst want and obscurity."[2]

Filled with ambitious plans for conquest, he descended again on Boston in the spring of 1795, ostensibly to practice law, but apparently most successful as a dashing young man about town and a litterateur of conspicuous promise. He contributed critical essays on the Boston theater and on Harvard College to *The Federal Orrery,* recently established by young Thomas Paine, who had graduated two classes behind him at Cambridge, and was something of a scapegrace who had incurred the displeasure of his patrician family by having recently married an actress. With Paine and among others of the young elite of Boston, Dennie was soon recognized as "a most charming companion, brilliant in conversation, fertile in allusion and quotation, abounding in wit, quick at repartee, and of only too jovial a disposition." Josiah Quincy remembered "gay dinners" to which Dennie would "summon the flower of the youth of Boston," and at which "the festivity which set in at the sober hour of two would reach far into the night."[3]

In May he began a periodical of his own, a weekly called *The Tablet,* described as "a miscellaneous paper devoted to the belles lettres." It survived for only thirteen issues between 19 May and 11 August 1795 but like Paine's *Federal Orrery,* almost as short-lived, is a landmark for identifying the postwar activities of young men who would establish a literary reputation, if not for the new United States, for themselves. Modeled on the *Spectator* and the *Tatler,* on Dr. Johnson's *Rambler* and *Idler,* and of a kind with Washington Irving's later *Salmagundi,* the first of its four pages presented each week an essay from "The Farrago" series, most of them reprinted from the *Morning Ray* or the *Eagle;* the last page, "The Parterre," was given over to verse, anecdotes, and epigrams; and the two middle pages contained items, usually brief, of biography, literary intelligence, and original criticism, the latter probably by John S. J. Gardiner, in what Dennie as editor described as "the first attempt at critical disquisition in America" (19 November 1795). Five contributions "From the Shop of Colon and Spondee" were lifted from the *Eagle,* one of which (19 May 1795) poked daring good fun at Col. David Humphreys, the tediously prolific maker of verse which seemed to echo aristocratic aspirations of the military and commercial complex which threatened domination of the new national establishment, warning that

> When the muses' death bell tolls
> A requiem to *poor* Poets' souls,
> Let worm to brother worm declare,
> "Expect to-day Duke Humphreys' fare."

Dennie prided himself on being able to distinguish good literature from bad. His letters are sprinkled with testimony to the
self-proclaimed superiority of his taste, his reading in Cervantes
and Shakespeare, Fielding, Swift, Addison, Chesterfield, and with
especially great admiration, Oliver Goldsmith. He applauded the
Scottish James Beattie for his "rich, fertile, and cultivated imagination" and the "energy and dignity of his language," but particularly for his pristine correctness and his exquisite taste.[4] Those
qualities, thought Dennie, were precisely what his provincial
countrymen lacked. Was not the failure of *The Tablet* to be
blamed on the dullness and tastelessness of Bostonians, on the
almost universal "waywardness of the times" and, said Dennie,
"the infancy of my savage country"? It would have succeeded
anywhere, he said, but in a vile democracy.[5]

He retreated then again to the Connecticut valley, to Walpole in
New Hampshire, where he would try his hand once more at law,
but found himself instead first a contributor to and then the editor
of the *New Hampshire Journal, or Farmer's Weekly Museum.*
"The Lay Preacher" essays which appeared in that newspaper
from 12 October 1795 to 21 August 1799 were widely reprinted
in other periodicals and brought him almost instant national fame.
They were pleasantly informal, attempting to blend the familiarity of Franklin's style with the quick simplicity of Sterne's
in homilies which counseled thrift, industry, and recognition that
men were not, in truth, created equal but owed it to themselves
and to the welfare of their country to maintain themselves at the
level to which they had been born. Conservative readers seem to
have reacted well to what "The Lay Preacher" said of the subversive infidelities of Tom Paine and of other fuzzy-headed
"democratic projectors" who interfered with rationally controlled
progress. Collected in a volume in 1796, and again posthumously
in 1817, these essays provided Dennie his first platform from
which to deliver corrective admonitions to his countrymen. By
the time he left Walpole after almost five years' residence there,
the newspaper which he edited was known as *The Farmer's
Museum, or Lay Preacher's Gazette.*

As an editor with admittedly superior taste, Dennie expressed a low opinion indeed of native newspaper editors in general. They were mere subalterns, perpetrators of "a gross and slovely system of plagiarism" (15 April 1799); they were "ignorant, blind, grovelling," without comprehension of even "the lowest elements of taste" (22 April 1799). But they accurately and inevitably reflected attitudes of most of their countrymen. The few native Americans who were interested in the arts, like Sir Benjamin Thompson from New England and Sir Benjamin West from Pennsylvania, were forced to look abroad for encouragement. Even the small handful of praiseworthy native poems, like Timothy Dwight's *Greenfield Hill*, Joel Barlow's "The Hasty Pudding," and Peter Markoe's *The Times*, had "been left by America for Great Britain to criticize" (22 April 1799). The poet in the United States, as much as the manufacturer of cloth goods, "has found a plenty of raw materials, each has made good homespun ware, and each had failed in raising that fine nap, and giving that brilliant colour to their manufactures which strike the eye of people of fashion" (1 April 1799).

Dennie from the beginning was unashamedly hortatory. The *Farmer's Museum* presented a varied display of edifying extracts from transatlantic writers which might serve as touchstones for aspiring native readers. And he kept up to date, becoming apparently the first in the United States publicly to welcome the *Lyrical Ballads* of Wordsworth and Coleridge. On 2 September 1799, just one year after the publication of that volume in England, he reprinted from it Wordsworth's "Goody Blake and Harry Gill," describing that poem as "in the genuine spirit of ancient English song," demonstrating, "by proof irrefragable, that simplicity and the language of ordinary life may be connected with the most exquisite poetry." No more than almost anyone else at that time, did he know who were the authors of the volume, but he was certain that this poem was "indited in the very language of nature," avoiding "the French paste and tinsel of the childish Coleridges, Southeys, and Merrys of the age." It derived certainly from no leveling Jacobin source: "It is written by an English gentleman and relishes of the character."[6]

So extreme was Dennie's advocacy of the simple, tasteful decencies of English manner and Federalist views that he soon found himself, not unhappily, caught in the cross fire of partisan politics. The dedicatedly democratic *Independent Chronicle* of Boston said of him that

> If love of England, monarchy, or gold,
> Could bribe a native to betray his country,
> There sits the pampered wretch would sell her to him.[7]

But others found him, though "rigidly aristocratic, and probably monarchial," not only "a judicious critic, and an excellent moralist, but an elegant writer," worthy on every count of "the appellation of the American Addison."[8]

In person he seems to have been something of a dandy, disdainful of his rural neighbors, a gentleman from sole to crown, shorter than most men and impeccably slender. A fellow villager described him as in "the highest note of fashion," fastidiously turned out "in a pea-green coat, white vest, and nanking small-clothes, white stocking," his "*pumps* fastened with silver buckles, which covered at least half the foot from instep to toe. His small-clothes were tied at the knees with ribands . . . in double bows, the ends reaching down to his ancles." His hair was "frizzled, or *craped*, and powdered," augmented "by a large *queue*" which, wrapped "in some yards of black riband, reached half way down his back."[9] No wonder that when he ran for Congress in the summer of 1798, he received only six votes. "I was disgusted," he then said, "with the levity and weakness of the *people*." He held "the *herd* of society" in "profound contempt."[10]

When late in 1799 Dennie's skill as an editor, the popularity of his "The Lay Preacher" essays, and his forthright political views brought him to Philadephia as successor to John Fenno in editing the obediently Federalist *Gazette of the United States* and to a position as clerk in the office of the secretary of state, he found himself among more agreeable associates. There in the nation's capital, he discovered what he called "rational pleasure" and "solid fruits of friendship" most often "in the company and conversation of Englishmen, or friends of Englishmen." For the "English character," he said, "is the most honest, the most generous, the most frank and liberal." How "foul is that day and our calendar," he went on, and how "bitterly are those *patriotic*, selfish . . . traitors to be cursed who instigated the 4th of July, as a day of Independence." He wished that he might have been an Englishman himself, for then his literary ambitions might have been realized.[11] Englishmen like William Cobbett fed his ambition and his pride. Dennie, said Cobbett, "would shine in almost any country but America," where "he casts his rays among the sleepers and the blind."[12] When in 1800 Cobbett fled to London, pursued by democratic suits for libel, he invited Dennie to go with him. By now, however, other plans were under way.

For "the spirit of literary adventure," said Dennie, "is not easily quenched." When in December 1800 he presented a prospectus for a new weekly paper to be called the *Port Folio*, which would be conducted pseudonymously by "Oliver Oldschool, Esq." for the entertainment of "the rich, the well-born and the able," Dennie approached the pinnacle of his influence as an arbiter of public taste. He promised "not to make his paper a *carte blanche* on which any knave or fool may scribble what he wishes"; he would "not strive to please the populace"; he could not "gratify the malignity of fanatics" by aspersing anything English, nor would he espouse "the Fairy-Tales of France, that *all* men are kings and emperors, and nobles, and judges and statesmen." He would not attempt to please "by infusing into every ill-balanced and weak mind, a jealousy of rulers, a love of inovation." He would avoid "reveries of liberty, equality, and the rights of man."[13]

Dennie was proud of his newly assumed position as a cosmopolite, and he was proud also of the friends he made among young men of sophisticated taste in Philadelphia. Association with well-connected people allowed him to present what he thought to be first printings of poems by Thomas Campbell and Leigh Hunt.[14] When Thomas Moore visited Philadelphia in 1804, he not only contributed to the new publication, but also recorded, "In the society of Mr. Dennie and his friends, I passed the few agreeable moments which my tour through the states afforded me." In spite of the "ignorance and corruption" which surrounded him, "Mr. Dennie has succeeded," said the English poet, "in diffusing through his cultivated little circle that love of literature and sound politics which is so rarely characteristic of their countrymen."[15]

Yet, except for a reprinting of sixteen of "The Farrago" series and of some sixty of "The Lay Preacher," plus a dozen new essays in that series, little in the *Port Folio* can be confidently assigned to Dennie. He may have contributed to the section which appeared irregularly as "An Author's Evenings," and his hand certainly appeared in some of the items identified as "From the Shop of Colon and Spondee." It may be assumed that as editor he was responsible for much of the "Literary Intelligence" which appeared in almost every issue, and for most of the headnotes which introduced miscellaneous contributions. A temptation to attribute many of the unsigned literary essays to him is lessened by the testimony of one of his associates "that in the whole course of his editorship," extending over a period of twelve years, "there are scarcely as many original essays from his pen."[16]

It may be supposed, however, that as editor Dennie set the tone and temper of the *Port Folio*, certainly from 1801 to 1809 while it remained a weekly over which he was actively in control, and in some degree from that time, when it became a monthly, until shortly before his death in 1812. Its contents can be thought to reflect literary judgments of which he approved.[17] And these judgments, set forth in a style which, though often primly magisterial and sometimes dominated by political considerations, went far in shaping attitudes toward literature in the young republic.

The *Port Folio* was not primarily intended as a show place for native wares, but as a cosmopolitan display of the correct best of classical and European literatures intended to "improve the taste and intelligence of the nation," to "enlarge and correct" its "notions of excellence" (12 September 1807). It was not addressed to "the lower classes of our motley vulgar, too often composed of scoundrels of all nations, perpetually restless and rebellious" (3 January 1801). John Quincy Adams who contributed generously to its early issues, hoped that it might "take off that vile stain of literary barbarism which has so exposed our country to the reproach of strangers, and to the derision of enemies."[18]

Its native contributors, however, included some of the more distinguished among the elite of the new nation. Not only John Quincy Adams, but his brother Thomas Boyston Adams, both sons of the former president, were among them, as were Nicholas Biddle, Samuel Ewing, Benjamin and Richard Rush, and Clement Moore. Old friends were there, like Royall Tyler and Thomas Greene Fessenden at whose father's house Dennie had boarded in Walpole, and newer friends in Philadelphia also, like Charles Brockden Brown and John Blair Linn.[19] Native writers, when of the right kind, received a fair share of commendation. David Humphreys's mechanical couplets were derided (3 November 1804), but lines by Timothy Dwight received editorial approval (13 October 1804), and the collaborative corrective satire of the Connecticut Wits aimed at "our political visionaries" was reprinted with delight (14 January 1802). Warren Dutton's Yale commencement poem on *The Present State of Literature* which pointed toward "the neglect or abuse of letters in America," was quoted at length (10 January 1801). But Dennie set precise standards. More than once he announced the return of a poem or an essay to its contributor because it was incorrect in tone, word, or meter.

Large space was given to Samuel F. Jarvis's Phi Beta Kappa oration on "Want of Patronage the Principal Cause of the Slow Progress of American Literature" (11–25 April 1807), which Dennie described as an effectively "caustick satire upon the degraded and unprotected state of letters in this licentious country," and to the anonymous "An Examination of the Causes Which Have Retarded the Progress of Literature in the United States" (20 June 1807), each of which pressed hard on native lack of learning and discipline, the failure of education in inculcating refined taste, the almost universal busy pursuit of wealth rather than culture among Americans, and the rampant vulgarity of its political demagoguery. Fessenden's *Democracy Unveiled* was applauded for "tracing the poison of Jacobism to its source, by portraying the character of all our demagogues and exposing the depravity and absurdity of a vulgar and short-lived system." In Dennie's judgment, writings such as this, and of his other friend Thomas Moore, gave promise that "the commencement of the nineteenth century bids fair to rival any of its predecessors" (18 January 1806). To prove it, he reprinted a long and laudatory English review of Fessenden's Hudibrastic satire (17 May 1806).

For Dennie was generous to his friends. The writings of John Blair Linn deserved, he said, "the notice and encouragement of every American reader" (17 January 1801). Robert Treat Paine, Jr., whom he had known in Boston as Thomas Paine, was an "eminent poet," to be admired especially for his descriptions of native scenery (23 May 1807). Royall Tyler's *The Algerine Captive* was recommended to all men of taste and judgment (28 April 1804). Charles Brockden Brown's "scrupulous purity of style" was applauded (24 August 1804), and Dennie noted with pride that Brown's fiction had attracted the attention of British readers "who have a taste for a purer style of English composition than is common in this gothic country (28 April 1804). Even Brown's friend William Dunlap, who had been chided for having translated plays by the irresponsibly romantic German dramatist Kotzebue, was excused as not having "willingly exhibited what is hostile to pure manners and good taste" (29 March 1806).

To Dennie, political error bred literary error: "The republican faction not only think erroneously," he said, "but write incorrectly" (6 November 1802). But a retired republican like Philip Freneau might be safely commended, at least for what he had done which was correct. From 31 October through 28 November 1807, a long four-part review of his poems appeared in the *Port Folio*, the first extended critique which the veteran poet had received. Freneau's versatility was praised, his sensitivity to nature, and his understanding of Indian character. He was placed on a level with William Falconer and Capt. Edward Thompson as a writer of the sea. He was compared, and not unfavorably, with Collins, Cowper, and Swift. But he was censured for his Jacobism and the occasional democratic vulgarity of his language. Finally, the critic, with what may now seem lack of nice discrimination, made a list of seventy-five poems by Freneau which in his estimate deserved preservation which did not include either "The Wild Honey Suckle" or "The House of Night." Though this essay in criticism has sometimes been attributed to Dennie, it seems to be neither in his style nor manner. He did, however, provide a headnote which attested, "For the *politicks* of the author it is pretty well known that we have no particular partiality, but of the *poetry* of this versatile bard we must say that, by the impartial, it will be at length entitled to no ordinary place in the judicious estimate of American genius" (31 October 1807).

For Dennie liked to assume a posture of judicious impartiality. When *The Columbiad* of Joel Barlow, who was in no way retired and who was a confidant of Thomas Jefferson, was attacked as lacking plot or unity, "a sort of poetical magic lantern," an "immense discordant mass of characters, facts and descriptions" set forth with "barren lack of invention" (January 1809), Dennie, who complained of having often been "rebuked for his fancied prejudice against the literature of his country," denied authorship of the review. "Any idea of deliberate hostility to this work" because it was an American production was, he said, absurd. "We know Mr. Barlow only as a poet, and in that capacity he is amenable at the Bar of Criticism" (May 1809). To prove lack of partisanship, Dennie silently reprinted from the *London Monthly Magazine* seventeen pages of more favorable reaction.

There were limits, however, to what Dennie, even half-heartedly, could approve. Benjamin Franklin, whose familiar style had been praised only a few years earlier in "The Farrago" and "The Lay Preacher" essays, was now chastised in the *Port Folio* as a despoiler of language who "attempted to degrade literature to the level of vulgar capacities in writings suited only to the capacity of apprentice boys and maid servants." Franklin was reviled as a base and penny-pinching man with a "low and scoundrel appetite for small sums," who had been among "the first to lay his head in the lap of French harlotry" (14 February 1801). His "hackneyed deism and muck-worn philosophy" was attacked (23 May 1801), his indelicacies and smirking immoralities, and his indecent audacity in passing off as "Franklinisms" the aphorisms which he had pilfered from other men (10 October 1801): "ever since the era of Dr. Franklin the love of proverbs has waxed exceedingly fervent among our countrymen," resulting in "debasement of the dignity and elegance of diction" and in an increase in the "woeful insipidity of the simple style" (12 March 1803).[20]

There was not, and there should not be, anything like an American language, as vulgarized by Franklin, stump orators and mob-rousing editors. Noah Webster, whose correct simplicity Dennie had also once publicly admired,[21] became as a lexicographer a favorite target. His dictionary was "an asylum for fugitive words" where "the idiotisms of his countrymen might find refuge" (21 November 1807). Dennie ridiculed Webster's proposed spelling reforms and cautioned contributors and printers alike to reply instead on the orthographic niceties approved in England by Samuel Johnson (7 November 1807). He promised always "to cherish the classical and established forms of diction, and preserve the purity, and resort to the standards of English style" (28 November 1801). He offered encouragement to "every American writer who is studious to emulate the finest authors of England" (31 August 1805). For himself, he wished "to be schooled in no other choice or combination of words than those which are derived from the country of his ancestors, and which constitute the *English* style. . . . Let others make a new language from the colloquies of our clowns, from the drawling cant of provincial idioms, and the turbid oratory of the *Town* meeting." He would have nothing to do with "nauseous, impure, and vulgar diction which has no authority in the *British Classics*" (19 April 1806).

For it was the classics which he admired, and the spirit of the classics, not the new poetry of English romantics. He printed translations from Juvenal and Horace, and various versions of Anacreon; biographical sketches of Livy, Plautus, Seneca, and Terence; and essays on Aeschylus, Horace, Ovid, Platon, Virgil, and Xenophon, hoping that "the rising geniuses of Columbia, the gentlemen and cavaliers, all the ambitious, all the aspiring" young men of the New World might learn to leave "the vile trash of literature to . . . the *swinish multitude*," to relish instead "the enchanting waters of antiquity" as much beside "the romantic Schuykill" as "by the side of the gentle Thames" (8 August 1807).

Rousseau was the arch villain who had unsettled men's minds. To Dennie, he was an "eloquent lunatic," a "splendid scoundrel," dangerous because persuasive (10 August 1805). From people like him derived the vile new French style of writing in "gross gibberish, the mother tongue of every low bred rebel" (23 June 1804). In his wake came that loathsome *"creeping-thing* called Tomas Paine" who was "a drunken atheist, and the scavenger of faction," the idol of the unenlightened (27 November 1802) and the protégé, no less, of that "speculative philosopher" Thomas Jefferson whose thoughts "when weighed in the scales of reason, against the practical wisdom of Edmund Burke, kicked the beam, like a gossamer, that floats in the air, balanced with a wedge of bullion" (12 June 1801). William Godwin was a lunatic, intent on beguiling with a "fantastic project of perfectibility" (14 September 1805). Joseph Priestley was a trickster intent on disrupting the government of honest men (3 January 1801). The "necromantic realms of German extravagance" were condemned (19 December 1801), as were the supernatural prodigalities of Anne Radcliffe and all her imitators (9 July 1803). Dennie announced himself "notoriously adverse to the hobgoblin style of writing." He promised to use the "mace of ridicule . . . to batter down the castles of horrible romance" (1 May 1803).

Wordsworth seemed less corrupted by malice or silly affectation, as did William L. Bowles whose sonnets were "incomparably the best in the English tongue, . . . neither in tenderness nor sweetness inferior to those of Petrarch" (15 July 1803). In early numbers of the *Port Folio,* Wordsworth was several times praised for his "language of simplicity" which avoided pitfalls of extravagance and sentimental ardor (19 December 1801). He had the "rare talent of unmasking many of the minuter operations of Nature, and of describing them at once in the simplest, and yet most interesting manner" (1 October 1803). He was an "amiable and humane man" who had "found a new walk in poetry" (24 March 1804). Dennie reprinted several of his poems (even attributing one by Coleridge to him), and seems to have encouraged contributors to imitate the Wordsworth manner.

But as more was learned of Wordsworth's politics, especially as revealed in the preface to the second edition of *Lyrical Ballads,* attitudes toward him altered. Though his "flashes of poetic imagination" were said still "to excite . . . admiration," he was now censured as "among the foremost of those English bards who have mistaken silliness for simplicity; and with a false and affected taste, filled their pages with the language of children and clowns" (March 1809). His "earlier effusions of poetical genius were not unworthy of the muse. But of late, he has extended so far his theory of simplicity in writing that it degenerates into burlesque and puerility" (May 1810).

Wordsworth had been thought to be an admirable poet because "he talks like *a man of this world*" (2 July 1802), but Southey and Coleridge, "mutually inflamed with France," wrote incendiary poems which attracted a "whole tribe of dissenters, innovators, wishers for parliamentary reform, and haters of church and king" (29 August 1801). Theirs was "flimsy poetry and abominable politics" (10 October 1801). Southey was "a romantic adventurer," with disdain of established rules sanctioned by the quiet good sense and "unerring experience of mankind" (January 1809). Coleridge was more to be admired "for the originality of his thoughts, than for the correctness of his opinions" (15 August 1801). He was "the boast of many a vulgar mind," honored by commoners, but rejected by aristocratic men of taste (12 October 1805). Yet there was good in Coleridge, for "however erroneous his political creed and however hairbrained his Pantisocratic dream of "migrating to the woods of Pennsylvania," he was at root "a man of genius and a poet." When his prospectus for *The Friend* appeared, the *Port Folio* supposed him to have reformed, thinking "that Time, Experience, and Observations, have totally changed the colour of this gentleman's mind, and that the rigor of right principle is restored," but Coleridge was nonetheless chided for the "affected negligence, not to say slovenliness" of his language (September 1809).

Even Charles Lamb came in for a small share of condemnation as a writer beguiled by the new school of loose liberality (10 October 1801). Byron's *Hours of Idleness,* though containing poems "written with spirit and force . . . and much sweetness," was marred by "faults of versification and . . . sins against grammar" (September 1809). For correctness was the byword, emphasized by instructive examples from the writings of such masters of impeccable language as Samuel Johnson, Smollett, Cowper, and Burke. Addison had set standards, said Dennie, to which "I have endeavoured to conform" (24 December 1803). "The Lay Preacher" essays were modeled on the "design of Addison," but in imitation also of "the harmless and playful levity of Goldsmith" (3 January 1801). For when pushed to make a distinction, Dennie placed the admirable author of the *Spectator* no higher than second place.

Unlike Addison, Goldsmith was "never careless, or indistinct." His writings were "admirable models for him, who is serious, of a style easy, but not colloquial; free, but not wanton; and exact, though not elaborate" (24 January 1801). Goldsmith remained "faithful to nature"; he was "correct and elegant, and at the same time free from every species of affectation" (19 March 1803). His language was "the very reverse of that revolutionary jargon so much in vogue" (24 February 1804). What could be better suited to "rectify the bad taste, and to purify that provincial diction, with which we are sometimes reproached" than the publication in the United States of an inexpensive edition of the writings of Goldsmith which every earnest American could carry in his pocket to read with profit during idle moments (22 October 1808). "Every line of this fascinating writer is to our eyes as a string of pearls, or a signet of carbuncle, set in gold" (5 April 1806).

Goldsmith's manner became the hallmark which guaranteed excellence. Much of Dennie's early admiration for Wordsworth apparently derived from his observation that "Wordsworth seems to follow Goldsmith in the easy and agreeable track of simplicity" (3 September 1803). Thomas Moore was praised for having "caught both the tenderness and general cadence" which "so gloriously distinguished his countryman" (2 August 1807). Like Goldsmith, he was "endowed with the enchanting privilege of expressing the warmest and tenderest thoughts, in a style at once brilliant and simple, like the wild flower of the mountains" (30 June 1804). Walter Scott's *Lay of the Last Minstrel* was "the most beautiful poem that has appeared since the days of Goldsmith" (27 August 1807). *Salmagundi*, edited by "a confederacy of man of wit and men of the world" in New York, contained matter which, "without servility, very successfully emulates Goldsmith's manner" (16 May 1807).

No wonder then that young Washington Irving, in imitation of Dennie's Oliver Oldschool, took as his first pseudonym the equally retrospective name of Jonathan Oldstyle. It is possible to believe that Irving may have contributed to early issues of the *Port Folio*. Certainly he met Dennie in Philadelphia in 1807, and sketched him in sympathetic caricature as Launcelot Langstaff in *Salmagundi*.[22] James Fenimore Cooper extended at truculent length some of Dennie's notions of Americans, the vulgarity of their popular press, the rapacity of their ways to wealth, and the demagoguery of their quite too democratic politicians. But it was Irving, whose *Life of Goldsmith* was admired and who cherished the reputation of being "the Goldsmith of his age,"[23] who provided the inevitable, though far less truculent, extension of Dennie's literary attitudes. As the dean of native letters during much of the half century that followed Dennie's death in 1812, Irving was the tone imparter who proved indeed that writing in the United States could be as genteel and charming and assiduously correct as writings in the motherland. Not until 1850, at the beginning of what people of our day have been schooled to recognize as the American Renaissance, was the dominance of Irving's attitude effectively contested. It was Melville who asserted that "there is no hope for us in these smooth pleasing writers" who "but furnish an appendix to Goldsmith." We want, he said, "no American Goldsmiths."[24]

Dennie need not be remembered as an important writer. His essays do not stand the test of time. His literary judgments were often warped by political considerations. He was charged with opportunism by contemporaries who did not like him:

> Does he aim at reformation—
>   Ah! know ye not, Joe Denny:
> What 'ere he may prate
> About the state;
>   He means but *to turn the penny*.[25]

He withstood trial for inflammatory and seditious libel in 1805 which failed to blunt the vigor of his attacks against fallacies of Jacobism and of literature written vulgarly for ordinary people. He sometimes struck out so boldly that he lost the support of friends like John Quincy Adams who mediated better than he. His health was never good, and his habits were perhaps not exemplary. By 1811 William Dunlap, who had once admired the sparkle of his wit, was shocked to discover "Dennie, the editor of the Port Folio, the American Addison, a driveller & a sot! . . . the ruin of a tasteful & polished edifice."[26] But he was there, a large and lasting influence who, if he did not establish, certainly effectively reflected an attitude toward literature which long outlived him. If, as Thomas Jefferson said, Philip Freneau saved our Constitution when it was galloping fast toward monarchy, Joseph Dennie may be said to have provided a following countervailing force in the dialogue between plebeian and patrician which continues to enliven our lives and literature.

NOTES

1. Laura Green Pedder, *The Letters of Joseph Dennie, 1786–1812* (Orono, Maine, 1936), p. 15. Details of Dennie's life are set forth by Harold Milton Ellis, *Joseph Dennie and His Circle* (Austin, Tex., 1915).

2. Pedder, *Letters*, p. 123.

3. Edmund Quincy, *Life of Josiah Quincy* (Boston, 1867), p. 31.

4. Pedder, *Letters*, p. 55.

5. Ibid., pp. 151, 153, 157.

6. See Lewis Leary, "Wordsworth in America," *Modern Language Notes* 57 (May 1943): 391–393.

7. 11 December 1797; quoted in Joseph T. Buckingham, *Specimens of Newspaper Literature* (Boston, 1852), 2: 304.

8. James Elliott, *Poetical and Miscellaneous Works* (Greenfield, Mass., 1798), pp. 229–231.

9. Buckingham, *Specimens*, 2: 196.

10. Pedder, *Letters*, p. 172.

11. Ibid., pp. 179, 182. Something might be made of essential similarities between Dennie's coming to Philadelphia in the dual role

of partisan editor and government clerk and Philip Freneau's experience almost a decade earlier in the same capacities but with very different political persuasion; each young man wished more than once that he had been born or could go to London, where writers, he thought, were allowed to flourish.

12. *Porcupine's Gazette*, 19 April 1799.

13. *Prospectus for a New Weekly Paper Submitted to Men of Affluence, Men of Liberality, and Men of Letters* (Philadelphia, 1800), pp. 1–2.

14. See Lewis Leary, "Leigh Hunt in Philadelphia," *Pennsylvania Magazine of History and Biography* 70 (July 1946): 270–280.

15. Ellis, *Joseph Dennie and His Circle*, p. 171.

16. John E. Hall, *The Philadelphia Souvenir* (Philadelphia, 1826), p. 59.

17. The present essay was in draft before I had opportunity of seeing Randolph C. Randall's expertly marshaled "Joseph Dennie's Literary Attitudes in the *Port Folio*, 1801–1812," in *Essays Mostly on Periodical Publishing in America*, ed. James Woodress (Durham, N.C., 1973), pp. 57–91, an essay to which I am nevertheless indebted.

18. *The Writings of John Quincy Adams*, ed. Worthington C. Ford (New York, 1913–1917), 2: 521.

19. See Randolph C. Randall, "Authors of the *Port Folio* as Revealed by the Hall Files," *American Literature* 11 (January 1940): 379–416.

20. See Lewis Leary, "Joseph Dennie on Benjamin Franklin: A Note on Early American Literary Criticism," *Pennsylvania Magazine of History and Biography* 72 (July 1948): 240–246.

21. Milton Ellis, *The Lay Preacher of Joseph Dennie* (New York, 1943), p. 17.

22. Ellis, *Joseph Dennie and His Circle*, p. 221.

23. Pierre M. Irving, *The Life and Letters of Washington Irving* (New York, 1869).

24. Herman Melville, "Hawthorne and His Masses," *New York Literary World*, 24 August 1850.

25. *Philadelphia Aurora General Advertiser*, 2 July 1801.

26. *The Diary of William Dunlap*, ed. Dorothy C. Barck (New York, 1930), 2: 430.

James Fenimore Cooper's Lover's Quarrel with America

❧ ❦

ONE Saturday afternoon in the summer of 1832 James Fenimore Cooper, who had spent four hours that day sitting for a portrait sketch by the Dutch painter Eugene Joseph Verboeckhoven (whose name he could not spell), recorded in his journal that "as is usual with nearly every artist who has attempted to give a resemblance of me, he has not succeeded. The character of the face has quite escaped him."[1] Cooper was a plainspoken person, sure of his opinion, on portraits or anything else. Not only did painters fail to please him, but critics also who attempted to delineate the features of his thought or art, or his attitudes toward America. "There may be better writers than I in the country," he said, "but there is certainly no one treated with so little deference."[2]

Some denounced him because he had lived abroad since 1826, but that was a personal matter, having to do with the education of his children and the protection of his rights as a novelist against transatlantic pirates who might reprint his books without paying him. It was certainly of no legitimate or logical concern of critics at home; Cooper would match his patriotism against any man's. Yet during these years in Europe he had not seen one "frank, manly, gentlemanly allusion" to himself in any American publication. And during that period he had published many books, each of which was meant to demonstrate the superiority of American to European ways. He was heartsick, he said, and "tired of wasting life, means, and comfort on behalf of those who return abuse for services." One thing seemed certain: "I am not with my country—the void between us is immense—which is in advance time alone will show."[3]

If time is ever to make a final judgment on Cooper's long lover's quarrel with America,[4] *Home as Found* (1838) must be examined with care. America's first detailed novel of manners, it presents the summation of an honest man's patriotic indictment. It appeared five years after Cooper's return to the United States, the last of a bombardment of books directed against shortcomings among his countrymen. To a man who had lived abroad, Americans seemed provincial, self-seeking, arrogant and complacent, thinking of liberty as a means rather than an end. Forgetting principles on which their nation was founded, they plunged without foresight toward chaos and corruption. Money-mad, they spoiled the land of its goodness, their voices strident in a single tone: "the mass has become so consolidated that it no longer has any integral parts; . . . the individual is fast losing his individuality in a common identity."[5]

At the center of Cooper's complaint was America's increasing deficit in integrity. His countrymen were losing pride in self, in being each a person with his own single nature or character. Only a few years later, Ralph Waldo Emerson would urge them to self-reliance, a term which Cooper did not like because it seemed to deny the instructive power of experience; he preferred to speak of self-confidence built securely on knowledge of the world and recognition of each person's ordered place within it. Like Ezra Pound a century later, he pressed irritatingly on sensitive areas, such as America's lack of originality and her misguided conception of wealth. But Cooper was not a subtle nor a complex person. He shared with most men the uneasy assurance that he had more to say than words to say it with, so that he repeats himself and contradicts and stumbles. That is perhaps why one of my friends advises undergraduates not to read Cooper until they are older, because Cooper is difficult to understand. What he means, I think, is that Cooper is deceptively easy to understand incompletely and therefore incorrectly.

He can be made to seem a bumbling romancer of forest and sea, who, as Mark Twain reminded us, did not always write well. He can be seen through D. H. Lawrence's eyes as the creator of lovely frontier idyls, or through Leslie Fiedler's eyes as revealing a pervasive psychic flaw which compels American men to flee women for the more comfortable companionship of their own sex. Cooper created our myth of restless expansion, of brave men pushing aside the wilderness, subduing it, but never themselves subdued. His Leatherstocking is an ancestor, not only of Huckleberry Finn and Faulkner's Ike McCaslin and Hemingway's emotionally abbreviated males who learn a right relation to nature, but also to each of the tall men who pack guns for righteousness' sake in celluloid sagas of adventure.

In this vein, Cooper has been read and will continue to be read as the writer of stories which almost every reader improves—in boyhood play, in daydream, by rewriting, or by varieties of critical interpretation. Hardly one of his forest romances is not more compelling in the memory of it than in the reading. Those rockbound adventures when war whoops pierce the quiet of a shadowed lake, the click of twigs or tell tale rustling of prairie grass, the cannily built campfires, the buffalo steaks and trout, the swift bark canoes and the trusty long rifles—remembrance snatches at these as bright threads from which new patterns are woven, forgetful of the dreary marches through the tangle of Cooper's prose. Yet when Cooper spoke of wishing to write American novels, it was not of these things that he thought. No more than Melville would he wish to be remembered only as a man who lived among adventures. The woodsman's competence and humanity, the red man's friendship or treachery, the race and chase and capture, were vehicles meant to carry larger meanings. Even in his earliest novels, he had something to say which was not always understood.

Above everything else Cooper wanted to be taken seriously. A man of intense pride and imperfect sense of humor, he plodded, as if with fists clenched, through the writing of each of his books. Born in Burlington, New Jersey, on 15 September 1789, he had grown up on his father's frontier lands at Cooperstown on Lake Otsego in upper New York state. After tutoring by an English clergyman in Albany, he entered Yale in 1803, where he learned to dislike New Englanders and was expelled before the end of his second year. For further training, he was sent to sea, first as an apprentice sailor on a merchantman, then as a midshipman and officer in the navy. At twenty, on his father's death, Cooper inherited extensive lands on the shores of Lake Otsego. Two years later, he married, left the navy, and settled into what he and everyone else expectd to be a career as landed squire and devoted husband and father. For a few years the Coopers lived near Mrs. Cooper's relatives in lower Westchester County, which he did not like; then they moved to Cooperstown, which she did not like; finally, they built a home at Scarsdale, where, quite by accident, Cooper began writing his first novel.

Tradition fostered by Cooper's daughter claims that he wrote *Precaution* (1820) on a dare from his wife. He himself explained that he put it together to amuse Mrs. Cooper at a time when she grieved over the death of her mother. He wrote on industriously until, finding the manuscript swelling to "rather unwieldly size," he counted the pages of *Ivanhoe* to discover how long a novel should be, and then adjusted his to that measure.[6] What resulted was a moral tale, set in rural England, which warned readers, among other things, of the danger of reading novels. Many people thought an Englishwoman, someone like Jane Austen, had written it. But of Cooper's second novel, done to show that he could do better and be original, no such mistake could be made. *The Spy* (1821) was native and masculine and filled with patriotic adventure. By trial and error, Cooper in his thirties was learning a new trade. "The task of making American manners and American scenes interesting to an American reader," he confessed, "is an arduous one."[7]

The Pioneers (1823), much of its plot borrowed from Shakespeare's *King Lear*, was laid near Lake Otsego and introduced Natty Bumppo, an aging woodsman who mourned the coming of civilization to his former hunting grounds. It told of the misfortunes of the Effingham family which had been Tory during the Revolution, and so had lost its lands. Through fortitude, manly skill, and marriage, they regained their property, but that fact becomes the least part of the book, which is an idyl of its author's boyhood and, after *Home as Found*, Cooper's most personal testament—a tranquil recollection of older times when men of all ranks worked together for a common purpose without any person forgetting the privileges or obligations appropriate to his position. Young Oliver Effingham had been trained to virtues of straight shooting and straight talking by the aging woodsman. He got the girl and the land because he was the kind of fellow who asked nothing and expected nothing of which he was not worthy by nature and training. Rags did not disguise his natural nobility.

This was characteristic of the American, to know his place, and to accept or claim it as his democratic freeman's right. Of different social station from young Effingham, but his equal in manly virtue had been Harvey Birch in *The Spy* (1821) and was Tom Coffin in *The Pilot* (1823). Each was a stout-spirited man, adroit, and excellently prepared for what he had to do. Each knew his place, and filled it with distinction, a useful, contributing member of wartime or shipboard society. Natty Bumppo, who appeared again in *The Last of the Mohicans* (1826) and *The Prairie* (1827), knew his place also, and maintained it against all temptation to become something other than what he was. Years before Emerson spoke of it more plainly, Cooper understood that human excellence required recognition of one's gifts and of one's inevitable limitations.

These five last-named books made Cooper's reputation. His country was proud of him, and he of it. "If I am able to create an excitement that may rouse the sleeping talents of the nation," he confided to Richard Henry Dana in 1823, "and in some measure clear us from the odium of dulness, which the malice of our enemies has been quick to insinuate, . . . I shall not have labored in vain."[8] Travelers from Europe, however, had not been kind in what they reported of America, its vulgarity, Franklin-bred penny-pinching, and inept imitation of European manners. For years Americans had lashed back with counterattacks, like Royall Tyler's *A Yankey in London* (1809) or James Kirke Paulding's *The United States and England* (1815). Even mild and conciliatory Washington Irving spoke sharply in *The Sketch Book* (1819) of "English Writers on America."

While living abroad, Cooper joined the fray with *Notions of the Americans, Picked up by a Travelling Bachelor* (1828), which attacked "falsehoods and calumnies" uttered against his homeland: "The European," he said, "has a great deal to unlearn before he can begin to learn correctly." Minimizing the odd or eccentric, Cooper concentrated on the decency, competence, and goodwill found among citizens of the New World. "What the peasant gains, the gentleman must in some measure lose," but, all in all, democracy was more elevating than leveling: "I would defy any nation on earth to produce as many men (and women too) . . . who have reached a credible moral elevation of character." The most "irresistible evidence of the general tone of decency" in America was the "great freedom" of her press. As for imitation, "America is beginning to receive with great distrust fashions and opinions from England." New York, to be sure, might impress a stranger as excessively commercial, but New York was not the United States.

In discussing native literature, however, Cooper expressed misgivings. There were in his homeland, he said, "no annals for the historian; no follies (beyond the most vulgar and commonplace) for the satirist; no manners for the dramatist; no obscure fictions for the writer of romance; no gross and hardy offenses against decorum for the moralist; nor any of the rich artificial auxiliaries of poetry."[9] Cooper did not mean to be insulting, any more than Nathaniel Hawthorne or Henry James did, who were later to say much the same thing. His *Notions* was intended as eulogy, but not blind eulogy. "It has ever been and still is my fixed opinion," he wrote to his publisher, "that America is of all countries one of the least favorable for all sorts of works of the imagination."[10]

Having exhausted native subjects—the settlement, the Revolution, the sea, and the frontier—Cooper therefore turned to writing other novels, no longer of American things, but illustrative of American democratic ideas. *The Bravo* (1831), laid in Venice, told of moral disintegration within a republic built on wrong principles. How different, he meant to imply, might be the situation in the United States. But critics at home found great fault with the book, and with *The Heidenmauer* (1832), which displayed the tyranny of German nobles, and *The Headsman* (1833), which revealed evils of hereditary aristocracy in Switzerland. What kind of American is this, who turns to foreign scenes for his fictions? asked the New York reviewers. What arrogance! What superiority he pretends!

When, after almost eight years abroad, the Coopers returned to America late in 1833, they must have seemed aloof and aristocratic, their attitude insinuating criticism of American ways. Everything about them was strange, their clothes, the furniture they imported, their foreign servants, and the manners of the children—"Even the cat was French." To them, New Yorkers appeared to be suspicious and resentful. The press continued to find fault with Cooper's writings, emphasizing elements which seemed to him unimportant or untrue, like his lumbering style and his disdain for unpolished people. Exasperated, he dismissed the reviewers as bothersome insects, "as nimble as fleas, and about as honest." If forced to choose, said Cooper, "give me the fleas."[11]

Then in a short-tempered essay, *A Letter to His Countrymen,* he wrote a brusque valedictory. Badly treated, he would write no more. "The American who wishes to illustrate and enforce the peculiar principles of his own country, by the agency of polite literature, will, for a long time to come, I fear, find that *his* constituency, as to all purposes of distinctive thought, is still too much under the influence of foreign theories to receive him with favor. It is under this conviction that I lay aside my pen."[12]

But the habit of writing and the desire to vindicate himself could not be put aside. If romances would not do, something else might. In *The Monikins* (1835) he attempted a roughly sketched, partially Swiftian satire, which took a liberal young Englishman, who thought that he should advance on his own merits and not because of the "stake in society" which he had inherited from a wealthy father, to a land where monkeys reigned, sure of their superiority over humans who were less than they because humans had no tails. Cooper pressed cumbersomely through every opportunity which the theme offered. Every sensible monkey knew his tail the seat of intelligence. When monkeys were to be punished, they were not beheaded, but decaudalized. Some lived in Leaphigh (England), where one was known as better than another by the number stamped on his rump; others lived in Leaplow (America), where discarded bits of Leaphigh tail were sold in great packages to newspapermen and society-minded up-starts.

There is something Olympian about this man who chastised his country because he wished it well. So serious and intense, with little laughter in him, he beat about him wildly with heavy strokes which bruised without piercing. Readers now spoke of his dull malignity, his clumsiness, his bad temper. *The Monikins* seemed "such a writing as a Bedlamite might produce, except that it lacks the vivacity and excitement of the madhouse." Imagine comparing men to monkeys or thinking that "politics can be associated in any way with romance."[13]

The travel books which appeared at this time—the five volumes of *Sketches of Switzerland* and *Gleanings in Europe*—made matters worse. Cooper plainly admired the graciousness, courtesy, and free intellectual play of Europeans, the excellence of Italian art, the quiet charm of London ladies, beside whom American women sounded like "nightingales roaring."[14] American society was distorted by a "secret, profound, and general defer-ence" for money, which is worshiped as "the very base of all distinction. . . . Men will, and do, daily, *corrupt themselves* in their rapacious pursuit of gain."[15]

Such remarks did not make friends in busy nineteenth-century America. Cooper's worst blunder, however, was made among his neighbors at Cooperstown. All the time he had been away, the villagers had used a piece of land which jutted into Lake Otsego as a picnic ground and bathing place. Most of them had forgotten that Three-Mile Point was not public property, but part of the Cooper estate. In order to protect himself legally, soon after his return to America the novelist had a chain strung across the entrance and a notice placed in a local newspaper asserting his right to the land. People in Cooperstown rose in indignation. Cooper's books were ordered removed from the pub-lic library. The press attacked him as an arrogant man and a bad writer, and he retaliated with one libel suit after another, some of which stretched on for years.

Even when he returned with *The Pathfinder* (1840) and *The*

Deerslayer (1841) to themes and adventures which readers liked, Cooper failed completely to recapture public favor. In the Littlepage trilogy, made up of *Satanstoe* (1845), *The Chainbearer* (1845), and *The Redskins* (1846), he again stubbornly asserted the rights of landed gentlemen to property which their ancestors had wrested from the wilderness. From this time forward, until his death in 1851, Cooper was known as a cantankerous man, ill-tempered and prejudiced indeed beside the urbane Washington Irving, who had also lived abroad but did seem to like America best, or Ralph Waldo Emerson, who also scolded his neighbors, but with kindly assurance that they could and would do better. Manifestly destined for greatness, young America grew and grew. Neither Herman Melville nor Mark Twain had arrived to invite it to a second look at what it might become.

Without their subtlety or skill, Cooper did. His *The American Democrat* (1838) played native counterpoint to Tocqueville's *Democracy in America* which appeared in translation during that year. Lacking the Frenchman's perceptive objectivity, Cooper scolded his contemporaries in essays written with bluntness not unlike that which H. L. Mencken would manage a century later. Democracy was right and good, but it depended on people, and people were not always to be trusted: they must "be watched in this country, as in other countries kings and aristocrats are to be watched," lest they escape sensible control and become tyrannical. Only in a special and limited sense was one man as good as another. Culture was needed, and manly experience, birth, and breeding.

The American Democrat had been called the intellectual scenario for Cooper's complaint against his countrymen in *Home as Found*, an account which started as one novel, but which broke into two, and which introduced for the first time into American fiction the kind of self-conscious judgment of native art and manners which later novelists who wrote better and thought more clearly would more successfully contrive.

Cooper's intention was plain—to set forth the character of their native land as seen by travelers returning from an extended residence abroad. He began his account with their taking ship in

England, but then became so involved in maritime adventure that he had written a novel's length before the passengers arrived at Sandy Hook, where he had originally planned their observations to commence. Never a man to begin over or deprive readers of adventure, Cooper published what he had written as *Homeward Bound* in the spring of 1838, and proceeded to provide it with a sequel, which was the book he first intended.

In some respects *Homeward Bound* is the better book of the two: it has more plot and more excitement and more explicit representation of character and Cooper is correct in warning that a reading of *Home as Found* "will be bootless" without knowledge of the book which preceded it.[16] The adventure is of minor importance, but not the characters—as in most Cooper novels, those who are good play their parts bravely, each according to his gifts; the man who drinks too much, though valiant, dies; the cowardly newspaperman who runs from battle with Arabs on the coast of Africa, lives on to be ridiculed further in the sequel.

On board the *Montauk* as she sails from Liverpool are the Effinghams, two cousins, John and Edward, and the latter's daughter, Eve. The girl has often attempted to sketch her father, but, like the Dutch painter who attempted a likeness of Cooper, finds the subtle character of the face continually to elude her. Edward Effingham lives on income derived from land, "which attached him to this world of ours by kindly feelings."[17] He is a cultured gentleman, amiable and winning. "Independence of situation had induced an independence of thought; study and investigation rendered him original and just, by surely exempting him from the influence of passion. . . . He loved his native land, while he saw and regretted its weaknesses; was its firm and consistent advocate abroad, without becoming its interested and mawkish flatterer at home" (1: 62–63). Many readers have thought that Cooper attempted a self-portrait.

John Effingham is richer than his cousin Edward, but John's money has come from commerce and speculation. As a result, he is forbidding, distant, even repulsive: his aquiline nose seems "to possess an eagle-like and hostile curvature—his compressed lip, sarcastic and cold expression . . . caused strangers usually to avoid him." Eve sketches him often "with great facility and truth" (1: 12). His father had been a Tory during the American Revolution, and he himself had sympathized with the British during the War of 1812, but John Effingham is not now so Anglophile as he had once been, "though the range of his old opinions were still to be noticed lingering (1: 12–13). He is sour and caustic, suspicious of the intentions of everyone, except his cousin's pretty daughter.

Eve Effingham is clearly Cooper's portrait of a lady, an older sister of Henry James's Isabel Archer. A "fair-haired, lovely, blue-eyed girl," much like Cooper's own daughters, she presents a softened reflection of her father's "sentiment, intelligence, knowledge, tastes, and cultivation, united to the artlessness and simplicity of her sex and years" (1: 10–11). Eve is twenty, and has been in Europe since she was eleven. She knows music, art, and languages——French, German, Italian, and impeccable English. Too well-bred "to run into the extravagant freedoms which pass for easy manners in America," she is "natural and unembarrassed in her intercourse with the world, and she had been allowed to see so many different nations that she had obtained a self-confidence . . . and great dignity of mind" (1: 12).

With her traveled as companion Mlle Viefville, daughter of one of Napoleon's officers, whose name the clownish captain of the *Montauk*, John Truck of Connecticut—a very different character from the sagacious seaman of *Home as Found*—insists on pronouncing "V.A.V." With her also is Ann Sidley who, like Mlle Viefville, appears unintroduced in the sequel. Nanny Sidley is a person who knows her place. "She had been born a servant, lived a servant, and was content to die a servant." One mark of her station is her inability to learn or like foreign languages. Another is that she is loyal and loving and innocent of "the vulgar scramble and heart-burnings, that, in the mêlée of a migrating and unsettled population, are so injurious to the grace and principles of American life" (1: 16).

In contrast stands Steadfast Dodge, "an American in a European mask" (1: 20), perhaps after Natty Bumppo Cooper's most memorable character, to be resurrected by Melville twenty years later as a model for Frank Goodman in *The Confidence Man*. When first seen, Steadfast is a pretentious scarecrow dressed in rags and tatters of European memorabilia—his cap from Berlin, his boots from Paris, his watchguard from Geneva, his coat from Frankfort, his pipe from Dresden. A traveler of six months, he had seen Paris, Geneva, the Rhine, and Holland, and thinks he had seen all Europe: "Mr. Dodge had come abroad quite as green as he was going home ripe" (1: 22). He has opinions on every subject, especially on democracy. Renowned in America as a journalist because of his Johnsonian style and Chesterfieldian taste ("even Walter Scott might not be ashamed to own some of his descriptions"), Steadfast sends accounts of his travels to his newspaper, the *Active Inquirer*. "His opinions," said a fellow editor, "meet with our unqualified approbation, being sound, American, and discriminating. We fancy these Europeans will begin to think in time that Jonathan has some pretty shrewd notions concerning themselves, the criturs!" (1: 47).

Though never given an identifiable habitation, Steadfast—of "pious ancestry" (1: 99)—can be supposed to be a New Englander come to New York and thence to Europe. Readers may have wondered if he was not a caricature of someone like Nathaniel Parker Willis whose *Pencillings by the Way* (1835) fed contemporary American appetites with tidbits of European scene and society. Steadfast is a "great stickler for the rights of the people. . . . Majorities were his hobbies"—he will have seamen vote on whether to obey commands of their captain. "So much and so long had Mr. Dodge respired a moral atmosphere of this community-character and gregarious propensity, that he had, in many things, lost all sense of individuality": No man, he thinks, has a "right to any of his senses without popular sufferance" (1: 99). Swollen with "the conceit of a vulgar and inflated man," he is "so far blinded . . . as to think his opinion of importance" (1: 189). Yet

> no asiatic slave stood more in terror of a vindictive master than Mr. Dodge stood in fear and trembling before the reproofs, comments, censures, frowns, cavilings, and remarks of every man in his county, who happened to belong to the political party that just at that moment was in power. . . . In a word, Steadfast Dodge was a man that wished to meddle

with and control all things, without possessing precisely the spirit that was necessary to leave him master of himself; he had a rabid desire for the good wishes of everything human.

(1:100)

Cooper wrote so much and so well of Steadfast Dodge in *Homeward Bound* that there was little more to say of him in the sequel. This is also true of Mr. Monday, whose packet of letters provides the denouement of *Home as Found*. He is a shrill-voiced cockney traveling salesman, devoted to sherry and champagne, who is brave when bravery is needed, and who knows his place. All his life a carrier of other men's goods and opinions, he is a decent person who would be pleased, we think, that his mysterious bundle of letters would bring happiness to such a sensible pair of superior lovers as Paul and Eve.

Young Paul Powis, or, as he is first introduced, Mr. Blunt, is from the beginning a man of mystery. He speaks so many languages that Eve thinks him first a German, then an Englishman, until his informed arguments in opposition to Steadfast Dodge's egalitarian notions and his defense of federal democracy identify him as an American, more worthy than most. With him on shipboard is a young Englishman, well-mannered but not bright, known as Mr. Sharp, a pseudonym he had playfully taken on learning that his real name of Sir George Templemore has been appropriated by an imposter who turns out to be an embezzler and the reason why the *Montauk* is chased across the Atlantic by an English sloop of war, the *Foam*, under command of Captain Ducie who, on finally overtaking the American vessel, arrests the imposter and also, with no reason explained, Paul Powis.

Here *Homeward Bound* ends, except for a final chapter which allows the Effinghams to land in New York and drive up Broadway, "a street that every American will tell you is so crowded as to render respiration impossible." How rustic, how cluttered and dirty it seemed. " 'Is *this* Broadway?' cried Eve, fairly appalled" (2: 247).

Home as Found is a package carelessly wrapped, but filled with good things. Each of Cooper's accumulated treasures is crammed inside, and his oldest, most treasured convictions. The fragile ribbon of plot which binds it is hastily tied in the last chapters with a handsome double lover's knot. However insistently a reader may be caught up by the intricacies of Paul Blunt-Powis-Assheton-Effingham's blood relationship to Eve, he realizes that Cooper married these two members of "the class of the chosen few"[18] not only because they were well matched, but because, the essential matter of the novel being done with, the story must be brought to an end. It would be monstrous to suspect that he considered the possibility that a union between two young people, so closely kin and so much of a kind, might lead to sterility. In advance of his time or behind it, Cooper did not maneuver well within conscious subtleties.

Yet in a real sense the book moves painstakingly about these two and their discovery of the necessity of an ordered life. Anticipating Melville's more dramatic presentation in *Billy Budd* half a century later, the new bridegroom informs his bride: "The etiquette of a vessel of war is rigid certainly, and wisely so" (p. 447). Appearances can deceive. Names like Blunt, Powis, Assheton, or Effingham are interchangeable—Mrs. Abbott, the gossip of Templeton, even agrees to lend hers to a friend who does not like her own. What matters is to know the rules, and to play confidently within their restrictions. Not self-reliance, such as once trapped John Effingham and which directed people like Aristabulus Bragg or Steadfast Dodge, but "absolute confidence, caution in drawing conclusions, and a just reliance on each other" (p. 447)—only these can provide proper balance. Like Hemingway's good people, Paul and Eve have learned restraint and expertise.

Tucked in all around this uncomplicated formulation are Cooper's sorrowful impressions of his homeland revisited. With so fair a promise, her principles set forth in a constitution which guaranteed rights to all men, the United States had become within eight years a conglomeration of opportunists, apish in servility and swaggering in pretensions of superiority. No more than the later Henry James or Henry Adams could Cooper square his convictions of America's innate superiority with his observations of her shortcomings: "no country has so altered in so short a time." Dividing himself between Edward Effingham, who loves his country, and John Effingham, who sees it through jaundiced eyes, he allowed the latter to advise his cousin, "Look about you, Ned, and you will see adventurers uppermost everywhere; in the government, in your villages, in the country even" (p. 223). Nor can gentle Edward Effingham "conceal from himself . . . that his native country had undergone changes since he last resided in it, and that some of these changes were quite sensibly for the worst."

Cooper's indictment against America was based on five counts. First, she was subservient to European opinion, especially to British opinion, and made herself ridiculous by imitating what she thought to be European manners. Second, instead of keeping a foothold in the land, she engaged in restless speculation, seeking quick wealth, unequally and dishonestly distributed, so that power shifted from the landholder to the entrepreneur. Third, her press, once free, was now shackled by special political or commercial interests. Fourth, she no longer managed her affairs according to regulations of law or constitution, but was led willy-nilly by mass opinion which shifted according to whim or pressure. Finally, and not least, she pretended to be what she was not, failing to recognize her manifest limitations and her unique destiny.

Cooper might not have liked Thoreau's later assumption that the majority is always wrong, but he did say that in America "the gross mistake has been of supposing, that because the mass rules in a political sense, it has a right to be listened to in all matters—a practical deduction that can only lead, under the most favorable exercise of power, to a very humble mediocrity" (p. 317). Though differing from Emerson in other things, Cooper would have agreed with the younger man that what America needed was not a mass, but cultivated men, wise to know and bold to perform.

Born a Federalist, but by uneasy conviction a Jeffersonian turned Jacksonian democrat, Cooper believed that "the heart and strength of the nation" was its rural population. "No government that is essentially ruled by commerce," he had said in *The Monikins*, "has ever been otherwise than exclusive and aristocratic."[19] The rule of property, he said in *Sketches in*

Switzerland, is "the most corrupt, narrow, and vicious form of polity that has ever been devised."[20] And in *The American Democrat* he stated: "Of all the sources of human pride, mere wealth is the basest and most vulgar minded. Real gentlemen are almost invariably above this low feeling."[21] That is why Edward Effingham, whose fortune is in land, is superior to his cousin who "did not own the ground to bury him." What endangered America was domination by an upstart commercial oligarchy. "The present political struggle in this country," Cooper told a friend in 1838, "appears to be a contest between men and dollars."[22]

"Though majorities often decide wrong," he admitted in *The American Democrat,* "it is believed that they are less liable to do so than minorities." Pressure groups deformed America—agents of special interests, the socially ambitious, politicians, speculators, corrupt newspapermen: "I have never yet been in a county in which what are called the lower orders have not clearer and sounder views than their betters of the great principles which ought to predominate in the control of human affairs."[23] Thus, as Arthur M. Schlesinger, Jr., has said, Cooper was torn between "two pervading revulsions: on the one hand, the self-constituted aristocracy of the American Whigs, with their pretensions and snobberies, their servility toward the British, their hatred of 'that monster' General Jackson, and their scorn for the lower classes; on the other, the menace of the democratic demagogue."[24]

No one has ever formulated Cooper's precise political alignment, not even himself. His temper and pride came between him and what he wanted to say. He never had words enough to frame the ideas with which his head seemed bursting. Unable to speak them clearly, he never ordered them to patterns which he or we could completely understand.

But in *Home as Found* he poured them forth without reserve, creating the third part of a trilogy which includes *The Pioneers* and *Homeward Bound,* books which bring the reader closer to Cooper than any others. Readers of *Home as Found* were expected to know these preceding two, the adventures at sea and the experiences of the earlier Effinghams who in *The Pioneers* inherited the prodigious house which Hiram Doolittle (from New England) and pudgy Richard Jones (a relative) had designed for Judge Temple. Some would recall that these Effinghams had been Tories, enemies to America, and tongues must have clicked in relating Cooper to the family in a later generation. Others must have wondered whether they or their friends were caricatured in *Home as Found,* as social pretenders, chauvinistic litterateurs, politicians, or journalists. Certainly many must have sympathized with the barber in Templeton who insisted that even Effinghams must come to his shop if they wish to be shaved.

There are excellent things in *Home as Found,* of which the self-conscious section on the Three-Mile Point controversy is not one. Baseball buffs will suspect that the national pastime is here mentioned for the first time in our literature, though not by name (pp. 158–159). Aristabulus Bragg will be recognized as forerunner of characters like Casper Goodwood whom Henry James portrayed more subtly, or George F. Babbit who clowned successfully for Sinclair Lewis. But Cooper's hand was heavy, and his humor missed many easy marks. He knew nothing of Mark Twain's secret, that the satirist is safest within the satire, so that it becomes, not what fools *these,* but what fools *we* mortals be.

Structurally the novel breaks into two unequal parts. The first seven chapters, which satirize the pretentions of New Yorkers and their carelessness in burning themselves up, contain a crowded series of vignettes of city people, done with none of the jovial lightness with which Dickens in *Pickwick Papers* had begun two years earlier to ridicule London manners. Never before had so many Americans been so completely anatomized, and most of the silliest among them were women, as if Cooper anticipated people like Philip Wylie in discovering his country dominated by females. The prodigality and vainglorious parade of New York society created an "intensity of selfishness which smothers all recollection of the past, and all just anticipations of the future, by condensing life with all its motives and enjoyments, into the present moment" (p. 110). To a free spirit like Eve such bad taste and extravagance became inevitably wearisome: "The town life of an American town offers little to one accustomed to a town life in older and more permanently regulated communities" (pp. 110–111).

So the Effinghams move northward toward their family estate, through two chapters which allow Cooper to compare the natural beauties of the Hudson River with what man has done to spoil it with architectural monstrosities. With their arrival at Cooperstown, called Templeton, the Effinghams are really at home, and Cooper also. He proudly shows off its unique wonders—the great echoing rock, the tree-fringed lake, the breath-taking vistas of forest and fertile fields, the solemn pines and the Rembrandt-like hemlocks. Any person might be proud of such a countryside, lush and beautiful and swollen with promise. Cooper labored lovingly over these descriptive passages—and the reader who skips them lightly is deprived of fine pleasure. Perhaps only William Faulkner, or Thoreau who, like Leatherstocking, could talk with wild things, has more successfully evoked the land which man threatens to despoil, in Cooper's words, of "whatever there is of poetry" (p. 133).

That Templeton had also changed was Cooper's final and heartbroken indictment. Filled with new people, birds of passage restlessly there until they could move on elsewhere, the village is no longer the idyllic place of which he wrote in *The Pioneers*. Working people, coolly impudent, neither know their place nor respect the superior place of others. Any man can aspire to any office. Uninformed men, like the ingenuous Mr. Howell, are enamored of an England which they only know through books. Years before Whitman did, Cooper here scolded Sir Walter Scott for writing undemocratic, un-American fiction. Other uninformed men, like Mr. Wenham, constantly praised native achievement, especially in literature—allowing Cooper to satirize and give name to the Young America movement—*la jeune Amérique*, he called it (p. 173)—which, said an equally censorious Edgar Allan Poe, praised bad books because, sure enough, their badness was American.

Fewer characters clutter these final thirty chapters set in Cooper's village. The pace is more leisurely, the criticism more particularized and scattered over a greater variety of subjects.

Just as one begins to tire of it, the plot picks up momentum, mystery deepens, young men move closer to young ladies, and wedding bells begin to ring. Cooper ties loose strands with clumsy competence as each character steps forward with a final bow.

Best in *Home as Found* is not the ridicule of foibles in manners, conversation, politics, literature, or religion, not even the sensible remarks on functional architecture which Cooper learned from his artist friend Horatio Greenough, but the passage in which Captain Truck and the Commodore drift happily on Lake Otsego, their talk becoming brighter with every swig at the jugs which keep them company. Here, if Cooper had found words to phrase it, is the effective center of the book, with nature quietly a background and the spirit of Natty Bumppo and the sogdollager informing the old men's wise, befuddled talk. Cooper was seldom as relaxed or mellow. He had too much on his mind to say.

Saying it with a rush of words which he had neither practice nor skill to order to art, he made America's first extensive novel of manners, its formlessness itself anticipatory of a native trend. If we accept the distinction underlined by Richard Chase between romance which is likely to speak indirectly through symbols and fiction which speaks realistically of society, *Home as Found* can be thought of as our first novel. Realizing, said Cooper, how desperate an undertaking it was to attempt a *roman de société*, such as he had known in France, about a country which had no society (p. xxviii), he nevertheless roughed out a pattern which later writers like William Dean Howells and Henry James would improve. He died without knowing that they would find better models provided by English ladies like Jane Austen or George Eliot, by upstart men of no background like Charles Dickens, or foreigners from Russia and France.

NOTES

1. James Franklin Beard, ed., *The Letters and Journals of James Fenimore Cooper* (Cambridge, 1960), 2: 285. There is no satisfactory complete study of Cooper as man and writer, but see Thomas R.

Lounsbury, *James Fenimore Cooper* (Boston, 1882); Donald A. Ringe, *James Fenimore Cooper* (New York, 1962); or Robert E. Spiller, *James Fenimore Cooper* (Minneapolis, 1965). Cooper's younger years are, however, set forth in detail in Maurice Clavel, *Fenimore Cooper: sa vie et son oeuvre; la jeunesse, 1789–1826* (Aix-en-Provence, 1938). The best single critical volume is James Grossman, *James Fenimore Cooper* (New York, 1949).

2. Beard, ed., *Letters and Journals,* 2: 237.

3. Ibid.

4. Cooper's attitudes toward his countrymen and his countrymen's attitudes toward him have been variously set forth in Robert E. Spiller, *Fenimore Cooper: Critic of His Times* (New York, 1931); Dorothy Waple, *The Whig Myth of James Fenimore Cooper* (New Haven, 1938); and, most recently and most satisfactorily, Kay Seymour House, *Cooper's Americans* (Columbus, Ohio, 1965).

5. James Fenimore Cooper, *Home as Found,* ed. Lewis Leary (New York, 1961), p. 225.

6. Spiller, *James Fenimore Cooper,* p. 13; see also Beard, ed., *Letters and Journals,* 1: 42.

7. Beard, ed., *Letters and Journals,* 1: 44.

8. Ibid., 1: 94.

9. *Notions of Americans Picked up by a Travelling Bachelor,* ed. Robert E. Spiller (New York, 1963), 1: xvii, 100–102; 2: 106, 127, 142.

10. Beard, ed., *Letters and Journals,* 2: 169.

11. Ibid., 2: 110.

12. *A Letter to His Countrymen* (New York, 1834), pp. 99–100.

13. *New-England Magazine* 5 (August 1835): 48; *Knickerbocker Magazine* 6 (August 1835): 152–153.

14. *Gleanings in Europe,* ed. Robert E. Spiller (New York, 1928–1930), 1: 239.

15. Ibid., 1: 296.

16. Leary, ed., *Home as Found,* p. xxvii.

17. *Homeward Bound; or, The Chase. A Tale of the Sea* (Philadelphia, 1838), 1: 13. Further quotations from this novel will be identified within parentheses in the text.

18. Leary, ed., *Home as Found,* p. 272. Further quotations from this novel will be identified within parentheses in the text.

19. *The Monikins; Edited by the Author of "The Spy"* (Philadelphia, 1835), p. 408; see also *A Letter to His Countrymen* (New York, 1834), pp. 65–67.

20. *Sketches of Switzerland. By an American. Part Second* (Philadelphia, 1836), 2: 181.

21. *The American Democrat; or, Hints on the Social and Civic Relations of the United States of America* (Cooperstown, N.Y., 1838), pp. 131–132.

22. Beard, ed., *Letters and Journals*, 3: 317.

23. *The American Democrat*, p. 46.

24. *The Age of Jackson* (Boston, 1946), p. 379.

Washington Irving

AN END AND A NEW BEGINNING

✿❧ ❦✿

EW writers have successfully stretched a small talent farther than Washington Irving. He was an alert, ingenuous
man who liked to be liked, and who tried to write what
other people expected of him. His success was at once the measure
of his own placid adaptability and of assurance among most of
his contemporaries that literary excursions should be pleasantly
trivial, skipping over surfaces without disturbing deeper matters
of trade or politics, the opening of the West or decisions on what
democracy should be. People who spoke their minds sharply,
like Philip Freneau or James Fenimore Cooper, held Irving in
great scorn, but almost everyone else admired him. He was
comfortable to have around, for he seldom raised his voice, and
he flattered his countrymen's assumption that they were, in
truth, gentlefolk who could sip appreciatively on Old World
culture at the same time that they built new traditions of strength
and hardihood.

Irving made himself heard at a time when his country needed
someone like him. No longer was quizzical Ben Franklin, sage
but uncouth, to represent the best in native accomplishment.
People had already begun to talk of him as a despoiler of polite
language and cultivated taste. His influence made for penny-
pinching vulgarities so that even poetry from the New World
often spoke of commerce as a be-all and end-all. Many Englishmen of discrimination seemed to agree with Dr. Samuel Johnson
that there was something degenerate about most Americans. Few
were surprised at the scorn in Sydney Smith's tone as he asked in
1820, "Who reads an American book?"[1]

When Washington Irving's *The Sketch Book* appeared at just
that time, as if to provide by its popularity an answer to the

question, literature of the United States gave first promise of eventual maturity. It had lived through a difficult, war-torn childhood, and for years was to struggle through an awkward adolescence. Clothed often in cast-off garments, pampered, and praised for the wrong things, nurtured more often in parlor or library than in its spacious backyard, it nonetheless grew, its voice wavering and cracking, until finally, by the time of Irving's death in 1859, it had learned to communicate with authenticity and persuasion. During the years between, when Emerson and Hawthorne spoke most clearly, when Thoreau was thought strange and Poe shocking, when Melville and Whitman wrote of matters beyond the experience of many men, then Irving was more famous and respected than any of these, the dean indeed of American letters, envied by Cooper, admired by Longfellow, whose deft extensions of Irving's moods made him seem his logical successor.

Neither Irving nor Longfellow is esteemed so highly now, but neither is forgotten. The latter's songs still occasionally gladden or gently lull, and Irving, at the very least, has presented his country with the inestimable gift of two characters and a name. Either Rip Van Winkle or Ichabod Crane would be recognized at once if he walked down almost any American street. Their adventures have become as much a part of native lore as Captain Smith's rescue by Pocahontas, Tom Sawyer's slick whitewashing deal, or Paul Bunyan's gargantuan strength and appetite. In much the same sense, the word *knickerbocker* has become, through Irving's use of it, more than a designation for a baggy Dutch garment: it describes a period in the history of native culture, and an attitude toward literature and life; it appears today almost one hundred times in the Manhattan directory, to identify, among others, a fashionable corps of cadets, a brewery, a book-shop, a professional basketball team, and a manufacturer of plastics.

But Irving's reputation during his lifetime rested on greatly more than this, and a candid revaluation of his writing today suggests more also. He had two effective voices. As Diedrich Knickerbocker, he spoke of native themes, with crusty vigor— almost everything of Irving's which is most affectionately re-

membered is put in the worlds of that unpretentious and sometimes impolite old gentleman. As Geoffrey Crayon, he was decorous and superbly polished, beloved as an ambassador of good
will between the New World and the Old, who lifted the literary
embargo on both sides by proving that "a man from the wilds of
America" could, after all, "express himself in tolerable English."[2] Praised by Scott and Byron and Moore, Irving became a
solid, cheerful, adaptable symbol of what a proper man of letters
might be. As much as Franklin, he studied the way toward
success.

Like Franklin also, he was the last son born in a large family,
but without forebears deeply rooted in colonial America, as
Franklin's had been.[3] Irving's dour Presbyterian father had come
to New York from Scotland only two decades before the birth
of his youngest son on 3 April 1783, just as the Revolution
drew to a close. In spite of wartime troubles, William Irving
had prospered, and was assisted now by his oldest son and name-
sake, already at seventeen active in the family wine, sugar, hardware, and auctioneering business. The next son, Peter, was two
years away from entrance to Columbia College, where he would
receive preliminary training toward a medical degree which he
was never to use. Seven-year-old Ebenezer was musical, but
already promised to be the steadiest of them all, destined for a
career in trade. John Treat, five years older than the youngest
Irving, would also attend Columbia, to prepare in law. The three
sisters married early and moved away, but wrote affectionate
letters home which testify to close-knit family ties.

As the youngest, Washington Irving seems to have been a
spoiled child, precocious, moody, and sensitive, and subject to
alarming bronchial attacks. "When I was very young," he remembered, "I had an impossible flow of spirits that went beyond
my strength. Every thing was fairy land to me." From the age
of six to fifteen, he was doomed, he said, "to be mewed up the
lifelong day in that purgatory of boyhood, a schoolroom."[4] Thereafter, instead of entering college, he read haphazardly in whatever books came to hand, and explored nooks and crannies of
little New York: "I knew every spot," he said, "where a murder

or robbery had been committed, or a ghost seen." More often, he wandered about the countryside, seeking health, it was explained, in the open air. Sometimes he adventured along the banks of the Hudson River, even above Spuyten Duyvil and Yonkers, through Dutch villages to Tarrytown, where his brother William's wife's family, the Pauldings, lived, "adding greatly to my stock of knowledge," he said, by noting rural habits and customs, and conversing with country people.[5] Passing through Sleepy Hollow to the Pocantico Hills, he could look across the river to the legend-haunted headlands of the lower Catskills.

Between excursions, after 1799, he read law intermittently, finally with Josiah Ogden Hoffman, who had two attractive daughters. During the summer of 1803, he made a long journey with the Hoffmans, by boat and oxcart into Canada, squiring the girls, playing his flute, reciting Shakespeare, and filling notebooks with impressions of moonlight over the Hudson, of trading with Dutch farmers for milk and cheese, of squalid frontier lodgings and overland travel through deep-rutted forest roads, alert for whatever was comic or picturesque or appealed to sentiment.

For he had already, at nineteen, become known to contemporaries as a person of "extraordinary . . . literary accomplishments," deserving of the best "admiration and esteem."[6] When the previous autumn his brother Peter had become editor of the new *Morning Chronicle* in New York, Irving contributed a series of nine sportive letters, from 15 November 1802, to 23 April 1803, over the signature of "Jonathan Oldstyle, Gent." They played with grave pleasantry over the state of manners, dress, and marriage in New York, but with greatest enthusiasm over the state of the theater. The jingoistic drama of the time— brave American sailors in love and at war—was lampooned; actors were caricatured, and musicians who with "solemn and important phizes"[7] produced discordant noise; the managers were chided for not keeping the playhouse clean or the playgoers quiet; and critics were taunted as "pests of society" (p. 37) who attended performances only to lounge away an idle hour.

Jonathan Oldstyle was so merry and vulgar an old gentleman that a more sedate Irving was later to be ashamed of him,[8] but he spoke zestfully, and colloquially well. He disliked candle-grease dripping on his jacket from the theater chandeliers, and he became tired of dodging apple cores thrown by rowdies in the gallery. Jonathan discreetly ogled the belles who smiled flirtatiously from the boxes, their charms set off to most alluring advantage—here an arched look, there a simper, everywhere bewitching languish. He was sorry that spyglasses were no longer used to observe them more closely. And the critics—"ha! ha!"—how foolish and subversive: "they reduce feelings to a state of miserable refinement, and destroy entirely all the enjoyments in which our coarser sentiments delighted" (p. 21).

Much of what Irving would do best is foreshadowed in these juvenile essays: the physical caricature, which Dickens would admire and imitate—the dapper Frenchman, the persnickety spinster, the talkative old gentleman, the suave but foolish gal-lant, and the honest countryman "gazing in gaping wonder"; the pose of nostalgia—"Nothing is more intolerable . . . than innovation" (p. 2); the rich delight in describing food and feasting—"the hissing of frying pans, winding the savoury steams of roast and boiled" (p. 42). Most predictive, however, are the style and manner: the tailored sentences, well buttoned with adjectives; the jocular good humor, vulgar sometimes, but seldom ribald; the quip and the laugh and the quick retreat before feelings are deeply hurt; and through all the sense that Irving liked the people at whom he flicked his whimsically bantering wit—"that quiet, shrewd, good-humored sense of the ridiculous" which contemporaries recognized as setting Irving apart "from every other writer in our language,"[9] but which never of itself was enough to ensure him a place as a major writer.

Perhaps because they did prick republican pretensions and looked shrewdly down their noses on native manners, the Old-style essays established young Irving as a kind of social arbiter for young America. Charles Brockden Brown, fresh from minor triumphs as a novelist, invited him to contribute to his *Phila-delphia Literary Magazine*.[10] Joseph Dennie, who conducted the *Port Folio* as "Oliver Oldschool," recognized and applauded the literary kinship implied by his choice of pseudonym.[11] During the spring of 1804, Irving almost certainly contributed to Peter's short-lived, astringent *Corrector*, and he continued his precocious career as a wit among men and a favorite with the ladies. His health, however, did not withstand even such pleasantly diversified pastimes, and he was packed off in May for a recuperative voyage to Europe.

The traveling did him good, in health and spirit. He made new friends and learned new manners, and filled notebook after notebook with careful records of what he saw and did, whether reverently viewing castles and cathedrals or in hairbrained escapades with his companions. He endured pirate attacks, excursions through bandit-infested hills, rough rides, bad lodgings, and poor food, picking up smatterings of French, Spanish, and Italian, reading volume after volume of travel adventures written by other men, and flirting with exotic women, now with novices in a convent, at another time with country damsels at a wayside tavern.

In Rome he met Madame de Staël, and was astonished that any woman could talk so much and so well. In Genoa he met Washington Allston, the American artist, who almost persuaded him to remain in Italy to study painting. In Paris he visited the tailors and the theater, and was thrilled to be accosted on the street by handsome, predatory young women. In London he saw Mrs. Siddons at Convent Garden—in fact, he saw every play he could and wrote home about them enthusiastically in detail. By the end of twenty-three months, however, Irving admitted that "one gets tired of travelling, even in the gay and polished countries of Europe. Curiosity cannot be kept ever on the stretch; like the sensual appetites, it in time becomes sated." He was happy therefore "once more [to] return to my friends, and sink again into tranquil domestic life."[12]

Back in New York he entered a scattered round of activities, reserving just enough time for the study of law to allow him to pass his bar examinations late in 1806. He helped Peter translate a travel book from the French; he contributed to the *Literary Picture Gallery*, a periodical dedicated to activities of visitors at Ballston Spa; he wrote occasional verse, including doggerel lines for the opening of the New Park Theater. Perhaps it was of himself that he spoke when later he allowed a character to confess: "I had too much genius for study . . . so I fell into bad company, and took to bad habits. Do not mistake me. I mean that I fell into the company of village literati, and village blues, and took to writing village poetry. It was quite the fashion in the village to be literary."[13]

They were gay blades, those "lads of Kilkenny"—Peter and Gouverneur Kemble, Henry Brevoort, Henry Ogden, James Kirke Paulding, the Irving brothers, Peter and Washington and sometimes William—the "worthies" who met for literary pow-wows at Dyde's tavern, and for "blackguard suppers" at a porter-house on Nassau Street: "sad dogs" indeed, fond of conscientious drinking and good fun.[14] Among their favorite haunts was the old Kemble mansion on the Passaic River, about a mile above Newark, which they renamed Cockloft Hall; they transferred to it much of the fictitious adventure set forth in *Salmagundi*, a periodical which, when it appeared in twenty numbers irregularly from 24 January 1807 to 25 January 1808, became the talk and wonder of the town. "If we moralize," they promised, "it shall be but seldom, and on all occasions, we shall be more solicitous to make our readers laugh than cry; for we are laughing philosophers, and truly of the opinion that wisdom, true wisdom, is a plump, jolly dame, who sits in her arm-chair, laughs right merrily at the farce of life—and takes the world as it comes."[15]

Who wrote it was soon suspected—the Irvings, Washington and William and perhaps Peter, and William's brother-in-law, James Kirke Paulding; but who wrote what has never been determined, so mixed and various but unified in temper was the matter set forth as "the whim-whams and opinions of Launcelot Langstaff, Esq., and others." Usually "Anthony Evergreen, Gent.," commented on fashionable society; "William Wizard, Esq.," handled theatrical and literary criticism; "Pindar Cock-loft" contributed verse; and Launcelot Langstaff, as proprietor, roamed at will over all subjects. "In hoc est hoax, cum quiz et jokesez. Et smokem, toastem, roastem folksez, Fee, faw fum," they asserted on the title page in a cryptic motto, which was obligingly translated as "With baked and broiled, stew'd and toasted, and fried, boil'd, smok'd and roasted, we treat the town."

"As everybody knows, or ought to know," the first issue began, "what a SALMAGUND is, we shall spare ourselves the trouble of an explanation; besides we despise trouble as we do everything low and mean, and hold the man who would incur it unnecessarily as an object worthy of our highest pity and contempt" (1: 13). Most people, however, have been tempted to look up the word, to discover that it describes an appetizer made of chopped meat (raw), pickled herring, and onions, liberally seasoned with olive oil, vinegar, and cayenne pepper—excellent, some find, with cocktails or beer. No less savory were the elements compounded in *Salmagundi,* expertly mixed to encourage "genuine honest American tastes" rather than fashionable "French slops and fricasseed sentiment" (1: 17). For the convenience of readers, it was printed "on hot-pressed vellum paper, as that is held in highest estimation for buckling up young ladies' hair" in size just right for fitting "old ladies' pockets and young ladies' work bags."[16]

The ladies came in for a great share of attention as the young men from Cockloft Hall labored to "instruct the young, reform the old, correct the town, and castigate the age." The ladies of New York were "the fairest, the finest, the most accomplished, the most ineffable things that walk, creep, crawl, swim, float, or vegetate in any or all of the four elements" (1: 19), but how alarmingly they dressed—in flesh-colored stockings and off-the-shoulder gowns: "*nudity* being all the rage" (1: 69). Actors and critics received sharp flicks, and fashionable upstarts like "Ding Dong," "Ichabod Fungus," and "Dick Paddle." Open war was declared against local folly and stupidity, especially in the letters of "Mustapha Rub-a-Dub Khan," written unashamedly in imitation of Oliver Goldsmith's "Citizen of the World" essays. Boorish English travelers and foppish French dancing masters were laughingly derided; even so popular a favorite as Thomas Moore, recently a visitor to America, was reproved for having "hopp'd and skipp'd our country o'er,"

> Sipped our tea and lived on sops,
> Revel'd on syllabubs and slops,
> And when his brain, of cob-web fine,

Was fuddled with five drops of wine,
Would all his puny loves rehearse,
And many a maid debauch—in verse.[17]

All was good humor, laughingly sustained, even when the
satire turned political, like that directed against Thomas Jefferson, his embargo, his red riding breeches (1: 42), and his
scientific interest in "impaling butterflies and pickling tadpoles"
(1: 64–65). More bitter invective was reserved for literary
rivals, like Thomas Green Fessenden, an outlander, recently
from New England, who in his *Weekly Inspector* dared criticize
Salmagundi as a frothy imitation of Addison and Steele. "From
one end of the town to another," he complained, "all is nonsense
and 'Salmagund.' America has never produced great literature—
her products have been scrub oaks, at best. We should, then,
encourage every native sapling; but when, like *Salmagundi*, it
turns out to be a *bramble*, and pricks and scratches everything
within its reach, we naturally ask, why it encumbereth the
ground."[18]

Quarreling which turned bitter was not to the taste of the
lads from Cockloft Hall; it was certainly not to Irving's, who
for all his wit was more fond of conciliation than of argument.
Salmagundi was intended only as "pleasant morning or after-
dinner reading, never taking too much of a gentleman's time
from his business or pleasures." It was calculated for the mood
of New York, "where the people—heaven help them—are the
most irregular, crazy-headed, quick-silver, eccentric, whim-
whamsical set of mortals that were ever jumbled together."[19]
Though frivolous and derivative, *Salmagundi* was expertly done.
If it were possible to know what parts of it Washington Irving
wrote, they would probably be recognized as almost as good as
anything he ever did.

Not only did *Salmagundi* hurt feelings; it was also not profitable—or so the young men claimed when they suspended publication after a year. Footloose again, Irving enjoyed his friends
in Washington, Philadelphia, and New York, where he played
lightly in chaste drawing-room flirtations with lovely ladies in
the highest society and, with gentlemanly disdain, in politics.
At Richmond, he helped Josiah Hoffman defend Aaron Burr

in his trial for treason. He wrote occasional verse and squibs, and perhaps contributed political commentary to the newspapers, composing what was expected of him—usually at someone else's request. But ever since the decease of *Salmagundi*, he had been casually at work on a book of his own.

He and Peter had started it together, as a parody of a guide-book to New York, but when Peter was called abroad as manager of the family business in Europe, Washington Irving completed it alone—in grief, it has been said, and sadness. For on 26 April 1809—a date which he never forgot—young Matilda Hoffman died, she on whom Washington Irving's errant attentions had at length settled. His heartbreak was so great, and finally so well known, that it has become a commonplace to suppose that Irving remained all his life a bachelor because of loyalty to Matilda Hoffman's memory: "her image was continually with me, and I dreamt of her incessantly."[20]

But, however sorrowful the months through which Irving brought it to completion, *A History of New York from the Beginning of the World to the End of the Dutch Dynasty*, which appeared in December 1809, remains his first unified and his most joyous book. He wished it thought to have been written by a strange, inquisitive little gentleman named Diedrich Knicker-bocker, who had disappeared, leaving behind him the manuscript of this volume, announced on its title page as the "only authentic history of the times that hath been or ever will be published." Fact was jumbled with fiction, some dates were wrong, some foot-notes spurious, but it was a gay, mirth-filled book. What its title page further identified as the "unutterable ponderings of Walter the Doubter, the disasterous projects of William the Testy, and the chivalric achievements of Peter the Headstrong" had New York in an uproar; when they reached England, they made Walter Scott's sides, he said, "absolutely sore with laughter." But many people of Dutch descent resented it: horsewhipping was spoken of, and ostracism. Emerson was later to disapprove of Knickerbocker's "deplorable Dutch wit," and Whitman of his "shallow burlesque."[21] More feelings were hurt than Irving had intended.

Yet Knickerbocker's *History* continues lightheartedly to beguile readers of later generations, who enjoy its lovely comic pose—its effervescent youthful verve of madcap exaggeration—without being bothered by attempts to identify every victim of Irving's satire. John Adams may be recognized, and perhaps James Madison; no one will miss Thomas Jefferson, who is ridiculed for his "cocked hat and corduroy small clothes,"[22] and his eccentric, democratic manners. What lives, however, are not these things, any more than what lives in *Gulliver's Travels* are the political allusions which scholars discover there. Byron prized Knickerbocker's *History* for its copious style; Dickens is said to have worn out his copy with eager reading; and Coleridge to have stayed up all one night to finish his.[23] Not every modern reader will respond as heartily, but none will find Irving more consistently pleasant to be with than in this boisterous book which he completed at the age of twenty-six.

His laughter is directed at historians, explorers, plump Dutch matrons, and robust Connecticut girls, at Yankee skinflints and parsons, cock-fighting Virginians, the cozy pleasures of bundling and overeating (in luscious detail). As a resident of "the beloved isle of Manna-hata," Knickerbocker looked with suspicion on New Englanders as "pumpkin-eating, molasses-daubing, shingle-splitting, cider-watering, horse-jockeying, notion-peddling" (pp. 177–178) creatures. Colonists to the south "lived on hoe-cakes and bacon, drank mint julips and brandy toddy," and amused themselves with "slave-driving, tavern-haunting, Sabbath-breaking, and mulatto-breeding" (p. 188). Frontiersmen were "a gigantic, gun-powdery race of men . . . exceedingly expert at boxing, biting, gouging, tar and feathering" (p. 188)—"half man," they were, "half horse, half alligator" (p. 254).

The extravagance, mock gravity, and vast irreverence which was to characterize American humor from Sam Slick through Mark Twain to Faulkner are anticipated as Irving describes a sunbeam falling on the giant red nose of Antony the Trumpeter as he leaned over the side of a ship plying the Hudson, then bouncing off, "hissing hot," into the water "to kill a mighty sturgeon that was sporting beside the vessel" (p. 263). Wouter van Twiller, "exactly five feet six inches in height and six feet five inches in circumference" (p. 123), was a man of such extraordinary wisdom that he avoided disturbances of the world by closing his eyes for hours at a time, his active intelligence producing all the while "certain guttural sounds, which his admirers declared were merely the noise of conflict made by his contending doubts and opinions" (pp. 124–125).

Irving's weapon was less often the rapier than what Stanley Williams has described as a "true Dutch blunderbuss, shooting off in all directions."[24] More often than not, the humor is broad, sometimes mirthfully vulgar, as when brave Peter Stuyvesant, harassed in a duel, falls backward "on his seat of honor," to land kerplunk on a meadow "cushion, softer than velvet, which providence or Minerva, or St. Nicholas, or some kindly cow, had benevolently prepared for his reception" (p. 288). No wonder his countrymen were scandalized when Irving compared a Dutch ship to a maiden from New York: "both full in the bows, with a pair of enormous cat-heads, a copper bottom, and a most prodigious poop!" (p. 90).

Legend is created and local legend is utilized as Irving shaped from whatever came to his quick-moving hands a mirage of tradition, through which characters moved in quixotic grandeur, their noble pretensions made absurd, though no less noble, because of the provincial background against which they suffered inevitable, comic defeat. His reading was ransacked for archetypal patterns against which native heroes could be measured: at the Battle of Fort Christina, "immortal deities, who whilom had seen service at the 'affair' of Troy—now mounted their feather-bed clouds and sailed over the plain," until "victory in the likeness of a gigantic ox-fly, sat perched upon the cocked hat of the gallant Stuyvesant" (p. 289). How ludicrously small the deeds of warriors in this New World "when contrasted with the semi-mythic grandeur with which we have clothed them, as we look backward from the crowned result, to fancy a cause as majestic as our conception of the effect." With these words, James Russell Lowell was perhaps the first to recognize that Irving, as much as Cooper, though with lighter touch, produced a "homespun and plebian mythos"—in Fielding's terms a "comic epic"—in which gallant protagonists tested ideals of the Old World against the frontier requirements of the New.[25]

There was theme and scheme behind the caricature of Knicker-bocker's *History*. The *Monthly Anthology* of Boston greeted it as a book "certainly the wittiest our press has ever produced." In Philadelphia the *Port Folio* praised its "drollery and quaint-ness," its "copious and natural style." Neither recognized it, as did the *Athenaeum* in London a few years later, as "an honest and manly attempt to found an American literature. Those who read it must have exclaimed involuntarily, 'Yes, this is the work which was wanted. The umbilical cord is severed. America is indeed independent.' "[26] For not even Irving quite knew what he had done; when he revised the *History* a few years later, he cleansed it of much colloquial coarseness, and of caricature which might wound, apparently so intent on being liked that he failed to realize that he had written the first American book capable of outliving the man who made it. Only Franklin's *Autobiography* claims precedence, for reasons quite different.

Irving's book is more irresponsible, more fun, and more liter-ary. Source hunters have searched libraries to discover every influence on it, and none has done the job to another's satisfaction. Sterne and Fielding were certainly on Irving's mind, imitated or parodied; Swift, Cervantes, Shakespeare, Rabelais, the King James Bible, Aesop, Homer, Thomas Malory, and Thomas Paine are all present, in allusion or idiom; Arthurian legend, Greek myth, and the ponderous supposings of Cotton Mather's *Magnalia Christi Americana* jostle one another in exuberant disarray. Historians have derided or defended his adaptation of fact to fancy, sometimes locating in some half-forgotten volume in Latin, French, or Dutch the phrase or incident which Irving wove into a fabric not quite like any other.

Knickerbocker's *History* brought some profit (two thousand dollars) and more renown: "I was noticed, caressed, and for a time elated by the popularity I had gained"; but "this career of gayety and notoriety soon palled on me. I seemed to drift with-out aim or object."[27] A second edition was called for in 1812, another in 1819; it was translated to French and German, and adapted for the stage. But it marked the end of one phase, the most carefree and lavish, of Irving's career. Not again would he write with such abandon; seldom would he write so spontaneously well. Grief or circumspection, or the enervating deceleration of spirits called growing up, sobered Irving.

In 1810 he became a partner in the family hardware business, but was apparently expected to devote little time to its routine affairs. Instead, he went to Washington as a lobbyist against restrictions in trade, and there he spent many hours in seeing the town with Paulding, and attending official balls, where he became a favorite of Washington's favorite hostess, Dolly Madison. Back in New York he prepared a brief biographical introduction for an American edition of the poems of Thomas Campbell, declaring that in "an age when we are overwhelmed by an abundance of eccentric poetry, it is really cheering and consolatory to behold a writer . . . studiously aiming to please."

Irving's consistent demand of literature was that it should please, and more by familiarity than strangeness. As editor for two years beginning in January 1813 of the *Analectic Magazine*, he warned readers against Wordsworth's "new and corrupt fashion of writing," preferring instead the comfortable rhythms of Scott and Byron, the "warm sensibilities and lively fancies" of Thomas Moore.[28] Friends complimented him for having "sacrificed his elegant leisure" thus to contribute to the literary advancement of his country, but Irving was bored and restless. He grumbled about the routine of editorial work and the quality of materials he found to print: "I really stagger under the trash."[29] Paulding contributed an occasional short story, and joined the editor in a series of sketches of naval heroes. Irving himself conducted a column of "literary intelligence," wrote undiscriminating reviews, and published a handful of sketches, among them the "Traits of Indian Character" and "Philip of Pokanoket," which he would later resurrect to fill out the pages of *The Sketch Book*.

Finally, in 1815, "weary of everything and myself," he set out again for Europe, determined "to break off . . . from idle habits and idle associates and fashionable dissipation." There he hoped to "pursue a plan I had some time contemplated, of studying for a while, and then travelling about the country for the purpose of observing the manners and characters of various parts of it, with a view to writing a book which, if I have any acquaintance with my talents, will be far more . . . reputable than anything I have yet written."[30]

In England he visited with relatives and old friends, explored romantic byways of London, called on Campbell and Moore, breakfasted with Samuel Rogers, went on literary pilgrimages to Kenilworth, Warwick, and Stratford, but most reverently to Abbotsford, where Scott welcomed him cordially. He studied German so that he could read legends which Scott admired. He wrote some tales of his own and assiduously noted impressions, in words or deftly sketched drawings, of each new scene. He helped whenever necessary with the family business, filling in as he could for Peter who was increasingly unwell. When, toward the end of 1817, the commercial enterprises of the Irving brothers faced bankruptcy, William, now in Congress, tried to get government positions for the two brothers stranded in England, and did manage an appointment for Washington, who turned it down, because, he said, "My talents are purely literary. . . . I require much leisure and a mind entirely abstracted from other cares and occupations."[31]

Faced now, in his mid-thirties, for the first time with the necessity of depending on himself for support, Irving took stock of his literary wares: he reworked Knickerbocker's *History* for new publication, thumbed through his journals for usable materials, and reminisced with friends about incidents which might be turned to account. He feared, however, that his mind had lost much of its cheerfulness—"Fancy, humor—all seemed to have gone from me."[32] When early in March 1819 he sent home a packet of manuscript, he apologized, "I have attempted no lofty theme, nor sought to look wise and learned. I have preferred addressing myself to the feeling and fancy of the reader rather than to his judgment. My writing, therefore, may seem light and trifling."[33]

But with the appearance in New York two months later of the first number of *The Sketch Book of Geoffrey Crayon, Gent.*, Irving's reputation rose at once to a level from which nothing he had done before or would do again would budge it. A pamphlet of ninety-three pages, in gray-brown paper covers, it contained five sketches, the first four skillfully done but commonplace, and the fifth, "Rip Van Winkle," the slender, indestructible peg on which much of his fame has ever since been hung. Six more numbers were issued in New York, irregularly over the next sixteen months, until September 1820, each greeted with applause and admiration.

When parts of *The Sketch Book* began to appear, without permission or profit, in English periodicals, Irving early in 1820 arranged for a London edition of the whole, first done at his own expense; but soon—thanks to assistance from Scott, to whom in gratitude (or perhaps to set right those readers who supposed Scott had written the pseudonymous work) the edition was dedicated—it was issued by John Murray in two attractive volumes which sold prodigiously well in printing after printing. Of its thirty-two essays and sketches, twenty-six were about England, six of them descriptive of London scenes and five celebrating old-time Christmas festivities at an English country house; two were asides—"The Voyage" and "The Spectre Bridegroom"; and four were on American themes, two of these the Indian sketches from the *Analectic* which had not appeared in the periodical publication of *The Sketch Book* in New York.

Scott thought the book delightful, not so "exclusively American" as Knickerbocker's *History* and *Salmagundi;* William Godwin admitted that he hardly knew an Englishman who could write so well. Few contemporary readers seemed to agree with Wordsworth that *The Sketch Book*, "though a work of talent, is disfigured by an abundance of affectations"; more thought Irving, as Southey did, "a remarkably agreeable writer," with touch light enough "to conciliate any reader."[34] These pleasantly diverting samples from Geoffrey Crayon's portfolio were shaded with humor and delicately colored with sentiment, not studied "with the eye of a philosopher; but rather with the sauntering gaze with which humble lovers of the picturesque stroll from one shop window of a print shop to another; caught sometimes by the distortions of caricature, and sometimes by the loveliness of landscape."[35]

Familiarity added to the charm of the sketches. Scott's influence was plain throughout, his fastidious archaizing and untidy eloquence, later so distasteful to Mark Twain. Strokes learned from Addison were clearly discernible, and moods borrowed from Goldsmith's *The Deserted Village,* Thomson's *The Seasons,* Cowper's *The Task,* and Crabbe's somber rustic vignettes. So soft and adroitly accommodating was his touch that Irving was constantly compared to someone else, as if he had not manner or substance of his own—to Sir Thomas Browne, Fielding, Smollett, Sterne, Swift, Defoe, and even Scott, but especially to the ruminative and moralizing essayists of the eighteenth century. As an artist, he seemed copyist rather than creator: his literary offspring, said one unkind commentator, "resemble a family of sickly, but pretty children,—tall, feeble, and delicately slender, with white hair and white eyes,—dressed in jaconet muslin, trimmed with pink ribbon."[36]

In England his "eye dwelt with delight on neat cottages, with their trim shrubberies and green grass plots," on "the mouldering abbey overgrown with ivy, with the taper spire of a village church rising from the brow of a neighboring hill" (p. 19). His landscapes were stylized in the manner of the Flemish colorists whom he admired. Broad, traditionally evocative strokes pictured

> vast lawns that extend like sheets of vivid green, and here and there clumps of gigantic trees, heaping up rich piles of foliage: the solemn pomp of groves and woodland glades, with deer trooping in silent herds across them; the hare bounding away to the covert; or the pheasant, suddenly bursting upon the wing; the brook, taught to wind in natural meanderings, or expand into a glassy lake: the sequestered pool, reflecting the quivering trees, with the yellow leaf sleeping on its bosom, the trout roaming fearlessly about its limpid waters; while some rustic temple or sylvan statue grown green and dank with age, gives an air of classic sanctity to the seclusion. (Pp. 79–80)

More important than the scene was the mood which it called forth, of serenity—"classic sanctity," wherein each once free-flowing brook is *taught* to wind in what are made to seem, but which are not, "natural meanderings"; or made to "expand into a glassy lake" which calmly reflects the lethargic quiescence which the scene suggests. Geoffrey Crayon's still waters have little depth; the irrepressible bright flow of language with which

Diedrich Knickerbocker spoke of old New York had been taught to conform to London manners. Though he admired, Irving said, the elegance and strength, robustness, manliness, and simplicity of the English gentleman, these were not traits which he easily transferred to his laboriously correct, embellished prose. He was not, it can be said, to the manor born.

Even the portraiture which as Geoffrey Crayon he now contrived was less vibrant, and the humor more timidly mannered. A line or two, whimsically suggestive because stylized, was often enough to represent a person—"the little swarthy Frenchman," for example, "with a dry weazen face, and large whiskers" (p. 156). Sometimes the portrait is briefly elaborated, like that of the angler in "broad-skirted fustian coat perplexed with half a hundred pockets; a pair of stout shoes, and leathern gaiters; a basket slung one side for fish; a patent landing net, and a score of other inconveniences" (p. 412). What people looked like was more important than what they were. Even in detailed "character," like that of "John Bull," Irving assiduously balanced every blemish with some appealing trait.

Careful now that feelings should not be hurt, his comic pose was altered. "Wit, after all," he explained, "is a mighty tart, pungent ingredient, and much too acid for some stomachs; but honest good-humor is the oil and wine of a merry meeting." In a world so roiled, who was he to venture a disturbing idea? "If, however, I can by some lucky chance, rub out one wrinkle from the brow of care, or beguile the heavy heart of one moment of sorrow . . . I shall not have written in vain" (p. 315).

Exactly what happened to Irving's comic sense has not been adequately explained. Perhaps it was caution—once burned, twice shy; or perhaps it was maturity, which may be the same thing, or a desire to be liked, which is not. Always dependent on crutches made of other men's literary manner, Irving once had agility enough sometimes to dance a little jig of his own, using the rubber-tipped supports to beat out a muffled accompanying rhythm; or, like some temporarily crippled athlete, had swung from them a breathtaking two steps at a time up some hazardous stairway of ridicule. Now he learned to use them more sedately, careful that his own feet, once bruised by criticism, should touch the ground no more often than necessary, but with his gait so well adjusted to other people's that they hardly noticed his using crutches at all. Some even remarked that he got on very well without them when he adventured in American themes.

But even when he spoke as Diedrich Knickerbocker, Irving was accused of plagiarism. The plot of "Rip Van Winkle" was shamelessly stolen. Passages from the old German tale of "Peter Klaus" have been placed side by side with passages from Irving's narrative, to reveal imitation so blatant that much of Rip's unhappy experience seems little more than direct translation. But such bookish detective work may miss much of Irving's intention. "I wish in every thing I do," he once declared, "to write in such a manner that my productions may have something more than mere interest in narrative to recommend them, which is very evanescent; something, if I may use the phrase, of classic merit, *i.e.,* depending on style . . . which gives a production some chance for duration beyond the whim and fashion of the day."[37]

Something more than style, however, has kept Rip Van Winkle alive, on stage, on screen, and in the hearts of his countrymen. He has become their "muse of memory." Hart Crane once said, their " 'guardian angel' of the journey into the past,"[38] and he remains their conscience, accusing and amusing at the same time. As Irving gave local habitation to a myth, perhaps as old as any which has beguiled the mind of man—that of Epimenides, Endymion, Sleeping Beauty, and the seven sleepers of Ephesus— he added such other familiar elements of popular lore as the thunder of the gods, birds of ill omen, a magic potion, man's canine best companion, and dwarfs who are spectral spirits, transporting Valhalla and the Brocken to the Catskills, where Rip still triumphantly postures as the man-boy American (Huck Finn and Anse Bundren) who never grows up, the New World innocent who yearns to return to prelapsarian freedom from work and responsibility, to retire like Franklin at forty and fly a kite. "A child playing with children," he has been called, "a kid with a dog."

Before James Fenimore Cooper or Mark Twain, Henry James, Sinclair Lewis, or William Faulkner, Irving created—it may be thought inadvertently—a symbol of the mythic American, presenting, as Philip Young has pointed out, a near-perfect image of the way a large part of the world looks at us: likeable enough, up to a point and at times, but essentially immature, self-centered, careless and above all—and perhaps dangerously—innocent. Even more pointedly Rip is a stereotype of the American male as seen from abroad, or in some jaundiced quarters at home: he is perfectly the jolly overgrown child, abysmally ignorant of his own wife and the whole world of adult men—perpetually "one of the boys,"[39]

a Lazarus come back from the dead, as if to warn his countrymen, and yet a comic figure, in spite of the tragedy of a life slept away. His son is like him, and his grandson is another Rip.

Irving himself was surely not consciously so devious a contriver —it is the critics who have found him out. When in "The Legend of Sleepy Hollow," he adapted parts of Bürger's *Der Wilde Jäger*, and perhaps Robert Burns's "Tam O'Shanter" also, Irving admitted the tale "a random thing, suggested by scenes and stories about Tarrytown"; its borrowed plot was "a mere whimsical band to connect descriptions of scenery, customs, manners."[40] Yet in creating Brom Bones and Ichabod Crane, and the contest between them, he has been recognized as "the first important American author to put to literary use the comic mythology and popular traditions of American character which, by the early nineteenth century, had proliferated widely in oral tradition," demonstrating that "Dutch rowdies of the upper Hudson Valley were frontiersmen of the same stamp as the Ohio riverboatmen and Missouri trappers."[41]

The Dutch of "The Legend of Sleepy Hollow" are indeed different from the chuckle-headed, indolent, pipe-smoking, stoop-sitting Dutch burghers of Irving's earlier writings. Brom is a frontier braggart, burly and roistering, "a Catskill Mike Fink, a ringtailed roarer from Kinderhook." He is the sturdy backwoodsman who tricks the tenderfoot, acting out for the first time in our literature, says Daniel G. Hoffman, a theme which "has proliferated ever since: in Davy Crockett, in Mark Twain, in thousands of dime novels and popular magazines in which the yokel gets the best of the city slicker."[42] Ichabod, a jack of many trades—schoolmaster, singing teacher, farmer, and eventually a successful lawyer—is rightly designated as Irving's Connecticut Yankee, a comic and less spectacular ancestor of Mark Twain's mechanic, a more optimistic witness to the common man's fate than Melville's Israel Potter. Obtrusively pious, this psalm-singing son of New England, naive and superstitious, but shrewdly ambitious, his head filled with daydreams of quick wealth through union with the "blooming" Katrina and setting out with her toward riches of the frontier, "for Kentucky, Tennessee, or the Lord knows where" (p. 435)—bloodless Ichabod is father to many confident, untrained, blundering, successful native heroes, and is the American cousin certainly of Dickens's Uriah Heep.

Almost all of Irving's better remembered tales thus celebrate victory for the practical man, defeat for the dreamer—as if they were modest or masochistic sardonic parables of his own career. Men like Brom, who understand or defy superstition and know that visions are illusory, come out well. Fancy must be replaced by common sense as one grows older: tales of goblins, or even of high adventure and romance, are for children or childish men. What an ironic twinkle must have accompanied Irving's post-script notification to readers that even an ungainly visionary like Ichabod Crane turned out well, when he left daydreaming, as Irving had not, and turned to law.

As Diedrich Knickerbocker rather than Geoffrey Crayon speaks, the technique of broadly sketched caricature is managed with surer touch: readers do not forget Ichabod Crane astride his boney nag, the short stirrups bringing "his knees nearly up to the pommel of the saddle; his sharp elbows stuck out like grass-hoppers'; he carried his whip perpendicularly in his hand, like a sceptre, and, as his horse jogged on, the motion of his arms was not unlike the flapping of a pair of wings" (p. 443). Dickens seldom displayed more gustatory fervor than Irving when he described "the ample charms of a genuine Dutch country tea-table"—the "doughty doughnut, the tender oly koek, and the crisp and crumbling cruller," abundance of pies and meats and poultry, and "delectable dishes of preserved plums, and peaches, and pears, and quinces . . . all mingled higgledy-piggledy" (p. 446).

Not Hawthorne or Balzac or Frank Norris at his descriptive best could better have presented Mynheer Van Tassel's spacious farmhouse, over which "a great elm tree spread its broad branches . . . at the foot of which bubbled up a spring of the softest and sweetest water in a little well formed of a barrel; and then stole sparkling away through the grass to a neighboring brook that bubbled along among alders and dwarf willows" (pp. 433–434). Beneath its low-projecting eaves were "flails, harness, various utensils of husbandry, and nets for fishing"; inside the house were "rows of resplendent pewter, ranged on a long dresser" (p. 435).

> In one corner stood a huge bag of wool ready to be spun; in another a quantity of linsey-woolsey just from the loom; ears of Indian corn, and strings of dried apples and peaches, hung in gay festoons along the walls, mingled with the gaud of red peppers . . . claw-footed chairs and dark mahogany tables shone like mirrors; and irons with their accompanying shovel and tongs, glistened from their covert of asparagus tops; mock-oranges and conch-shells decorated the mantel-piece; strings of various colored birds' eggs were suspended above it; a great ostrich egg was hung from the centre of the room, and a corner cupboard, knowingly left open, displayed immense treasures of old silver and well-mended china. (P. 436)

Without Rip Van Winkle and Ichabod Crane, and Diedrich Knickerbocker to tell their stories, *The Sketch Book* would still be a pleasantly diverting, but an undistinguished, collection. The Christmas sketches, the observations on country customs, the descriptions of Westminster Abbey, Stratford-on-Avon, and Boar's Head Tavern contain painstakingly colored vignettes of people and of venerable scenes. "The Art of Bookmaking" is a good-natured spoof of the manner in which Irving himself culled from writers of the past. His remarks on "The Mutability of Literature" are engaging rephrasings of melancholy certainties about there being no end to the making of books, or to mute, inglorious authors who are fated to write unknown. In his mild rebuke to "English Writers on America," Irving comes perilously close to expressing ideas which might offend.

From this time on, the spirit of Geoffrey Crayon almost completely took charge, and manner became increasingly more important than matter. "I consider the story," Irving repeated a

few years later, "merely as a frame on which to spread my materials. It is the play of thought, and sentiment, and language; the
weaving in and out of characters lightly, yet expressively de-
lineated; the familiar and faithful presentation of scenes of common life; and the half-concealed vein of humor that is often
playing through the whole;—these are what I aim at."[43] But his
aim was uncertain: when friends advised him to try longer fiction,
he objected that anyone could write a novel—"the mere interest
of story . . . carries the reader through pages and pages of careless writing, and the author may be dull for half a volume at a
time, if he has some striking scene at the end of it." In composition such as he preferred, the "author must be continuously
piquant; woe to him if he makes an awkward sentence or writes
a stupid page."[44]

Yet like Poe, who also disputed the effectiveness of longer
fiction, Irving did not turn aside from the novel until he had
tried to write one and discovered that he did not do it well.
Though *Bracebridge Hall; or, The Humorists* was offered in
1822 as a "medley" of fifty-one sketches centered about an
English country house, it is in fact a novel manqué, faintly
derisive and winsomely derivative. Squire Bracebridge may have
been modeled, as Irving once suggested, on Walter Scott, but
General Hardbottle, Lady Lillycraft, the village antiquary, and
the faithful family retainers come direct from memories of characters better drawn by Goldsmith and Sterne. Ghost stories, bits
of village gossip, essays on falconry, fortune-telling, and love
charms are strung almost haphazardly on a slender thread of
romance, which ends with the wedding of Fair Julia, a shy,
exemplary English girl, adroitly a caricature of heroines of sentimental fiction.

But most endearing of the sketches in *Bracebridge Hall* are
not the village tales which form its substance but the fillers, the
stories told as evening pastime at the ancient country house. Sus-
pense is artfully created in "The Stout Gentleman," and exotic
charm in "The Student of Salamanaca," but not as successfully
as in "Dolph Heyliger" and "The Storm Ship," both re-creations
of Hudson River lore drawn "from the MSS. of the late
Diedrich Knickerbocker." Once again, however, these native tales

were exceptions, for the New World offered little of appeal comparable to that of Europe. In America, Irving explained, all was "new and progressive, and pointed to the future rather than to the past"; there all "works of man gave no ideas but of young existence," without historical associations such as Irving found in England, where he wandered happily, "a grown-up child," he said, "delighted with every object."[45]

"Never need an American look beyond his own country for the sublime and beautiful of natural scenery," he had said in *The Sketch Book* (p. 10).

> But Europe held forth charms of storied and poetical associa-
> tion. There were to be seen the masterpieces of art, the refine-
> ments of highly-cultivated society, the quaint peculiarities of
> ancient and local custom. My native country was full of youth-
> ful promise: Europe was rich in the accumulated treasures of
> age. Her very ruins told the history of times gone by, and
> every mouldering stone was a chronicle. I longed to wander
> over the scenes of renowned achievement—to tread, as it were,
> in the footsteps of antiquity,—to loiter about the ruined castle,
> —to meditate on the falling tower,—to escape, in short, from
> the commonplace realities of the present, and lose myself
> among the shadowy grandeurs of the past. (Pp. 10–11)

Irving meant what Cooper, Hawthorne, Henry James, and Van Wyck Brooks later were to mean when they spoke of what America lacked which Europe had—the sustaining sense of history, and a decorum bred by tradition; but, perhaps because he said it first, he did not say it as clearly as they.

He searched through Europe now for more tales to retell, in a series of new collections—a German sketchbook, an Italian, a Spanish, a French, filling more notebooks with observations on quaint ceremonials, boar hunts, old castles, and bright national costumes—anything calculated to delight the eye or excite the imagination. But he worked by fits and starts, for he was not well, and he was forty and often wearied of the task. In Dresden he puttered over translations, entertained himself and his friends with amateur theatricals, and courted young Emily Foster, who thought him too old. In Paris, where French editions of his writings made him seem a man of importance, he collaborated with John Howard Payne on plays, none of which was successful; he considered a book on Napoleon, worked over a series of American tales, planned an edition of English classics and a play based on the life of Shakespeare.

After two dilatory years, hounded by his publisher for new materials but unable to collect enough of any one kind for a new book, in the summer of 1824 Irving threw together what he had into *Tales of a Traveller*—a mélange of German stories, tales of Italian banditti, an abortive novelete, and more American sketches "found among the papers of the late Diedrich Knicker-bocker." Though containing some of the liveliest writing which Irving had done since leaving America, and presenting in "The Devil and Tom Walker" his third-best native tale, the collection was not well received. We have heard these stories all before, said *Blackwood's:* the characters are corpses in clumsy new clothing. Irving was called "indisputably feeble, unoriginal, and timorous; a mere adjective of a man, who had neither vigor nor courage to stand alone."[46]

If it were to bring such dubious returns, further travel seemed a wearisome prospect. Irving considered writing a life of Byron, of Cervantes—tempted now to suspect that he was by nature of biographer, which he was; and he worked long hours over a projected American sketchbook—and then either destroyed or lost the manuscript. His talent, he thought, was blighted, the romance of life past. When early in 1826 he was invited to join the staff of the American Legation at Madrid, he welcomed the opportunity to settle in one place. He vowed again to work assiduously, and for three years he did.

Irving was wanted in Spain, not as a diplomat, but as a writer, to translate Don Martín de Navarette's recently published collection of documents relating to Columbus. The work was congenial and appealingly sedentary: Irving rummaged with such zeal through old libraries for collateral materials that when Longfellow called on him that spring, he was astounded at the older man's energy—up at six, at his desk through the day.[47] Incidents from Navarette's book were elaborated with bits and pieces from other chronicles, and the whole was polished until it shone attractively as a straightforward narrative of exotic color and maritime adventure. But by the time the four volumes of *The Life and Voyages of Christopher Columbus* were issued in the summer of 1828, Irving was excitedly involved with another book, more surely his own, which he hoped might recapture, though with circumspection, something of the ironic tone of Knickerbocker's *History*.

Assuming the pseudonym of Fray Antonio Agapida, a zealot monk, who distorted history to make it conform to his religious convictions, Irving presented *A Chronicle of the Conquest of Granada* in 1829 as something of an experiment: a book made out of old chronicles, embellished by the imagination, and adapted to what he considered the romantic taste of his day—something between history and romance. William H. Prescott and Francis Parkman were to do this kind of thing better; but Irving did it first, mingling romance and satire with historical details as he told the story of Boabdil, last Moorish king of Granada, a dashing man in love or battle. But irony filters only dimly through these corpse-strewn fields lighted by flashes of sunlight on the tyrant's bloody scimitar; as halls resound with shrieks and fountains run red with blood, the spirit of old romance excitingly illuminates each of its one hundred brief and chiseled chapters.

The *Voyages and Discoveries of the Companions of Columbus*, in 1831, was another modified translation, expertly done and well received. Meanwhile, however, Irving had been traveling again —through the rugged valleys and long, sweeping plains of southern Spain, where he was captivated by the hardy, country people, and by the stories they told and the songs they sang; and he had settled in the old Moorish castle of the Alhambra. Through most of the spring and into the summer of 1829, Irving threw all his energies into a Spanish sketchbook which, when published in 1832 as *The Alhambra*, would revive his reputation as a favorite among the reading public, an artist with a true and tender eye for the unusual or picturesque, with feeling for scene at once precise and emotionally expansive.

The luxuriant southern sun, quiet countryside, and remains of oriental splendor in the ancient Moorish stronghold seemed "too beautiful to be real": "As I loiter through these oriental chambers and hear the murmur of fountains and the song of the nightingale, as I inhale the odor of the rose and feel the influence of the balmy climate, I am almost tempted to fancy myself in the paradise of Mahomet."[48] He admired the refinement of those elegant Moorish princes who had reigned there in Oriental splendor when the rest of Europe was still in a state of barbarism, their achievement in art and education, their benevolent administration of justice. How splendid was the "transient gaiety and loveliness" (p. 77) of a past, when "lovers of the gay sciences resorted to Cordova and Granada, to imbibe the poetry and music of the East; and the steel-clad warriors of the North hastened thither, to accomplish themselves in the grateful exercises and courteous usages of chivalry" (p. 59).

Irving's love of ancient lore, his feeling for scenery, his sentiment for people as simple, tranquilly suffering, but well-meaning and ultimately good, seldom had been better exercised than in *The Alhambra*, which for generations has vied with *The Sketch Book* as the most popular of his works, anticipating Flaubert, Pierre Loti, Stevenson, and Lafcadio Hearn in luxuriant sensuality. If all seems surface polish and prettiness; if dark areas are lighted with too soft a glow; if "manly defiance of hardships, and contempt of effeminate indulgence" (p. 19) again seem traits inappropriately honored by a person of Irving's haphazard sensibility, *The Alhambra* nonetheless does present him at his burnished best and at his wayward worst. The story of Peregil, the water carrier, in the "Legend of the Moor's Legacy" combines pathos and humor with narrative skill, to produce another minor masterwork; the rest of *The Alhambra* blends to a deliquescent glow which is remembered as pleasant long after details are forgotten.

Fame now completely engulfed Washington Irving, celebrated in the press of two continents as a purveyor of culture from the Old World to the New, and as the good-natured explainer of American idiosyncrasies to Europe: his writings went through half a hundred editions, and were translated into a dozen languages. On leaving the Alhambra in the later summer of 1829, Irving returned to London as secretary to the American

Legation there. The next year, he received a medal from the Royal Society of Literature, and he edited Bryant's *Poems* for publication in England, changing some of the words to make them conform to British taste. The year after that, he was awarded an honorary doctorate at Oxford. Then, following a final tour to Stratford and Kenilworth, he set out for home, something he had contemplated doing every year, he said, for the past seventeen years.

His return was triumphant, but his effective literary career was virtually over. He had succeeded for more than two decades in presenting himself to the world, as William L. Hedges has so well explained, as a "somewhat puzzled and alienated observer," beset by whimsy and beguiled by grotesquerie of kinds which during the next twenty years would find more complete expression in the writings of Nathaniel Hawthorne, Herman Melville, and Edgar Allan Poe. The essential characteristic of Irving's early, and better, tales and sketches is, says Mr. Hedges, "that they are told by a man who is not altogether sure of himself"; his fiction "is a fiction of dream, fantastic symbolic projections; it is heavily loaded with imagery functioning as metaphor. . . . It alternately sympathizes with, laughs at, and turns in fear from the stranger, the homeless or orphaned young man, the provincial abroad, the recluse, the eccentric scholar, the teller of tales." Irving had confessed himself "a poor devil of an author," torn by tensions he never completely understood.[49] But he had discovered now a style and a manner. From this time on he would be able to achieve something of composure by capitalizing on his reputation and repeating tested formulas. He would become less harried, more at ease with himself, and less consistently successful.

On 23 May 1832 he once again saw "the bright city" of his birth. New York provided him a hero's welcome, with a ceremonious dinner at the City Hotel, where the halls "rang with bravos, handkerchiefs were waved on every side, three cheers given again and again," as Irving, tears in his eyes, announced that he was home to stay, and that, above all, he loved America: "It was the home of the heart."[50] He visited Saratoga Springs and Niagara

Falls, and as the result of a chance meeting with a commissioner to the Indians, made a four-month trip into the Pawnee country of the Southwest, recording excitedly in his journal each new scene of picturesque interest.

Back in New York that winter, among friends now as sedate but not nearly so famous as he had become, plaudits continued to be showered on him. He declined nomination to Congress, as he would later decline nomination by Tammany Hall as candidate for mayor of New York and appointment by President Van Buren as secretary of the navy. Instead he engaged himself to John Jacob Astor—for a tremendous sum, it was rumored—for the purpose of going over that self-made millionaire's papers, to make a book from them about the opening of the West and the fur trade. In 1836 he moved to an old Dutch farmhouse below Tarrytown, which he first named "Wolfert's Roost," and then "Sunnyside," a "little, old-fashioned, stone mansion, all made up of gabled ends, as full of angles and corners as an old cocked hat."[51]

The Crayon Miscellany had appeared in 1835, most of it taken up with the lively *A Tour on the Prairies,* but pieced out with memorials of Abbotsford and Newstead Abbey to make it of book length. Often reprinted as another minor American classic, a book to be placed beside Parkman's *The Oregon Trail* or even Mark Twain's *Roughing It,* Irving's *Tour* has gone through more than thirty editions in English and twenty in translation. Because, in Irving's words, it is "a simple narrative of everyday occurrence," with "no wonders to describe, nor any moving accidents by flood or field to narrate,"[52] it represents to readers with little patience for whimsy or sentimental humor the crown of Irving's work. It offers them a rugged Irving, with trousers tucked inside his boots, gun in hand, fording streams, sprawled (elegantly perhaps) beside a campfire.

Unlike *Astoria,* in 1836 ("Not even WASHINGTON IRVING," said one reviewer, "can beat furs into eloquence"), or *Adventures of Captain Bonneville,* in 1837, both of them, like the Spanish histories, suavely adapted from other men's accounts, *A Tour on the Prairies* recounted Irving's own discovery of the frontier West. He noted the "gypsy fondness" (p. 30) of Creek

Indians for brilliant color and gay decorations, the proud independence of the Pawnee—"sons of Ishmael, their hand is against everyone" (75)—and the fine, Roman features of the Osages; their manly independence reminded him, almost twenty years before Thoreau expressed the same thought in *Walden,* that "We in society are slaves, not so much to others as to ourselves; our superfluities are the chains that bind us" (p. 34). Some forecast of the tone of Lambert Strether, who also learned in his middle years that he had never really lived, creeps into Irving's voice when, over fifty, he admits, "We send our youths abroad to grow luxurious and effeminate in Europe; it appears to me that a previous tour of the prairies would be more likely to produce that manliness, and self-dependence, most in unison with our political institutions" (p. 55).

But, though he spoke of trappers as a "rabble rout of non-descript beings" who hover like bats "about the frontiers between civilized and savage life"; though he described his half-breed guide as "one of the worthless brood engendered and brought up among the missions," who "fancied himself highly connected, his sister being concubine to an opulent white trader" (p. 23); and though he sometimes caught in dialogue the clipped colloquialism of the native woodsman ("Next to my rifle, I'd as leave lend you my wife" [p. 77]), Irving's old manner of piquant phrase and romantic extension crept often into his record of these frontier experiences, especially when he retold at second hand the stories of hunting and Indian warfare, tall tales recounted by trappers, and Indian legends which had "a wild romantic interest heard from the lips of half-savage narrators" (p. 104). His brief chapter on "The Bee Hunt" may deserve comparison with William Bartram's account of Florida alligators, or Thoreau's description of the battle of the ants; but the brief vignette of forest rangers in bivouac, in a "wild bandit" or "Robin Hood" atmosphere, is another set piece of the kind at which Geoffrey Crayon had always excelled—an assemblage of particularized notations, memoranda in an artist's field book:

> Some were cooking at large fires made at the feet of trees; some were stretching and dressing deer skins; some were shooting at a mark, and some were lying about in the grass.

Venison jerked and hung on frames, was drying over embers in one place; in another lay carcasses recently brought in by the hunters. Stacks of rifles were leaning against the trunks of trees, and saddles, bridles, and powder-horns hanging above them, while the horses were grazing here and there among the thickets. (Pp. 47–48)

But pictures like this, carefully drawn from observation, seldom appeared in what Irving now considered his more important work. He grumbled about imitators who climbed toward fame with sketchbooks of their own, none quite done in his painstaking manner, not even Longfellow's *Outre-Mer* in 1834, which spoke of Europe and its legends. John Pendleton Kennedy's *Swallow Barn* in 1832 seemed simply a Virginian adaptation of *Bracebridge Hall*, not to speak of Cooper's *The Pioneers* nine years earlier, which told of an old family mansion on the frontier, and James Hall's *Legends of the West*, which skimmed most of the good stories from that region. Nathaniel Parker Willis had done a *Pencillings by the Way*, and Augustus Longstreet a boisterous *Georgia Scenes*, both in 1835. Irving had no heart for continuing in competition with any of these, or with the younger men like Hawthorne, who admired him, or Poe, who thought him pallid, or Emerson, whose remarks on self-reliance and throwing off shackles of the past may have seemed a rebuke.

Instead, at Sunnyside from 1837 to 1842, Irving rummaged through old notebooks for materials capable of being reworked, "writing away *like fury*," said Longfellow, on "remnants—odds and ends,—about Sleepy Hollow, and Granada. What a pity!"[53] Another Spanish book was on his mind, a history of the conquest of Mexico, but he gave that up when he learned that Prescott was engaged with the subject, turning instead to an even more "American" theme—a life of George Washington which, like the *Columbus*, might examine roots of New World tradition, providing indisputable evidence that strength and resolution and solid sense and gallantry had been from their beginnings characteristic of the best of his countrymen.

To the *Knickerbocker Magazine* in New York he contributed sketches and tales—"a hodgepodge of his experiences from the age of eighteen to fifty-eight," which were to be collected in *Wolfert's Roost* in 1855 and in the posthumous volume of *Spanish Papers*. "Mount-Joy: or Some Passages out of the Life of a Castle-Builder" made good-natured fun of transcendentalists "who render many of our young men verbose and declamatory, and prone to mistake aberrations of their fancy for inspirations of divine philosophy,"[54] and both "The Great Mississippi Bubble" and "The Early Adventures of Ralph Ringwood" are sprawling narratives of frontier life which look tentatively toward the lustier ironic realism of Mark Twain.

These better things were few, however, and not greatly different from other contributions by younger Americans who now vaunted their devotion to native scene and theme; but the Irving stamp was on them, certifying their authenticity by a style which shaped whatever subject to his familiar moods. He reworked his biography of Campbell and the sketch of Goldsmith which he had first done in Paris fifteen years before. Few books written during these decorous years were more popularly applauded than his sentimental *Biography and Poetical Remains of the Late Margaret Miller Davidson* of 1841, in which Irving spoke tenderly about the yearnings and aspiring verse of a tremulous, tubercular girl who had died at the age of sixteen, only a year younger than Matilda Hoffman had been when she died.

Early in 1842 Irving accepted appointment as minister plenipotentiary to the court of Spain, a position which came to him as the result of an apparent political about-face which had James Fenimore Cooper—just then caged about by legal controversies with Whig opponents—growling in disgust. During the next few years, briefly in England and then in Madrid, Irving played a modestly important role as a diplomat, lending his prestige and suave good humor to negotiations over Cuba, the Oregon boundary dispute, and defense of his country's attitude in the Mexican war. But public life put a strain on his never too robust health. By the late summer of 1846 he was happy to be back once more at Sunnyside, which he would not leave for long again.

"In the early part of my literary career," he remembered, "I used to think I would take warning by the fate of writers who kept on writing until they 'wrote themselves down,' and that I would retire while still in the freshness of my powers—but . . . circumstances have obliged me to change my plan, and I am likely to write until the pen drops from my hands."[55] Day after day at Sunnyside, he tinkered over old writings and projected new. In 1849 he arranged with George P. Putnam for a revised edition of his works, which would finally grow from fifteen to twenty-one, then to twenty-seven volumes. *Mahomet and His Successors,* over which he had been worrying for almost a quarter of a century, appeared in 1850, to be followed by the miscellaneous *Wolfert's Roost* five years later, a book which it pleased him to find praised in the London *Spectator* as filled with "as much elegance of diction, as graceful a description of natural scenery, as grotesque an earnestness in diablerie, and as quiet but telling a satiric humor, as when Geoffrey Crayon came before the English world, nearly forty years ago."[56]

Meant as praise, these words describe much of Irving's literary fortune, and foretell the inevitable decline of his reputation. For forty years there had been no change. This man of limpid style was without a subject, except as he could find it ready-made, available for transforming to language adroitly adapted to popular taste. Adventures as revealed in old tales or old documents, nostalgic recollection of bygone scenes, and the fallible, lovable, admirable characteristics of people—these were the themes which brought Geoffrey Crayon fame. Diedrich Knickerbocker could do better, and did, slipping into each miscellaneous volume a tale or two giving it body, usually through the creation of characters indelibly drawn.

For it was finally people who interested Washington Irving most—whimsical people, droll manifestations of popular whim-whams; people who drifted as he had drifted, from one project to another, searching for the key to success; or successful people, the heroes of whom Carlyle had written, and the representative men of whom Emerson spoke. Irving's life had been checkered with plans for biographies never completed, of Byron, Napoleon, Cervantes. The lives of the English poets which he had supplied as hackwork introductions spurred his ambition to do something larger. The popular success of the little book about Margaret Davidson made him think he could do even better.

He did do greatly better with *Oliver Goldsmith*, one of the most appealing literary biographies of the first half of the nineteenth century. It was "a labor of love," said Irving, "a tribute of gratitude to the memory of an author whose writings were the delight of my childhood, and have been a source of enjoyment to me throughout life." Done in three versions, first in Paris in 1825 as an introduction to the Goldsmith volume in Galignani's series of English Classics, expanded in 1840 as *The Life of Oliver Goldsmith, with Selections from His Writings* in Harper's Family Library, it was published in final form as *Oliver Goldsmith: A Biography* by Putnam in 1849. Though much of its material is drawn from Sir James Prior's and John Forster's more complete studies, Irving's *Oliver Goldsmith* outlives either, partly because, as Hazlitt recognized, its author "binds up his own portrait with Goldsmith's."[57]

Irving admired "the artless benevolence" of Goldsmith, the "whimsical, yet amiable views of human life and nature; the unforced humor, blending so happily with good feeling and good sense, and singularly dashed at times with a pleasing melancholy"[58]—all characteristics which readers for so many years had been accustomed to associate with Irving's own writing. Each, it has been said, looks "at human nature from the same generous point of view, with the same kindly sympathies, and the same tolerant philosophy"; each has "the same quick perception of the ludicrous, and the same tender simplicity in the pathetic"; in each runs "the same quiet vein of human, and the same cheerful spirit of hopefulness."[59] Irving defended his own literary intentions when he praised Goldsmith's writings because they "sweeten our tempers, and harmonize our thoughts; they put us in a good humor with the world, and in so doing they make us happier and better men."[60]

Veneration and a sense of responsibility got in the way, however, as Irving devoted his final, failing energies to the *Life of George Washington*, the first volume of which appeared in 1855. Planned for three volumes, the work dragged on, filled with fact and anecdote and with massive descriptions of military events; too seldom graced even with vestiges of Irving's former easy prose, it moves by fits and starts, as if pushing desperately toward completion. "The shadows of departed years," he confided to a friend, "are gathering over me." But, he said, "I must get through with the work which I have cut out for myself. I must weave my web, and then die."[61]

Scarcely six months after seeing the fifth and last volume of the *Life of George Washington* through the press, on 28 November 1859, Washington Irving died. At his funeral "thousands from far and near silently looked for the last time on his genial face, and mourned his loss as that of a personal friend and national benefactor."[62] His grave in Sleepy Hollow Cemetery is still carefully attended, and flowers are placed in Christ Episcopal Church in Tarrytown each year on the anniversary of his death. The old house at Sunnyside has been restored, and schoolchildren make pilgrimages there to see the room where Washington Irving wrote.

For his reputation does live on, not perhaps among somber critics, for Irving was not in their sense a dedicated or committed person. But for those who accept in literature what they find there, and who know it well enough not always to expect too much, refreshing discoveries are to be made in reviewing his writings. It will not do to think of Irving as a complicated man, yet with quick eye, ready tongue, and alert recognition of absurdities, he stretches quietly toward both ends of the American literary spectrum—an expatriate seeking reverently in Europe for sources of culture and at the same time a native myth maker who weaves indigenous lore into comic tales which become fables. His country's first, though not her best, romantic historian; an early but unsatisfying impressionistic biographer; an exotic local colorist before Flaubert popularized the term; a mildly boisterous, thigh-slapping, sidesplitting rural humorist, a comic realist before Thackeray, a caricaturist before Dickens—Irving was tentatively all of these. He writes better than anyone who has written about him, in praise or condemnation, and he shares with each critic the handicap of having quite too little of final importance to write about.

Yet he is certainly not an unattractive figure, seated there, though complacently, at the threshhold of what we have been proud to call the American Renaissance. Emerson early wrote him off as ephemeral, and Melville found him only a charming echo, but there he does sit, pleasantly charming still to those who briefly visit him. An echo, yes; but a placid portent also of new beginnings.

NOTES

1. *Edinburgh Review* 33 (January 1820): 79.

2. "The Author," *Bracebridge Hall; or, The Humorists, a Medley*, author's rev. ed. (New York, 1858), p. 9.

3. The standard biography of Irving is Stanley T. Williams, *The Life of Washington Irving* (New York, 1963), 2 vols. For briefer treatments, see George S. Hellman, *Washington Irving, Esquire: Ambassador at Large from the New World to the Old* (New York, 1925), and Edward Wagenknecht, *Washington Irving: Moderation Displayed* (New York, 1962). The best critical study is William L. Hedges, *Washington Irving: An American Study, 1802–1832* (Baltimore, 1965); see also Lewis Leary, "Washington Irving," *The Comic Imagination in American Literature*, ed. Louis D. Rubin, Jr. (New Brunswick, N.J., 1973).

4. Williams, *Life*, 1: 8, 19.

5. "The Author's Account of Himself," *The Sketch Book of Geoffrey Crayon, Gent*ⁿ, author's rev. ed. (New York, 1858), p. 9.

6. Williams, *Life*, 1: 41.

7. *Letters of Jonathan Oldstyle, Gent.* (New York, 1824), p. 23. Further quotations from this volume are identified within parentheses in the text.

8. Irving was irritated in 1824 at the unauthorized reprinting of the *Letters* (see n. 7 above), apparently thinking that the crudities of Jonathan Oldstyle might detract from his newly won fame as Geoffrey Crayon; when preparing in 1848 a revised edition of his writings, he wrote after the last three of the *Letters*, "not to be reprinted" (Williams, *Life*, 1: 35).

9. Williams, *Life*, 1: 41, quoting from *Blackwood's Magazine*, January 1825.

10. Pierre M. Irving, *The Life and Letters of Washington Irving* (London, 1882), 1: 24.

11. *Port Folio* 3 (8 January 1803): 13.

12. Irving, *Life and Letters*, 1: 109.

13. This quotation is from the perhaps semiautobiographical sketch "Buckthorne," *Tales of a Traveller* (Philadelphia, 1834), 1: 139.

14. Williams, *Life*, 1: 76–77.

15. *Salmagundi; or, The Whim-Whams and Opinions of Launcelot Langstaff and Others* (New York, 1835), 1: 18. Further quotations from this volume are identified within parentheses in the text.

16. "Publisher's Notice," *Salmagundi* (Paris, 1824), pp. vii–viii.

17. Quoted in Williams, *Life*, 2: 398. These verses were deleted both in the Paris, 1824, and the New York, 1835, reprints of *Salmagundi*.

18. *Weekly Inspector*, 14 February 1807, p. 1. For more on the brief controversy, see Porter G. Perrin, *The Life and Works of Thomas Greene Fessenden* (Orono, Maine, 1925), pp. 117–120.

19. *North American Review* 9 (September 1819): 334.

20. Williams, *Life*, 1: 106.

21. Ibid., 2: 274–276.

22. *A History of New York*, ed. Edwin T. Bowden (New York, 1964). Further quotations from this volume, which is presently the most easily available edition, are identified within parentheses in the text.

23. Williams, *Life*, 1: 116.

24. Ibid.

25. *Among My Books* (Boston, 1870), p. 231.

26. These and other estimates are quoted in Williams, *Life*, 2: 274–277.

27. Williams, *Life*, 1: 119.

28. For a discussion of these and other literary preferences which Irving expressed at this time, see Williams, *Life*, 1: 137–139.

29. Williams, *Life*, 1: 137.

30. Ibid., p. 144.

31. Irving, *Life and Letters*, 1: 310.

32. Williams, *Life*, 1: 172.

33. Irving, *Life and Letters*, 1: 314.

34. For these and other early estimates of *The Sketch Book*, see Williams, *Life*, 1: 176–177, 188–191; 2: 278–279.

35. *The Sketch Book*, p. 11. Further quotations from this volume are identified within parentheses in the text.

36. Gorham A. Worth, *American Bards* (New York, 1919), p. 51.

37. Irving, *Life and Letters*, 2: 20.

38. *The Letters of Hart Crane, 1916–1932*, ed. Brom Weber (New York, 1952), p. 306.

39. "Fallen from Time: The Mythic Rip Van Winkle," *Kenyon Review* 22 (August 1960): 550.

40. *Letters of Washington Irving to Henry Brevoort*, ed. George S. Hellman (New York, 1918), p. 390.

41. Daniel G. Hoffman, "Irving's Use of American Folklore in 'The Legend of Sleepy Hollow,'" *Publications of the Modern Language Association* 68 (June 1953): 427.

42. Ibid., p. 425.

43. *Letters of Washington Irving to Henry Brevoort*, pp. 398.

44. Ibid., pp. 399–400.

45. "The Author," *Bracebridge Hall*, p. 13.

46. For this and other commentary on *Tales of a Traveller*, see Williams, *Life*, 1: 276–277; 2: 294–297.

47. Williams, *Life*, 1: 317.

48. *Tales of the Alhambra* (Granada, 1961), p. 68. Further quotations from this volume are identified within parentheses in the text.

49. Hedges, *Washington Irving*, pp. 147, 161.

50. Irving, *Life and Letters*, 2: 224–226.

51. Ibid., p. 277.

52. *A Tour on the Prairies*, ed. John Francis McDermott (Norman, Okla., 1956), p. 9. Further quotations from this volume are identified within parentheses in the text.

53. Williams, *Life*, 2: 107.

54. *Wolfert's Roost and Other Papers, Now First Collected* (New York, 1855), p. 98.

55. Williams, *Life*, 2: 190.

56. Ibid., p. 227.

57. Ibid., p. 219.

58. *Oliver Goldsmith: A Biography* (New York, 1869), pp. 13–14.

59. Williams, *Life*, 2: 220.

60. *Oliver Goldsmith*, p. 14.

61. Williams, *Life*, 2: 234.

62. *New York Times*, 7 December 1859, p. 1.

A Basic Bookshelf

IN EARLY AMERICAN LITERATURE

Becker, Carl L. *The Heavenly City of the Eighteenth-Century Philosophers* (New Haven, Conn.: Yale University Press, 1952).

Bercovitch, Sacvan. *Typology and Early American Literature* (Amherst: University of Massachusetts Press, 1970).

Bridenbaugh, Carl and Jessica. *Rebels and Gentlemen: Philadelphia in the Age of Franklin* (New York: Reynal and Hitchcock, 1942).

Carroll, Peter N. *Puritanism and the Wilderness: The Intellectual Significance of the New England Frontier* (New York: Columbia University Press, 1969).

Cassirer, Ernst. *The Philosophy of the Enlightenment* (Princeton, N.J.: Princeton University Press, 1951).

Charvat, William. *Literary Publishing in America, 1790–1830* (Philadelphia: University of Pennsylvania Press, 1959).

Cook, Elizabeth C. *Literary Influences in Colonial Newspapers* (New York: Columbia University Press, 1912).

Davis, Richard Beale. *Intellectual Life in Jefferson's Virginia, 1790–1830* (Chapel Hill: University of North Carolina Press, 1964).

Emerson, Everett, ed. *Major Writers of Early American Literature* (Madison: University of Wisconsin Press, 1972).

Gay, Peter. *A Loss of Mastery: Puritan Historians in Colonial America* (Berkeley and Los Angeles: University of California Press, 1966).

Granger, Bruce I. *Political Satire in the American Revolution, 1763–1783* (Ithaca, N.Y.: Cornell University Press, 1960).

Haller, William. *The Rise of Puritanism* (New York: Columbia University Press, 1938).

Haroutian, Joseph. *Piety versus Moralism: The Passing of the New England Theology* (New York: Henry Holt, 1932).

Howard, Leon. *The Connecticut Wits* (Chicago: University of Chicago Press, 1943).

Jantz, Harold S. *The First Century of American Verse* (Worcester,

Mass.: American Antiquarian Society, 1944; New York: Russell and Russell, 1962).

Jones, Howard Mumford. *The Literature of Colonial Virginia* (Charlottesville: University Press of Virginia, 1968).

——. *O Strange New World: American Culture, the Formative Years* (New York: Viking, 1964).

Koch, G. Adolph. *Republican Religion: The American Revolution and the Cult of Reason* (New York: Henry Holt, 1933).

Lemay, J. A. Leo. *Men of Letters in Colonial Maryland* (Knoxville: University of Tennessee Press, 1972).

Messerole, Harrison T., ed. *Seventeenth-Century American Poetry* (Garden City, N.Y.: Doubleday, 1968).

Miller, Perry. *Errand into the Wilderness* (Cambridge, Mass.: Harvard University Press, 1956).

——. *The New England Mind: From Colony to Province* (Cambridge, Mass.: Harvard University Press, 1953).

——. *The New England Mind: The Seventeenth Century* (New York: Macmillan, 1939; Cambridge, Mass.: Harvard University Press, 1954).

Miner, Louie B. *Our Rude Forefathers: American Political Verse, 1783–1788* (Cedar Rapids, Iowa: Torch, 1937).

Morais, Herbert M. *Deism in Eighteenth-Century America* (New York: Columbia University Press, 1934).

Morison, Samuel Eliot. *Builders of the Bay Colony* (Boston: Houghton Mifflin, 1930).

——. *The Intellectual Life of Early New England* (New York: New York University Press, 1956).

Nye, Russell B. *The Cultural Life of the New Nation* (New York: Harper, 1960).

Parrington, Vernon L. *Main Currents in American Thought: The Colonial Mind* (New York: Harcourt Brace, 1927).

Pearce, Roy Harvey. *The Continuity of American Poetry* (Princeton, N.J.: Princeton University Press, 1961).

Petter, Henri. *The Early American Novel* (Columbus: Ohio State University Press, 1970).

Piercy, Josephine K. *Studies in Literary Types in Seventeenth-Century America* (New Haven, Conn.: Yale University Press, 1939).

Richardson, Lyon N. *A History of Early American Magazines, 1741–1789* (New York: Thomas Nelson, 1931).

Schneider, Herbert. *The Puritan Mind* (New York: Henry Holt, 1930).

Shea, Daniel B. *Spiritual Biography in Early America* (Princeton, N.J.: Princeton University Press, 1968).

Silverman, Kenneth, ed. *Colonial American Poetry* (New York: Hafner, 1968).

Taft, Kendall B. ed. *Minor Knickerbockers* (New York: American, 1947).

Tyler, Moses Coit. *American Literature during the Colonial Time, 1607–1765* (New York: G. P. Putnam's, 1897; Ithaca, N.Y.: Cornell University Press, 1949; Gloucester, Mass.: Peter Smith, 1963).

————. *The Literary History of the American Revolution, 1763–1783* (New York: G. P. Putnam's, 1897; New York: Barnes and Noble, 1941; New York: Frederick Ungar, 1957).

Waggoner, Hyatt. *American Poetry from the Puritans to the Present* (Boston: Houghton Mifflin, 1968).

Wright, Louis B. *The Cultural Life of the Early American Colonies, 1607–1763* (New York: Harper, 1955).

————. *The First Gentlemen of Virginia* (San Marino, Cal.: Huntington Library, 1940).

Wright, Thomas G. *Literary Culture in Early New England* (New Haven, Conn.: Yale University Press, 1920).